"This collection makes a powerful case for putting Bob Young at the heart of the intellectual maelstrom which led to the creation of Science and Technology Studies, a programme of engaged scholarship from whose history he has too often been excluded."

David Edgerton, *Hans Rausing Professor of History of Science, Kings College London, UK*

"This is a rich collection of essays that cover the extraordinary range of Bob Young's intellectual and political engagements. The contributions introduce Young's psychopolitical concerns and simultaneously extend his thinking, thereby illustrating the continuing relevance of his theoretical endeavours. This book is highly recommended, as reading it will provide rich rewards."

Amal Treacher Kabesh, *University of Nottingham, UK*

"Whenever I reminisce about Robert Young, an image of Leonardo da Vinci pops into my mind. An esteemed clinician, historian, scholar, publisher, editor, author and critic, Bob Young – more than anyone else in the psychoanalytical community – deserves to be recognised as a true 'Renaissance Man'. Thankfully, Kurt Jacobsen and R. D. Hinshelwood have curated a masterpiece of riveting tributes to this remarkable gentleman who challenged the 'elitism' of psychoanalysis and who dared to speak out bravely and boldly with wisdom and fortitude. Professor Young will be much missed but, happily, due to this magnificent book, he will always be remembered."

Professor Brett Kahr, *Senior Fellow, Tavistock Institute of Medical Psychology, London; Honorary Director of Research, Freud Museum London, UK*

"This multi-voiced volume is a fine tribute to a remarkable man. Robert Young's unorthodox, ever-questing brilliance sparked young historians of science in the 70s and went on to inspire new ways of thinking with psychoanalysis and about science and technology for the rest of his long and engaged life. In probing Young's work, these elegant, disputatious essays by leaders across a variety of fields themselves illuminate a spectrum of ideas key to the formation of our times."

Lisa Appignanesi, *OBE, FRSL; author,* Freud's Women *(with John Forrester),* Mad, Bad and Sad *and* Everyday Madness

"Anyone remotely interested in the fields of Science and Technology Studies and/or psychoanalysis – especially if they are interested in changing as well as understanding the world – will be inspired by this collection of essays honouring the polymathic scholar and activist Bob Young. Over a fifty-year career Young challenged his students, colleagues and comrades to rethink the foundations of their beliefs and practices through his seminal writings and interventions, initially as an historian and social analyst of science, and later as a psychotherapist and teacher of psychoanalytic theory. By assessing Young's career and intellectual legacy, the distinguished contributors to this volume are offering a new generation of scholars and activists some powerful tools to demystify their disciplines and sustain their struggles to make a better world."

Dr Gary Werskey, *University of Sydney, Australia*

Psychoanalysis, Science and Power

Psychoanalysis, Science and Power reexamines the current state of psychoanalysis and science and technology studies as they have been influenced by Robert Maxwell Young's work.

Robert Maxwell Young, a Texas émigré to Britain, was a scholar, publisher, TV documentarian, psychoanalytic psychotherapist, journal editor, conference organiser and political activist. Young urged that psychoanalysis, particularly in its Kleinian incarnation, illuminated new aspects of science and technology studies, and vice versa. This volume not only provides an overview of Young's life and interests by a stellar cast of scholars and practitioners but also commemorates the many and intersecting streams of his contributions, reasoning for their continuing relevance in the contemporary studies of psychoanalysis, biological sciences, technology and Darwinian thought.

Presenting perspectives that are rigorously analytical and yet often poignant, *Psychoanalysis, Science and Power* will be an important read for students, analysts and analytic therapists of all orientations who are interested in broadening their understanding of their practice.

Kurt Jacobsen is co-editor of *Free Associations* journal and research associate in the Political Science Department at the University of Chicago, USA. He also is an award-winning documentary filmmaker.

R. D. Hinshelwood is a Fellow of the British Psychoanalytical Society, previously Professor at Centre for Psychoanalytic Studies, University of Essex (now Emeritus, Department of Psychosocial and Psychoanalytic Studies), UK. He was Consultant Psychotherapist in the NHS for many years, and Director of the Cassel Hospital, 1993–1997. He has a long association with *Free Associations*.

Psychoanalysis, Science and Power

Essays in Honour of Robert Maxwell Young

Edited by
Kurt Jacobsen and
R. D. Hinshelwood

Routledge
Taylor & Francis Group

LONDON AND NEW YORK

Designed Cover Image: © Kurt Jacobsen, c.2015

First published 2023
by Routledge
4 Park Square, Milton Park, Abingdon, Oxon OX14 4RN

and by Routledge
605 Third Avenue, New York, NY 10158

Routledge is an imprint of the Taylor & Francis Group, an informa business

British Library Cataloguing-in-Publication Data
A catalogue record for this book is available from the British Library

ISBN: 978-1-032-06871-8 (hbk)
ISBN: 978-1-032-06870-1 (pbk)
ISBN: 978-1-003-20424-4 (ebk)

DOI: 10.4324/9781003204244

Typeset in Times New Roman
by codeMantra

Contents

Editors

Robert D. Hinshelwood is a Fellow of the British Psychoanalytical Society, previously Professor, Centre for Psychoanalytic Studies, University of Essex (now Emeritus, Department of Psychosocial and Psychoanalytic Studies), UK. He was Consultant Psychotherapist in the NHS for many years and Director of the Cassel Hospital, 1993–1997. He has a long association with *Free Associations* and published several books with Free Association Books, including the *Dictionary of Kleinian Thought* (1989) and *Clinical Klein* (1993).

Kurt Jacobsen is co-editor of *Free Associations* and research associate in Political Science at the University of Chicago. He is author of *Freud's Foes: Psychoanalysis, Science and Resistance, International Politics and Inner Worlds: Masks of Reason under Scrutiny, Pacification and Its Discontents* and co-editor of *Experiencing The State* and of *Reconsidering American Power*, among a number of other books. He was a visiting scholar at the London School of Economics and a Teaching Fellow at the Center for the Study of History of Science, Medicine and Technology, then at Imperial College. He is an award-winning documentary filmmaker and is book review editor for *Logos: A Journal of Modern Society & Culture*.

Contributors

Peter Barham has been engaging in the field of madness for more than 50 years. His work straddles clinical research, historical inquiry, mental health activism and filmmaking. He has a PhD in Modern History from Cambridge and in Abnormal Psychology from Durham. His books include *Schizophrenia & Human Value* (1984); *Relocating Madness: From the Mental Patient to the Person* (1991); *Closing the Asylum: The Mental Patient in Modern Society* (1992, new edition Process Press 2020) and *Forgotten Lunatics of the Great War* (2004). He was on the staff of the Tavistock Institute of Human Relations and a visiting teacher at the Tavistock Institute & Clinic. He was the founder of the Hamlet Trust, which between 1990 and 2007 pioneered grassroots mental health reform in Central and Eastern Europe. He is a founder member of the Guild of Psychotherapists and a chartered psychologist and a fellow of the British Psychological Society. Laterly, he was an associate member of the history faculty at Oxford.

Karl Figlio is a senior member of the Psychoanalytic Psychotherapy Association and a clinical associate of the British Psychoanalytical Society. He was the founding Director of the Centre for Psychoanalytic Studies (now the Department of Psychosocial and Psychoanalytic Studies) at the University of Essex and for several years a managing editor of *Free Associations*. Recent publications include *Remembering as Reparation: Psychoanalysis and Historical Memory* (Palgrave 2017), and "Fundamentalism and the Delusional Creation of an Enemy." In Steffen Krüger, Karl Figlio and Barry Richards, (eds) *Fomenting Political Violence: Fantasy, Language, Media, Action* (Palgrave, 2018); "On the Roots of Absolutism," *Free Associations* (December 2018).

Paul Hoggett is Emeritus Professor of Social Policy at UWE, Bristol. He is a psychoanalytic psychotherapist and has been involved in training and consultancy to public and voluntary organisations for many years. He was a founding co-editor of the journal *Organisational and Social Dynamics*. He is the Chair of the Climate Psychology Alliance which seeks to bring insights from depth psychologies to our understanding of collective paralysis in the face of dangerous climate change.

Les Levidow is a senior research fellow at the Faculty of Arts and Social Sciences, The Open University. In the mid-1970s, he participated in US activities around *Science for the People* magazine. After moving to London, he became a managing editor of the *Radical Science Journal* in the 1980s. He is a co-founder and editor of its successor journal, *Science as Culture*. His books include *GM on Trial: Testing European Democracy*, and (coedited with Robert Young) *Science, Technology and the Labour Process*.

Maureen McNeil is Professor Emerita affiliated with the Sociology Department, Lancaster University. Bob Young supervised her PhD thesis research which provided the basis for her book – *Under the Banner of Science: Erasmus Darwin and His Age* (1988). She was a member of the Radical Science Collective and edited *Gender and Expertise* (1987) which was a special issue of the *Radical Science Journal*. Her subsequent publications include *Feminist Cultural Studies of Science and Technology* (2007).

Barry Richards is Professor of Political Psychology at Bournemouth University and a former editor of *Free Associations*. His many books include *The Psychology of Politics* (2019), *What Holds Us Together: Popular Culture and Social Cohesion* (2017), *Emotional Governance: Politics, Media and Terror* (2007), *Disciplines of Delight: The Psychoanalysis of Popular Culture* (1994) and *Images of Freud: Cultural Responses to Psychoanalysis* (1989).

Michael Ruse is Professor of Philosophy at Florida State University. His books include *The Philosophy of Biology, Sociobiology: Sense or Nonsense?, The Darwinian Revolution* and *Darwinism Defended*.

Ann Scott is a senior member of British Psychotherapy Foundation (Psychoanalytic Psychotherapy Association), a training therapist for the Independent Psychoanalytic Child and Adolescent Psychotherapy Association (IPCAPA – BPF) and was editor-in-Chief of *British Journal of Psychotherapy*, 2009–2022. She worked as an editor at Free Association Books (FAB), 1985–1989 and as a managing editor of FAB, 1991–1994. She is the co-author, with the late Ruth First, of *Olive Schreiner: A Biography* (1980); with the late Mary Barnes, of *Something Sacred: Conversations, Writings, Paintings* (1989); and author of *Real Events Revisited: Fantasy, Memory, Psychoanalysis* (1996). She is the literary executor of Isabel Menzies Lyth.

James A. Secord is Emeritus Professor of History and Philosophy of Science and Director of the Darwin Correspondence Project at the University of Cambridge. His books include *Controversy in Victorian Geology* (1986),

Victorian Sensation (2000), and *Visions of Science* (2014). He is co-editor of *Cultures of Natural History* (1996) and *Worlds of Natural History* (2018).

Timothy Sim is a PhD candidate in History of Science at Cambridge University.

Valerie Sinason, PhD, is a poet, writer, child psychotherapist and adult psychoanalyst. She is also the Director of the Clinic for Dissociative Studies and specialises in working with abused/abusing and dissociative patients including those with a learning disability. She was Consultant Child Psychotherapist at the Tavistock Clinic from 1987 to 1999, Consultant Psychotherapist at both the Anna Freud and Portman Clinics from 1994 to 1997 and Consultant Research Psychotherapist/Psychoanalyst at St George's Hospital Medical School, University of London, from 1994 to 2006. Valerie is Honorary Consultant Psychotherapist at the University of Cape Town's Child Guidance Clinic.

Roger Smith is Reader Emeritus in the History of Science at Lancaster University and honorary associate of the Institute of Philosophy of the Russian Academy of Sciences in Moscow. He obtained his PhD in the History and Philosophy of Science in 1971, with Bob Young as his supervisor, and taught in the Department of History at Lancaster for 25 years. He is the author of *Trial by Medicine: Insanity and Responsibility in Victorian Trials* (1981), *Inhibition: History and Meaning in the Sciences of Mind and Brain* (1992), *The Fontana History of the Human Sciences* (1997), *Being Human: Historical Knowledge and the Creation of Human Nature* (2007), *Between Mind and Nature: A History of Psychology (2013), Free Will and the Human Sciences in Britain, 1870–1910* (2013), *and The Sense of Movement: An Intellectual History* (2019). *He was a founder of the journal, History of the Human Sciences.* From 1998 until the Ukrainian war, he lived in Moscow.

Introduction

Kurt Jacobsen and R.D. Hinshelwood

Robert Maxwell Young (1935–2019), a Texan transplant to the UK in the 1960s, was a scholar, writer, publisher, TV documentarian, psychotherapeutic psychoanalyst, journal editor, conference organizer, and political activist. Bob was an inveterate yet purposeful iconoclast who accepted nothing on any authority's say-so, something of a leftist entrepreneur, a daring thinker engaged in the "ruthless criticism of everything existing," a dedicated anti-follower of fashion, and a besotted pursuer of the "life of the mind" who nonetheless acutely understood that we were here not merely to interpret the world but to change it, hopefully, for the better. Did we mention that Bob also was a Texan?

Bob barrelled around London on a huge *Wild One* motorcycle, commanded a meeting room whenever he cared to, and, in later years, grew into an imposing Falstaffian presence with an irrepressible brio. Unlike Falstaff, Bob was no timorous soul or player of the odds. At considerable personal cost, he championed ideas – big and inherently subversive ideas like truth, justice, and social relevance – wherever they took him and his sometimes nervous associates. Bob reveled, however slyly, in his Texas origin with its mythicized mandate for living large, roaming free, and, slightly less characteristic of the hardy breed, thinking uninhibitedly.

In most respects, except relocations (Manhattan versus London), his own concerns resonated strongly with those of fellow Texan emigre and savant C. Wright Mills, who also had a serious thing for motorbikes, scholarship, and gutsy thought. They were eminently kindred spirits and both deserved to leave a lasting scholarly legacy. Like Mills, whom he held in high esteem, Bob operated at his best at the edges of the academy. As one of the costs of their profound rebel views, Mills was marginalized at Columbia University at the time of his early death in 1962 while Bob exited Cambridge University under pressure in the 1970s – eventually to return to scholarly posts decades later.

In the lengthy interval between academic appointments, Bob amassed an extraordinary list of accomplishments as writer, author, publisher, and documentary filmmaker. This volume commemorates the many and

DOI: 10.4324/9781003204244-1

intersecting streams of his contributions and argues for their continuing relevance in studies of science, especially Darwin studies, and to the trickier realm of psychoanalysis, which he always treated in a critical yet appreciative way.[1] To fill, or fill out, missing intellectual spaces, Bob perforce became something of a radical entrepreneur though, for lack of an acquisitive nature or knack, he frankly was a terrible businessman, Bob played a key role in founding *Radical Science Journal* (now *Science as Culture*), *Free Associations* journal and Free Associations Books, the lattermost of which he was relieved by craftier business heads.

Nothing was alien to him, except cruelty and hypocrisy, and nothing was above scrutiny. He was just plain fun in any conversation, if one could keep up with his vast range of references. If not, one suddenly found oneself either in an engaging impromptu tutorial or else gestured toward a bookshelf containing a vein of knowledge he urged you to begin to master. Bob was instinctively heretical. One remembers most of all his unflagging enthusiasm for the "life of the mind" and his heartfelt moral concerns in this world of too, too solid flesh. Naturally, he rubbed a good few conventional scholars the wrong way, and he also paid the price, willingly, if also grousing about it during down moments.

This collection accordingly intends to intervene boldly into several disciplines that ought to overlap even if they do not always do so in academic practice. All contributors have been deeply influenced in some way by Bob Young's work, which provides cues, but not necessarily rules, for the ways they conduct their sprightly forays into the contemporary states of philosophy of science, psychoanalysis, and science and technology studies (STS). Young was content to spur challenging thought, not to set down tiresome recipes for how to accomplish subversive ends. He wasn't interested in cloning himself. Over time, Young's meta-theoretical musings and urgings were so thoroughly embraced that they became common features in scholarship, as if there forever (and not in need of footnoted credit). Nonetheless, much of Young's work goes unappreciated and unabsorbed in the fields in which he laboured. Those gaps require some acknowledgment and repair, and academe will be the better for it. That power permeates everything we do and think, and that science is social relations, remain propositions that need explicit recognition in our work as scholars and/or therapists.

Bob hailed from a modest family home nestled on the edge of a wealthy community in Dallas, Texas. He and one older sister were raised as much or more by a cherished black servant as they were by an emotionally troubled mother. When Bob viewed the 2011 movie *The Help*, he enthused that it depicted what he lived out in Dallas, including his beloved black upbringer becoming emboldened by the civil rights movement that the whites he knew reviled. His rowdy associates included future oil heirs, who he found wanting in every respect except cash flow. Bob, after dallying with visions of a valiant military career, serendipitously slipped away on a swimming scholarship to

Yale in the mid-1950s where, unlike the parched privileged legacy kids like George W. Bush, he fell head over heels in love with scholarship, philosophy above all. While at Yale, Bob spent a Summer as a care worker at an Arizona "snake pit" sanitarium, which left an indelible mark – a bone deep distrust of reigning psychiatric models and of institutions based on them. Yet, he always saw such institutions as in dire need of rigorous humane reform, not abolition.

After Yale, Bob attended the University of Rochester Medical School with the intention of becoming a psychoanalytical psychiatrist but in his second year, he snagged an irresistible research fellowship to Cambridge, which gave him an intoxicating freedom to explore whatever medical subject he chose. He decided to remain in Cambridge to finish a PhD with a remarkable dissertation which appeared in 1970 as the Oxford University Press book *Mind, Brain, and Adaptation in the Nineteenth Century.* The correspondence theory of localized brain area to specific behavior that he demolished there is evident again today in a related form in stubborn genetic determinist enterprises. Peter Gay, among many others, pronounced it a "classic."

Bob was invited to stay on as a Cambridge don and soon became the first head of the Wellcome Unit for the History of Medicine there. He followed up *Mind, Brain, and Adaptation* with the ground-breaking Darwin essays that he eventually collected and published in 1985 as *Darwin's Metaphor*, wherein he situated Darwin squarely in his Malthusian Victorian socioeconomic context. This enterprise led him further into what is today dubbed STS where Bob of course jousted with every other "school" in the field. "I consider Robert Young to be one of the central founders of critical science and technology studies," Donna Haraway attested. "His pursuit of the issues where they led, rather than his pursuit of an orthodox academic career, has, in my view, been his greatest strength." The late Cambridge Professor of history and philosophy of science John Forrester said that he and Roy Porter were "inspired by Bob Young, a larger-than-life Texan historian of the brain sciences and Darwinism who moulded an entire generation of Cambridge historians of science."

A staunch opponent of positivism (which "depoliticises whenever qualitative and evaluative aspects are made less prominent than the numerical representation"), Bob's arguments have taken hold in some high places but the word has yet to get through in others – and backsliding was always possible. "It is probably the case that all 'facts' are theory laden, but it is certainly true that some facts are more theory-laden than others," Bob argued early on.

> The reader who comes to [pop science texts] for guaranteed social and political wisdom supported by the authority of science is making a very grave mistake. Let us have the debate on the social meaning of biology, but we must strip it of the specious aura of scientific objectivity.

Science, Bob contended, is social relations, far from immaculately detached from the interest-riven milieus in which it is conducted. "I am in no sense recommending an anti-rational, much less an irrational, activity." Bob explained.

> The aim is to open up more aspects of science and its context to public debate so that conflicting values can be discussed as such. Science is no substitute for morality or politics, nor is it independent at any level from them.

At the core of his critique was a deeply democratic notion of how science should proceed. He identified three key themes:[2]

> The first is the strategic exhortation that we move on, both in theory and in practice. The second is the conception of an alternative cosmology or counter-hegemonic world view, which I offer as a large step beyond recent preoccupations with questions which still lie inside an ontology and an epistemology which contain and express our alienated world view in modern science and society ... The third theme concerns the lives of radical scientists and technologists and argues that those lives should involve prefigurative struggle toward socialism by getting priorities right and letting other activities find their own level.

The relentless questing, questioning spirit of the late 1960s and early 1970s worked its way into a highly receptive Bob's life, as did an intense new interest in Marxism, which many colleagues would find unwelcome. Bob, under some duress, left Cambridge in 1975 to roam outside the strictures of the academy. Bob really thought that the liberatory leftward social thrust of the era would flourish. He did not reckon with the relentless counterrevolutionary neoliberal project signaled by the arrival of Margaret Thatcher in the UK and Ronald Reagan in the US, slowly steamrollering everything in its path ever since.

Bob's earlier science studies work pervaded everything he did as a Kleinian psychotherapist, a historian, and as a social science theoretician. Bob entered analysis after a jarring and disheartening brush with the cynical, sharp-elbowed culture in British television during his production of the brilliant ten part "Crucible: Science in Society" series in the early 1980s (to be found in the BFI archives). (Thatcherites in the industry saw to it that it was broadcast just the once.) Yet, Bob happily plunged into the welcoming depths of especially Kleinian psychoanalysis, and soon became a practitioner himself. Psychoanalysis, with its concerns about reflexivity and its penetration into unconscious presuppositions, could not have been a more congenial addition to his repertoire. In his writings, he became a sort of fusion reaction of the best elements of the two fields of science studies and psychoanalysis, employing the keenest instruments in one field to interrogate and improve the other.

Bob had a great long run. He started Free Associations Books (turning out several hundred titles) and, after losing control of it, continued with Process Press, ran the aforementioned journals, formed the Radical Science Collective, produced and narrated a TV series on science issues in society, trained as a psychotherapist, headed the celebrated Psychoanalysis and the Public Sphere conferences from 1987 to 1998, resumed academic life at firstly the University of Kent, and then as professor at Sheffield University, published *Mental Space* and *Whatever Happened to Human Nature* plus three edited volumes on science and technology (two with Les Levidow), and influenced a long stream of colleagues, associates, and readers. He developed an extensive website of his own papers and presentations (and of others he admired). Many of these papers of his were not conventionally published, but a formal collection is now in preparation posthumously, with Process Press. He believed that publishing should and would move to the digital world, and he was deeply committed to the free publication of materials, often ignoring copyrighting principles that would constrain others. Bob was a wonderfully engaging writer who always had worthwhile things to say.

"I continue to believe," Bob wrote in 1996, "that in the beginning was the value – not the word, nor the fact – and that all institutions, theories and practices are embodied politics." Those were fighting words when he started out and in some quarters they remain so. In revising his collection of Darwin essays in the 1980s, he provocatively stated that he had cause to thumb again through the Bible (as literature, not doctrinaire guide), which perhaps seemed even worse to many academics than taking Marx seriously, and argued that it provided

> a coherent frame of reference for the issues he addresses – origins, human frailty, temptation, the birth of knowledge, sin, pain, evil suffering, and the beginning of the sort of social order to which I wish to relate scientific knowledge – living and doing our best on the east of Eden.[3]

Hard to bridle at that. Bob did his best and it was much more than (*pace* Winnicott) good-enough.

The purpose of the intersecting and thematically coherent contributions by a group of distinguished scholars is to reexamine the current state of psychoanalysis and of STS in light of Young's work. Bob always reckoned and urged that one field (psychoanalysis, especially but not exclusively in its Kleinian incarnation) shed light on the other (STS) to the benefit of both. That is our objective here for fields that can always stand to be shaken up again for their own good. Now for the essayists:

Roger Smith argues that Young's passage from science studies to psychoanalysis was, as a critical enterprise, seamless, and sound. In the early and quite stellar stages of his career, Young already hauled a sharp scholarly knowledge of psychoanalysis to his historical research, while his cumulative acumen in the history and philosophy of science later informed a wary but deeply respectful approach to psychoanalysis as he navigated that highly conflictual domain too. One exacting field, through Young's bristling prismatic sensibility, informed the other and served the purpose of illuminating both. The indelible and overt moral aim behind Young's work in history of science as well as in psychoanalytic psychotherapy was to devise cogent ways to overcome the mind-body split – which he argued sacrificed understanding of the human subject for the sake of a counterfeit abstract grip on reality – and sought instead to "engage processes realizing human values in material actions."

E. A. Burtt and Alfred North Whitehead were intellectual mainstays for Young in that they squarely targeted the "incoherence" of the mind-body split, which "divided the processes going on 'inside' from the processes going on 'outside' a person, culture from nature, values from facts, the observer from the observed, the sacred from the profane, the individual from the collective." This pungent diagnosis posed, as Smith states, an intellectual theme for a lifetime. For Young, psychoanalysis became immensely attractive as a way of thinking that explores how the "internal" and the "external" relate in shaping human subjectivity. His 1994 book *Mental Space* tapped Kleinian psychoanalysis to reckon with the rampant dehumanization Young saw as intrinsic to a science which, Procrusteanly, limited itself to description of mind as functions of the brain Behold the reductionist program, which in its positivist form Burtt regarded as an "exceedingly subtle and insidious danger" to scientific thought.[4]

Smith stresses the antidote of relational theory, which Marxism, as Young expansively construed it, qualified as one example, signifying an analytical approach in which the elements investigated "are said to possess meaning by virtue of their relations to other elements." Any such framework is emphatically anti-dualistic: "There are no things, including persons, 'in-themselves,' but, rather, relational properties. Relational theories take process (or event, or act) to precede entities – to be ontologically prior." Hence, Smith establishes the vital continuity between Bob's work as scholar and, later, as therapist (and still a scholar).

Jim Secord critically assesses Young in his early scholarly posts at Cambridge, focusing on his tasks, ultimately, of exploding the theory of cerebral localization to kingdom come, and flushing into the open Thomas Malthus' influence on Darwin. The field of history of science in which Young worked was especially useful "in revealing the ideological foundations required for change." At the time, though, spotting Darwin's reliance on political economists' work was close to "anathema." The demonstrable influence of Malthus, dark patron saint of population studies, upon Darwin, Secord notes, was downplayed or resisted for their very different reasons by both conventional Marxists and languid liberals. Secord accordingly recounts Young's academic travails, some perhaps of his own making. Secord, turning the tables, aptly discusses the social context for Young's own scribblings, and in doing so also highlights the key question that Young raised ever afterward, which is, "why defer" to great men, to scientists, historians, and so on? Young, by all accounts, was a large and striking personality. He could have been more clubbable and gotten ahead faster except such a person is unlikely ever to have dared to devise or advance his theoretical contributions in the first place.

Secord chides Young's narrow focus in *Mind Brain and Adaptation,* but for Young, the insidious influence of Gall's "concepts and his empirical approach remain highly significant" in adjacent fields such as genetics where one still encounters breathtakingly naive deterministic propositions.[5] Applying a Latourian view to lab work in the nineteenth century is an interesting thought exercise but would not affect Young's conclusions. Secord justifiably notes Young's "frustrated and repetitive glosses" on his early work, from which many scholars have suffered because their earlier work wasn't absorbed and understood the first time around. Young never strived to fit Darwin into an ideological template nor use Malthus's influence as a spur toward devising a more radical view of science, he instead revealed these conditions as realities and took the lessons forward into subsequent projects.

Secord tartly observes that it

> would have been hard to imagine Young, the historical theorist, reading papers about the fossil remains of mammals, the dissection of the frontal cortex, or the reproductive organs of the platypus, but that was where the politics of science was most profoundly expressed.

That's a viewpoint, but here we inevitably bump up against what E. H. Carr termed a kind of archivist conceit.[6] Not everything in musty archives accurately reflects the reality of the times, and much of that material can seriously mislead us. Young contended that it was the conceptual mindset that scholars brought to archives that mattered most, not the data gleaned. Data does not interpret itself and reads very differently according to the assumptions we bring to it.

In assaying the impact of Young's first book *Mind, Brain, and Adaptation,* Timothy Sim astutely excavates the modern archives and finds a mother lode of fascinating controversy. On the strong supporters' side, Denis William raved that the book "must be the most important work upon the evolution of thought upon the results of cerebral localization written in the decade now ending."[7] *Science* labeled it a volume of "unusual excellence." Others, though, such as Samuel Shortt, defensively espied a barbarian cavorting at the gates. Sims' article examines "how and why such a multiplicity of readings was made possible." Such a multiplicity implies as much a sort of Rorschach test for the reviewers as it does for Young's work. "Meanings emerge," as Sim observes, "from an interplay between content and context, between the author's goals and the reader's social, cultural, and intellectual assumptions." Curious and disputatious things then inevitably arise. The neurologists read Young as a devotee of their work versus psychology when that was the last thing Young invidiously aimed to be.

By framing phrenology as an inextricable starting point for modern brain science, Young destabilized neat dichotomies of speculative versus scientific, old versus modern, and repressive versus trustworthy. Some readers simply did not understand that Bob was not rehabilitating Gall as a "true" scientist but showing that what many regarded as true blue science at the time had ample room for Gall, which should give us pause as to what may be happening in precincts of science today. "To avoid falling into the same traps as their forebears," Sim sums up Young's concern, "it was necessary for the historically-minded scientist to study phrenology's failings."

Finally, in this section, Michael Ruse offers a critical yet effervescent appreciation of the depth and impact of Young's Darwin studies, which still reverberate and incite, even if a sediment seems to have formed over latter-day citations. One qualification to Ruse's lively essay is that Young was Marxist only in an incipient way at the time of his Darwinian studies. His interest in Marxist studies was spurred by research expeditions into the intellectual crevices of Gall and Darwin and did not precede them. Young in those years, by his own amused admission, knew the Bible far better than he did *Das Kapital*.

In the next section on Young's radical science enterprise after he departed Cambridge, Kurt Jacobsen examines the explicitly dialectical disposition running throughout his writings. a cunning reflexivity, which, given its intensifying yet undogmatic Marxist influence, sent a few would-be disciples scurrying to more comfortable arenas. Today, much of what Young brought to STS survives because the "relational studies" approach he advocated absolutely was needed and valued, so long as it was politically neutered. Young had no taste for concessions to convention and so arguably soon found himself left behind because he was so far ahead. Like Donna Haraway, whom he admired, Young saw science as a "contested narrative field," from which repressed but ever present values needed to be acknowledged and accounted for.[8] Little wonder he would find psychoanalysis so compelling.

Maureen McNeil in a more illustrative experiential mode, as both a student and colleague of Young, zeroes in on key lessons, principles, and rules of thumb that Young disseminated regarding STS. "If we don't prefigure, we'll reproduce the existing society." "The critique of the factory applies equally to the laboratory" and, our favorite, "Marxism needs freaks" – because every discipline requires genuinely out-of-the-box people to progress and to stay in touch. Wilfred Bion would have heartily agreed. McNeil's chosen essay title axiom "Science *is* social relations" – a shockingly radical assertion at the time – precedes a reflective meditation on this key building block in Young's analytical strategy.

In an ensuing essay entitled with another Young exhortation, Les Levidow revisits the Radical Science Journal collective, linked with the Conference of Socialist Economists and the British Society for Responsibility in Science. What "moving on" meant, Levidow explains, was "a friendly invitation with a sometimes scary challenge to contest and abandon conventional concepts" and "a joint task to substitute different concepts and practices prefiguring a post-capitalist society." The corrosive solvents upon a recalcitrant official reality were to be Critical Theory, labour process perspectives, and psychoanalytic Marxism. How do we de-fetishize, and – again – why do we defer? are two presiding questions Young brought to every inquiry. We investigated how capitalist social relations were designed within and manifested as forces of production, which Marx understood broadly as "the general intelligence." Here Levidow links Young's project to psychoanalysis: "As this perspective suggests, capitalist value systems become naturalised through subconscious processes, which can be understood through various psychoanalytic concepts." What Jurgen Habermas portrayed as methodical self-reflection is what Young and like-minded scholars sought and championed.

Psychoanalysis forms the base and fulcrum for the rest of Young's multifarious career and thus forms the largest section of this volume. Young in his London decades was still a scholar and prolific writer as well as a documentary filmmaker, a book publisher, a conference organizer ("Psychoanalysis and the Public Sphere"), a journal editor (multiply), and whatever else he had time for in a colorful personal life. Young also revisited the academic arena for considerable spells.

Barry Richards offers an intimate account of Young's activities; among them, the founding of *Radical Science Journal* and its transmutation into *Science as Culture*, and the founding of Free Associations Books and then the journal *Free Associations*, which both marked a "return to Freud equipped with a sympathetic feminism and with political sensibilities shaped by the Vietnam War, the Cold War, and the deepening of consumer culture." Richards mentions Young's "impulse toward confrontation" with the "establishment," but affirms that these encounters stemmed from sound grounds for grievance.[9] Young's libertarian Marxism may appear oxymoronic to those unversed in the tradition, but "Bob recommended that we all should hold our concepts loosely and wear them lightly." Richards cites factional divides which a project promoting a socially engaged and left-oriented psychoanalysis inevitably engendered. Still, that project encouraged clinicians to apply their professional skills to phenomena outside the consulting room, "which fed into changes within the psychoanalytic world, in which there is now much more sociological reflexivity and political consciousness than there was forty years ago," giving rise to psychosocial studies in the 1980s.

Ann Scott likewise provides an intimate, vivid and, in her case, ambivalent account of experiences with Young, a "large, generous charismatic presence" at first sight at a Cambridge commune in 1971, and with whom she worked most closely as an editor at Free Associations Books in the 1980s and early 1990s. An all-in commitment to pursuit of the will-o-the-wisp of truth clearly tends to pair with what some associates take as a bruising lack of tact or politesse on occasion. The publisher with the acute eye for psycho-analytic talent also was, by anyone's standards, an appallingly inept busi-nessman who eventually lost his FAB company to shrewder agents, though of course he continued publishing through the holding company Process Press. Readers who knew Young will make up their own minds as to the piece but it ultimately is a touching and revealing portrait.

Young rued the estrangement of human nature from the natural world, and all its culturally impoverishing consequences. "Since money, as the ex-isting and active concept of value, confounds and confuses things" as Marx decried, Karl Figlio confronts money as the supreme everyday instrument of alienation, with the "drive to amass wealth" as its apotheosis.[10] Figlio detects that "pathological narcissism is the internal dimension of the in-filtration of abstract market relationships into every corner of human life, so extreme in neo-liberalism" today. (Ferenczi's graphic case illustration of anal-eroticism, referenced here, ought to be wry reading for anyone who deals with what Senator Bernie Sanders calls the "billionaire class.") Marx's sardonic portrait of money is rendered psychoanalytically intelligible and becomes strikingly useful as such. "The sphere of indebtedness, debt and fertility," Figlio avers, "is a situation in which social disquiet converges with the private world of the consulting room, and the analysis proffered by the social scientist converges with that of the psychoanalyst."

Peter Barham reappraises schizophrenia in light of the critique of scien-tific naturalism, a withering critique Young shared because it severed "the links between the suffering of mental patients and the wider human commu-nity of which they are part in the name of a supposedly neutral and value-free line of enquiry." The thrust of the diagnosis was to make a threatening source of incoherence seem coherent. The trouble is that the label itself was incoherent, fabricated from a medley of prejudices, ideologies, and institu-tional inertia. Noxious notions of degeneration and eugenics pervaded what medicine made of these sufferers. Schizophrenia, Barham argues, is bet-ter understood as a sociological matter rather than a biomedical disorder. Sufferers "were palpably reflecting the unacknowledged troubles of a larger system but were, instead, mostly spurned, treated as isolates, and inhibited or obstructed from making, or exploring, potentially productive connec-tions or from playing responsible roles." Unfortunately, deinstitutionaliza-tion abruptly led to abandonment, not revisioning the mental hospital as a means for "engaging with madness as a social problem."

Robert Hinshelwood follows the earlier direction that human and so-cial values are the context for all scientific, intellectual, professional and especially academic disciplines. The details of finely tuned human values direct and control the directions science and social sciences take. No knowledge exists without its context of sets of meanings and values of the human mind. Psychoanalysis offers an enduring and time-tested set of principles for connecting the meanings and values of the inner world of the human mind, and the mental expression in the external world of our investigations and habitual sets of behaviour and attitudes. Just as interesting is the way in which Young's principle of contextual values sets psychoanalysis itself in an interaction with its cultural context. As Young would say, there is no possibility of taking an above-the-battle position. And this challenges the idea that the unconscious mind is somehow outside the vagaries and slings and arrows of the cultural context our minds exist within – a challenging view for many psychoanalysts.

Taking a leaf from Young's *Mental Space* and also recalling Young's activities in Group Relations, Paul Hoggett addresses the stark ecological effects of alienation of man from nature. Conspiracy theories such as QAnon twaddle accordingly abound. Hoggett asks the oft-neglected question: "What social conditions support or militate against the love of truth?" *Apophenia*, too much in evidence, is "the tendency to perceive a connection or meaningful pattern between unrelated or random things." Yet, apophenia flourishes because citizens – or those representing them – ignored meaningful patterns in upward redistributions of wealth, unchecked public and private surveillance, legalized political corruption, and rigged markets where culprits get swiftly bailed out. As Hoggett laments, the links and connections that should be made are not made. Still, people don't make these dodgy connections unaided. In describing a palpable "structure of feeling for our age," the catastrophic anxiety Hoggett describes presupposes a layer of heedless superior agents between the citizenry and the problems to be solved who will not act, or at least not until they can offload the cost onto everyone else.

Finally, Valerie Sinason adds a concise and heartfelt tribute to Young, offering a warm, witty, and ebullient recollection of his inspiring and supportive effects on her life and career. "Bob's understanding that we were all embedded in socio-political situations and identities meant" that he could entertain and examine subjects not regarded in other precincts as "proper psychoanalytic thinking" – and advance, or help others advance, thinking in underexplored areas.

As a coda, readers are invited in the appendix to hear Bob's story in his own voice in a wide-ranging interview conducted at his London flat in 2015. (No penalties or tut-tuts for reading it first.) We trust readers familiar with Young's work will enjoy revisiting and reassessing his oeuvre, and that those to whom Robert M. Young is now merely a remotely familiar name will be duly informed, inspired, and encouraged in their own quests.

Notes

1 For a superb analytic blending of these two disciplines by one of Young's close associates, see Karl Figlio, "The Mentality of Conviction: Feeling Certain and the Search for Truth." In N. Minchev and R. D. Hinshelwood, eds *The Feeling of Certainty: Psychosocial Perspectives on Truth and Certainty*. London: Palgrave Macmillan, 2017. pp. 11–30, and his "Certainty, Doubt and Discovery" (paper presented at Anna Freud Centre Academic Faculty, London 2018).
2 R. M. Young, "Science *is* social relations", *Radical Science Journal* 5 (1977), p. 66.
3 R. M. Young, *Darwin's Metaphor*. Cambridge: Cambridge University Press, 1985, p. ix.
4 E. A. Burtt, *Metaphysical Foundations of Modern Science*. New York: Double-day Anchor Books, 1955, p. 225.
5 R. M. Young, *Mind Brain and Adaptation in the Nineteenth Century*. Oxford: Oxford University Press, 1970, p. 3. For an example of this exasperatingly re-silient mindset at work see D. Plomin, *Blueprint: How DNA Makes Us Who we Are*. Cambridge: MIT Press, 2019. See Jay Joseph's riposte review at. https://cpb-us-e1.wpmucdn.com/sites.ucsc.edu/dist/0/158/files/2021/10/FinalJay-Joseph-Review-of-Blueprint-Manuscript-AJP-Revised-9-17-2021.pdf. Also see E. Joyce, Blueprint – The Stealthy Return of Scientific Racism? https://blogs.bath.ac.uk/eric/2018/09/28/blueprint; and Nathaniel Comfort, Genetic Determinism Rides Again. *Nature* 25 September 2018.
6 See E. H. Carr, *What is History?* New York: Random House, 1961, pp. 5–35.
7 D. Williams, "Review of the book *Mind, Brain, and Adaptation* by R. M. Young]", *Brain 93* (1970), pp. 655–656.
8 "Deeds, as opposed to words, are the parents of facts." Donna Haraway argues, "That is, human action is at the root of what we can see as a fact, linguistically and historically." Haraway, *Primate Visions: Gender, Race and Nature in the World of Modern Science*. London: Routledge, 1990, pp. 3, 6.
9 See D. Kirsner, *Unfree Associations: Inside Psychoanalytical Institutes*. London: Process Press, 2000.
10 K. Marx, *Economic and Philosophical Manuscripts of 1844*. Moscow: Progress Publishers, 1959, p. 11.

Part 1

Darwin and Malthus

The Cambridge years

Chapter 1

Relations

History of science and the thought of the therapist

Roger Smith

Bob Young trained and worked as a psychoanalytic psychotherapist in the second half of his life. In the first half, he was by turns medical student, writer of a PhD on the history of brain science, academic lecturer in history and philosophy of science and politically radical activist, of a libertarian Marxian persuasion, in biological science and medicine. All the same, it seemed to me during his life, and it seems to me now, that there was no marked break in this career and, in particular, no break with the turn to psychotherapy. Rather, as I have written in a preceding essay, there was a common trajectory.[1]

This contribution to the festschrift is in two parts. The first part amplifies comment on the intellectual background in the history of science, in order to show the importance it had for Bob's work in psychoanalytic psychotherapy. There was a common concern with humanizing science and human relations. The second part turns to my own writing on the sense of movement, writing long tied to Bob's interests, for the reason – as I shall argue – that this sense has been thought pivotal to the value-laden experience of persons in relations to other people, to the world around them and to power. The link between history of science and psychotherapy has substance.

I want to make clear the reasons I have for writing. I am a retired academic, not a therapist, an intellectual historian and historian of the human sciences, a specialist in the history of psychology and beliefs about mind and brain. Because of what I first learned with Bob, and, if intermittently, by exchanges with him over half a century, I may have something to say about the intellectual resources Bob brought to therapeutic work. I studied with him – first as an undergraduate and then with him as my PhD supervisor at Cambridge, 1966–1970 – during his period as Assistant Lecturer in the sub-department of the History and Philosophy of Science. I had an independent academic career, and in later years we talked about his relations with the academic world which he had left. My own research and teaching included work on the history of psychiatry, psychology and psychoanalysis, and on Victorian evolutionary debates, creating resources for perspective on the movements in which Bob participated. Recently, I published a large-scale

DOI: 10.4324/9781003204244-3

study of the sense of movement, or kinaesthesia, and, in ways which I shall explain, this goes back to work I did in Cambridge. It has a lot to do with the very notion of relations. The book, *The Sense of Movement: An Intellectual History*, was in course of publication with the small press Bob set up, Process Press, now run by Em Farrell, at the time of his death.[2]

I

Bob moved into psychotherapy in the 1980s along with a significant number of other people radicalized politically in the late 1960s or early 1970s. Faced with the shift in national politics away from anything resembling the hopes for socialism in which they had invested their intellectual understanding and passion, people understandably attempted to maintain theory, ideals and models of practice in working with individuals, groups and relevant institutions. There was an urgent need to create ways of life, forums and media capable of sustaining this. One result, which Bob inspired, was the set of conferences on 'Psychoanalysis and the Public Sphere' in the 1980s, brought back to life in 2020.[3] Bob left Cambridge and the academic life in 1974/5, but he brought with him an intellectual framework, indeed a kind of worldview, informed by his pioneering and inspirational work in the history and philosophy of science. The work done in Cambridge was, in turn, a response to experiences he had had as a medical student, experiences which convinced him that medical learning addressed neither the needs of the whole person with mental illness nor his own subjective need for wholeness. He came to think this in the late 1950s at the prestigious medical school in Rochester, New York State, where the teaching included psychoanalysis. Bob did not complete his training but instead turned to intellectual study of the problems he thought mental medicine faced. He believed that inadequacies in medicine, and more widely in ways of being human, were a legacy of the split between thought about body and thought about mind. He conceived of the ideal of a science able to do justice to the realities, as he saw them, of *both* biology and the sensuous, subjective world, that is, the qualitative riches, purposiveness and ethical aspirations of the mental world. Intensely ambitious and fiercely committed, and a staunchly moral humanist, he set out to understand the historical and philosophical origins of the split. He always viewed this quest as *the* morally serious intellectual project. It led him personally to Cambridge, England and to the history and philosophy of science.[4]

In this chapter, I explore the intellectual content of this thinking, so as to suggest that, when Bob turned to the practice of psychotherapy in the 1980s, he was, in effect, *re-turning* to the moral and intellectual interests that had driven him all along. These interests have lost none of their pertinence over the decades. I open up a large perspective in which the history of science is relevant to psychotherapy.

From his first years as a young scholar to his last years as a therapist, it was Bob's intellectual habit to cite E. A. Burtt and A. N. Whitehead on the origins of modern science. The framing argument of Burtt's book on *The Metaphysical Foundations of Modern Physical Science* (originally published in 1924) was a touchstone for Bob. He thought Burtt had stated the theme that was, or should be, of basic importance in inquiry into human nature: the connection between intuition of what it is to be human (in shorthand, mind) and modern scientific knowledge (in shorthand, body). In general terms, Bob looked to psychoanalytic thought to make this connection clear, and it was his acute awareness that it had not done this that, in part, led to his disillusionment with medical education in Rochester. What readers of Burtt and Whitehead also learned was that the mind-body split in thought has the same roots, and in some sense is the reason for, the split in the modern age ('modernity') between values and facts. We moderns supposedly have 'real knowledge' by virtue of science; but because it is the unscientific world of subjective belief and emotion which confers values, we do not have knowledge of values. Thus, the argument goes, modern life is effective in material terms but all at sea, directionless, and in connection with human values politically disastrous. This theme lay behind the work in history of science, the radical politics and the psychoanalytic psychotherapy. The task, in each register, was to find the means to overcome the split and engage processes realizing human values in material actions.

Bob cited Burtt because he thought Burtt had shown how the split should and could be critically investigated through the intellectual history of science. Burtt was a US philosopher whose study of the scientific revolution in astronomy and mechanics argued that the Revolution (earlier but not now usually graced by scholars with a capital letter) was a revolution in the metaphysics at the foundations of Western thought. For Burtt, whatever the triumphs of physical science, the Revolution was a disaster for philosophy and civilized culture. The new way of thought, he argued, made it impossible for there to be systematic knowledge, that is, a true science, of the mental world of the individual or of the expression of mind in culture. Bob often cited a passage in which Burtt accused early natural scientists of achieving explanatory success at the expense of understanding people: 'Did it never cross their minds that sooner or later people would appear who craved verifiable knowledge about mind in the same way they craved it about physical events, and who might reasonably curse their elder scientific brethren for buying easier success in their own enterprise by throwing extra handicaps in the way of their successors in social science?'[5] The young Bob Young indeed 'craved verifiable knowledge about mind' and thought it essential for medicine. In his dissertation research at Cambridge, he searched in the history of attempts to relate mental functions to regions of the brain ('localization') in order to understand why such knowledge has not been forthcoming. He researched a history of nineteenth-century physicians, scientists and intellectuals relating mental functions (reason, emotion, memory, desire, etc.) to the physical world by localizing them in regions of the brain. (This is a programme very largely recreated, if with new technology, in contemporary neuroscience.) Bob argued that the localization of mental functions in the brain was the key step in the attempt to create a science of (non-spatial) mind in the material (spatial) body, thus making possible a biological approach to human nature. There were other large dimensions to the history which Bob did not discuss, notably the concept of reflex action, but he successfully made an entrée into the history of approaches to create biological science encompassing mind. The historical and philosophical irony is that the notion of body denotes a spatial entity, while the notion of mind denotes a non-spatial 'something'. As a consequence, the actual direction natural science has taken has tended to exclude reference to mind rather than successfully to integrate it. This leaves reference to mind – and values and subjectivity – without foundations.

Attempting seriously to grapple with historical knowledge led Bob to an appreciation of 'the context', to the study of the social and cultural circumstances in which statements about knowledge have meaning and consequence. This prepared his thinking, then influenced by the events of the late sixties and intensive reading of Marxist literature, for a radical political reading of 'context' and for the application of conclusions drawn to specific issues (like the use of evolutionary biology to support reactionary causes). From first to last, Bob's thinking was notably prescriptive as well as interpretive: he assumed intellectual work was work in the world, embodied work, and that it should contribute to the emancipation of how people live. Through the years in Cambridge, I surmise, he retained an ideal vision of psychoanalysis as *the* domain of real knowledge in which biology, psychology, medicine and social science come together in support of humane values. But his activity then was elsewhere.

In Whitehead, Bob found an authority, of unimpeachable scholarly credentials, to cite for the reasons why modern science and a humane vision were adrift, even opposed. Whitehead's still widely read book, *Science and the Modern World* (originally delivered as lectures in 1926) is comparable with Burtt's, though Whitehead also developed his arguments in the form of a profound, and notoriously difficult to read, metaphysics – a set of logically consistent claims about the nature of reality. Bob, like a number of his contemporaries who were literary scholars and humanist critics of modern culture, used passages from Whitehead to state that the philosophical foundations of modern natural science have isolated objective knowledge from subjective feeling. While science states facts about matter and motion, the values of love, beauty and feeling generally drift in a subjective world without foundations in knowledge. Such values are left to the poets. Re-expressed in the language of moral and political critique (Whitehead himself never used a political voice), the argument was that science has fostered thought which legitimates the treatment of people as objects, their treatment in ways cut off from each person's worth. The kernel of Whitehead's reasoning was the claim that science has established *abstract knowledge*, not knowledge of the world filled with values and subjective qualities as known in everyday activity and experience. In an oft-quoted phrase, Whitehead referred to the *'misplaced concreteness'* of 'the scientific scheme of the seventeenth century'.[6] For Whitehead, followed in this respect by Bob, the concrete is the presentational immediacy of the world as it exists in an actual person's perception, a world of colour, warmth, feeling and, in Whitehead's word, 'worth'.[7] Bob added that presentational immediacy is intrinsically constituted at a particular socio-political time and in a particular socio-political place.

Whitehead himself shaped a new metaphysics, sometimes called process philosophy, intended to replace the framework passed down from the seventeenth century and to do justice to the individual and collective experience modern science dismisses as subjective. It was not Bob's way to step back and attempt systematically to elaborate philosophy.[8] Rather, he referred to Whitehead, as he referred to Burtt, to legitimate historical and critical analysis of science, to expose dehumanizing thought about people across the biological, psychological and social sciences (broadly, the human sciences). These were public issues familiar to people across the educational spectrum in the 1960s in the form of debate about 'the two cultures' (the title of the famous lecture given by C. P. Snow in 1959).

Burtt and Whitehead made plain the incoherence of post-seventeenth-century Western ways of describing body separate from mind, and mind separate from body. This incoherence *mattered*: it divided the processes going on 'inside' from the processes going on 'outside' a person, culture from nature, values from facts, the observer from the observed, the sacred from the profane, the individual from the collective. It was indeed an intellectual theme for a lifetime. For Bob, it framed psychoanalysis as a way of thinking, as he hoped, that would explore how the 'internal' and the 'external' relate in the processes of individual development. This became the substance of his book, *Mental Space* (1994), which established links between the Kleinian tradition of psychoanalysis and the dehumanization Bob though intrinsic to science which was limited to description of mind as functions of the brain (the reductionist programme). Elaborating the theory of projective identification, he searched to delineate 'the space' in individual people's everyday lives that might contain forces working for developing humane relations.[9] He was therapeutically, politically and personally very well aware of 'the space' of destructive forces.

Though numerous biographical details about Bob's early career are not known precisely, Burtt and Whitehead possibly had a place in inspiring his trajectory as well as becoming reference points for critique. At university, he first studied philosophy at Yale, and he remembered Whitehead, 'to whom

I have continued to return as a guide since I first read him as a second-year undergraduate'.[10] Bob's PhD work, published as his first book, *Mind, Brain, and Adaptation in the Nineteenth Century* (1970, republished with new Preface, 1990) on the history of localization of mental functions in the brain could, in principle, have derived from Burtt.[11] Burtt had concluded his book with an illustration of the mess of mind-body dualism by examining the question, where can it be said we feel our sensations. It is, he argued, only the prejudice of belief, deferring to the Newtonian explanation of events in terms of change of motion in time and space, which makes people say that feelings are in the brain. Ordinary language, in contrast, locates the feel in the relations of a person with the object of perception, e.g. the pain is 'in' the finger where the knife cuts, not 'in the brain'.[12] It is a question with potential to disrupt the whole scientific tradition of locating mental functions in the brain. Awareness of this entered into Bob's choice for the title of his Kleinian book, *Mental Space*.

In the second half of the 1960s, after completing his PhD, this concern with biological approaches to mind, along with the opportunities for teaching which opened up at Cambridge, led Bob into scholarly work on the Victorian debate around Darwin's theory of evolution by means of natural selection. If any theory provides systematic grounds for seeking biological knowledge of mind, it is surely evolution: if humans have evolved from biological nature, their mental characteristics share that nature. What this argument actually involves and what conclusions it legitimately leads to agitated the Victorians, it agitated Bob and it has continued to agitate public intellectual culture down to the present. Bob's book on *Mind, Brain, and Adaptation* gave considerable attention to Herbert Spencer's 'Synthetic Philosophy' of evolution – a large influence (along with the work of Alexander Bain, also given a chapter in Bob's book) on the shift of interest in psychological thought to behaviour as functional adaptation. He extended his research to encompass Darwin, and, working as a historian, examined the way the Victorian interest in 'man's place in nature' (in T. H. Huxley's expression) was bound up with the question of science and religion and with political and economic argument.[13] The Darwin scholarship had great influence, and the relevant papers were subsequently collected in *Darwin's Metaphor: Nature's Place in Victorian Culture* (1985). The Darwin work also provided the scholarly model for Bob's wider, explicitly politically involved studies of science as culture, carried out both before and after he left Cambridge.

As I have commented, Bob's scholarly practice was always prescriptive. He was heir, in this like Freud, to the Enlightenment project: knowledge is to improve the human estate. Bob was brought up in a Presbyterian family, with strongly articulated moral principles, in Dallas. He was something of a preacher. Interestingly like Burtt, he spoke and wrote in a voice which was at one and the same time historically descriptive, philosophically critical and morally prescriptive. One of his better known papers, which began life as his papers so often did, as an inspirational lecture, opened: 'I begin, rather as a clergyman would, with a text ...'[14] As in a life directed by religious faith, Bob understood the way people think and the way people live to be inseparable. His references to Burtt and Whitehead were 'texts' for his message. If one believes in the identity of knowledge and practice, as Bob more and more self-consciously asserted as he became politically radical, the failure of a general framework of thought is a failure of a way of life. For the Christian believer, which Bob was not, though he knew something emotionally about what personal belief might mean, the general framework of modern science deprived people of their 'worth'.[15] Burtt had posed the issue in rather melodramatic humanistic terms: had it 'been worth the metaphysical barbarism of a few centuries to possess modern science'?[16] It was not a large step, in the early 1970s, to reformulate this question (in my words): 'Was it worth social, political and military barbarism to possess modern science', and to translate the issues at stake into the practice of 'radical science'. When Bob became an activist, he in effect declined to be a Cartesian mind, a philosopher or scholar using abstract reason as if reason stands independently of the biologically and socially embedded, particular and individual, body. He sought instead to expose reason's activity *in actual work*, including actual scientific work. Bob retained from his early teacher at Yale, Richard Rorty, an understanding that learning is not passive but is the consequence of what we do.[17] His voice was therefore compelling, confrontational, not abstract, analytic and detached. This turned on some and turned off others.

It was a driving preoccupation with Bob, even before his politics became radical, that nineteenth-century argument continues in present argument. It was, after all, perceived difficulties in relating mind and body in the present that had led him to work in the history of science in the first place. The argument that the history of the biological and human sciences exposes the limits of reductionist natural science as the basis for humane living ran through all the work in Cambridge. It was no great step from this to political engagement in response to the role of modern science and technology in political violence – mass violence, as in the Vietnam War, or individual violence, as in physical therapies in mental illness. The intellectual position derived from Burtt and Whitehead merged with belief in the inhumane alienation inherent in the capitalist labour process. The attempt to pursue the human sciences could not succeed, according to Marxian argument, unless the sciences ground themselves in the constitution of the human in the actual history of the relations of production. The argument was reflexive: historical scholars and scientists should understand the material conditions of their own labour. Radical science sought to expose the ideological nature of belief in the transcendental objectivity of science. As Bob asserted, 'science *is* social relations'.[18]

Bob brought all this background with him when he turned to psychoanalytic psychotherapy. This was evident in his written and especially in his spoken style, for example, in the inaugural lecture he gave as Professor of Psychotherapy and Psychoanalytic Studies at the University of Sheffield in 2000. The therapeutic demand to respond to the highly individual particularities of each case, however, brought a new kind of discipline to the articulation of relations between theory and practice. It also brought Bob into intensive engagement with the literature of Kleinian and object relations thinking, giving specific content to the notion of the material, historical conditions of human lives. Bob had no doubt that there was a biological content to these processes – he was, for instance, sympathetic to the emphasis on the innate aggressiveness of the child's earliest relations that Klein had delineated. At the same time, he focused intently on the social processes mediating the actual particularities and subjective qualities of these contents. His ability to speak suggestively about how the biological and the social relate, often using a personal, emotionally coloured voice, ensured an audience. For many within the therapeutic professions, the value psychoanalytic approaches have lies precisely with this capacity to show how the biological and social relate in individual lives. Karl Figlio circulated a paper, "'The lineage of the superego": a psychoanalytic view of entrenched beliefs', which explored the psychic roots of prejudice, and (as I read it) exemplified this potential.[19]

II

The second part of the paper draws on my work on the sense of movement in order to deepen argument connecting the history of science and psychoanalytic psychotherapy. The starting point is once again Burtt and, especially, Whitehead. The sense of movement may sound marginal, even esoteric, but it is not.

Cartesian dualism involved incoherent talk about a non-spatial mind acting in, and having knowledge of, a spatial world. Some of the difficulties this entailed were apparent to Descartes himself, while they were to preoccupy many people in different activities in subsequent centuries.[20] Descartes set out the ideal of mechanistic explanation of the natural world, and in doing so took the body and much of psychic life (e.g., the passions) to belong to this realm explicable in terms of matter and motion. Though explanation in mechanistic terms was widespread, and sometimes spectacularly successful from the late seventeenth century onwards, there also, however, continued to be ways of scientific thought that did not follow the explanatory pattern. Prominent examples include treatments of attraction at a distance (such as gravity) central to Newtonian science and also theories of life positing active powers and principles of organization. Studying life and death, health and illness, philosophically minded physicians referred widely to non-mechanistic notions, such as function and purpose, confounding dualist categories. This is still so – as in contemporary reference to mental functions. Bob cited Whitehead: 'In between [the concepts of mind and body] there lie the concepts of life, organism, function, instantaneous reality, interaction, order of nature, which collectively form the Achilles heel of the whole system [of scientific materialism]'.[21] There was and is a rich language articulating claims to knowledge not reducible to statements about mind or statements about body; this is a language which expresses events in terms of *relations*. We sustain this language in everyday and therapeutic talk about *persons* or *people*.

A relational theory is one in which the elements to which the investigator attends, be they physical, mental, mathematical, social or whatever, are said to possess meaning by virtue of their relations to other elements. Whitehead, discussing relations, referred to a philosophy of 'functional activity': 'By this I mean that every actual thing is something by reason of its activity; whereby its nature consists in its relevance to other things, and its individuality consists in its synthesis of other things so far as they are relevant to it'.[22] In the context of psychological discussion, relational theories are radically anti-dualistic, opposed to division of mind and body, self and object, thought and action, description and prescription, individual and society. There are no things, including persons, 'in-themselves' but, rather, relational properties. The social psychologist Kenneth J. Gergen's comment, 'the belief that the skin marks the separation of the body from the world is a useful fiction that we have developed together', is pertinent.[23] According to the thought behind this, we are 'we' by virtue of relations, and where a line is drawn at the skin between the self and what is not the self is a social and historical matter. Similarly, in my research, I have tried to demonstrate how commonly writers have invoked the sense of movement in maintaining that, at base, 'we humans' are phenomena in relations not entities of one kind or another. (For the purpose of this argument, it misses the point to seek to specify whether 'we' are spiritual, biological, social or something else in nature.) Relational theories take process (or event, or act) to precede entities – to be ontologically prior. I add the claim that the historical literature shows subjective awareness of movement or being moved, kinaesthesia, and of effort and resistance, to have had a large place in supporting such thought. In short, talk about relations has been intimately bound up with the sense that people are embodied subjects in movement.

Before explaining this, I should clarify the fact that psychologists may associate a relational approach with an emphasis in psychotherapy on the therapist's emotional, empathetic engagement with the notions of well-being distinctively relevant to the patient and the patient's socio-cultural background. 'Relational therapy' attends to the co-production of emotion and meaning in the therapeutic encounter. In the US, this links to the work of Jean Baker Miller. There is also the more phenomenologically oriented understanding of Thomas Fuchs, among others, as well as Gergen's distinctive work.[24] For someone outside the psychotherapeutic community who is familiar with the language of relations, the phrase 'relational therapy' appears tautological, since, after all, every encounter is in its nature relational. In context, however, the phrase of course refers to certain kinds of relations held to be therapeutically appropriate in the way objective relations (as maintained in orthodox psychoanalytic practice) are said not to be. The word 'relational' gains traction by pointing to the contrast of certain kinds of therapeutic relations with the observation 'at a distance' thought characteristic of emotionally neutral and visual interactions.

Relational therapy acknowledges a debt to the object relations theories in psychoanalysis deriving from Donald Winnicott and other analysts, and these theories include claims about the objective basis of relations in instinctual, biological processes. In the background are Kleinian insights into the developmental origins of the sensory world in foetal life in the womb, in the birth passage and in the initial contact between neonate and mother. As a number of psychologists have postulated, the foetus's first subjective awareness may in significant part originate with the sense of movement, the sense which, for this reason, can be posited as the first discernible instance of the relational co-constitution of the child's psyche. In the foetus, there is movement-resistance, in which process there are the beginnings of the differentiation of a new individual subjectivity.[25] Belief about the ontogenetic primacy of the sense of movement is at least not disconfirmed by phylogeny, as it is thought that basic proprioceptive mechanisms (the automatic and largely unconscious nervous basis of movement control) have an evolutionary history of at least 500 million years.[26]

It is nevertheless the case, that psychologists and everyday speakers alike rather pass over the sense of movement, treating it either as a sub-species of the sense of touch or as a vague bodily sense – 'dark feeling', as it is called in Russian.[27] Countering this lack of attention, I have argued that the appreciation and understanding of the sense of movement has long been central to the reasons people give for talking about humans as actors in processes, in relations, rather than for talking about people as minds or bodies (let alone as brains). Bob, anticipating the historical research, very much welcomed the direction of argument. Indeed, my interest in kinaesthesia, or sensed self-movement, actually goes back to the PhD I did under Bob's supervision. I am not suggesting anyone should return to a thesis completed (but not published) 50 years ago! All the same, there is a feeling of fitness in publishing the results of many decades of broadening and deepening the inquiry with the aptly named Process Press.[28] There is, it turns out, a much richer story to be told than either of us long ago imagined.

The argument is this. The sense of moving or being moved, including the sense of effort and of resistance to it, centrally contributes to the feelings constituting awareness of being an embodied subject. There is a history to the claim. Around 1800, various authors began to refer to a distinct sense of movement, then called the muscular sense and only later called kinaesthesia, and they related this sense to accounts of the origins of knowledge as well as to intuitions about the nature of the body. Language did not separate developmental psychology and philosophical statements, as twentieth-century practice was to attempt to do, but described knowledge building on the differentiation of the knowing subject, the self, and the known object, non-self (or world). This differentiation, it was argued, is given in phenomenal awareness (or consciousness) of activity-resistance. They developed a picture of the muscular sense as having a dual nature, at one and the same time expressing or representing active, effortful, and passive, modes.[29] In Jean Starobinski's figure of speech, this awareness lay behind the conceptualization of 'a couple', activity-resistance, as the foundation of relations with the world, including the relations called knowledge.[30] Conceptualization in these terms, for example, very much informed the psychology and philosophy of Spencer and of Alexander Bain, both of whom were important to Bob's early work on mind-brain localization.[31]

Writers on the senses described, and still do describe, the earliest inchoate sense of the body, given in the feelings of pleasure and pain and in feelings of movement and resistance to movement, as the source of subjective differentiation of self and other. Living activity engenders resistance, and reflective articulation of this process, activity-resistance, is the ground for awareness of being in relations. Such relational language is not language 'of mind' or 'of body' but of participation in a world. It disowns Cartesian dualism as a conceptual framework and instead promotes a feeling for integrated relations. It is the kind of language Bob looked for in promoting psychoanalytic theory informed by the givens of life (the biology, if you wish, like the sheer aggressiveness of the psyche Klein posited) *and* the phenomenology of 'worth' given in awareness of the value of being human.

There are other substantial dimensions to argument about the sense of movement. Here, I briefly point to four which are relevant to the intellectual background Bob brought to psychotherapy.

Firstly, there is a long-held contrast in the literature of Western culture between tactile knowing and visual knowing, the former associated with 'contact' and subjectivity – and with 'the primitive' and femininity, and the latter associated with 'distance' and objectivity – and with science and masculinity.[32] This contrast informs the history of the discipline required to achieve objectivity, a discipline, well known to the analytic therapist who looks and hears but does not touch (or smell?). Touching and being touched, which involve a sense of movement, create relations which, in many cultures and certainly in the contemporary Western world, are associated with intimacy, so much so that the sense is bound by complex, historically formed social rules. The situation facing therapists and patients in conditions of social distancing during the Covid-19 pandemic, where work proceeded online, was surely a large stimulus to thinking further about this. Online technology mediates communication at a distance, which would seem to be just what the analytic discipline requires. What, then, if anything, is at stake with the desire to have physical presence, even though it excludes touch, and the belief that it makes a difference to the therapeutic encounter?

Secondly, the structure of talk about action-resistance in the formation of knowledge suggests a striking parallel to the Fichtean and Hegelian dialectic. These philosophers described the spirit divided against itself and through the relations that thereby develop striving to integrate and fully realize its being in self-awareness or real knowledge. I think it can be shown that there are historical and structural links between belief in the sense of movement giving rise to embodied knowledge and Marxian notions of the process of the movement to satisfy basic material needs giving rise to reaction, and action-reaction generating historical change. At one stage, Bob put considerable effort into trying to think through Marxian arguments in order to understand science as a labour process.[33] He later approached the study of relations, the action and reaction in the individual's early development as the concrete, actual, particular site which mediates the dialectic in people's lives. There are, I suggest, reasons originating in the subjective sources of feeling for relations in movement why language refers to 'making a move' in human relations and to political 'movements' and to political 'resistance'. There is metaphor at work here (and Bob was interested in metaphor – 'mental space', 'natural selection' and so on), but I am referring not to just figures of speech but (again, like Bob) to historically formed interconnections between knowledge, or science, social structure and power. The language of the feeling of movement is richly meaningful because it is the language of *a feeling of powers, or forces, at work*, powers differentiated into those that are said to lie 'within' and 'without' a self. The phenomenology of this is central to modern notions of agency and identity. Think, for example, of the complex social play in debate around who, in a given situation, should make the first move.

This mention of powers or forces leads to a third line of argument, which I stress here because it confirms the connection in Bob's career between the history of science and psychotherapy. The language of forces or powers – besides being political language and the language used to describe awareness of action-resistance in sensed movement – was also the language of natural philosophy (or natural science, before specialization established the modern disciplines). There was extensive discussion of forces in eighteenth and nineteenth-century natural philosophy, which significantly disrupted dualistic categories of mind and body. Philosophers, physicians and non-specialist writers often referred to forces when they attempted to understand the qualitative phenomena of nature (life processes, gravity, electricity, chemical reactions and so on). Elsewhere, I have suggested that there was a circulation of reference and meaning between statements about the sensed activity-resistance thought intrinsic to touch and belief in the presence of active-resisting forces in the physical and living world.[34] Many writers agreed that imagination about forces at play in the physical world originated with subjective awareness of force-resistance in personal lives. To be sure, anthropologists and positivists, in the late nineteenth and early twentieth centuries, dismissed this imagination as 'primitive thinking'. Nevertheless, as the examples of both Whitehead and dialectical thought suggest, there was much more at stake in the underlying reasoning than crude anthropomorphism. The human manner of gaining knowledge of activity-resistance in effort and movement may constitute a kind of framework in terms of which a human, as opposed to an abstract, understanding of the human relation to nature is possible. This, for example, is the kind of argument to be found in the contemporary work of Tim Ingold and in varieties of ecological consciousness.[35] Once again, the very general point is that people are participants in, not neutral observers of, a world.

Lastly, there is a history connecting the sense of movement to the feel for reality. This extends to the argument that awareness of activity-resistance is the source of the very notion of reality.[36] In its best known form, the argument is that of Dr. Johnson, who 'struck' a boulder in order to refute the philosophical idealism of Bishop Berkeley. He performed a movement and established the presence of resistance in order to prove the presence of the physical world. Language, indeed, reflects a special relationship between touch (and sensed movement) and what people think real ('palpable reality'). One of the creators of modern dance, Martha Graham, is said to have declared: 'movement never lies'.[37] While this may be questioned as a theory of knowledge, it certainly says something of the greatest importance to dancers and to ordinary perception. Saying that a sensation of movement is not real would be like saying we don't have pain when we have a sense of pain. This is a sphere of inquiry of enormous contemporary interest because of fascination with and heavy investment in virtual realities, and because of the switch, greatly accelerated in the conditions of the Covid-19 pandemic, to digitalized communication without touch. The issues at stake in turn relate to the differences between live performance and recorded performance, as important to sport and teaching as to the arts, and to therapy, and to 'walking in' as opposed to 'looking at' landscape and so on. Since (as I have said) a number of modern psychologists suggest that the foetus's subjectivity begins with sensed movement, analytic accounts of what happens to this subjectivity would seem to relate to anything we might say about the feeling for reality. In a longer study, account would also have to be taken of the bodily feelings in general, sometimes called coenaesthesia.

III

It remains to conclude.

The potential interest of these ramifications of discussion of the sense of movement to a psychotherapist of Kleinian or object relations persuasion is,

I hope, apparent. If indeed the affective character of the phenomenal world in the first hours, days and months of life forms the pattern of all subsequent relations with events, things and people alike, then the senses that mediate the first relations constitute the means through which a person forms. The study of how relations then actually establish themselves, in each person's case, through such activity as projective identification, gives analysis its subject matter. Whether it will make a difference to analytic theory or practice to recognize the place of kinaesthesia in awareness then becomes a question. My supposition, though as someone who is not a therapist, is that it will. I would, for instance, suggest that there is something important to be learned from the fact that the everyday language of relations – at the level of personal intimacy, with objects and with social and political relations – is rich with figures of speech signifying the importance of touch and movement: 'a touching appeal', 'you don't move me', 'I grasp this', 'hands-on experience', 'don't touch', 'he's under her thumb', 'to join a political movement', 'freedom of movement' and much more. This language returns to a point already made, a point central to Bob's ambition for psychoanalysis. The language of 'moving', 'grasping', 'resistance' and so on is not language distinctive of discourse about mind or about body, but language fitting the life *of a person*, or the lives *of people* collectively, participating in a world. Each person's earliest awareness of, and subsequent reflection on, the sense of movement, and of resistance to it, enters into living out what this language actually means.

The common trajectory in Bob's intellectual career exemplifies the Enlightenment project to achieve a science of the human in the service of an equitable, just society. In late eighteenth-century terms, in the tradition developed by Kant, Feuerbach, Marx, Spencer and many others, the project is to establish an anthropology.[38] An anthropology (in this meaning of the word) requires knowledge true to the actual sensuous, passionate phenomenal world of being human, the world formed in individual subjectivity but inescapably shaped by the historically shaped social relations present at birth. Science must encompass as part of scientific knowledge the observing subject, the subject which, or who, produces knowledge. This means encompassing the historically specific, materially, technologically and economically particular subject as member of a social process. It also means encompassing the psychological subject, the self formed in the intimate but social relations of the earliest days and years. In this chapter, I have pointed to the significance of Western ways of thought which have found the source of feelings *for relations, and hence for meaning,* in the very movement of living beings, through action-resistance.

Bob was a realist in the theory of knowledge. Though accepting that he was a social constructionist, he was a realist in the sense Whitehead was a realist: knowledge must do justice to the shared, social, empirical realities with all their colour, feel, evaluative content and force. As a result, the Marxist concept of mediation became a very important part of his thinking, since it provided a framework for understanding how the material practices of daily life and of science alike result in ways of thinking about reason and feeling detached from material life. Material practices, he held, become embedded and form the self in the intimate relations that Klein and object relations theorists had elaborated. He wanted to integrate it all. This was reflected in his enthusiasm for biography as a genre of writing and, in his estimation, even the model genre for human self-understanding. He found in biography realist writing about *the constitution* of the person in relations. Understanding this required a language appropriately acknowledging the forces at work in a person's life: 'Nothing is ultimately contextual; all is constitutive, which is another way of saying all relationships are dialectical'.[39] Awareness of this 'dialectical' character, I argue through a history of the sense of movement, has been at the heart of a Western intellectual tradition – and, as it may be, other traditions as well – built around a sense of the participatory engagement of being human rather than around the abstraction required by objectivity.[40]

It is the fourth and last dimension of argument around the sense of movement which most obviously concerns Kleinian and object relations psychotherapy. Our feel for what is real and the very notion of embodied subjectivity appear tied to activity-resistance in touch and movement. For therapeutic purposes, the problems with realist theories of knowledge do not necessarily matter. What matters is the experiential content of feeling, apparently dating from the time of foetal life, the feeling traceable in the practice and language of 'contact'. Everything, in all its endlessly rich variety, that affects this may become relevant to a person – and just how it does so for a particular person is, of course, the business of analysis in the large sense.

There was intellectual and moral continuity between Bob Young's work as a historian of science and as a psychotherapist. If we speak of a common trajectory in his work, it is necessary to remember that he encountered psychoanalysis as a medical student, at the time when there was intense discussion in the US, especially around the work of David Rapaport, on the relation of psychoanalysis to mainstream scientific psychology. This coincided with historical research on the importance to Freud himself of his scientific training, of his early 'Project for a Scientific Psychology' and of his belief that he was creating psychoanalysis as a science. In a way, it might be said that Bob's writing on brain localization and on Darwin was one long path exploring the intellectual conditions and possibilities for a psychoanalytic discipline of the human. Turning to psychotherapeutic practice, which was also a re-turning, Bob envisaged a way of life in which knowing and doing, and the personal and the political, were a unity. He thought such a way of life required a philosophy and an anthropology, an appreciation of what is in the world that discerns 'worth' in the human state and not only matter and motion. Exploring these prospects requires an understanding of the history of science. That history, where it concerns the legacy of mind-body dualism and the search for systematic knowledge of being human, shows that the embodied phenomenology of movement, of action and resistance, has been a central source of meaning, at one and the same time personal and shared.

Notes

1 R. Smith, The quest for humane relations: the trajectory of an intellectual life. *Free Associations*, 80 (2020): 11–26. That essay, in a special issue of *Free Associations* dedicated to Bob as the journal's founding editor, included an obituary. In the present chapter, I draw on the earlier essay, though not repeating biographical detail, with the kind agreement of the Editors of *Free Associations*. The former essay began life as a contribution to the conference, 'Remembering Bob Young', Darwin College, Cambridge, 20 March 2020, and I appreciate and draw on the contributions of other participants and warmly thank Simon Schaffer, whose idea it was and who made it possible.

2 R. Smith, *The Sense of Movement: An Intellectual History.* London: Process Press, 2019. For the general history of psychology, see R. Smith, *Between Mind and Nature: A History of Psychology.* London: Reaktion Books, 2013.

3 Recreated by the editors of *Free Associations* Kurt Jacobsen and David Morgan and hosted online since 2019 by the Freud Museum: https://www.freud.org.uk/event/psychoanalysis-and-the-public-sphere-social-fault-lines.

4 R. M. Young, Science and the humanities in the understanding of human nature. *Inaugural Lecture* (2000) University of Sheffield. At: http://www.humannature.com/rmyoung/papers/paper131h.html (accessed 2010). Because Bob gave many talks in different settings, his papers, some published, others unpublished, are also scattered. He set up a number of online sites, aiming to be more systematic, including http://www.psychoanalysis-and therapy.com/rmyoung/index.html.

5 E. A. Burtt, *The Metaphysical Foundations of Modern Physical Science: A Historical and Critical Essay*, 2nd edn. London: Routledge & Kegan Paul, 1932: 318–319; cited, e.g. R. M. Young, The mind-body problem. In R. C. Olby et al. (Eds.), *Companion to the History of Modern Science.* London: Routledge, 1990: 702–711.

6 A. N. Whitehead, *Science and the Modern World.* Cambridge: Cambridge University Press, 1953: 70. For an excellent introduction to Whitehead and Whitehead scholarship: R. Desmet & A. D. Irvine, Alfred North Whitehead, *Stanford Encyclopedia of Philosophy* (2018). http://plato.stanford.edu/entries/whitehead/. I also introduced Whitehead: R. Smith, Alfred North Whitehead – against dualism. Философский журнал/ *Philosophy Journal* [Moscow], 5(4) (2020): 17–36.

7 A. N. Whitehead, *Modes of Thought.* Cambridge: Cambridge University Press, 1938: 149.

8 The closest he came to doing this was in an early article on primary and secondary qualities, R. M. Young, Persons, organisms ... and primary qualities [written 1969]. In J. R. Moore (Ed.), *History, Humanity and Evolution: Essays for John C. Greene.* Cambridge: Cambridge University Press, 1989: 375–401, a contribution to the festschrift for John Greene, another historian of science drawn to the field for its potential for insight into the relations of science and values.

9 R. M. Young, *Mental Space.* London: Process Press, 1994: 3–11, 168–171.

10 Young, "The Mind-Body Problem." Digital file [246].

11 R. M. Young, *Mind, Brain, and Adaptation in the Nineteenth Century: Cerebral Localization and Its Biological Context from Gall to Ferrier,* Reissue. Oxford: Clarendon Press, 1990.

12 Burtt, *Metaphysical Foundations*: 308–321 (this passage is from the completely rewritten concluding chapter of the 2nd edition.). For persuasive re-statement of the argument, see A. Noë, *Out of Our Heads: Why You Are not Your Brain, and Other Lessons from the Biology of Consciousness.* New York: Hill and Wang, 2009.

13 I will not go further into Bob's Darwin research. See James A. Secord's and Timothy Sim's contributions in this volume.

14 R. M. Young, Darwin's metaphor and the philosophy of science [written 1986]. *Science as Culture*, 3 (1993): 375.

15 He characteristically stated (Young 2000: digital file [10]): 'I am not a theist, though I sometimes nostalgically wish I could be. I am, however, a believer in the collective wisdom contained in religious traditions.'

16 Burtt, *Metaphysical Foundations*: 303.

17 Young, Darwin's metaphor and the philosophy of science.

18 The title of Young's radically experimental paper, Science *is* social relations. *Radical Science Journal*, 5: 65–131, the rhetoric of which Maureen McNeil discusses in this volume.

19 Circulated to participants at the conference 'Remembering Bob Young' (see note 1).

20 For example, my first book, a history of the defence of insanity in Victorian criminal law, R. Smith, *Trial by Medicine: Insanity and Responsibility in Victorian Trials.* Edinburgh: Edinburgh University Press. 1981, shaped an account of the decision, guilty/not guilty by reason of insanity in terms of the dualistic discourse on mind and body operating in legal institutions. For Bob's later brief (and rather disappointing) summary of the mind-body question, see Young, "The Mind-Body Problem."

21 Whitehead, *Science and the Modern World*: 71.

22 A. N. Whitehead, *Symbolism: Its Meaning and Effect.* Barbour-Page Lectures, University of Virginia 1927. Cambridge: Cambridge University Press, 1958: 26.

23 K. J. Gergen, *Relational Being: Beyond Self and Community.* New York: Oxford University Press, 2009: xxvii.

24 J. B. Miller, *Toward a New Psychology of Women.* Boston, MA: Beacon Press, 1986; T. Fuchs & S. C. Koch, Embodied affectivity: on moving and being moved. *Frontiers in Psychology*, 5 (2004): 1–12; T. Fuchs & H. De Jaegher, Enactive inter subjectivity: participatory sense-making and mutual incorporation. *Phenomenological Cognitive Science*, 8 (2009): 465–486; and Gergen, *Relational Being.* Gergen has been a central figure in North-American controversy in psychology about the viability of social constructionist theories.

25 For the claim to the priority of movement among the foetus's senses, see M. Sheets-Johnstone, *The Primacy of Movement*, 2nd edn. Amsterdam and Philadelphia: John Benjamins, 2011: 133, 228, 434; and S. Gallagher, *How the Body Shapes the Mind.* Oxford: Clarendon Press, 2005. For development, see P. Rochat, Five levels of self-awareness as they unfold early in life. *Consciousness and Cognition*, 12(4) (2003): 717-731. I presented my thought about these matters, in a paper written with psychologists in mind, in R. Smith, Human movement, kinaesthesia, dance. In W. Pickren (Ed.), *The Oxford Research Handbook of the History of Psychology.* New York: Oxford University Press, 2022.

26 J. C. Tuthill & E. Azim, Proprioception. *Current Biology*, 28(5) (2018): 194–203.

27 R. Smith, The muscular sense in Russia: I. M. Sechenov and materialist realism. *Journal of the History of the Behavioral Sciences*, 55 (2019): 5–20.

28 I published a brief statement of leading points, as I then understood them, in R. Smith, The background of physiological psychology in natural philosophy. *History of Science*, 11 (1973): 75-123.

29 How actually to characterize the content of mental processes – in terms of representations, images, ideas, acts, functions and so on – has been a huge issue; but there is no need to go into this here.

30 J. Starobinski, *Action and Reaction: The Life and Adventures of a Couple.* New York: Zone Books, 2003.

31 Young, *Mind, Brain, and Adaptation*, chs. 3, 5; Smith, *The Sense of Movement*, ch. 8.

32 On the discipline of scientific objectivity see L. Daston & P. Galison, The image of objectivity. *Representations*, 40 (1992): 81–128.

33 See Les Levidow, this volume.

34 R. Smith, Kinaesthesia and a feeling for relations. *Review of General Psychology*, 24(4) (2020): 355–368.

35 T. Ingold, Being Alive: Essays on Movement, Knowledge and Description. London: Routledge, 2011; A. Berque, *Thinking through Landscape*. Abingdon, OX: Routledge, 2013.

36 For philosophical work sensitive to the psychological importance of the connection between touch and a feel for reality, see M. Ratcliffe, Touch and situatedness. *International Journal of Philosophical Studies*, 16 (2008): 299–322, and M. Ratcliffe, Touch and the sense of reality. In Z. Radman (Ed.), *The Hand, an Organ of the Mind: What the Manual Tells the Mental.* Cambridge, MA: MIT Press, 2013: 131–157. Modern syntheses of the biological and phenomenological approaches recognizing the importance of movement include A. Berthoz & J-L. Petit, *The Physiology and Phenomenology of Action.* Oxford: Oxford University Press, 2008, and Sheets-Johnstone, *Primacy of Movement.*

37 As cited in C. Noland, *Agency and Embodiment: Performing Gestures/Producing Culture.* Cambridge, MA: Harvard University Press, 2009: 11. The words are actually those of Graham's father.

38 Though Bob used 'anthropology' in passing to describe his project in *Darwin's Metaphor: Nature's Place in Victorian Culture.* Cambridge: Cambridge University Press, 1985: 214, 243, he did not relate it to the term's German-language cultural roots in the eighteenth and nineteenth centuries, except indirectly through discussion of the Marxist theory of human nature. I attempted to unpack these issues in theories of human nature in R. Smith, *Being Human: Historical Knowledge and the Creation of Human Nature.* Manchester: Manchester University Press, 2007. Also see R. Smith, The senses of touch and movement and the argument for active powers. In B. Demarest, J. Regier & C. T. Wolfe (Eds.), *Animism and Its Discontents: Soul-Based Explanations in Early-Modern Natural Philosophy & Medicine.* Special issue, *History of Philosophy of Science*, online June 2021. https://doi.org/10.1086/715975.

39 Young, *Darwin's Metaphor*: 241.

40 The sense of movement is clearly important in other cultures. See, e.g., feeling the pulse and breath in Chinese and Japanese medicine: S. Kuriyama, *The Expressiveness of the Body: The Divergence of Greek and Chinese Medicine.* New York: Zone Books, 1999.

Chapter 2

Revolutions in the head

Darwin, Malthus and Robert M. Young

James A. Secord

> Anyone who thinks history and long arguments are mystifying can stop reading after two sentences from Jerry Rubin: 'The New Left sprang, a predestined pissed-off child, from Elvis' gyrating pelvis .... there can be no social revolution without a head revolution and no head revolution without a social revolution.'
>
> —Bob Young, 'Functions of rock', *New Edinburgh Review*, Dec. 1970, 5.[1]

What does historical writing have to do with political action? This essay highlights a moment when the history of science became part of the struggle for radical social transformation. In the late 1960s, intellectual history was the field on which battles about the meaning of science were fought. For many commentators, the values of post-Galilean science were the natural ally of enlightened liberalism. For radical socialists of the New Left, however, natural science either provided the justification for scientific socialism or alternatively had an ambiguous legacy as the source of environmental disaster, racial prejudice and military domination. As Theodore Roszak wrote in *The Making of a Counter Culture* (1969), 'Reason, material Progress, the scientific world view have revealed themselves in numerous respects as simply a higher superstition, based on dubious but well-concealed assumptions about man and nature'. Intellectual foundations really mattered.[2]

The early writings of Robert M. Young and their fate in subsequent decades offer a revealing window on the changing politics of history of science. Born in Texas in 1935, Young studied philosophy and religion at Yale. In the early 1960s, he did a PhD on history of psychology at Cambridge, where he taught history of science for a decade from 1964 and served as graduate tutor at King's College. In 1974, he left for London to engage in radical politics, publishing and eventually psychoanalytic practice. Like Jerry Ravetz, Gary Werskey and others in the radical science movement, Young brought American perspectives to bear on long-standing British controversies about the role of science in society – in his case, from pragmatic philosophy and

DOI: 10.4324/9781003204244-4

the history of ideas.[3] His lifetime goal was to understand human nature in the broadest sense.[4]

My focus is on Young's essays on the nineteenth-century disputes over the place of humans in nature, and particularly his most audacious claim, that the central theory of modern biological science originated as an answer to questions about politics, religion and economics. His celebrated article, 'Malthus and the Evolutionists: The Common Context of Biological and Social Theory', argued that Charles Darwin formulated the theory of evolution by natural selection as part of wide-ranging discussions of human nature and natural theology – particularly the controversy about Thomas Robert Malthus's *An Essay on the Principle of Population*.[5] For many commentators in the second half of the twentieth century, especially biologists, this was anathema. Young's article, presented in 1968 and published in *Past and Present* in the following year, has long been taught and cited throughout the English-speaking world, but in ways that fail to recognize its iconoclastic aims. Its history illustrates not only the political functions of academic writing at a moment of dramatic upheaval but also the ways in which the politics of understanding past science has changed since.

Storming the citadel

From the distance of 50 years, we can see Young's concern with Darwin, Malthus and the Victorian debate about 'man's place in nature' as the product of a specific historical juncture. The critical context was the Vietnam war. Notably, Young was one of the signatories of 'Bombing of North Vietnam', a letter to *The Times* in May 1966 from 21 Cambridge academics against the conflict, organized by the classicist Moses Finley.[6] For many, the war – with its use of napalm, Agent Orange and other science-based weapons – revealed the profound involvement of the sciences in what President Dwight D. Eisenhower had termed the 'military–industrial complex'. Science, shown by the war to be complicit in social injustice and imperial domination, could not claim to be neutral and value-free. Enquiring into the political origins of natural selection stormed the scientific citadel.

From this perspective, the kind of history of science that Young had been advocating since 1964 from his position as a lecturer at Cambridge could serve as a force for resistance and liberation. The extent of his radical conversion cannot be overestimated. Born into a once prosperous family in Highland Park, the wealthiest Dallas suburb, Young had served in the Reserve Officer Training Corps (ROTC), and until the age of 20 had shared his parent's Presbyterian religious views. He brought to the countercultural cause in England all the evangelical fervour of a Texan abroad. With motorcycle, big boots, strong libido and an abrasive unwillingness to conform, Young presented himself as an incorruptible maverick in a hidebound world of sherry and college dinners. From 1968, he retooled his approach to the problem of human nature through an increasingly uncompromising turn to Marxism and radical politics. The central concern always remained the difficult task of reconciling intellectual enquiry and social action.[7]

The tension between thought and action as political forms is clear in 'The New Nation?', an essay written by Young for the programme of the Bath Festival of Blues and Progressive Music in June 1970. This was a major event held in the wake of Woodstock, with an audience estimated at 150,000 and featuring bands from the Byrds and Jefferson Airplane to Pink Floyd and Led Zeppelin; it later became the inspiration for the annual gathering at Glastonbury. Young had already discussed 'the pop scene' on BBC radio and was emerging as a noted commentator on contemporary music and social transformation. The essay, retitled 'Functions of Rock', appeared again in December as the lead article in a special issue of the *New Edinburgh Review* on *The Underground* (Figure 1). For this version, Young added a new preface and conclusion, more sceptical in tone than the original.

Figure 2.1 New Edinburgh Review.

What, Young asked, was the relation between the 'head revolution' represented by rock and progressive music, and real-life social and political revolution? What did it mean when Jefferson Airplane's recently released 'Volunteers' advocated revolution in the streets or when Bob Dylan sang 'You don't need a weatherman to know which way the wind blows'?

This raises the question I have been posing in different forms throughout this article. How much has the music really freed people from oppression and repression, and how much is it a subtle accommodation with them? Gospel and blues, country & western, even folk and protest were consolations. They gave strength, they even helped to produce some changes in the real world, but they always led, in the end, away from total commitment to the kinds of integrated social and political and personal changes that people dream of when they invoke the word 'Revolution'. I don't know the elements of the structural critique that is required to achieve these changes, nor can I specify the role of rock and festivals in it. But I do know that we should be aware of an alternative interpretation of the function of rock and festivals, an interpretation which shows that we may very well be diverting our energies from achieving and implementing that critique. I'm not suggesting that we must choose between the music and the festivals on the one hand and hard-headed politics on the other. If we lose the spirit of the music, we lose the political and social and personal integration as well. But if we think the head revolution is enough on its own, we are leading ourselves into the same blind alley that earlier manifestations of the music have done.[8]

Just at this time, Young and his second wife Sheila Ernst were engaged in more direct forms of political action. They became leading figures in the international campaign on behalf of Rudi Dutschke, a German student activist recovering in Britain from an assassination attempt by a right-wing extremist. Young helped Dutschke apply for a PhD at King's College and worked with him in navigating a particularly rigorous process of admission to the University. Almost immediately after his arrival in the autumn of 1970, however, it became clear that Dutschke – who was seriously ill from bullet wounds to his brain – would get no peace at a college filled with undergraduates eager for advice about how to rebel against the university. Young arranged for him to move to Clare Hall, which had been recently established on as a graduate college outside the city centre.[9] Here, Dutschke was also less likely to be accused of violating the conditions of his admission to the UK, which prohibited him from engaging in politics. When the newly elected Heath government decided to deport Dutschke anyway for representing a danger to the state, Young arranged for legal counsel in a hearing that achieved attention across the world. After that appeal failed, he worked with others to organize mass demonstrations to protest what was widely seen as a travesty of justice. Dutschke and his family then moved to Denmark, where Bob, Sheila and several friends visited early in the summer of 1971.[10] Soon after that, Bob and Sheila joined with three other couples associated with King's to form a commune in their big house at 25–27 High Street in Chesterton, Cambridge. This was a revolutionary act, establishing a way of living that would point a way out of the contradictions of western capitalism.

The rapidly changing situation led to unusual conjunctions. At the same time as Young had been campaigning for Dutschke, his article on 'The Impact of Darwin on Conventional Thought' appeared in a collection of lectures published by no less staid an institution than the Society for the Promotion of Christian Knowledge. This essay was based on a talk he had given at the National Portrait Gallery in the winter of 1968.[11] For Young, participating in these diverse settings was part of a single process. 'History and long arguments' were not mystifications, but were essential to the movement's success. Just as music and social change could go hand in hand, carefully researched historical analysis could underpin efforts to change science, as part of the broader campaign for social justice. The key element was action. Young concluded the 'Afterthoughts' added to 'Functions of Rock' in the *New Edinburgh Review* by noting that 'strategy and tactics must be appropriate to the objective conditions in Britain, and there is no substitute for *political* action, however much we should leaven them by the soul and values of rock music'.[12] In terms of tactics, history of science was relevant, in an even broader way, in revealing the ideological foundations required for change. But history was useful only if it led to action.

What mattered for the committed historian of science was the history of ideas, an approach that inspired Young while he was an undergraduate at Yale and motivated his entire intellectual career. This may come as a surprise to many who assume that intellectual history was the exclusive preserve of anti-Marxist defenders of the West during the Cold War.[13] Yet, all sides in the debate saw the foundations of science as conceptual. The dominance of this view was partly a response to the perceived crudity of 'vulgar' Marxism, in which the scientific superstructure grew directly out of the economic and technological base. That approach was usually typified by 'The Social and Economic Roots of Newton's *Principia*', a paper by Boris Hessen from the Russian delegation at the famous International Congress of the History of Science and Technology in July 1931. Hessen's argument, although far from following a party line (he was executed in 1936), came to symbolize the failures of the Soviet Union under Stalin.[14] Instead, Young looked to the early Marx and writers such as György Lukács and Herbert Marcuse, who were at this time widely influential in the academic New Left.

Intellectual history was the chosen medium not only for the leading voices of liberal historiography (including Charles Gillispie and Thomas Kuhn in the United States, and Rupert Hall and Alistair Crombie in Britain) but equally for those who looked to see the establishment overthrown. The aim was to uncover *The Metaphysical Foundations of Modern Physical Science* (1924), to quote the title of a book by Edwin Burtt that shaped the intellectual trajectory of the postwar generation. This approach, developed by writers ranging from Alexandre Koyré and Emile Meyerson to Arthur Lovejoy and Alfred North Whitehead, involved analysing the concepts expressed by leading thinkers. The key participants were seen to be the handful of white male authors who wrote systematic treatises and dominated public discussion.

The centrality of the search for an integrating picture of the world is clear from Young's first published essay, which had appeared in a student periodical during his senior year at Yale in 1956. Here, Young recalled how his fundamentalist Christianity, 'the faith of our fathers', was undermined in lectures at the Divinity School. In his notes, Young marked a 'D' (for 'dispute') next to claims that the Scriptures contained inconsistencies, or that Jesus was merely 'a good *man*'. Confronted by these challenges, he suffered the shock of disillusionment. Christianity, it appeared, relied on a dogmatism characteristic of all the intellectual systems in history, whether derived from Aristotle, Freud, Hegel, logic or contemporary science. In this chaotic marketplace of ideas, students were invited to 'shop, select, and choose' among the products of what Young termed 'an ideological hysteria'. 'But such shopping', he stressed, 'does not satisfy disillusionment'. The only answer was a constant, highly personal search for integration. What mattered was not the final answer, but the paths along the way to 'an integrated life', combining feelings, words and actions. 'What we seek is an open ended road for inquiry. ... This is a busy process, because we are never finished'.[15]

Soon after taking up a post as temporary assistant lecturer in history of biology at Cambridge in 1964, Young began teaching a six-lecture course on Science and Public Debate in Britain, 1830–1870 to small groups of final-year natural-science students and others, as part of a Special Paper under the auspices of the History Faculty.[16] His approach crystallized as he worked on a (never-completed) study of the Victorian evolutionary debates, which allowed him to combine his formal role as a historian of the life sciences with his established interest in psychology and the human sciences. The most significant of his contributions, 'Malthus and the Evolutionists', was delivered to the prestigious Stubbs Society in Oxford on 2 February 1968, two days after the Viet Cong launched the Tet offensive, a turning point in the war.

The paper's overarching claim was that biology and society belonged to the same debate. This meant drawing a wide net around the texts to be studied, with attention given to utopian writings by William Godwin and the Marquis de Condorcet, the natural theology of William Paley and the authors of the Bridgewater Treatises, the political economy of Thomas Chalmers and Thomas Malthus, and the social philosophy of George Combe and Herbert Spencer. Young then showed that the theory of evolution proposed in Darwin's *On the Origin of Species* and in the writings of Alfred Russel Wallace was directly in dialogue with these authors.

The most controversial aspect of Young's argument was that reading Malthus was constitutive for Darwin's formulation of natural selection, the keystone of modern biology. Especially for biologists, grounding Darwin's discovery in a controversial work of political economy was anathema. The Malthusian law famously stated that human population growth, unchecked, increases geometrically, while the supply of food can at most increase arithmetically. The result is dearth, death and a struggle for scarce resources. In Young's interpretation, Darwin removed any possibility of 'moral restraint' (delaying marriage) in softening the impact of Malthus's doctrine. Darwin then extended it from humans to the whole living world and used it to explain how new adaptations (and ultimately new species) came into being. In making his case, Young assembled a barrage of quotations in which Darwin expressed his debt to Malthus, starting with the autobiography, moving backwards in time through the *Origin* and other published works and ending with passages from manuscript notebooks that had only recently been transcribed and published.[17]

The claim about natural selection was the pivotal move in uniting social and biological thought in a shared context. Young pointed out that writers on the left had traditionally prized apart Darwin and Malthus. In this tradition, Darwin was a hero of scientific socialism: as Marx had written to the German socialist Ferdinand Lasalle, the *Origin* 'provides a basis in natural science for the historical class struggle'.[18] In contrast, Malthus was condemned as a 'bourgeois fraud' who had naturalized the faults of a political system based on capitalism. Young profoundly disagreed with this separation.[19] As he summed up his argument:

> Instead of seeing Malthus as an influence outside of biology, I should like to indicate the ways in which his theory and its assumptions about nature were at once pervasive in the biological literature of the first decades of the century and a part of an ongoing debate within natural theology which was at least as important to Darwin and Wallace as the question of the mechanism of evolution. Finally, I want to suggest that the distinction between social and biological issues – which was, in turn, based on the distinction between man and animals which evolutionary theory was supposed to break down from 1859 onwards – was broken down in principle well before the turn of the century.[20]

The essay concluded by carrying the story to the present day. As Young noted with uncharacteristic indirectness, 'it is not unlikely that a future historian will find that the neat division between biological and social science which most current scientists believe to have been established, is less absolute than it now appears'.[21] The key issue was purity. Western scientists characteristically complimented themselves on separating biology from politics and social science, in contrast with the situation in totalitarian regimes such as the Soviet Union, where scientific theories developed in line with ideological orthodoxy. The standard example of the dangers of mixing science with politics involved the Soviet regime's support for the melioristic theories of inheritance advocated by Trofim Denisovich Lysenko. Young, however, believed that such cases were aberrations. This was not because science was otherwise always pure, but because the 'Lysenko affair' involved grotesque attempts by the state to enforce scientific orthodoxy. Imprisonment, torture and murder were not the only means through which politics could shape science. Young argued that the Soviet case could not be used to claim that 'well-attested scientific findings' such as the structure of DNA were beyond ideology.[22]

Within biology, Darwin was a critical figure during the 1960s, often treated as though he was a contemporary. These years were the high point of Francis Crick's 'central dogma' and the neo-Darwinian synthesis, which ruled out any form of somatic inheritance and stressed the comprehensive power of natural selection over all other evolutionary mechanisms. The emergence of a belief in the biological determinants of human behaviour gave a 'hard' interpretation of Darwin's theory a unique significance.[23] This was also the decade following the centenary of the *Origin* in 1959, which revived Darwin's reputation and sparked the enduring fascination in his life and writings. As the historian of science David Kohn later noted, 'only after biologists legitimated Darwin did historians rush to study him'.[24] Young, of course, was not out to legitimate Darwin – far from it – but rather to use the remarkable prominence of the theory of natural selection to tackle current issues in the relations of biology and society, what Theodore Roszak would term 'the grizzly callousness of social Darwinism'.[25] Understanding the genesis of natural selection thus held a key to understanding science in society.

Malthus was the perfect battering ram. The argument that unchecked population growth would ultimately outstrip food supply had been a flashpoint for controversy since its inception, but never more so than in the period in which Young's article appeared.[26] The postwar years through the mid-1970s have been identified as the 'Malthusian moment', with a resurgence of interest in the problems his work had posed. In the United States, concerns about global overpopulation catalysed mass environmental movements.[27] In Britain, however, this 'green Malthus' had scarcely emerged, with debate centred instead on questions of religion, birth control and economic analysis.[28]

The prominence of the *Essay* in these polemics gave Malthus a fresh notoriety. His work was central to the distinguished Oxford geneticist Cyril Darlington's *The Evolution of Man and Society* (1969), which appeared soon after Young's *Past and Present* essay. In this widely discussed book (which Young furiously condemned in the *New Statesman*), Darlington reduced human history to biology, with selection between races and classes as the driving force of evolutionary progress. He ranked Malthus high in his 'succession of pioneers', although this was strictly for the mathematical law of population, which had to be disentangled from the theological and social views of an Anglican parson. The discovery of natural selection ('Darwin's rider' to the Malthusian law) had revealed competition for limited resources as the underlying principle of biology.[29] Malthus, in Darlington's view, thus provided the foundations for a racist history of humanity.

Most evolutionary biologists, challenged by the ascendency of molecular biology, were determined to demonstrate the purity of their science, so the influence of Malthus on Darwin was downplayed just as it had been among the Marxists. The centennial celebrations of the *Origin* in the late 1950s made the wealthy embryologist Sir Gavin de Beer the most influential commentator on Darwin in the English-speaking world. De Beer, who drove daily in his Rolls Royce to the British Museum (Natural History) even after he had ceased to be its director, consistently maintained that Darwin was untainted by Malthusian political economy or natural theology. The great naturalist's accomplishment – achieved in splendid isolation and purely on the basis of observation – was to move evolutionary theorizing into the realm of science. Without Darwin, de Beer stressed, evolutionary theorizing 'was ringing wet with politics'.[30]

De Beer's self-confessed status as a 'high-priest of Darwin' was crowned in 1960 with publication in the *Bulletin of the British Museum (Natural History): Historical Series* of the transmutation notebooks, the records of Darwin's thoughts on species in the crucial years after the *Beagle* voyage. Frustratingly, this edition was incomplete, as Darwin had excised pages for later use, and among those missing appeared to be the record of his first reading of Malthus's *Essay*. In October 1962, de Beer was present when a black metal box of Darwin's papers, previously in possession of the family, was hammered open. As was his usual practice, de Beer delegated the reading, sorting and transcribing of these extraordinarily complex materials to an Austrian-born secretary at the British Museum (Natural History), Maria Skramovsky. As de Beer acknowledged, it was Skramovsky who 'found, recognized and showed me' the page from 28 September 1838 recording Darwin's initial reaction to Malthus's *Essay*.[31] The page she found was first quoted by de Beer in his 1963 biography of Darwin, and soon afterwards was the centrepiece of an article by him in *New Scientist*, outlining 'How Darwin came by his Theory of Natural Selection'.

With triple underlining and extensive interlineation, the notebook page was clearly significant, and Young's article would quote it as 'unequivocal evidence of Malthus's rôle in the actual formation of Darwin's theory'.[32] We do not know what Skramovsky thought about her discovery, but for de Beer and other biologists, the explanation remained unchanged. Malthus had no constitutive part in the origins of natural selection; the *Essay* provided nothing more than an enhanced appreciation of the mathematics of selection pressure – as well as an unproven 'banal slogan' about geometrical versus arithmetical rates of increase.[33] To the end of his life, de Beer continued to resist any significant role for Malthus, and he vetoed publication of Darwin's notebooks on metaphysics and mind, seeing these as outside proper scientific interests. Skramovsky had wanted her transcriptions to appear as a follow-up to the notebooks on species, but was overruled.[34]

As in the natural sciences, Darwin was recognized in the humanities as a significant figure, although the analysis of his work typically fell into the chasm separating what the novelist C.P. Snow had identified in 1959 as 'the two cultures'. During the years immediately after 1959, no professionally trained historians of science in Britain were seriously studying Darwin or the development of evolutionary theory.[35] In Cambridge, the history and philosophy of science, as part of the Natural Sciences Tripos, stressed rigorous analysis of concepts in the physical sciences and in philosophy, and technical work on the history of astronomy. The subject was not yet conducted in a distinct department, but through a 'committee' with members scattered across the university. Young was initially placed in the Department of Experimental Psychology, but he looked to the History Faculty, then dominated by historians of politics and religion, for intellectual orientations. The history of political thought as developed by Quentin Skinner, John Dunn and others – although seen by Young as a crucial resource – in retrospect can be seen to have almost completely ignored the natural sciences.[36]

There were, however, places in Cambridge where the research Young was advocating could be pursued, such as a path-breaking seminar series in 1968–1969 at the King's Research Centre. This monthly seminar, which brought together many future leaders of the field and a remarkable array of approaches, was co-organized with Piyo Rattansi, who had moved from Leeds to Cambridge on a four-year fellowship at King's which had been brokered by Young. Soon after his appointment as assistant lecturer, Young had learned about Rattansi's work on seventeenth-century English scientific debates from a key mentor, the sinologist Joseph Needham, who was based in Gonville and Caius College.[37] Young also maintained good relations with the History Faculty and opposed combining history of science with philosophy of science in a separate department, as occurred in 1972.[38] He was friendly with Raymond Williams in English and Martin Richards in Social and Political Sciences. But most of these connections proved fragile, as when he and John Dunn fell out over Marxism. As another one-time associate Martin Bernal recalled, Young 'achieved a great deal but has antagonized almost everybody he has encountered'.[39] The person with the closest intellectual interests would have been John Burrow, whose doctoral thesis provided the basis for the still standard *Evolution and Society: A Study in Victorian Social Theory* (1966), which Young praised in the *Cambridge Review* and assigned to students.[40] Burrow, however, had earlier failed to obtain a position in the faculty, leaving Young as the only senior academic in Cambridge pursuing the intellectual history of the modern period.

The situation was more promising for seventeenth-century studies and elsewhere in the country, largely through approaches pioneered by Rattansi, Ted McGuire and Charles Webster at Leeds and the Marxist seventeenth-century historian Christopher Hill and others at Oxford. History was changing rapidly, with a stress on hitherto marginalized groups and the critical revaluation of traditional narratives. Notably, it was at Oxford, not Cambridge, that 'Malthus and the Evolutionists' had its main public airing in 1968 at the Stubbs Society. Young's name had been put forward by the historian of science Alistair Crombie, who quickly regretted his suggestion. Oxford was also the home of *Past and Present*, and the assistant editor Timothy Mason, a Marxist historian of Nazi Germany, invited Young to submit to the journal after attending the seminar.[41] Among historical periodicals, *Past and Present* was unusual in being run by a collective board, combining Marxists such as Hill and Mason and liberals such as Lawrence Stone.[42] Rapidly emerging as the most prestigious journal of its kind in the English-speaking world, it was publishing not only material from the left but also occasional pieces on the history of science, although the latter had exclusively dealt with seventeenth-century topics.

'Malthus and the Evolutionists' – together with the thesis book on *Mind, Brain, and Adaptation in the Nineteenth Century* (1970), and the other essays on 'man's place in nature' from this time – established Young's reputation within the academy. This was just at the moment, however, when he became increasingly frustrated by the limitations of a university career. Young had failed to gain a permanent lectureship when one was advertised in 1967, despite his evident promise at this early stage.[43] Further attempts had been made to promote him two years later, but his continuing lack of publications at this date clearly made his case open to attack from those who wished to get him out of Cambridge. Even so, Young had strong support from the University's Vice-Chancellor Eric Ashby and others. 'My own judgment', the philosopher of science Mary Hesse wrote early in 1969, 'is that he far outweighs in intellectual quality other persons who are now Lecturers in the department'.[44]

In 1971, Young was appointed to an untenured post directing a Wellcome-funded Unit for the History of Medicine in what soon became the Department of History and Philosophy of Science, but this proved a source of conflict and administrative logjams. Fired by conviction, he became increasingly combative. As the Provost at King's, the eminent anthropologist Edmund Leach, wrote soon afterwards:

I think that Bob Young will always throw himself with great energy into any task that he undertakes; his intellectual capacities are not of the very first order but they are quite up to those of a normal career academic. This quality is however somewhat marred by the fact that Bob Young himself has a very exalted idea about his capacities and tends to assume that anyone who fails to recognise this great ability is motivated by prejudice. He can be very rude and is sometimes a bit of a bully, on the other hand the kind of student who responds to enthusiasm can be greatly stimulated by his exhibitionist manner and be fired to enthusiasm in turn. In the past, in King's, he has evoked strong friendships and strong enmities... he is not the sort of person who passes by unnoticed.[45]

Leach admitted that this dismissal was 'a personal reaction' and he was 'not Bob Young's "favourite Provost"'.

The really divisive issue had become the overt political commitment that Young now brought to everything he did. This was most apparent in the formation of the commune at Chesterton by four couples from King's and their children during the summer of 1971.[46] The first meeting agreed that everyone would sleep in the same room, as an expression of group solidarity. Cooking, cleaning, decision-making and childcare were to be equally shared. One of the men proposed a sexual rotation to challenge the patriarchal assumptions of monogamy, to which nearly everyone – both women and men – agreed. Almost immediately, however, 'all hell broke loose' (as Young later put it) as the group was riven by gender politics, personal betrayals and struggles over authority.[47] Within three days, Bob and Sheila's marriage had broken down and by Christmas, he was living in separate quarters, with sexual liaisons including a regular partner from outside, whom the rest of the communal group perceived as being placed too close to the traditional role of a 'mistress'.

The commune, although lasting only months, expressed the profound hope of all its members that radical politics, feminism and the counterculture could be united in a revolutionary transformation of daily life. It served as a hub for local radical political activity, supporting striking miners, the anti-war struggle, the liberation of Northern Ireland and the burgeoning feminist movement. American GIs stationed at nearby military bases, on trial for advocating peace in Vietnam, stopped by the commune's kitchen for conversation. The women were particularly active in grass-roots political movements, with an extended sit-in at government offices as part of a campaign for unsupported mothers to have rights to Social Security payments. They also joined in a women's squat in nearby housing owned by King's. Books central to the radical canon were shared among the group, with authors ranging from Marx and Marcuse to Jerry Rubin, Abbie Hoffman and the sexual libertarian Wilhelm Reich. There was great interest in social anthropology, with three members of the group studying in that field, and in psychotherapy and psychiatry. Franz Fanon's anticolonial autoethnography *Black Faces, White Masks* (1952) was avidly discussed. As senior member of the group (and the only one with an established career), Young contributed primarily through theoretical work and charismatic inspiration rather than institution-building in the community or action on the streets.[48]

By the early 1970s, Young had already begun the work that led to the founding of the *Radical Science Journal* and the British Society for Social Responsibility in Science. With John Dunn and then the ethologist Patrick Bateson, he led seminars at King's that brought radical politics into academic discussions of society and science. In 1974, Young made a brave decision to pursue initiatives along these lines in a wider sphere, move to London and abandon the security of university and college positions.[49] He subsequently produced science programmes for television, began several important journals, founded two publishing companies, and eventually studied to become a psychoanalytic psychotherapist. While continuing actively to write and publish, Young increasingly left the history of science behind.

Changing perspectives

If Young 'moved on', to use one of his favourite phrases, his central argument about Darwin and Malthus remained available in the pages of *Past and Present*, where it was widely cited and read. The essay was reprinted for students in a series produced by the American publisher Bobbs-Merrill, which indicates just how extensively it was used in teaching. In 1985, it was republished in *Darwin's Metaphor: Nature's Place in Victorian Culture*, which collected Young's articles from 1969 to 1973.[50] Three settings were crucial for the reception of Young's argument: historical studies of Charles Darwin, the social history of nineteenth-century British science and the emergence of sociologically inspired studies of scientific practice.

'Malthus and the Evolutionists' appeared at an early but pivotal period in the scholarly re-evaluation of significant figures such as Newton, Galileo, Freud and Darwin. This movement was delayed in the history of political economy: the increased public prominence of Malthus had been accompanied by editions of his writings and occasional articles, but the only book-length account of the debate remained Kenneth Smith's largely descriptive and anti-Malthusian *The Malthusian Controversy* of 1951.[51] In contrast, the 1959 centennial of the *Origin* had sparked an explosion of celebratory publications about Darwin. Even so, serious research into primary sources had barely begun. Indications of the riches of the manuscript collections, deposited mainly in the University Library in Cambridge, were available in publications by Darwin's granddaughter, Nora Barlow, of the autobiography and various documents from the *Beagle* voyage, and in the piecemeal appearance of the transmutation notebooks between 1959 and 1967. Access to the collection was mediated by the embryologist Sydney Smith and the archivist Peter Gautrey. A succession of scholars, largely from North America, began to make the pilgrimage to the Fens that marked one as a true expert.[52]

The examination of this rich archive by professionally trained historians was transformative. No longer was it easy to say, as de Beer had done (and continued to maintain), that Darwin already had the theory of natural selection before reading Malthus in September 1838. Nor did it make sense to claim, as passages in the autobiography and in letters can be interpreted, that Darwin had seen artificial selection in action but needed to understand how to apply it to nature. Instead, the reading of Malthus's *Essay* led Darwin to realize the power not just of competition between species but also of competition between individuals of the same species. This argument, made by Sandra Herbert in her Brandeis PhD dissertation of 1968 and a brief article in 1971, had the potential to give Young's broader claims vital specificity and content.[53]

The other key revelation, developed in the late 1970s and early 1980s especially by David Kohn, was that Darwin had 'a theory to work by' based on reproduction, well before the reading of Malthus. Darwin was searching the literature on breeding, not to find an analogue in nature for artificial selection, but to answer questions about generation, growth and heredity. On reading the *Essay*, Darwin initially expressed the force of intra-species competition through a violently mechanical metaphor of wedging; only in the following months did he reconceptualize his new vision in terms of softer analogies between 'artificial' and 'natural' selection.[54]

'Malthus and the Evolutionists' came out remarkably well from these studies. As Kohn wrote in a phrase that Young liked to quote, 'The work of one recent commentator, Robert M. Young, stands out as nearly definitive'.[55] Yet in significant respects, Young never appreciated the potential of what authors such as Kohn and Herbert had done for the historiographic politics of the Malthus question. While quoting the relevant passages and stressing the relevant contexts, Young had been surprisingly vague on the critical issue of what Darwin took away from the *Essay*: 'It seems that Malthus legitimized the idea of a law of struggle, impressed Darwin with the intensity of struggle, and provided a convenient natural mechanism for the changes which Darwin was studying in the selection of domesticated varieties'.[56] From this perspective, Malthus gave new emphasis to the concept of struggle, already familiar from other works; but this was a change of degree rather than of kind. And Young also expressed the traditional view that before Malthus Darwin had no theory, but instead was searching for a natural analogy with artificial selection.

In other words, at this level of detail, 'Malthus and the Evolutionists' simply repeated the standard line familiar from de Beer's Darwin biography. Young admitted as much in the mid-1980s, noting, 'my own reading of what Darwin "got" from the *Essay* is remarkably close' to what de Beer and other biologists had said. Young derived much of his understanding of the transmutation notebooks from conversations with Sydney Smith, who (like de Beer) did not see Darwin's reading of Malthus as a decisive turning point. What mattered to Young was the broader context.[57] However, the existence in the notebooks of a pre-Malthusian theory for speciation and the distinction between 'inter-specific' and 'intra-specific' competition were not just details, but ways of placing individual competition and capitalist political economy at the heart of the theory. Although de Beer, Mayr and other biologists continued as sceptics, the broader significance of Malthus was suddenly harder to dismiss, which made Young's argument much more directly significant.[58]

For all that, the turn to manuscripts had major downsides. The work in what was becoming known as the 'Darwin industry' became increasingly esoteric, inward-looking and out of touch with more general trends in science studies in being resolutely focused on a single individual. As Young reflected after attending a major meeting organized by Kohn at the Villa di Mondeggi in Florence in 1982,

> The zeal with which current scientist-historians seek to separate Darwin's genius and achievements from the work, ideas, and influences of Spencer, Chambers, and Wallace seems to betray a pathetic, sycophantic hagiography – Great Man history – which I thought was waning in the history of science, as historians of science thought of their discipline in terms of the history of ideas, the history of culture, and the history of society. Indeed, one distinguished biologist-historian [Ernst Mayr] concluded his comments by saying that Darwin was the author of 'the greatest and most universal revolution ever experienced in the history of human thought'. I found myself asking, why do we defer to great men? Why do we defer to working scientists who are part-time historians? Why do we defer to great men in the history of science? Why do we not consider the social processes of scientific change in their broadest contexts? Where have these questions gone in the past decade?[59]

Although close studies of the manuscripts often ended up supporting the connection between Malthus and Darwin, specialist monographs and long articles in the *Journal of the History of Biology* and the annual *Studies in History of Biology* seemed to have lost interest in the metaphysical foundations of a debate about humans in nature that extended to the present day. Historians of biology, in their attempts to establish rigour and appease practising scientists, had too often overlooked the political context in which their work was embedded. Young would not have been surprised to know that Mayr, an honoured presence at the Florence meeting, privately supported Darlington's view that human history was the product of biological competition between lesser and more advanced biological races. As Mayr had written in a letter to Darlington,

> I am delighted you have said all these things which are so true but which are simply suppressed in the 'egalitarian' mass media ... I am frank to say, your bias, or I should say government policies based on your bias, should promise a far better future for mankind than the ruling bias.[60]

Young collected his old essays directly in response to the Florence gathering. By his own admission, he had left the history of science well behind, and ironically, his academic reputation as a historian became retrospectively limited to that of a leading 'Darwin scholar'.[61] His jaundiced view was coloured by the fact that the Darwin/Malthus literature was almost the only subject in nineteenth-century science he tracked closely. He was disappointed by its increasing narrowness and lack of political bite. Although vastly more was known about Darwin, the literature seemed – sometimes unwittingly, sometimes not – simply to reinforce notions of genius and singular greatness.

There was, of course, a lot else going on. Although there were only limited indications of this in Florence, the institutional and social history of British science was blossoming. This work was produced by a diverse array of participants spread across the English-speaking world, especially in the north of England, as part of a much broader move to cultural history among historians generally.[62] The resulting studies vastly increased the range of participants in British science and offered for the first time a secure institutional framework for understanding their activities and status.[63] The dominance of a few leading men was no longer a taken-for-granted feature of intellectual life in the nineteenth century, but understood as a product of the individualistic bias of British scientific culture.

A later generation carried this project further, dismantling monolithic conceptions of 'popular science' and revealing new spaces for science populated by women, artisans and other hitherto marginalized groups. After these writings, no one could say, as Young had, that popular phrenology and mechanics' institutes could be demarcated from the study of an 'intelligentsia'.[64] (He had never even considered the idea of women, other than George Eliot, playing any significant role.) His insistence that the agenda should be 'broadened' to include figures such as Herbert Spencer and Robert Chambers looked out of touch, even in the very specific context of research into Darwin.[65]

As John Christie said in reviewing *Darwin's Metaphor* in 1988, there was no particular reason why 'heavy-duty social history' could not be combined with a 'broad-based intellectualist historiography'.[66] Young did know about the transformation of the social history of Victorian science, but from his perspective, it was bound always to be peripheral; with characteristic candour, he admitted to not having read Jack Morrell and Arnold Thackray's *Gentlemen of Science: The Early Years of the British Association* (1981), probably the most significant work in this tradition.[67] He had always made it clear that what mattered were the writings of 'the intelligentsia', not what he explicitly dismissed as 'the social history of ideas conceived as the study of low-brow popular opinion'.[68] In fact, Young's focus was always even more specific, on some 20 'major thinkers' and 'major' reviews of their works. His essays referred extensively to the periodical press, but never discussed, say, something so fundamental as the political orientation of the *Edinburgh Review* compared with the *Quarterly*. Young's polemical farewell to his Cambridge years, published in 1973, pointed towards the need for what he called a 'social intellectual history'.[69] This, however, remained an aspiration, in important respects not easy to reconcile with his overall political project.

Within the history of science generally in the 1970s and 1980s, even more important than the retooling of the social history of science was a move from the history of ideas to the history of practice. This was a political change of tactics, as analysis moved from science as ideology to science as work.[70] The inspiring sociological studies were about life in laboratories, showing how the contents of science could be the subject of sociological analysis.[71] From Young's perspective, as with many on the left who emerged from the debates in the 1960s, the new sociology of knowledge only rarely put to the fore questions of overt political use and ideology. Partly for that reason, this work never seemed particularly important to Young, even as his own concerns moved towards studies of the labour process.[72] He never applied these approaches to the Victorian debates, nor did he appreciate work that did this.

Yet, the new methods did have a political foundation. It had simply proved too easy to see the 'social' as an optional add-on.[73] Thus, Malthus could be seen as critically important to the making of Darwin's evolutionary theory, but could arguably not carry the ideological baggage of political economy and its draconian applications in the 1830s, let alone provide an argument for radical action today. Such connections could scarcely bear the weight of Young's increasingly frustrated and repetitive glosses on his early work. As Frank Turner complained in reviewing *Darwin's Metaphor*, 'that commentary really has little or nothing to do with what Young has written or taught us'.[74]

Even more critically, too much of Darwin's science seemed hard to fit into an ideological template. What about writings on barnacles, orchids and coral reefs, the research that gave Darwin's evolutionary theory its authority and power? This is a point that Thomas Kuhn had raised in discussing the problem soon after the *Past and Present* essay appeared, and one that Jonathan Hodge pressed at the Florence meeting. Young always resisted the idea of a 'scale' of purity moving from science to ideology, and repeatedly castigated Edward Thompson and others for separating the polemicist Thomas Henry Huxley from the supposedly neutral scientist Darwin.[75] However, Young's own unwillingness to look closely at scientific work in the laboratory and field tended towards precisely that conclusion. He did not read any papers in zoological, botanical and natural-history journals, so these arenas seemed outside the discussion. Thus, in dealing with geology, Young was willing to adopt Martin Rudwick's view that stratigraphy, surveying and other subjects could be studied within the parameters of a well-demarcated disciplinary community, insulated from considerations of economic management or imperial control.[76] Only when the documents revealed specifically religious, political or otherwise 'ideological' concerns did Young show any interest. As Kuhn commented on the paper, 'far from being a barrier breaker, it belongs to a standard historiographical tradition which has done much to preserve the very separation Young deplores'.[77]

For many historians of science writing in light of the sociological work unintentionally inspired by Kuhn's *Structure of Scientific Revolutions* (1962), the key political imperative was to tackle the detailed contents of science. There were important moves towards this during the mid-1970s, as in studies of laboratory research schools by Jack Morrell and Gerald Geison, and early interest in the sociological work of Harry Collins, particularly his 1975 article on the replication of experiments in gravity waves, 'The Seven Sexes'.[78] The key developments in bringing scientific practice and social history together for the nineteenth century date from Steven Shapin's classic paper in the *Sociological Review* of 1979 on phrenology, tellingly titled 'The Politics of Observation'. Shapin's previous essays in this area had mapped support for phrenology onto ideology and social class, using models of interest theory combined with work in prosopography. The new work looked at practices of observation and dissection. By 1982, Shapin had brought together a host of studies under this umbrella in an influential paper, 'History of science and its sociological reconstructions'.[79]

The same impulse was evident in work close to Young's areas of original concern. Adrian Desmond's *Archetypes and Ancestors: Palaeontology in Victorian London* (1982) and *The Politics of Evolution: Morphology, Medicine, and Reform in Radical London* (1989) combined fiercely fine-grained studies of scientific and medical periodicals with an understanding of political positions, to unmask the ideological underpinnings of disputes about animal bodies and structures. Instead of a 'common context' of debate among 'the intelligentsia', Desmond revealed a society riven by controversies.[80] Similar work in a variety of fields was carried out at the same time: Crosbie Smith and Norton Wise on thermodynamics and electromagnetism, Evelleen Richards on evolution and development, Simon Schaffer on astronomy.[81] These outlined precisely the kind of mediations that Young had called for, but for which his methods were not particularly well suited. It would have been hard to imagine Young reading papers about the fossil remains of mammals, the dissection of the frontal cortex, or the reproductive organs of the platypus, but that was where the politics of science was most profoundly expressed.

More generally, Young remained deeply dissatisfied with the direction of academic life in Britain and America. Darwin studies had turned largely inward; from his perspective, the new social history of science didn't tackle the big issue of 'man's place in nature' – a topic that, despite praise for a few studies by former students, he saw as dominated by theologically inspired waffle about 'science and religion' from lapsed evangelicals.[82] And for all the references to politics, much of the historical work inspired by sociology of knowledge was narrowly targeted at professional audiences, so that its potential significance was obscured.[83] As has become clear in the intervening years, the pioneering work by sociologists provided superb resources for dealing with issues inside laboratories, but was less effective in connecting to wider concerns. In retrospect, this 'new internalism', evident in some but by no means all of the work, can be seen to reflect a caution induced by the hostile climate faced by academics in the years after 1980. Much of the sociological literature became mired in discussions of epistemology, leading to the fruitless conflicts of the science wars during the late 1990s. The moment in which an author could hope for a heavily researched academic paper in *Past and Present* to connect with direct political action had passed.

Conversely, when Adrian Desmond and Jim Moore offered a 'defiantly political' portrait of Darwin in their bestselling biography of 1991, Young slammed it in a long review for being too smooth and accessible.[84] An argument intended to provoke outrage had transmuted into new orthodoxy, a racy narrative that could be advertised to commuters on the London Underground. From Young's perspective, rough authenticity had been sacrificed for commercial surface, as had happened in the 1960s as rock music compromised with corporate capitalism – blunting the edge of revolution through repressive sublimation. To quote again from his essay on 'The New Nation?' in 1970, 'How much has the music really freed people from oppression and repression, and how much is it a subtle accommodation with them?'[85]

It was all too easy. To Young's dismay, there was no sense of historiographical debate in the Darwin biography, of what was at stake in the link with Malthus. Young saw more hope for the field through the work of Donna Haraway, which was both deeply engaged and rough around the edges (but accessible only to a tiny fraction of the audience). Whether his response to the biography was justified, the review expressed perfectly why Young had abandoned academia in the first place.

Conclusion: the long march

I met Bob Young on six occasions, the last time in May 2016 at the memorial conference for the much-missed historian of the human sciences John Forrester. So, unlike the others who spoke at a workshop in Cambridge held in Bob's honour following his death in 2019, I never knew him well. For me as for many who entered history of science in the 1970s, Robert M. Young was without question a figure to be reckoned with, but almost entirely through his writings. The first serious book in history of science I owned was his 1973 Festschrift for the sinologist Joseph Needham, *Changing Perspectives in the History of Science*, co-edited with Mikuláš Teich. I bought this volume in London a couple of years after it came out and was nearly arrested at Foyles bookshop by a security guard midway on an escalator having failed to understand the bizarre system of paying for books which operated there at the time. Young's long essay, 'The Historiographic and Ideological Contexts of the Nineteenth-century Debate on Man's Place in Nature', was like nothing I had ever read. Not only did it introduce me to what he later termed 'the corruption, opportunism, and hypocrisy of certain colleagues and patrons' in Cambridge,[86] it also opened my eyes to the breath and significance of the subject.

Although I did not know Young at all well, in an important respect, I have a unique relationship with him. Ever since arriving in the Department of History and Philosophy of Science in Cambridge in 1992, I have taught courses that are direct descendants of his lectures on Science and Public Debate. For decades, I have been hammering home lessons about Malthus, Darwin, natural theology, the 1834 New Poor Law and similar issues to undergraduates in the Natural Sciences Tripos. Every spring, I read out the relevant passages from Darwin's notebooks and stress that natural selection was not articulated in isolation in the Galapagos, but on Great Marlborough Street in London, in the midst of a passionate debate about the place of humans in nature. And yet I always suspected that Young thought I was too 'soft', willing to work within a system that he condemned as too corrupt and constraining for the intellectual ventures he wished to undertake.

For what it is worth, my view is that Young never fully appreciated the leverage for change that institutions can bring. Particularly after the advent of Thatcher and Reagan, with the decimation of the labour movement and the systematic destruction of many of the structures on which earlier campaigns had depended, the universities offered one of the few remaining platforms for the expression of alternative views. Young certainly contemplated the role of existing structures on many occasions, recalling Dutschke's celebrated call for 'a long march through the institutions'.[87] That is one of the reasons for Young's own partial return to academic life, first through a visiting professorship at Kent (1991–1994) and then as professor of psychoanalytic studies at Sheffield (1995–2000). These appointments acknowledged what was by then a substantial body of work in psychology and the human sciences, and his status as a psychoanalytic psychotherapist. And it is also true, of course, that even places like Cambridge, which remain deeply traditional, have changed during the past half-century, most clearly in attitudes towards diversity. Like Young himself, they have 'moved on'.

For all their grounding in the distant days of the 1960s, Young's writings continue to serve as a disciplinary conscience. The dichotomies he argued against – between science and society, nature and culture, mind and body, internal and external – are still as pervasive as ever, and the forces supporting them have become even more powerful. At the same time, his call to overcome these divisions, and for using the power of history to contribute to breaking them down, are urgent in new ways and for different reasons. Today, we see both Malthus and Darwin in wider contexts involving race, gender, immigration and cross-cultural exchange.[88] The debate about the place of humans in nature is a question not only of belief among the leaders of thought, but of survival. I can thus end with one of Young's favourite quotations from George Eliot: as Dorothea Brooke's uncle says in *Middlemarch*,

'I went into science a great deal myself at one time; but I saw it would not do. It leads to everything; you can let nothing alone'.[89]

Acknowledgements

This paper is significantly expanded and revised from an article with the same title in *British Journal for the History of Science* 54 (2021): 41–59. It was first presented at the Remembering Bob Young workshop organized by Simon Schaffer at Darwin College in March 2020. I wish to thank the many people who answered queries, contributed reminiscences and commented on drafts of this paper, including John Brooke, Louisa Brown, Rebecca Fallas, Sandra Herbert, Richard Hesse, Jerry Kutcher, Chris Lawrence, Bernard Lightman, Patricia McGuire, Patrick Parrinder, Evelleen Richards, Martin Rudwick, Roger Smith, Gillian Sutherland and Jon Topham. I am especially grateful to Anne Secord, the editors of this volume, the referees from the *British Journal for the History of Science,* and members of the Longest Nineteenth Century Reading Group and to Sarah Greaves for her recollections of Cambridge life in the early 1970s.

Notes

1 Reprinted by permission of the publishers Birlinn Ltd., Edinburgh.
2 Theodore Roszak, *The Making of a Counter Culture: Reflections on the Technocratic Society and Its Youthful Opposition* (New York: Anchor Books, 1969): 164. For science and technology in the 1960s see Jon Agar, 'What Happened in the Sixties?', *British Journal for the History of Science* 41 (2008): 567–600; Everett Mendelsohn, 'The Politics of Pessimism: Science and Technology circa 1968', in *Technology, Pessimism and Postmodernism*, ed. Y. Ezrahi, E. Mendelsohn and H. Segal, 151–173 (Dordrecht: Reidel, 1994); and Jerome R. Ravetz, 'Orthodoxies, Critiques and Alternatives', in *The Companion to the History of Modern Science*, ed. Robert Olby, Geoffrey N. Cantor, John R.R. Christie and Michael Jonathan Sessions Hodge, 898–908 (London: Routledge, 1990).
3 Simone Turchetti, 'Looking for the Bad Teachers: The Radical Science Movement and Its Transnational History', in *Science Studies during the Cold War and Beyond*, ed. Elena Aronova and Simone Turchetti, 77–101 (New York: Palgrave Macmillan, 2016), esp. 82–84. Unless otherwise mentioned, biographical information is taken from Young's website, http://psychoanalysis-and-therapy.com/rmyoung/index.html, accessed 10 Apr. 2020.
4 See especially Christopher J. Lawrence, 'Robert M. Young's *Mind, Brain, and Adaptation* Revisited', *British Journal for the History of Science* 53 (2021): 61–67, and the other papers in this volume, especially Roger Smith, 'The Quest for Humane Relations in the Trajectory of an Intellectual Life'. For early recollections see Bob Young, 'Growing Up in Texas in the 1950s', *Ideas and Production: A Journal in the History of Ideas* 9–10 (1989): 31–43.
5 Robert M. Young, 'Malthus and the Evolutionists: The Common Context of Biological and Social Theory', *Past and Present* 43 (May 1969): 109–145.
6 *The Times*, 3 May 1966, 17, col. 3. Other signatories included John Dunn, Gillian Sutherland (as Gillian Thomas), Joan Robinson, Terry Eagleton and Raymond Williams. Overviews of the period, although with little about science, are in Mark

Donnelly, *Sixties Britain: Culture, Society and Politics* (London: Routledge, 2013); and Arthur Marwick, *The Sixties: Social and Cultural Transformation in Britain, France, Italy and the United States, 1958–74* (Oxford: Oxford University Press, 1998).

7 For Young's perspective on these issues, see Robert M. Young, 'The Historiographic and Ideological Contexts of the Nineteenth-century Debate on Man's Place in Nature', in *Changing Perspectives in the History of Science: Essays in Honour of Joseph Needham*, ed. Mikuláš Teich and Robert M. Young, 344–438 (London: Heinemann, 1973).

8 Bob Young, 'The New Nation?', *Bath Festival of Blues & Progressive Music* (June 1970), 29–33, at p. 33.

9 Interview with Sir Brian Pippard by Duke Henry Ryan, 17 June 1996, Clare Hall Archives, Rudi Dutschke collection. Thanks to Elizabeth Stratton, the archivist at Clare Hall, for providing this information; also Gretchen Dutschke, *Rudi Dutschke: Wir hatten ein barbarisches, schönes Leben* (Köln: Kiepenheuer & Witsch, 1996): 251.

10 Dutschke, *Rudi Dutschke*, 251, 267; 'Student Protest over Dutschke Expulsion Flops', *Daily Telegraph*, 19 Jan. 1971, 13.

11 Robert M. Young, 'The Impact of Darwin on Conventional Thought', in *The Victorian Crisis of Faith*, ed. Anthony Symondson, 13–35 (London: Society for the Promotion of Christian Knowledge, 1970).

12 Bob Young, 'Functions of Rock', *New Edinburgh Review*, Dec. 1970, 4–14, 14, original emphasis. The particularities of the situation in Britain are addressed in Stuart Mitchell, 'You Say You Want a Revolution? Popular Music and Revolt in France, the United States, and Britain during the Late 1960s', *Historia Actual* 8 (2005): 7–18.

13 The limitations of this view are cogently presented in Robert Fox, 'Fashioning the Discipline: History of Science in the European Intellectual Tradition', *Minerva* 44 (2006): 410–432.

14 For discussion and further references see Simon Schaffer, 'Newton at the Crossroads', *Radical Philosophy* 37 (1984): 23–28; and Gary Werskey, 'The Marxist Critique of Capitalist Science: A History in Three Movements?', *Science as Culture* 16 (2007): 397–461.

15 Robert M. Young, 'The Process of Belief', *Criterion* 1 (1956): 19–24, *passim*. Thanks to Jessica Becker and others in Manuscripts and Archives at Yale for locating this article in the first issue of a journal for student discussion. See also Young, 'Meliora?', which appeared in *Reflection* 1 (1959): 3–8, a student publication arguing for changes to the curriculum and teaching ethos at the University of Rochester Medical School. Thanks to Meredith Gozo of the Miner Library at Rochester for a copy of this article.

16 John Brooke recollects the course in an interview with Paul Merchant, 'Science and Religion: Exploring the Spectrum', in *National Life Stories*, British Library, at https://sounds.bl.uk/related-content/TRANSCRIPTS/021T- C1672X0008XX-0000A1.pdf, accessed 30 Nov. 2020. For the correct date of Young's appointment as assistant lecturer, see *Cambridge University Reporter* 95 (1 Oct. 1964): 13; the post was advertised in the *Reporter* 94 (22 Apr. 1964): 1541–1542. I acknowledge the assistance of Kathryn Jennings in the Cambridge University Library for all references to this source.

17 Young, 'Malthus', 125–130. The relevant passages first appeared in Gavin de Beer, *Charles Darwin: Evolution by Natural Selection* (London: Nelson, 1963): 99–100. See also Gavin de Beer, Maldwyn Jones Rowlands and Bertha Maria Skramovsky (eds.), 'Darwin's Notebooks on the Transmutation of Species. Part VI. Pages Excised by Darwin', *Bulletin of the British Museum (Natural History) Historical Series* 3 no. 5 (1967): 129–176.

18 K. Marx to F. Lasalles, 16 Jan. 1861, in *Marx–Engels Collected Works*, vol. 41 (Moscow: Progress Publishers, 1975): 246–247, 138–139.
19 Young, 'Malthus', 138–139.
20 Young, 'Malthus', 110–111.
21 Young, 'Malthus', 140.
22 Young developed this perspective in more detail in Robert M. Young, 'Getting Started on Lysenkoism', *Radical Science Journal* 6–7 (1978): 81–105.
23 Stephen Jay Gould, 'The Hardening of the Modern Synthesis', in *Dimensions of Darwinism: Themes and Counterthemes in Twentieth-Century Evolutionary Theory* Marjorie Grene, 71–93 (Cambridge: Cambridge University Press, 1983), and Erika Lorraine Milam, *Creatures of Cain: The Hunt for Human Nature in Cold War America* (Princeton, NJ: Princeton University Press, 2019).
24 David Kohn, 'Introduction: A High Regard for Darwin', in *The Darwinian Heritage*, ed. Kohn, 1–5 (Princeton, NJ: Princeton University Press in association with Nova Pacifica, 1985), 2.
25 Roszak, *Making of a Counter Culture*, 101.
26 Robert J. Mayhew, *Malthus: The Life and Legacies of an Untimely Prophet* (Cambridge, MA: Harvard University Press, 2014).
27 Thomas Robertson, *The Malthusian Moment: Global Population Growth and the Birth of American Environmentalism* (New Brunswick, NJ: Rutgers University Press, 2012).
28 Robert J. Mayhew, 'The Publication Bomb: The Birth of Modern Environmentalism and the Editing of Malthus's *Essay*', in *New Perspectives on Malthus*, ed. Mayhew, 240–266 (Cambridge: Cambridge University Press, 2016), esp. 259–260.
29 Cyril D. Darlington, *The Evolution of Man and Society* (London: George Allen and Unwin, 1969), 61, 680. Robert M. Young, 'Understanding It All', *New Statesman* 78 (26 Sept. 1969): 417–418.
30 Gavin de Beer, 'How Darwin Came by his Theory of Natural Selection', *New Scientist* 21 (23 Jan. 1964): 216–218, at p. 217. 'Perched on a pile of cushions, [de Beer] daily sallied forth from the Museum in his Rolls Royce into the tide of traffic with an unassailable (and in the event justified) faith that it would part at his coming'. William T. Stearn, *The Natural History Museum at South Kensington* (London: William Heinemann, 1981): 339.
31 De Beer, 'How Darwin Came by his Theory', 218. Born in Vienna in 1914, Bertha Maria Skramovsky had emigrated to Britain and after the Second World War became a naturalized citizen. She worked initially as a housekeeper, but her language skills and evident abilities gained her employment in London in increasingly senior clerical posts at the museum. For the birthdate, see National Archives, Kew, Piece Number Description 086: Internees at Liberty in UK 1939–1942: Sk-Spe. Skramovsky was naturalized in 1947 (see *London Gazette*, 21 Nov. 1947), retired from the museum at the end of 1967, married in 1970 and died on 11 December 2006 at the age of 92. I am grateful to Kathryn Rooke of the Natural History Museum, and to Anne Secord, for information about Skramovsky.
32 Young, 'Malthus', 127.
33 De Beer, 'How Darwin Came by his Theory', 218.
34 Sandra Herbert, 'The Darwinian Revolution Revisited', *Journal of the History of Biology* 38 (2005): 51–66, at p. 55. Only in 1974, two years after de Beer's death, did the M and N notebooks appear in an edition by Paul Barrett. For an overview of the history of the manuscripts, see Sydney Smith, 'Historical Preface', in *Charles Darwin's Notebooks, 1836–1844*, ed. Paul H. Barrett, Peter J. Gautrey, Sandra Herbert, David Kohn and Sydney Smith, 1–5 (London and Ithaca, NY: British Museum [Natural History] and Cornell University Press, 1987).

35 Bert James Loewenberg, 'Darwin and Darwin Studies, 1959–63', *History of Science* 4 (1965): 15–54, surveys the work being carried out.

36 For Young's view of the situation in Cambridge, see Young, 'Historiographic and Ideological Contexts'. For other perspectives see Gerd Buchdahl, 'Twenty-five Years of History and Philosophy of Science at Cambridge', *Cambridge Review* 10 (1989): 167–171; and the overview in Anna-K. Mayer, '"I have been very fortunate": Brief Report on the BSHS Oral History Project: "The History of Science in Britain, 1945–65"', *British Journal for the History of Science* 32 (1999): 223–235.

37 Raphael Uchôa, interview with Piyo Rattansi, *Circumscribere* 23 (2019): 1–76, 16–17, on the seminar see 48–49.

38 Fox, 'Fashioning the Discipline', 425.

39 Bernal, *Geography of a Life*, 327.

40 Robert M. Young, review of J.W. Burrow, *Evolution and Society, Cambridge Review* 89 (1967): 409–411. The book is on the reading list for the course, as evidenced by notes made at the time by Patrick Parrinder, who kindly provided a full transcript (personal communication, 18 Mar. 2020).

41 Anna-K. Mayer, interview with Robert M. Young, 10 Feb. 1998, British Society for the History of Science Oral History Project, Special Collections, Leeds University Library. Cited with the permission of the President and Council of the British Society for the History of Science.

42 Christopher Hill, Rodney H. Hilton and Eric J. Hobsbawm, 'Origins and Early Years', *Past and Present* 100 (1983): 3–14; and Jacques Le Goff, 'Later History', *Past and Present* 100 (1983): 14–28.

43 *Cambridge University Reporter* (1 Mar. 1967) 97, 1002–1003. Martin Rudwick was appointed to the position.

44 Mary Hesse to Eric Ashby, 30 Jan. 1969, King's College Archives, semi-current records: Fellows' files. Quoted by permission of Richard Hesse.

45 Edmund Leach to Noel Annan, 13 Mar. 1973, semi-current records: Fellows' files'. Quoted by permission of Louisa Brown, Edmund Leach's daughter and literary executor.

46 For accounts of the commune, I am deeply grateful to Sarah Greaves, personal communication, emails 3 Apr. 202, 21 Apr. 2021, 1 May 2021. Later recollections of the commune vary, but all stress that it was driven by deeply held conviction.

47 Robert M. Young, 'Psychoanalysis and the Public Sphere' (1987) http://www.psychoanalysis-and-therapy.com/human_nature/papers/ppsl.html, accessed 1 Apr. 2021; also Martin Bernal, *Geography of a Life* (Bloomington, IN: Xlibris, 2012): 341.

48 Sarah Greaves, personal communication, emails 21 Apr. 2021 and 1 May 2021. For the political activities pursued especially by women, see Helene Curtis and Mimi Sanderson, *The Unsung Sixties: Memoirs of Social Innovation* (London: Whiting and Birch, 2004).

49 Young resigned from his King's fellowship and his post as assistant director of research in the Wellcome Unit, effective 31 December 1974. For the date, which is incorrectly stated in most sources, see 'University Offices Vacated during the Academical Year 1974–75', *Cambridge University Reporter* 106 (8 Oct. 1975): 84.

50 The essays (with revisions and additions) were collected in Robert M. Young, *Darwin's Metaphor: Nature's Place in Victorian Culture* (Cambridge: Cambridge University Press, 1985).

51 Mayhew, 'The Publication Bomb', 262 n. 13, speaks of 'an explosion of interest', but the volume of scholarly historical publication before Patricia James's *Population Malthus: His Life and Times* (London: Routledge, 1979) appears modest.

52   For an insightful analysis of Young's relation to these later writings, see Inge-
     mar Bohlin, 'Robert M. Young and Darwin Historiography', *Social Studies
     of Science* 21 (1991): 597–648. The literature is summarized in David Oldroyd,
     'How Did Darwin Arrive at His Theory? The Secondary Literature to 1982',
     History of Science 22 (1984): 325–371. and also Piers J. Hale, 'Finding a Place
     for the Anti-Malthusian Tradition in the Victorian Evolutionary Debates', in
     New Perspectives on Malthus, ed. Mayhew, 182–207. The most valuable general
     survey up to the mid-1980s remains Antonello La Vergata, 'Images of Darwin:
     A Historiographic Overview', in *Darwinian Heritage*, ed. Kohn, 901–972. For
     an especially incisive account see Gregory Radick, 'Is the Theory of Natural
     Selection Independent of its History?" in *The Cambridge Companion to Darwin*,
     ed. Jonathan Hodge and Gregory Radick, 147–172, 2nd edn (Cambridge: Cam-
     bridge University Press, 2009).
53   Sandra Herbert, 'The Logic of Darwin's Discovery', Brandeis University PhD
     dissertation (1968); Herbert, 'Darwin, Malthus and Selection', *Journal of the
     History of Biology* 4 (1971): 209–217.
54   David Kohn, 'Theories to Work By: Rejected Theories, Reproduction, and Dar-
     win's Path to Natural Selection', *Studies in History of Biology* 4 (1990): 67–170, at
     p. 142.
55   Kohn, 'Theories to Work By', 142.
56   Young, 'Malthus', 130.
57   Robert M. Young, 'Darwinism *is* Social', in *Darwinian Heritage*, ed. Kohn, 609–
     638, 634. Young ('Malthus', 71) declares his debt to Smith.
58   For a thorough discussion of this issue, see Bohlin, 'Robert M. Young', 627–634.
     Young explicitly rejected the significance of any of these distinctions in 'Malthus
     on Man: In Animals No Moral Restraint', in *Malthus, Medicine, and Morality:
     'Malthusianism' after 1798*, ed. Brian Dolan, 73–91 (Amsterdam: Rudolfi, 2000).
59   Young, 'Darwinism *is* Social', 633.
60   Mayr to Darlington, 28 Nov. 1978, quoted in Solomon Harman, *The Man Who
     Invented the Chromosome: A Life of Cyril Darlington* (Cambridge, MA: Harvard
     University Press, 2004), 261.
61   See the editor's title of the obituary by Roger Smith, 'Robert M. Young, 'Science
     Historian and Darwin Scholar Who Wielded Great Influence on the Cultural
     Left', *The Independent*, 19 Aug. 2019. John Durant's assessment of Young as
     'the world's leading Darwin scholar' is prominently featured on Young's website
     at www.psychoanalysis-and-therapy.com/rmyoung/pubs.html, accessed 18 Apr.
     2020.
62   For the development of cultural history in relation to social history, see William
     H. Sewell, 'The Political Unconscious of Social History', in *Logics of History:
     Social Theory and Social Transformation*, ed. Sewell, 22–80 (Chicago: The Uni-
     versity of Chicago Press, 2005).
63   David Philip Miller, 'The Social History of British Science: After the Harvest?',
     Social Studies of Science 14 (1984): 115–135.
64   Robert M. Young, 'Natural Theology, Victorian Periodicals, and the Fragmen-
     tation of a Common Context', in *Darwin to Einstein: Historical Studies on Science
     and Belief*, ed. Colin Chant and J.R. Fauvel, 69–107 (London: Longman/Open
     University Press, 1980), 74.
65   One way in which a wider perspective took hold was, paradoxically, through
     complete publication of the notebooks in 1987 and the volumes of the Darwin
     correspondence from 1985. The Darwin Correspondence Project, begun in
     1974 by the American philosopher Frederick Burkhardt with the assistance of
     Sydney Smith and a small team of researchers, proposed to issue only letters
     from Darwin, but eventually was funded to publish letters to him as well. This

changed what would have been a monument to a great man into a resource for understanding the Victorian debates, involving some 2,000 correspondents from across the world. For this point, see Evelleen Richards, 'Democratizing Darwin', *Annals of Science* 52 (1992): 509–517, at p. 512.

66 J.R.R. Christie, review of R.M. Young, *Darwin's Metaphor*, *Social Studies of Science* 18 (1988): 187–189, at p. 188.
67 Young, *Darwin's Metaphor*, 365.
68 Young, 'Natural Theology', 74.
69 Young, 'Historiographic and Ideological Contexts', 351–352. For recognition that his own work had not accomplished this integration see Bob Young, 'Desmond and Moore's *Darwin*: A Critique', *Science as Culture* 4 (1994): 393–424, at p. 399.
70 Agar, 'What Happened in the Sixties?', 594–595, cites Young as providing 'a masterclass in the new sociology of science' at the 1970 meeting of the British Society for Social Responsibility in Science, but his emphasis was very different than that being developed in Edinburgh, even if some of the motives were related.
71 For these developments see Jan Golinski, *Making Natural Knowledge: Constructivism and the History of Science*, 2nd edn (Chicago: The University of Chicago Press, 2005).
72 See, for example, Young, 'Science is a Labour Process', in *Science for People* 43–44 (1979): 31–37; and Turchetti, 'Looking for the Bad Teachers', 84–87.
73 For example, see the autobiographical preface by Steven Shapin to Daniel S. Greenberg, *The Politics of Pure Science*, 2nd edn (Chicago: The University of Chicago Press, 1999); and Steven Shapin's comments on Young in 'History of Science and its Sociological Reconstructions', *History of Science* 20 (1982): 157–211, at pp. 178–179.
74 Frank M. Turner, review of Robert M. Young, *Darwin's Metaphor*, *Isis* 7 (1986): 727–728, at p. 728.
75 Young's remarks on the question of a scale would appear to be somewhat contradictory, but see Young, 'Historiographic and Ideological Contexts', 194.
76 Young, 'Historiographic and Ideological Contexts', 364–365. Rudwick later wrote essays that did place geology in wider contexts, especially in relation to political economy and antiquarianism. See the articles collected in Martin J. S. Rudwick, *Lyell and Darwin, Geologists: Studies in the Earth Sciences in the Age of Reform* (Aldershot: Ashgate, 2005).
77 Thomas S. Kuhn, 'The Relations Between History and the History of Science', *Daedalus* 100 (1971): 271–304, at p. 302. For related criticisms, see Jan Golinski, 'Lost in Mediation: The Social Component of Darwin's Science', *History of the Human Sciences* 2 (1989): 95–103.
78 Harry M. Collins, 'The Seven Sexes: A Study in the Sociology of a Phenomenon, or the Replication of Experiments in Physics', *Sociology* 9 (1975): 205–224. For research schools, see J. B. Morrell, 'The Chemist Breeders: The Research Schools of Liebig and Thomas Thomson', *Ambix* 19 (1972): 1–46; and Gerald L. Geison, *Michael Foster and the Cambridge School of Physiology: The Scientific Enterprise in Late Victorian Society* (Princeton, NJ: Princeton University Press, 1978).
79 Steven Shapin, 'History of Science and its Sociological Reconstructions', *History of Science* 20 (1982): 157–211.
80 For a contemporary survey, see James A. Secord, 'Natural History in Depth', *Social Studies of Science* 15 (1985): 181–200.

81 Crosbie Smith and M. Norton Wise, *Energy and Empire: A Biographical Study of Lord Kelvin* (Cambridge: Cambridge University Press, 1989); Evelleen Richards, articles collected in *Ideology and Evolution in Nineteenth Century Britain: Embryos, Monsters, and Racial and Gendered Others in the Making of Evolutionary Theory and Culture* (London: Routledge, 2021); Simon Schaffer, 'Scientific Discoveries and the End of Natural Philosophy', *Social Studies of Science* 16 (1986): 387–420; and Schaffer, 'Astronomers Mark Time: Discipline and the Personal Equation', *Science in Context* 2 (1988): 115–145.

82 For the praise of former students, see Young, *Darwin's Metaphor*, 162–163.

83 Steven Shapin, 'Hyperprofessionalism and the Crisis of Readership in the History of Science', *Isis* 96 (2005): 238–243. On the politics of science studies, see the special issue edited by Evelleen Richards and Malcolm Ashmore, *The Politics of SSK: Neutrality, Commitment and Beyond, Social Studies of Science* 26 no. 2 (1996): 219–468.

84 Young, 'Desmond and Moore's *Darwin*'. For reflections on this episode, see James Moore, 'Metabiographical Reflections on Charles Darwin', in *Telling Lives in Science: Essays on Scientific Biography*, ed. Michael Shortland and Richard Yeo, 267–281 (Cambridge: Cambridge University Press, 2008). Young's concern about the politics of popular biography were shared by others; see Richards, 'Democratizing Darwin', 518; Ingemar Bohlin, 'Popularizing Darwin', *Science as Culture* 4 (1994): 425–439, at p. 419; and Paul White, 'Desmond/*Huxley*: The Hot-blooded Historian', *Studies in History and Philosophy of the Biological and Biomedical Sciences* 35 (2004): 191–198, italics in original.

85 Young, 'The New Nation?', 33.

86 Young, *Nature's Metaphor*, x.

87 Young, 'Psychoanalysis and the Public Sphere'. See Jermi Suri, 'The Rise and Fall of an International Counterculture, 1960–1975', *American Historical Review* 114 (2009), 45–68, and Boris Buden, 'To Make the Long March Short: A Short Commentary on the Two Long Marches that have Failed their Emancipatory Promises', *Crisis & Critique* 5 (2018), 128–141.

88 See, for example, Alison Bashford and Joyce E. Chaplin, *The New Worlds of Thomas Robert Malthus: Rereading* The Principle of Population (Princeton, NJ: Princeton University Press, 2016); and Marwa Elshakry, 'Global Darwin: Eastern Enchantment', *Nature* 461 (28 Oct. 2009): 1200–1201.

89 Robert M. Young, 'Darwin's Metaphor: Does Nature Select?', *The Monist* 55 (1971): 442–503, at p. 503.

Chapter 3

The reception of Robert M. Young's *Mind, Brain, and Adaptation in the Nineteenth Century*[1]

Timothy Sim

Introduction

When Robert Young finished his 100,000 word PhD thesis on cerebral localization in 1965, he could scarcely have known that it would become a foundational text in the history of the brain sciences. In some ways, he was an unlikely candidate for this distinction, for he had stumbled into the history of science by accident rather than intention. He had studied philosophy and psychology at Yale with the aim of becoming a psychiatrist. The rush of starting medical school in 1958, however, was quickly overshadowed by "the confusion in current attempts to relate the concepts used in the explanation of normal and abnormal behaviour to the physiology of organisms."[2] Personal issues at home added further strain, but an opportunity to resolve this situation appeared in the autumn of 1960: with the offer of a Cambridge fellowship in the history of medicine, he crossed the Atlantic for a one-year visit that expanded into a four-year PhD project.[3]

Lacking formal training in history, but under the tutelage of the neuropsychologist Oliver Zangwill, Young devoted his time to exploring the conceptual history of localizing functions in the brain, for "the history of various concepts of function *is* the history of psychology."[4] By the end of his research he was convinced that psychology indeed had progressed by moving from philosophy to physiology, but at the cost of reducing meaningful, adaptive functions to mere sensory-motor reactions. History revealed the problem, and history provided the solution: modern science had to learn from Gall's pseudoscientific phrenology, and combine physiological analysis with "a biologically significant set of functions" derived from psychology.[5] Impressed by his work, the Faculty of Moral Sciences (later Faculty of Philosophy) promptly awarded him his doctorate.

Five years later, as Fellow of King's College and Director of the Wellcome Unit for the History of Medicine, Young reduced the academic title of his thesis, *Cerebral localization and its biological context from Gall to Ferrier*, to the simple, if less specific *Mind, Brain, and Adaptation in the Nineteenth Century* (1970).[6] The impact of this change is uncertain, but the acclaim it

DOI: 10.4324/9781003204244-5

received is not. From a quantitative perspective, the citation index Web of Science records more than 5,000 citations of *Mind, Brain, and Adaptation* by almost 250 publications as of March 2020. Its reception transcended disciplinary boundaries, with 69 citations in the History of Science, 61 citations in Neuroscience, 64 in Psychology, and 28 in Clinical Neurology and Psychiatry.[7] From a qualitative perspective, the view is similar: in *Brain*, Denis William raved that "It must be the most important work upon the evolution of thought upon the results of cerebral localization written in the decade now ending."[8] *Science* labelled it a volume of "unusual excellence,"[9] while *The British Journal for the History of Science* "could offer nothing but praise for this scholarly study."[10] Even the *New York Review of Books* chipped in, calling his book "a model for the writing of the history of science."[11]

Hidden within this sea of general positivity, however, were many different – often contradictory – interpretations of Young's work. For some, *Mind, Brain, and Adaptation* legitimated the current status of science, but for others, it motivated reform. Some argued that it guided the present by clarifying the past, but others replied that it could not help future research at all. His historiography was variously applauded, dismissed, or denounced.

This chapter examines how and why such a multiplicity of readings was possible. Studying the reception of a work necessitates examining both the contexts of reading and the contents of the book, for readers and writers are in constant conversation.[12] Writers address implicit audiences, anticipate responses, and defend against probable criticism. While writers frame and constrain, readers take liberties with their work, infusing new meanings within their interpretive communities. Meanings emerge from an interplay between content and context, between the author's goals and the reader's social, cultural, and intellectual assumptions. As Secord concluded in *Victorian Sensation*, "meaning is understood as the product of reading, undertaken in a context of struggles for authority over interpretation."[13]

This framework reveals that the sheer range of interpretations of *Mind, Brain, and Adaptation* derived from a combination of disciplinary relevance and textual ambiguity. *Mind, Brain, and Adaptation* spoke to a diverse set of issues produced by the disciplinary ruptures of the 1970s. In the brain sciences, boundaries between neurology and psychology were being drawn, even as the coherence of the "pre-paradigmatic" psychology was questioned. In psychiatry, the patient's rights movement of the 1960s was challenging the methods, places, and ethics of treatment. And in the history of science, ferocious debates about historiography occurred amidst professionalization and Cold War politics. These diverse backgrounds fostered a variety of responses to *Mind, Brain, and Adaptation*, from celebration and mobilization to condemnation and rejection.

Complementing this was the significant amount of ambiguity woven into the work, which had been slightly revised before publication. While the bulk of the book was a verbatim repackaging of his 1965 thesis, in 1970, Young added an entirely new introduction, a few lines in the preface, and a final paragraph in the conclusion. All these changes sought to strengthen the book's implicit (and often inconspicuous) claims about current science. For example, a new section in the preface reads:

> In raising this issue here, *I want to allude to a theme implicit in my argument* [emphasis mine]: the problem of providing functional or purposive explanations within the context of Cartesian mind-body dualism set constraints on the study of cerebral localization which were not overcome within the period which is treated here; and, it seems to me, the problem is no less acute today.[14]

Thus, *Mind, Brain, and Adaptation*'s conclusions were asserted with heightened strength and fervour only five years after its writing. That is not to say that Young's PhD thesis was entirely free of argumentative force (the claim that history should inform modern psychology was unchanged), but it was certainly "tacked on" to the front and end of the book, framing the historical analysis rather than constituting it. This disjunction meant that readers, if they wished, could (and did) separate Young's history of localization from his conclusions about the state of modern science. Further ambiguity resided even within the analytical portions of the book, for it was written at a time that Young later claimed lacked any "clearly-conceived historiography."[15] As a result, his history incorporated aspects of presentist, historicist, and sometimes even sociological approaches, resulting in a complex and multivocal product.

Because of the limitations of space, this article will not provide a detailed outline of the contents of Young's book; instead, its contents will be introduced in tandem with reviewer's interpretations. I first discuss the initial reception to Young's work in the sciences and the history of science, before focusing on the changing interpretations of Young's analysis of phrenology between 1970 and 1990. It will become clear that evaluations of *Mind, Brain, and Adaptation* were closely linked to wider optimism, crisis, or professionalization in the various disciplines.

The meaning of history: reception in the sciences

Neurology

Since *Mind, Brain, and Adaptation* detailed the transformation of psychology into a mature science of "general biology," it appealed to neurologists at a time when they were increasingly distancing themselves from psychology. To many contemporaries, it was obvious that neurology was the winner of this divorce. With the post-war boom in biological funding, the proliferation of new instruments like the string galvanometer, and the standardization of systems like the giant squid axon, neurology was flourishing.[16] By the 1960s, the proliferation of specialists journals such as *Electroencephalography and Clinical Neurophysiology* (founded in 1949) and the *Journal of Neurochemistry* (1956) motivated calls to unify the "neurosciences," through initiatives like the Brain Research Association in Britain and the Neurosciences Research Program at MIT.[17]

Against this backdrop, it was all too easy to read *Mind, Brain, and Adaptation* as a straightforward tale of how bad psychology had become good neurophysiology, despite Young's worries about the current state of brain research. In the *British Journal of Psychiatry*, the neuropathologist William McMenemey marvelled that Young's work showed the "metamorphosis of the embryonic subject of psychology into a true science."[18] In *Science*, the esteemed neurophysiologist Mary Brazier elaborated that:

> "Psychology," said Norbert Wiener, "is like a tapeworm that keeps losing segments to physiology." This is essentially the message of this absorbing book, which traces the history of the concepts of cerebral localization of function and (in much less detail) of the relation of organisms to their environments.[19]

In fact, for these neurologists, the tale was not triumphant enough – why weren't the experimental advances of neurology privileged over the confused investigations of psychology? Brazier remarked that it was "surprising to find a whole chapter given to [the association psychologist] Bain, who contributed nothing of substance to our knowledge of cerebral localization or of evolution." For her, the true turning point was instead in Fritsch and Hitzig's electrophysiological investigations, where "speculation finally gave way to experiment," and "objective localization" was made possible.[20] McMenemey was more guarded, but he agreed: the experimental investigations of Fritsch and Hitzig and of Ferrier were the "important landmark."[21] Both Brazier and McMenemey also concluded their reviews by connecting Young's history with recent progress in neurophysiology and neurosurgery, respectively.[22] Evidently, both saw Young's work as legitimating neurological, rather than psychological, approaches to the brain.

Not all neurologists, however, believed that Young's history reified the present. Those discontent with the ongoing separation between neurology and psychology were quick to note Young's own ambivalence towards modern brain science, and his call to bring together neurological "analysis" with a "biologically significant set of functions" derived from psychology.[23] The Harvard neurology professor Norman Geschwind, who would later be hailed as the "modern father of Behavioural Neurology,"[24] concluded in *Nature* that "Young argues, in my view correctly, that a knowledge of the history and awareness of philosophical problems in this area is important for future advances."[25] Similarly, the clinical psychologist Richard Carolus

Oldfield noted in the *Journal of Neurology, Neurosurgery & Psychiatry* that "psychologists and neurologists alike are now hampered by lack of appreciation of their predecessor's interactions and their relationship to the biological advances of the nineteenth century." Young's reappraisal contributed to their "growing convergence" and "could prove vitalizing to neurology and psychology alike."[26] For these neuropsychologists, further progress in brain science could only be secured through the interdisciplinary projects they advocated.[27] Thus, depending on one's view of the disciplinary trajectory of neurology, *Mind, Brain, and Adaptation* could either legitimate the present or motivate reform.

Psychiatry

While neurologists may have disagreed on what Young's work meant for the future of the field, there was no question among practitioners that neurology was progressing. The same could not be said for psychiatry, which was facing increasingly strong critiques from the anti-psychiatry movement. This context birthed the most vicious evaluation of *Mind, Brain, and Adaptation* in Henry R. Rollin's review for the *British Medical Journal* (*BMJ*). Science, Rollin asserted, was dashing past the "varied and inconstant" speculations of philosophers, theologians, and phrenologists. Young's attempt to restore Gall was mere ideology:

> "That sink-hole of human folly and prating coxcombry" was how a contemporary writer... described phrenology, Gall's brainchild. Yet Dr. Young expends buckets of whitewash in an attempt to re-establish him in the record book of true scientists... in a particularly ham-fisted, intuitive way, Gall did introduce the concept of cerebral localization into scientific thinking. But it was left to Jean-Pierre-Maire Flourens (1794–1867) to provide the first experimental demonstration of the localization of function in the brain. His prime failing was unfortunately to draw sweeping inferences...the begetting sin of many an experimental physiologist.[28]

Given the praise lavished by other reviewers, the *BMJ* review is remarkable for its hostility, and for ignoring Young's critique of Flourens' conclusions as "essentially theological" and "anatomically false and physiologically absurd."[29] Rollin's staunch alignment with experimental physiology (and against phrenology) can be traced to the urgent importance of distinguishing science from pseudoscience in psychiatry, whether or not this was always possible historically. Since the 1950s, anti-establishment activists argued that mental hospitals were more concerned with political control rather than scientific cure.[30] They alleged that physical treatments such as prefrontal lobotomy and insulin shock therapy were barbaric, especially since patients were held against their will. Complementing these critiques was the rise of psychopharmacology in the 1960s, which promised to shift psychiatry away from in-patient treatment at asylums to outpatient prescriptions at clinics. To many contemporaries, this signalled a new era of scientific, drug-based psychiatry that made de-institutionalization both a moral necessity and a professional advance.

Rollin was no exception. In his 22 years as Deputy Superintendent of Horton Hospital, one of the largest British mental hospitals of its time, he incorporated music therapy, dance, and sport in an effort to transform the hospital into a therapeutic rather than custodial space.[31] The anti-psychiatric movement resonated deeply with him, as did the promise of drug therapy – in later interviews about Horton hospital, he recalled that "some of the disasters of the era of physical methods were being replaced by the new, exciting era of psychopharmacology."[32] We can even glean some of these attitudes from his review of Young's book, where he lamented:

> How far then have we got? In truth, not very far. And yet the most important accolade for scientific discovery, the Nobel prize, was awarded in our time to the inventor of a blind, mutilating operation on the human brain. It is not only yesterday's scholars, who considered the brain to be the seat of the soul, who might rate this as an act of sacrilege.[33]

This "mutilating operation" would have been understood as referring to 1949 Nobel Prize in Physiology or Medicine, awarded to Antonio Moniz for pioneering lobotomy.[34] Rollin's acerbic comments point to his righteous belief that modern psychiatry was founded on a better empirical base – informed by science rather than "blind" speculation.

Rollin's desire to defend the scientific status of psychiatry (and hence, to distance it from phrenology) must have also been influenced by his past experience with psychoanalysis. In 1953, Rollin had won a Fulbright Fellowship to study psychiatry at Temple University, Philadelphia, at a time when psychoanalysis was at its peak in America.[35] Since psychoanalysis had never entered the mainstream in British psychiatry, Rollin was shocked at the "religious reverence" for it there, and he would later recall that "having in my life escaped the constrictions of both religious and political dogma, I wanted no part of it."[36] In the wake of the Rosenhan hoax of 1973 which shook psychotherapists of all stripes, Rollin must have felt vindicated.[37] By following science, rather than what he deemed dogma, Rollin could be assured that psychiatric treatment was reliable.

In light of these trends, Rollin's vehement rejection of Young's history probably reflected an embarrassment about psychiatry's questionable past and a desire to separate modern, "scientific" treatment from older, "speculative" ones. It was less important to recover the pseudoscientific origins of modern science than to emphasize the "quantum leap psychiatry has taken during the 20th century" that justified his transformation of Horton hospital.[38] Young's work, by framing phrenology as an inextricable starting point for modern brain science, destabilized these neat dichotomies of speculative versus scientific, old versus modern, and repressive versus trustworthy. If one accepted that science could grow from pseudoscience, how could one reject ineffective psychoanalysis or barbaric lobotomy? At a time when the fundamental principles of psychiatric treatment were being questioned and reformed, it is no surprise that Rollin saw Young's history as a threat.

Psychology

Like its medical counterpart in psychiatry, psychology was facing a crisis. At the same time that public faith in the progressiveness of the social sciences was waning, the field of psychology was becoming ever more fragmented.[39] Even at the undergraduate level, textbooks like Robert S. Woodworth's *Contemporary Schools of Psychology* (1931–1951, eight editions) and Edna Heidbredder's *Seven Psychologies* (1933) evinced the enormous diversity of what were often independent, if not mutually exclusive "schools" of psychology.[40] For instance, while behaviourism eschewed all mental states in favour of quantifiable behaviour, Gestalt psychology took for granted that the patterns and qualities of perception should serve as starting points for investigation. In a context where proponents of different factions would clash fervently and publicly over what constituted proper psychology, Thomas Kuhn's comments about the "pre-paradigmatic" nature of the social sciences seem like a polite understatement, although the not so implicit assumption that the human sciences should unify one day around one paradigm was perhaps unwise and inappropriate.[41]

The factionalism dominant within psychology directly shaped reviews of *Mind, Brain, and Adaptation*. Writing for *Contemporary Psychology,* the Professor Emeritus of the University of California, David Krech, praised Young's work for its emphasis on functional psychology: "I share so many of Young's biases that I will not even play devil's advocate."[42] On the other hand, the psychophysiologist J. P. Wierda bemoaned in *Janus* that Young's book was "*rather limited*" because it failed to give structural psychology its due. "The bibliography mentions two publications by TITCHENER, but in the index I found *neither* TITCHENER *nor structuralism!*"[43] This was disciplinary fragmentation writ large. Less obviously, but perhaps more significantly, this factionalism led to some deep engagement with Young's historiography. Krech, for instance, discussed at length Young's goal of clarifying modern psychology:

> As to the second question, how significant are these new interpretations for our understanding of the history of brain-behavior research, much depends upon one's philosophy of science and one's view of the

proper uses of history. And here I think I would quarrel with Young. I am among those who believe that almost each new major advance in science necessitates a rewriting of its history. A "breakthrough" not only opens up a whole new future for the science but discloses a whole new past... But Young seems to be of the opinion that his history is significant in helping us to understand the achievements, puzzlements, and promises of *contemporary* brain-behavior research—and there I think he is wrong, very wrong. No history of a currently active biological science written from 'within' the nineteenth century (as Young has done) can be very helpful.[44]

It is tempting to explain Krech's disregard as merely the problem of a scientist failing to understand the historical method, but this would be too hasty. His proposed historiography is unabashedly Whiggish, but this was part of a broader move in psychology to use history to legitimate the present.[45] These "internal" histories, written by psychologists rather than historians, could raise psychology's reputation in two ways. Firstly, they helped define the disciplinary borders of psychology by generating a "vertical synthesis" of the various schools. By showing complementarity between schools, problematic disunity could be restated as a fruitful diversity. Secondly, internal histories could legitimate newer schools by reconstructing a long and distinguished history. Wierda's review, with its overriding concern for structuralism and psychophysiology, is an example of the latter. It should come as no surprise that he dedicated the second half of his review to preaching the gospel of Titchener, Wundt, and Fechner, to the point of recommending alternate histories for the interested reader.

By 1970, the use of history to guide the present was already becoming institutionalized in psychology. Since 1950, nearly half of all American psychology university departments offered undergraduate courses in "systems and schools" and "history"; by the 1960s, the history of psychology had emerged as a speciality, with dedicated groups like Division 26 of the American Psychological Association that published in the *Journal of the History of the Behavioural Sciences*.[46] While the histories produced were becoming increasingly sophisticated, they were still ultimately about understanding the present. Thus a graduate program in the University of New Hampshire intended its course to "reveal a complex interaction over time of biographical, social and intellectual factors; by analogy, the student comes away with a truer sense of the development of his own professional identity."[47]

Seen in this light, Krech's motivations for rejecting Young's history become clearer: he rejected it not because it was wrong, but because it was not useful. As he wrote in his review, it was precisely because a presentist history "discloses a whole new past" and "opens up a whole new future" that it could stimulate contemporary research.[48] If Krech had to "outline [his] own history of brain research (from the standpoint of the 1970s)," he would have joined the neurologists in emphasizing modern psychology's experimental nature: "Gall and Bain and Spencer – and almost every psychologist of the nineteenth century – would play but minor roles, and Mueller and Flourens... would get their names in lights."[49] In failing to account for modern psychology's character, Young had limited the practical impact that his history could have. At a time of disciplinary crisis, history had to be used to legitimate the present rather than fulfil some needless academic curiosity. The pursuit of this goal was more fruitfully done by a presentist rather than historicist approach, no matter how sophisticated *Mind, Brain, and Adaptation* could be.

The writing of history: reception in history of science

Intellectual history

Krech's presentism might seem characteristic of a scientist muddling in history, but taking his views as representative obscures the fact that much of the best historical work was being done by "scientist-historians" who straddled science and history.[50] Young himself could be characterized as a scientist-historian: although his interest in history was deep and his work was sophisticated, he had been formally trained in psychology rather than history. The same could said for the majority of British historians of science from 1945 to 1965, who overwhelmingly entered the field with a science rather than arts background.[51]

The semi-professional nature of history of science (and of history of psychology in particular) explains why some scientists-historians were invited to review his book in history journals. Their evaluation of Young's historiography was almost completely opposite to Krech's: they praised his work precisely because of its historicism. The psychiatrist Richard Alfred Hunter wrote in *Annals of Science*:

> The author is a psychologist with a medical background. His aim is to clarify present-day confusion and obscurities in psychological thinking and research by tracing its origins. The method of advancing knowledge by historical research, paradoxical though it may sound, has already yielded fruits in related fields and may be expected to do so increasingly as science builds up a larger backlog. The reason is that the historical method provides perspective for evaluating modern trends not obtainable in any other way.
>
> He is not a historian but his approach is refreshing and his pen fluent.[52]

Hunter's pleasant surprise at the quality of Young's history shows that scientist-historians tended to distance themselves from those with only a passing interest in history.[53] Reviews in history journals reveal that scientist-historians and intellectual historians read *Mind, Brain, and Adaptation* in much the same way: as an exemplary history of ideas that could guide the present by clarifying the past. But contrary to Krech, they believed that it was historicism, and not presentism, that could illuminate modern science.

Hunter did not need to belabour the usefulness of historicism because Young had already done so in *Mind, Brain, and Adaptation*. On opening the book, the reader was greeted by two quotes in the preface: one by the eminent intellectual historian Arthur Lovejoy (from his 1936 *Great Chain of Being*) and the other by the leading medical historians Erwin H. Ackerknecht and Henry V. Vallois (from their 1956 history of Gall).[54] Both quotes were beautiful defences of the history of ideas. A section from Lovejoy's quote reads:

> But though the history of ideas is a history of trial-and-error, even the errors illuminate the peculiar nature, the cravings, the endowments, and the limitations of the creature that falls into them, as well as the logic of the problems in reflection upon which they have arisen...The adequate record of even the confusions of our forebears may help, not only to clarify those confusions, but to engender a salutary doubt whether we are wholly immune from different but equally great confusions.[55]

These were complemented by three epigraphs in the introduction by the philosopher Alfred North Whitehead and an in-text quote of Edwin Arthur Burtt's *The Metaphysical Foundations of Modern Physical Science* (1924).[56] All served to justify Young's project of making "a case for the use of historical method in the analysis of *current* problems in science."[57] The professional historian Bert James Loewenberg was so convinced of Young's success that he adduced more evidence to support Young's thesis. As he concluded in *Victorian Studies*: "Schools of psychology, dominant in contemporary thought, have yet to offer adequate explanations of thought and feeling. Evidence has been accumulating for fifty years; the concepts have already been formulated. But yesterday's assumptions remain to be dissolved."[58] It was left unsaid that works like *Mind, Brain, and Adaptation* were the solution.

In turn, *Mind, Brain, and Adaptation* could even be used as an argument for the importance of "internal" intellectual history over other kinds of history. As a prolific intellectual historian of evolution, Loewenberg's review had actually examined Young's work alongside Michael T. Ghiselin's *The Triumph of the Darwinian Method* (1969).[59] Noting that they were "fused in [the] scholarly purpose"[60] of clarifying modern thought, Loewenberg praised Ghiselin's study: "Intellectual growth and personal development are the twin solvents [of evolutionary theory], not arbitrary classification of specialist data or culturally conditioned disciplinary rubrics. Ghiselin's technique reveals Darwin's creative powers, his imaginative insights."[61] In just two sentences, Loewenberg both celebrated intellectual history and critiqued sociological ones. Only a history of the development of individual genius could explain the emergence of evolution; only a history of ideas could explain past events usefully.

Science and society

The *Isis* review by Norman Dain was significantly more cautious. Dain was Emeritus Professor of History at Rutgers University and a leading American historian of psychiatry.[62] Where the intellectual historians above focused on Young's study of ideas in science, Dain was more inclined to examine how "external" social factors could impact science. His first book, *Concepts of Insanity in the United States, 1789–1865* (1964) had traced the rise and fall of moral treatment in psychiatry by appeal to socioeconomic trends and the influence of humanitarianism.[63] In the last paragraph of the book, Dain argued that the "conditions for [moral therapy's] successful practice were complex, expensive, and sensitive to changes in the attitudes of the lay public and the medical profession."[64] In turn, he pleaded for a more humane treatment of lower-class patients to avoid similarly "dismal consequences for the insane."[65] The moral of Dain's history sprung not from a conceptual analysis of insanity, but from an evaluation of the relationship between science with society.

Given this background, Dain was more attuned to Young's discussion of how politics and ideology might have affected science. He wrote:

> Young makes a strong case for the inhibiting role of ideological, theological, and philosophical ideas in the advance of the science of psychology, a situation that has also been shown to have existed in psychiatry as well. Yet his own commitment to his thesis seems to have prevented him from looking for counter tendencies... might not a new generation of neurophysiologists have been influenced as well by a broader philosophical trend that reflected abandonment of or indifference to the traditional mind-body dichotomy?
>
> Young's emphasis on the implications of his study for contemporary psychology will no doubt meet with criticism. Psychologists may quarrel with his evaluation of their discipline; historians may question his polemical attitude (though this reviewer does not). Yet his thesis is ably defended and gives currency to his book. In any case, one need not accept his conclusions about the present to appreciate the value of his analysis of the past. He has dealt lucidly and meaningfully with a complex subject and contributed substantially to our understanding of the history of psychology.[66]

In the context of a field divided by the internalist-externalist debate and of the tendency to equate intellectual history with internalism and social history with externalism, it might seem surprising that the social historian in Dain was so respectful of Young's intellectual project.[67] A careful reading of *Mind, Brain, and Adaptation*, however, shows that even if the preface and introduction proclaimed its intellectual allegiance, in practice Young took immense pains to contextualize his actors and criticize them charitably. When discussing phrenology, Young noted that "Gall too was wrong, but his hypothesis was extremely plausible at the beginning of the last century" and was crucial for stimulating experimental study.[68] His method of naturalistic observation and corroboration misled, but "it would not make sense to ask that Gall use control procedures and statistical methods, or conduct his work in the light of a falsificationism view of scientific method" since they emerged at the end of the nineteenth century.[69] In any case, even Darwin and Wallace were in the business of using "great numbers of naturalistic observations and pieces of anecdotal evidence to support the theory...logically [evolution] was in the same position as phrenology for most of the nineteenth century," as Huxley's criticism revealed.[70] Similar judgements were made for other figures: Flourens was pioneering for his "technical contributions" but limited by theology,[71] Bain's work pointed both "forward to an experimental psychophysiology, and backward to the method of introspection," [72] and Ferrier "sacrifices the significance of functions to physiological accuracy."[73] This was no rational reconstruction of the past following Lakatos – in fact Young had denounced this approach in a 1966 article – it was a critical evaluation of the messiness of progress.[74] The psychologist David Krech summed it up as such: "His scholarship pervades but does not overwhelm, and despite his admiration for Gall, he can be critical of phrenological fantasies, i.e., he is 'sound.'"[75]

The curious balance of intellectual and social explanation in *Mind, Brain, and Adaptation* was because Young was still developing his historiographic approach in 1965. An examination of Young's 1966 article "Scholarship and the History of the Behavioural Sciences" illuminates both his historiography and Dain's response. In the article, Young rejected hagiographic or "great man" theories of history. While biographies helped explain the intellectual development of ideas, they were subordinate to conceptual analysis: "It would be a radical and retrograde step to separate biography and intellectual development from the history of scientific ideas, but a surgical separation of these approaches would be preferable to hero worship."[76] These approaches were common because of the early need for textbook histories in psychology, but the field "has passed through the useful but limited stage of amateurism" and had to investigate controversy rather than impose retrospective consensus.[77] Just a year after his PhD thesis was written, Young was espousing a refined form of intellectual history as a way of reforming the history of behavioural science.

Interestingly, Young's sophistication increased his desire to place science in its context. In an apparent contradiction to his stated aim in *Mind, Brain, and Adaptation*, Young dismissed the predominant view that researchers should focus on "the history of problems of *current* interest."[78] The tension between Young's views in 1966 and 1965/1970 arose because he supported the goal of a history for the present even as he indicted the methods it spawned. He wrote: "It is arguable that this [presentist] approach is most useful to these authors and their chosen audience, but the argument ultimately breaks down for two reasons."[79] For one, it generated "shockingly bad history" that considered writings "completely out of their context" and reduced history to a trivial collection of discoveries and anticipations.[80] More importantly, it failed to provide a contrasting perspective upon which "our own assumptions and our own vantage points" could be transcended.[81] Only a truly historicist approach could paradoxically inform the present. His rejection of a focus on current problems was thus a rejection of presentist *methodology* rather than presentist *purpose*. In a sense, *Mind, Brain, and Adaptation* was an attempt to perform this balancing act, by writing a retrospectively motivated history while placing its characters in their contexts. The result was a hybrid work that considered ideas and how they formed in their social and ideological contexts.

Of all the reviewers so far, Dain was the most careful by some margin, and he was poised to note that *Mind, Brain, and Adaptation* could be read as both an intellectual and social account of science. Indeed, Dain was the only reviewer to explicitly pinpoint the disjunction between *Mind, Brain, and Adaptation*'s body and the framing added to it later: as he noted, Young's polemical conclusions could be separated from his historical analysis. Consequently, Dain's critique of Young was less about his neglect of external influences on science, and more about Young's focus only on negative influences. To him, Young's history was a well-argued but one-sided presentation of the past. Unlike other reviewers, who celebrated the separation of science from speculation and politics, Dain's externalism led him to suggest positive roles for theology and philosophy. In asking Young to look for countertendencies to his argument, Dain seemed to believe that alternate, social histories of the mind could complement rather than undermine Young's thesis.

Phrenology, pseudoscience, and historiography

While contemporaries celebrated *Mind, Brain, and Adaptation* as a whole, it was Young's analysis of phrenology in particular that left the longest legacy. In the history of science, the changing evaluations of this analysis would mirror the steady shift from intellectual to sociological history.

When *Mind, Brain, and Adaptation* was first published, many scientist-historians were intent on uncovering historical precursors to modern theories. The pseudoscience of phrenology, which had long been dismissed out of hand, was beginning to look like a key precursor for modern brain science, and Young's work only added fuel to the fire. In the *British Journal for the History of Science* (*BJHS*), the neurologist Macdonald Critchley spent his entire review discussing how Young's work contributed to renewed interest in the origins of modern behavioural science: "Gall's influence upon contemporary views about cerebral localization of function is a subject of perennial interest, and Dr. Young joins the growing band of recent rehabilitators."[82] In *Isis*, the historian of psychiatry Norman Dain agreed: "In this serious consideration of Gall's ideas Young reinforces the contemporary rehabilitation of phrenology as a scientific effort, a forerunner of modern psychology."[83]

Young was aware of this interest because he had contributed to it. His 1966 article celebrated the nascent field of history of behavioural science and called for increased attention to phrenology.[84] In *Mind, Brain, and Adaptation*, Young had also foregrounded the analysis of phrenology as a major component of his history. The introductory overview of the book devoted almost two pages to discussing Gall alone; by comparison, the next closest figures in Bain and Ferrier were each given less than a full page.[85] This was reiterated at the end of the book: "The importance of phrenology in the development of adaptive and functional thinking in psychology has been one of the major themes of the present work...[it] has been one of the most interesting and significant results of my research."[86]

Contemporary reviewers enthusiastically agreed with Young's revisionist project. If his work was hardly hagiographic, it certainly reinstated Gall as an intellectual father of modern science. Loewenberg noted in *Victorian Studies* that "Gall is but one of the captivating figures whose life and thought enrich Young's work,"[87] while Critchley admired how "F. J. Gall has come alive."[88] The biographical nature of Young's investigations also provided strong handles for separating phrenology's actual scientific merit from its crass popularization. *Mind, Brain, and Adaptation*'s introduction proclaimed: "It is relatively incidental for present purposes that [Gall's] 'cranioscopic' method led to the pseudoscience of phrenology and was abandoned in favour of experimental cerebral localization. The influence of his concepts and his empirical approach remain highly significant."[89] Reviewers reiterated and strengthened this distinction. For instance, Critchley argued that Gall's phrenology was a sound science that had been co-opted by political agenda:

> That Gall has only too often been unkindly brushed aside as an exponent of a pseudo-science is true: perhaps the sins of his pupil Spurzheim were responsible for this. Indeed, Gall has been spoken of as "a great, though misguided, and perhaps even slightly ridiculous figure in the rise of a progressive science". Dr. Young correctly gives Gall credit for opposing an undue holistic conception of cerebral function which once obtained.[90]
>
> ... it must not be forgotten that Gall's work brought to an end a barren system of philosophy which seriously impeded progress. His

contributions to the anatomy of the central nervous system are of far-reaching importance, and to the physiology of the brain and to psychological theory he gave a new orientation and a new inspiration.[91]

In Critchley's reading, the truths and falsities of phrenological thinking could be distinguished not only at the level of theory but also in their very embodiment by different individuals. Gall was not in the business of phrenology, but rather in anatomy, physiology, and psychological theory. The disrepute of his science lay solely in the hands of "irresponsible followers" who twisted his speculations for "meretricious purposes."[92] Richard Hunter echoed this distinction in *Annals of Science*: "Remarkable too how much easier it seems to be to swallow a theory than to digest a fact and how readily mere verbiage is mistaken for realities."[93] Young's history showed that the scientific facts had always been sound, even if they had been corrupted by sophistry.

The parcelling up of Gall's work into craniology and phrenology, science and speculation, and truth and falsity, reflected the more general goal in intellectual history of clarifying the present by examining the confusions of the past. As Loewenberg put it:

> Transitions in knowledge are traced in copious detail...Young performs an inestimable service. He delineates, for example, the intricate history of cerebral localization and resuscitates Franz Joseph Gall in the process. Phrenology, despite its aberrations, emerges as a cutting edge of intellectual change and carrier of productive ideas.[94]

For these historians, then, the whole of phrenology was worth significantly less than the sum of its parts. A proper historical appreciation of phrenology had to cut through its flaws to isolate the kernel of scientific truth buried within. In turn, a sophisticated understanding of the past would clarify the confusion of the present, since as Hunter said, "all who practice in neuropsychiatry are bound to think to some extent phrenologically."[95] To avoid falling into the same traps as their forebears, it was necessary for the historically minded scientist to study phrenology's failings.

Reforming phrenology

By the late 1970s and early 1980s, however, the professionalization of the history of science had begun to erode the institutional allegiance between historians and scientists. Practitioners were increasingly working in dedicated university departments rather than within scientific ones.[96] As these historians began to write history for its own sake, talk of internal and external "factors" quickly became unsatisfactory. Contemporaneously, new inspirations for historiography drew on the emergence of the Sociology of Scientific Knowledge (SSK) in Britain, the anthropological approach in Latour's and

Woolgar's *Laboratory Life* (1979), and cultural or feminist histories such as by Martin Rudwick and Evelyn Fox Keller.[97] By 1985, Shapin and Schaffer's *Leviathan and the Air-pump* would provide a seminal (if initially neglected) model for historiography: one that criticized the unreflective use of an internalist-externalist dichotomy in favour of historical investigation into its very creation.[98]

This new cohort of historians saw Young's book as a dated history that needed to be transcended. In their eyes, Young's treatment of phrenology was too presentist and too asymmetrical: a good historian had to foreswear any knowledge of future "truth" in explaining the results of the past. Mitigating these criticisms was Young's sophistication: if he had not been symmetrical enough, at the very least, his seemingly charitable analysis had showed phrenology's intellectual consistency and its immense influence in nineteenth-century thinking.

In the wake of Young's book, phrenology became a topic *par excellence* for scholars to demonstrate their progressiveness. Where Young had confidently labelled phrenology as a pseudoscience, contemporary authors challenged this by placing it in inverted commas ("pseudoscience"). Amidst this revisionism, *Mind, Brain, and Adaptation* emerged as the referential standard upon which newer histories could be favourably compared. Well into the 1980s, authors like Angus McLaren and Michael Lynch would cite the book as the best recent history of the subject, before pointing to its shortcomings as starting points for their research.[99] In a 1976 article titled "Phrenology: The Provocation of Progress," Young's student Roger Cooter noted these trends explicitly:

> R. M. Young's study of Gall in *Mind, brain, and adaptation* (1970) has been a seminal influence for many scholars and his later publications (which attack the slightly Whiggish interpretation contained in the book) have stimulated much more interest in the role of phrenology in nineteenth century psychology in the broadest sense.[100]

Young's study was groundbreaking because it had helped transformed phrenology from an "amusing curiosity" to a respectable intellectual enterprise.[101] Once interest had been generated, however, the modern scholar supposedly had to recognize that phrenology was of historical interest primarily "because of the wide range of Victorian values, ideas and attitudes it appears to have mediated."[102] In short, phrenology was important because past actors thought it was important, not because it contributed to an understanding of later science which presumably could never ever err in that same systematic way again. This critique was intensified by the medical historian Samuel Shortt, who cited Cooter to reject Young:

> It was irrelevant that [phrenology] subsequently made notable contributions to cerebral localization. The significant point is that... in its

heyday it was accepted, its craniology as much as its sophisticated revision of associationist psychology, by leading psychiatrists in England and the United States.[103]

This offhand dismissal points to Shortt's conviction that *Mind, Brain, and Adaptation* belonged to an obsolete generation of history.

If most historians agreed with Shortt's historiography, they were less quick to discard Young's history, because in retrospect Young's historiography could look surprisingly similar to SSK. Many of the epigraphs to his chapters would not be out of place in a sociological textbook. E. H. Gombrich's quote in chapter three, for instance, touched on the social nature of classification: "science is born of itself, not of nature. There is no neutral naturalism. The artist... needs a vocabulary before he can embark on a 'copy' of reality."[104] In Chapter 8, John Dewey's quote underscored the importance of place: "Unless our laboratory results are to give us artificialities, mere scientific curiosities, they must be subjected to interpretation by gradual reapproximation to conditions of life."[105] Young had used this quote to reveal his dissatisfaction with reducing psychological functions to sensory-motor physiology, but it nevertheless underscored the problem of translating laboratory knowledge to the outside world.

These quotes were not merely programmatic, for Young did achieve an incomplete symmetry in practice, especially when analysing the methods of science. As noted above, he explained both Gall's success and failure by appeal to the method of naturalistic corroboration.[106] Although he evidently believed in the experimental method, he acknowledged that Gall had "excellent reasons" for critiquing them.[107] Asymmetry mainly arose when Young discussed external factors, such as when he dismissed Flourens' data interpretation as "essentially theological."[108] More grievously for contemporaries, Young never failed to assure readers what was really true based on modern science. His was a semi-symmetrical approach that highlighted the fallibility of science even as it reified its progressiveness.

For the new breed of historian, of course, half-hearted symmetry was inadequate. A proper history had to study credibility rather than truth. Instead of asking why Gall had gone wrong, one should ask why his craniology had been rejected by the broader scientific community. As Cooter's quote suggests, by the mid-1970s, Young himself was sympathetic to this re-evaluation. His work on Darwin from 1969 to 1973 and his political conversion to Marxism drastically changed his historiographic approach. Growing increasingly discontent with talk of "factors," but unable to offer a coherent alternative, Young claimed in 1973 that his early work had not been written according to any "clearly-conceived historiography."[109] After rejecting Lakatosian reconstruction, Kuhnian contextualism, and Mertonian sociology, he concluded that science, society, and ideology always had to be treated in concert.[110] In 1969, he expressed this as a "common context" between science and society; by 1977, in his *Radical Science Journal*, he was proclaiming that "Science is Social Relations."[111] Young saw himself as a radical historian in the years after *Mind, Brain, and Adaptation*, and his rejection of the internalist-externalist dichotomy motivated calls for symmetry. Critics questioned whether he succeeded, but the influence of his views was, as Jan Golinski put it, "seminal."[112]

In this light, most researchers who cited *Mind, Brain, and Adaptation* were more respectful than Shortt. Young's book might only be a partial foundation for future work, but it was a rich base that rewarded study. The famous social turned sociological historian Steven Shapin noted that his work was an intermediate step between intellectual history and sociological history. In his landmark 1979 article on the politics of observation, Shapin acknowledged that Young's book "fully detailed" the "intellectual structure" of phrenology.[113] However, he was critical of Young's retrospective approach to phrenology. He argued that one must not "prise apart what they regard as true and worthwhile in the phrenologist's anatomy from the 'illegitimate' interests with which the observations were associated."[114] Shapin believed Young was mistaken in focusing so strongly on Gall's anatomical investigations because this did not accurately reflect Gall's motivations.[115] Furthermore, an awareness of various social interests should not only reconstruct the "theoretical scaffolding" of science but also explain its "esoteric, and really detailed, scientific content."[116] It mattered not that *Mind, Brain, and Adaptation* showed the productivity of phrenology for modern science. What mattered was that it could be a foundation for properly sociological accounts of science in practice, which Young later disputed were adequate in the way Shapin conceived them.

Conclusion

Robert Young died in the summer of 2019. In obituaries and memorials, the foundational role of *Mind, Brain, and Adaptation* is noted only as preface to his controversial contributions to Darwin studies and radical science.[117] This quick and quiet recognition was encouraged by Young himself, in later years a much more Marxist historian who denigrated his early historiography for being too cautious. Yet, it was this very inoffensiveness and historiographical ambiguity that contributed to *Mind, Brain, and Adaptation*'s wide-ranging reception amongst all sorts of scientists and historians. It allowed readers to acknowledge the quality of his scholarship while accepting, rejecting, or ignoring his historiographic approach on grounds other than ideology.

At the same time, the story of *Mind, Brain, and Adaptation*'s reception is a story of disciplines, for its multivocal potential was realized only in concert with readers' assumptions and allegiances. The specific meanings that emerged provide a window into the state of neurology, psychology, psychiatry, and the history of science in the 1970s. For disciplines filled with optimism about the future, as Brazier and McMenemey in neurology exemplified, *Mind, Brain, and Adaptation*'s worries about modern science could be ignored, and its history fit within a broader narrative of progress. But optimism about the future could equally be paired with discontent about the present, as Geschwind and Oldfield's calls for interdisciplinarity showed, or with a rejection of the past, as Rollin's vicious attack on Young's "whitewashing" project revealed.

A more complicated understanding of Young's work surfaced in disciplines that grappled with the writing of history. Psychologists and intellectual historians (whether professional or scientist-historian) were united in their belief that a good history had to inform the present by clarifying the past, but disagreed over the balance of presentism and historicism that was acceptable. For psychologists facing a crisis of confidence and coherence, historicism was an interesting but ineffective way of achieving disciplinary synthesis and credibility; for intellectual historians like Hunter, Loewenberg, and the Young of 1966, it was precisely historicism, but not presentism, that could challenge contemporary assumptions. As the history of science continued to professionalize, new facets to the debate appeared – this time questioning the validity of any history that failed to respect actor's categories and to approach history symmetrically. For these sociological historians, now institutionally divorced from science, Young's work was not historicist enough, for it was motivated by the needs of the present rather than an appreciation of the past. Accordingly, Young's analysis of phrenology was deemed significant not for clarifying modern science, as he intended, but only for stimulating research into an influential intellectual enterprise of the nineteenth century. Regardless of its status as a "pseudoscience," phrenology was to be of intrinsic interest in the new history of science.

Seen generally, the multifarious receptions of *Mind, Brain, and Adaptation* mark an important shift in the relationship between science and its history. What was once a closely mutualistic enterprise, with scientists as well as historians reading and writing histories of science, has become parallel but distinct: scientists write scientific histories and historians write academic ones. For history of science the prize has been intellectual credibility, but the cost has often been isolation from science, as scientists tire of contextual, revisionist, and sociological "attacks" on progress – "The price of purity is privacy."[118] Written at a time when these barriers were not yet solidified, by a historian with only scientific training, and with a complex historiography that emphasized progress while placing it in context, *Mind, Brain, and Adaptation* belongs to a dying breed of impure yet celebrated history.

Notes

1 I am grateful to Jim Secord for supervising this as an undergraduate thesis in Cambridge HPS.

2 R. M. Young, *Mind, Brain, and Adaptation in the Nineteenth Century: Cerebral Localization and Its Biological Context from Gall to Ferrier* (Reprint ed.). Oxford University Press. (1990, original edition 1970), p. xxi; R. M. Young, *Cerebral Localisation and Its Biological Context from Gall to Ferrier* (PhD.5083) [Doctoral dissertation, University of Cambridge]. University of Cambridge, 1965.

3 The Cambridge visit was strongly motivated by his first wife's depression, which had worsened during his medical studies. For an account of his turbulent personal life, see Young. Robert Maxwell Young: Personal information. *Psychoanalysis and Psychotherapy* (n.d.). Retrieved 4 April 2020, from http://www.psychoanalysis-and-therapy.com/rmyoung/persinfo.html.

4 Young, *Mind, Brain, and Adaptation in the Nineteenth Century*, p. xxii.

5 Young, *Mind, Brain, and Adaptation in the Nineteenth Century*, p. 249.

6 In 1990, the book was reprinted unchanged, except for an additional preface. This article cites page numbers from the 1990 edition (which differ from the 1970 edition only in the original preface).

7 Web of Science 2020. For the category History of Science, I combined "History Philosophy of Science" and "History of Social Sciences"; for the category Psychology I combined "Psychology Experimental", "Psychology Multidisciplinary" and "Psychology". Web of Science. (2020). *Citation Report*. Retrieved 31 March 2020, from https://apps.webofknowledge.com/CitationReport.do?product=WOS&search_mode=CitationReport&SID=F166DpvCrHVbYSKLz2R&page=1&cr_pqid=7&viewType=summary.

    Web of Science. (2020). *Results Analysis: Web of Science Categories*. Retrieved 31 March 2020, from https://wcs.webofknowledge.com/RA/analyze.do?product=WOS&SID=F166DpvCrHVbYSKLz2R&field=TASCA_JCRCategories_JCRCategories_en&yearSort=false.

8 D. Williams, Review of *Mind, Brain, and Adaptation* by R. M. Young. *Brain* (1970) *93*, p. 656.

9 M.A. Brazier, Neurophysiological history [Review of *Mind, Brain, and Adaptation* by R.M. Young]. *Science*, (1971), pp. 1013–1014.

10 M. Critchley, Review of *Mind, Brain, and Adaptation* by R. M. Young. *The British Journal for the History of Science*, (1971) *5*(3), pp. 304–305.

11 P. F. Strawson, Brain Storm [Review of *Mind, Brain, and Adaptation* by R.M. Young]. *The New York Review of Books*, (24 September 1970), p. 35.

12 R. Darnton, What is the history of books? *Daedalus*, (1982) *111*(3), pp. 65–83.

13 J. A. Secord, *Victorian Sensation: The Extraordinary Publication, Reception, and Secret Authorship of Vestiges of the Natural History of Creation*. University of Chicago Press, 2000, p. 518.

14 Young, *Mind, Brain, and Adaptation in the Nineteenth Century*, p. xx.

15 R. M. Young, The historiographic and ideological contexts of the nineteenth-century debate on man's place in nature. In M. Teich & R. M. Young, (Eds.), *Changing Perspectives in the History of Science: Essays in Honour of Joseph Needham* (pp. 344–438). Boston: D. Reidel Publishing Co., 1973, p. 350.

16 D. J. Kevles & G. L. Geison, The experimental life sciences in the twentieth century. *Osiris*, (1995) *10*, 97–121.

17 R. W. Doty, Neuroscience. In J. R. Brobeck, O. E. Reynolds & T. A. Appel, (Eds.), *History of the American Physiological Society: The First Century, 1887–1987*. American Physiological Society, 1987, p. 428; J. M. Abi-Rached, From Brain to neuro: The brain research association and the making of British neuroscience, 1965–1996. *Journal of the History of the Neurosciences* (2012) *21*, 2; G. Adelman, The neurosciences research program at MIT and the beginning of the modern field of neuroscience. *Journal of the History of the Neurosciences* (2010) *19*(1), pp. 15–23.

18　W. H. McMenemey, Review of *Mind, Brain, and Adaptation* by R. M. Young. *The British Journal of Psychiatry* (1970) *117*, p. 592.

19　Brazier, Neurophysiological history, p. 1013.

20　Brazier, Neurophysiological history, p. 1014.

21　McMenemey, Review of *Mind, Brain, and Adaptation*, p. 592.

22　Brazier, Neurophysiological history, p. 1014; McMenemey, 1970, p. 593.

23　Young, *Mind, Brain, and Adaptation in the Nineteenth Century*, p. 249.

24　O. Devinsky, Norman Geschwind: Influence on his career and comments on his course on the neurology of behavior. *Epilepsy & Behavior*, (2009) *15*(4), p. 416.

25　N. Geschwind, Lumps and localization [Review of the book *Mind, Brain, and Adaptation* by R. M. Young]. *Nature*, (1970) *226*(5246), p. 665.

26　R. C. Oldfield, Review of the book *Mind, Brain, and Adaptation* by R. M. Young, *Journal of Neurology, Neurosurgery, and Psychiatry* (1970) *33*(6), p. 886.

27　Both Geschwind and Oldfield were especially interested in localizing the psychological functions of language to specific areas in the brain, see S. Sandrone, Norman Geschwind (1926–1984). *Journal of Neurology* (2013) *260*(12), pp. 3197–3198; O. L Zangwill, Obituary Notice: Richard Carolus Oldfield (1909–1972). *Quarterly Journal of Experimental Psychology* (1972) *24*, pp. 375–377 and O. L. Zangwill, R. C. Oldfield's contribution to neuropsychology. *Neuropsychologica* (1973) *11*(4). Oldfield was also close to the neuropsychologist Oliver Zangwill at Cambridge, as evidenced by Zangwill's two obituaries of Oldfield in the *Quarterly Journal of Experimental Psychology* and *Neuropsychologia*. Given that Zangwill had supervised Young's work as a thesis and was quoted in its conclusion (Young, *Mind, Brain, and Adaptation*, p. 252), Oldfield was likely predisposed to give a positive assessment of *Mind, Brain, and Adaptation*.

28　H. R. Rollin, Understanding the Brain: 19th Century Scientists [Review of the book *Mind, Brain, and Adaptation* by R. M. Young]. *British Medical Journal* (1970) *3*(5719), p. 394.

29　Young, *Mind, Brain, and Adaptation in the Nineteenth Century*, p. 74.

30　H. Freeman, Psychiatry and the state in Britain. In M. Gijswijt-Hofstra, H. Oosterhuis & J. Vijselaar, (Eds.), *Psychiatric Cultures Compared: Psychiatry and Mental Health Care in the Twentieth Century: Comparisons and Approaches* (pp. 116–140). Amsterdam University Press, 2005.

31　R. Bluglass, Dr Henry Rollin. *The Psychiatric Bulletin* (2014) *38*(3), p. 141; A. Forrester & Henry R. Rollin. *The Journal of Forensic Psychiatry & Psychology*, (2008) *19*(4), p. 634.

32　A. Kerr & Henry R. Rollin, In conversation with Alan Kerr. *Psychiatric Bulletin*, (1999) *23*, pp. 286–290, 289.

33　H. R. Rollin, Psychiatry in Britain one hundred years ago. *The British Journal of Psychiatry*, (2003) *183*(4), pp. 292–298, 394.

34　NobelPrize.org (n.d.). *Egas Moniz – Facts*. Retrieved 2 April 2020, https://www.nobelprize.org/prizes/medicine/1949/moniz/facts/.

35　G. N. Grob, The transformation of American psychiatry: From institution to community, 1800–2000. In E. R. Wallace & J. Gach (Eds.), *History of Psychiatry and Medical Psychology* (p. 645), Netherlands: Springer, 2008.

36　Forrester, A. Henry R. Rollin, p. 636.

37　D. L. Rosenhan, On being sane in insane places. *Science*, (1970) *179*(4070). In the hoax, Rosenhan sent pseudopatients to 12 different mental hospitals. Despite behaving normally after being admitted, it took between 7 and 52 days for them to be released. For a discussion of the hoax in wider context, see A. Scull, Contending professions: Sciences of the brain and mind in the United States, 1850–2013. *Science in Context*, (2015). *28*(1), pp. 131–161, 148.

38 Rollin, Psychiatry in Britain one hundred years ago, p. 298.

39 L. Graham, W. Lepenies & P. Weingart, (Eds.), *Functions and Uses of Disciplinary Histories*. Netherlands: Springer, 1983.

40 M. Ash, The self-presentation of a discipline: History of psychology in the United States between pedagogy and scholarship. In L. Graham, W. Lepenies & P. Weingart, (Eds.), *Functions and Uses of Disciplinary Histories* (pp. 143–189). Netherlands: Springer, 1983.

41 T. S. Kuhn, *The Structure of Scientific Revolutions*. Chicago: University of Chicago Press, 1962.

42 D. Krech, Four Sins and 248 Virtues [Review of *Mind, Brain, and Adaptation* by R. M. Young]. *Contemporary Psychology*, (1972) *17*(8), pp. 430–432, ix–x.

43 J. P. Wierda, [Review of *Mind, Brain, and Adaptation* by R. M. Young]. *Janus* (1970) *57*, p. 61.

44 Krech, Four Sins and 248 Virtues, p. 432.

45 Ash, The self-presentation of a discipline, p. 158.

46 Ash, The self-presentation of a discipline, pp. 158–160.

47 Ash, The self-presentation of a discipline, p. 172.

48 Krech, Four sins and 248 virtues, p. 432.

49 Krech, Four sins and 248 virtues, p. 432.

50 I use scientist-historian to refer to professional scientists with strong, rather than shallow historical credentials. An equally accurate term would be "amateur", but because of the professionalization of history of science the label is more derogatory than it was before, when amateurs were generally respected members of the diverse historical community.

51 A. K. Mayer, 'I have been very fortunate…'. Brief report on the BSHS Oral history project: 'The history of science in Britain, 1945–65. *The British Journal for the History of Science*, (1999) *32*(2), p. 225.

52 R. Hunter, Review of *Mind, Brain, and Adaptation* by R. M. Young. *Annals of Science,* (1971) *27*(2), p.207.

53 Hunter's own historical credentials included the mammoth *Three Hundred Years of Psychiatry 1535–1800* (1963) written with his mother Ida Macalpine, and his appointment as President of the history of medicine at the Royal Society of Medicine in 1972. More details are available in L. M. Payne & L. M. *Richard Alfred Hunter*. Royal College of Physicians: Inspiring Physicians. (n.d.) Retrieved 2 April 2020, from https://history.rcplondon.ac.uk/inspiring-physicians/richard-alfred-hunter.

54 Young, *Mind, Brain, and Adaptation in the Nineteenth Century*, p. xix.

55 Young, *Mind, Brain, and Adaptation in the Nineteenth Century*, p. xix.

56 Young, *Mind, Brain, and Adaptation in the Nineteenth Century*, p. 1.

57 Young, *Mind, Brain, and Adaptation in the Nineteenth Century*, p. xxii

58 B. J. Loewenberg, Review of *Mind, Brain, and Adaptation* by R. M. Young and of *The Triumph of the Darwinian Method* by M. T. Ghiselin]. *Victorian Studies,* (1971) *14*(3), pp. 344–345.

59 R. de la Rosa Campos & M. Reynolds, *Guide to the Bert James Loewenberg (1927–1974) Papers RG 10.3.* Sarah Lawrence College Archives, (2005). Retrieved 2 April 2020, from https://www.sarahlawrence.edu/archives/collections/finding-aids/b/bert-james-loewenberg-papers.pdf.

60 Loewenberg, Review of *Mind, Brain, and Adaptation*, p. 343.

61 Loewenberg, Review of *Mind, Brain, and Adaptation*, p. 344.

62 G. J. Makari, *Obituary: Norman Dain (1926–2015).* 29 April 2015. H-Madness. Retrieved 2 April 2020, from https://historypsychiatry.com/2015/04/29/obituary-norman-dain-1926-2015/.

63   M. R. Dearing, Review of *Concepts of Insanity in the United States 1789–1865* by
      N. Dain]. *The American Historical Review*, (1965) *70*(2), 477–478.
          J. S. Bockoven, Review of *Concepts of Insanity in the United States 1789–
      1865* by N. Dain]. *Journal of the History of the Behavioral Sciences*, (1965) *1*(4),
      pp. 384–386.
64   Quoted in Bockoven, Review of *Concepts of Insanity in the United States*, p. 385.
65   Quoted in Bockoven, Review of *Concepts of Insanity in the United States*, p. 385.
66   Dain, Review of *Mind, Brain, and Adaptation*, p. 593.
67   Golinski gives an excellent introduction to this debate in *Making Natural
      Knowledge: Constructivism and the History of Science.* Cambridge University
      Press, 1998. On the unstable meanings of "internalism" and "externalism", see
      S. Shapin, Discipline and bounding: The history and sociology of science as
      seen through the externalism-internalism debate. *History of Science*, (1992) *30*,
      pp. 333–369, and on the link to Cold War politics, see S. Shapin & S. Schaffer,
      Leviathan and the Air-Pump: Hobbes, Boyle, and the Experimental Life (Reprint
      ed.). Princeton University Press, 2011. Young was an externalist historian in that
      he emphasized how "non-scientific" political and economic ideas influenced sci-
      entific thought, but he was less interested in how funding or infrastructure could
      affect the detailed content of scientific theories.
68   Young, *Mind, Brain, and Adaptation*, p. 14.
69   Young, *Mind, Brain, and Adaptation*, pp. 40–41.
70   Young, *Mind, Brain, and Adaptation*, p. 44.
71   Young, *Mind, Brain, and Adaptation*, p. 74.
72   Young, *Mind, Brain, and Adaptation*, p. 133.
73   Young, *Mind, Brain, and Adaptation*, p. 247.
74   R. M. Young, Scholarship and the history of the behavioural sciences. *History
      of Science*, (1966) *5*(1), p.33.
75   Krech, Four Sins and 248 Virtues, p. 431.
76   Young, Scholarship and the history of the behavioural sciences, p. 3.
77   Young, Scholarship and the history of the behavioural sciences. p. 16.
78   Young, Scholarship and the history of the behavioural sciences. p. 18.
79   Young, Scholarship and the history of the behavioural sciences. p. 18.
80   Young, Scholarship and the history of the behavioural sciences. p. 18.
81   Young, Scholarship and the history of the behavioural sciences. p. 19.
82   Critchley, Review of *Mind, Brain, and Adaptation*.
83   N. Dain, [Review of *Mind, Brain, and Adaptation*]. *Isis*, (1972) *63*(4), p. 593.
84   Young, Scholarship and the history of the behavioural sciences, pp. 14–36.
85   Young, *Mind, Brain, and Adaptation*, pp. 3–7.
86   Young, *Mind, Brain, and Adaptation*, p. 250.
87   Loewenberg, Review of *Mind, Brain, and Adaptation*, p. 344.
88   Critchley, Review of *Mind, Brain, and Adaptation*, p. 304.
89   Young, M*ind, Brain, and Adaptation*, p. 3.
90   Critchley, Review of *Mind, Brain, and Adaptation*, p. 304.
91   Critchley, Review of *Mind, Brain, and Adaptation*, p. 305.
92   Critchley, Review of *Mind, Brain, and Adaptation*, p. 305.
93   Hunter, Review of *Mind, Brain, and Adaptation*, p. 207.
94   Loewenberg, Review of *Mind, Brain, and Adaptation*, p. 344.
95   Hunter, Review of *Mind, Brain, and Adaptation*, p. 207.
96   Shapin & Schaffer *Leviathan and the air-pump*, p. xxi.
97   P. Dear & S. Jasanoff, Dismantling boundaries in science and technology stud-
      ies. *Isis*, (2010) *101*(4), pp. 759–774; P. Dear, Cultural history of science: An
      overview with reflections. *Science, Technology, & Human Values*, (1995) *20*(2),
      pp. 150–170.

98 Shapin & Schaffer, *Leviathan and the Air-Pump*, p. 342.
99 A. McLaren, A prehistory of the social sciences: Phrenology in France. *Comparative Studies in Society and History*, (1981) *23*(1), pp. 3–22, endnote 4; M. Lynch "Here Is Adhesiveness": From friendship to homosexuality. *Victorian Studies*, (1985) *29*(1), endnote 10.
100 R. J. Cooter, Phrenology: The provocation of progress. *History of Science*, (1976) *14*(4), p. 212.
101 Cooter, Phrenology: The provocation of progress, p. 211.
102 Cooter, Phrenology: The provocation of progress, p. 213.
103 S. E. Shortt, Physicians, science, and status: Issues in the professionalization of Anglo-American medicine in the nineteenth century. *Medical History*, (1983) *27*(1), pp. 51–68, 59.
104 Young, M*ind, Brain, and Adaptation*, p. 101.
105 Young, *Mind, Brain, and Adaptation*, p. 234.
106 Young, *Mind, Brain, and Adaptation*, pp. 33–46.
107 Young, *Mind, Brain, and Adaptation*, p. 50.
108 Young, *Mind, Brain, and Adaptation*, p. 74.
109 R. M. Young The historiographic and ideological contexts of the nineteenth-century debate on man's place in nature. In M. Teich & R. M. Young, (Eds.), *Changing Perspectives in the History of Science: Essays in Honour of Joseph Needham* (pp. 344–438). Boston: D. Reidel Publishing Co, 1973, p. 350.
110 Young, The historiographic and ideological contexts, p. 436.
111 R. M. Young, Malthus and the evolutionists: The common context of biological and social theory. *Past & Present*, (1969) *43*, pp.109–110; R. M. Young, Science is social relations. *Radical Science Journal* (1977) *5*.
112 J. Golinski, Lost in mediation: The social component of Darwin''s science. *History of the Human Sciences*, (1989), p. 97. Golinski nevertheless argues that Young's social influences were often "lost in mediation". I. Bohlin offers a similar critique in his through Malthusian specs?: A study in the philosophy of science studies, with special reference to the theory and ideology of Darwin historiography [Doctoral dissertation, University of Göteberg]. University of Göteberg, 1995, pp. 202–210.
113 S. Shapin, The politics of observation: Cerebral anatomy and social interests in the Edinburgh phrenology disputes. *The Sociological Review*, (1979) *27*, pp. 139–178, 142.
114 Shapin, The politics of observation, p. 147.
115 Shapin, The politics of observation, p. 148.
116 Shapin, The politics of observation, p. 139.
117 K. Jacobsen, Robert Young obituary. *The Guardian*. Retrieved 2 April 2020, from https://www.theguardian.com/science/2019/aug/01/robert-young-obituary; R. Smith & R. M. Young, Science historian and Darwin scholar who wielded great influence on the cultural left. *The Independent*. 19 August 2019, Retrieved 2 April 2020, from https://www.independent.co.uk/news/obituaries/robert-young-death-academic-science-historian-scholar-darwin-psychotherapy-psychoanalysis-a9045206.html. Also, see the tributes to Young by R. Smith, K. Jacobsen & R. Cooter, *History of the Human Sciences* 6 July 2020. https://www.histhum.com/robert-maxwell-young-bob-young-26-september-1935-5-july-2019/; and the tribute by B. Kahr in *Associations* 2020.
118 S. Shapin, Discipline and bounding, p. 359.

Chapter 4

Robert M. Young's Darwinian aftermath

Michael Ruse

My thinking about Darwin and his portance was formed by and has persisted from a year (1972 to 1973) that I spent at Cambridge University attached to the Department of History and Philosophy of Science. I like to joke that I rarely agree with the opinions of the Marxist scholar Robert M. Young, and he never agreed with mine, but I still think that his was the most original mind that turned to the study of Darwin. His influence was reinforced by contact with the great historian of geology Martin Rudwick as well as by Roy Porter, then the equivalent of a post-doctoral student, and the future historian of medicine William Bynum. Across in the University Library, in charge of the Darwin Archives, was the ever-knowledgeable and helpful Peter Gautrey. Always available and willing to talk and share ideas was Sydney Smith of St Catharine's College, who concealed a keen intellect and immense background understanding behind the façade of being the archetypal, old English buffer.[1]

The historian of science

In the course of a long career – over 50 years – Bob Young was a practicing historian of evolutionary biology for less than a quarter of this time. Yet, it is hardly an exaggeration to say that he was (and still is) one of the most innovative and influential people in the field. I can say, unambiguously, Bob Young was by far the most important person in my own development as a historian of science, and his influence colours almost all I do to this day. Young came to Darwinism at a good time and in a good place. For the first hundred or so years after the publication of the *Origin of Species* in 1859, it seems not unfair to say that most that was written on Charles Darwin and his theory of evolution rarely reached the standards of professional historical writing. Darwin's son, Francis, did sterling work in publishing selections of his letters, and other contemporaries like Thomas Henry Huxley contributed their memories and reactions and analyses. Later, by the beginning of the twentieth century, most who wrote on Darwin were either retired scientists writing hagiographies of their hero or professional popular writers who

DOI: 10.4324/9781003204244-6

included Darwin in their canon along with other dignitaries like Gladstone and Lloyd George.

Then, in the 1950s, the history of science started to get professionalized – founding the department in Cambridge and a corresponding department at Harvard. Those trained in the field realized that archives must be opened up and consulted. Work done on the subject must locate itself in the historical corpus generally, not looking upon Darwin rather like the Archangel Gabriel come to earth for a few decades in the nineteenth century. Professional historians turned their interests towards Darwin and his theory, not always with the happiest results. Gertrude Himmelfarb's *Darwin and the Darwinian Revolution* is the Platonic Form of Hatchet Job.[2] On the one hand, Forms are universals, so there must be a Form of Hatchet Job, in which – to use Plato's terminology – Himmelfarb's book would have "participated." However, the Forms are good things – they derive from the Form of the Good, and it is questionable as to whether hatchet jobs are good things.

A major move forward came thanks to the enterprise of the embryologist Gavin de Beer. He uncovered, in the Darwin Archives in the University Library (UL) Cambridge, the unpublished private notebooks of Charles Darwin. These were written during the crucial years of 1836 and 1839, when Darwin became an evolutionist and then went on to discover his mechanism of natural selection. De Beer transcribed, edited, and published these notebooks at the beginning of the 1960s. (He also wrote his own hagiography of Darwin.)[3] There was material to work on and young scholars were attracted to the subject and started producing very much higher quality work than hitherto. It did not hurt that the *Journal of the History of Biology* was founded by Everett Mendelsohn later in the decade.

Young at Cambridge was perfectly placed to take advantage of the new winds. In major respects, he did to the full, although somewhat paradoxically he rarely walked out of the back of his college, crossed Queen's road and took the elevator to the Manuscripts Room of the UL, to look at any of its holdings. He used to claim that no one had to date looked at most of the published material, so why bother yet with the unpublished material! What he did bring to the field was a super-keen intelligence, an ability and willingness to look at huge amounts of that published material, both around the time of Darwin and later, and a critical sensibility that demanded that everything be put in social context. Darwin particularly, for had not Marx (in 1862) written to Engels: "It is remarkable how Darwin rediscovers among beasts and plants the society of England, with its division of labour, competition, opening up of new markets, inventions, and the Malthusian struggle for existence."[4]

This led to a huge burst of creative activity, with articles pouring forth, and then – almost as quickly as they had begun – five or six years later, it finished. Possibly, because Young thought he had all that he had to say. He could see younger scholars coming along who did go to the archives and the like, and that was just not his style. Possibly, because he was already starting to move on to other topics and other fields. Possibly, as noted above, because he was starting to feel disconnected from the style of English – especially Cambridge – academic life. I "left academic life in disgust at the corruption, opportunism, and hypocrisy of certain colleagues and patrons." (I confess the people in HPS always struck me as rather mild, friendly people.)

As noted, Young's interests then did not even extend to collecting and publishing his articles as a whole. This had to wait more than ten years. To be honest, the volume has a somewhat embarrassing, self-promoting fore-word. Friends tell him that his work is still "state of the art," and he tells himself that "my essays have suffered relatively little when tested against the careful sifting of the manuscript archives which has become the exclusive preoccupation of many scholars." But, you know, in many respects he was right!

> I remain certain it is not right to separate the Darwinian debate from broader cultural, ideological, political, and economic issues. Darwinism provides the unifying thread and themes from Malthus to the commod-ification of the smallest elements of living nature in genetic engineering.

An interlude about Bob Young's influence on a young philosopher

Since everything about Bob was personal – "corruption, opportunism, and hypocrisy" – let me explain how I got involved and why it made such a differ-ence. I was trained in the 1960s as a philosopher of science. A small group of us – notable leader, David Hull – had turned to biology for subject material, mainly on the excellent grounds that not much had been written on the sub-ject, and this existing work was pretty awful. The 1960s was, of course, the decade of Thomas Kuhn's *The Structure of Scientific Revolutions*. I think few philosophers – and, to be honest, not many historians – agreed with his thesis about paradigms and the non-rational nature of their change, but Kuhn did have a huge effect on many younger philosophers of science. We agreed with him entirely that, in order to do good philosophy of science, you had to do history of science. No longer was it good enough just to grab a couple of pop-ular accounts and get on with the job. You had to do history as seriously and as well as the historians. Naturally, given that it is the strong belief of every philosopher that we are the brightest people on campus, this was a challenge rather than a threat. Especially, those of us trying to create a modern philos-ophy of biology were much inspired to turn to the history of the subject, and what juicier topic could there be than Darwin and his Revolution?

My first sabbatical was in 1972 – I then worked in Canada – and what more obvious destination for one so fired up than to make my way to Cam-bridge. Obviously, on the one hand, there was the prospect of working in the Darwin Archives. For me, no less, was, on the other hand, the prospect of interacting with Bob Young. Why Bob Young? For five years, I had been reading the Darwin literature – his own writings, the five volumes of letters published by his son, the works of his contemporaries like Thomas Henry Huxley and Alfred Russel Wallace, and then a huge amount of secondary material. By 1970, younger professional historians were coming on line – Peter Vorzimmer and Sandra Herbert for instance – and other historians like Bob Olby were making related contributions.[5] So, I was getting comfortable in the field. Young for me, however, was something special. His writings simply were inspirational. He made you think, he challenged you, and he changed your perspective.

I won't say I wanted to sit at Bob Young's feet. I am pretty Oedipal about these sorts of things – I am quite convinced that a major reason why I am not a Christian is because I couldn't worship another human being. But I did want to learn from Bob Young. So Cambridge it was. As it happens, although Bob was welcoming, he was already transitioning out of his job, so he was not always the easiest of people to be around. But I learnt enough, and as I said in my quotation at the beginning of this essay, with the added attractions of Martin Rudwick – still the most brilliant historian of geology we have ever had – with Roy Porter – a graduate student (or something of that nature) but without doubt the most self-confident person I have ever known – the embryologist Sydney Smith, who knew just an incredible amount about Darwin – and add in a couple of philosophers like Mary Hesse (much interested in metaphor), I was in heaven.

"Darwin's metaphor"

Why was it that Young had this nigh mesmeric effect on me? Let me focus on what I think was his major and best paper, a long essay published in 1971 in the *Monist*: "Darwin's metaphor: does nature select?"[6] The paper is on the revolution brought about by Darwin's *Origin*. Although there is a reference to Kuhn, the discussion is not set in a particularly philosophical context. It is noted that Kuhn is interesting, but his thesis is brushed aside (without comment) as not very relevant to the Darwinian case. Young focuses on the state of play before the *Origin*, the state of play after the *Origin*, and the central metaphor of the *Origin* – natural selection a phenomenon modelled on the breeder's practice of artificial selection – and how that played out in what happened – or did not play out in what happened.

Straight off, you can see why a philosopher like myself was going to be so excited.[7]

> I shall concentrate on a very close analysis of the texts, attempting to show that the fine texture of the scientific debate directly involves theological and philosophical issues. These were constitutive, not

contextual, and historians of the philosophical, theological, and general intellectual history of the period may find that their interests should lead them to study these documents. In approaching the problem in this way I hope to show that the scientific heart of the theory raised fundamental philosophical and theological issues.

In the lingo of the time, Young intends to take an "externalist" approach, looking at cultural values broadly conceived, rather than a strictly "internalist" approach, looking basically at the science involved and judging things from the point of right or wrong, good or bad.

It is nigh impossible to be strictly internalist with the Darwinian Revolution – nothing about religion? – but it is fair to say that there was a break here. Retired scientists writing about their hero would naturally gravitate to their areas of interest and expertise, which are wholly internalist. In fact, Young took time out from his discussion to make a rather nasty crack about this sort of thing.

> I would continue to argue that Darwin's thinking drew on a wide context of Victorian ideas. One of the purposes of my writing the study of Malthus [an earlier paper, Malthus and the evolutionists"] was to help free the history of science from the internalist approach exemplified by de Beer's work.[8]

Others may have internalist failings, but let me say that, for a Kuhnian-influenced philosopher, I loved all of this. Encountering externalism was a thrilling revelation. I say this, despite the fact that, on looking back, Kuhn's discussion of paradigm change is remarkably internalist.[9] Not much about religion and that sort of thing.

"Darwin's thinking drew on a wide context of Victorian ideas."[10] Young showed that it certainly did. Most obviously there was the analogy – the metaphor – between the practice of the breeders of the day, selecting for the best livestock, and the actions of the chief mechanism of natural selection, possessors of favourable variations surviving and reproducing and others failing in life's competitions. Then, there was the thinking of the political economist Thomas Robert Malthus, whose idea of a "struggle for existence" found its way into the heart of the theory of the *Origin*. It was because of the struggle that one had a force driving the selection of favourable variations and the rejection of unfavourable variations. Added to this was Archdeacon William Paley. Young wrote of "the strong influence of the tradition of natural theology on the assumptions of science." Continuing: "In freeing himself from belief in the static, designed adaptations which he had found so appealing in his reading of William Paley as an undergraduate, Darwin retained the rhetoric of deliberate, piecemeal design." At one level, the distance between the approach of Paley and that of Darwin is much less than it appears to be.

And then, above all, there was the influence of the Scottish geologist, Charles Lyell. "The uniformity of nature." Bob seized on this.[11]

> At one level, then that of the principle of explanation by small changes in terms of the uniformity of nature Lyell was the main source of Darwin's assumptions. Darwin's intellectual mentor, Charles Lyell, had provided both the greatest helps and the greatest hindrances to any attempt to provide a satisfactory theory. He had insisted that only causes now in operation and in their present intensities could be used to explain the history of the earth and the history of life. When these stringent criteria were applied to the question of the mutability of species, Lyell's judicious exposition and analysis of the evidence led to the conclusion that there was no evidence that present causes were producing modifications which, given sufficient time, could accumulate directionally so as to produce new species.

This leads us from the first part of Bob Young's argument, to the second, middle part. Here, we have Darwin's move from artificial selection to natural selection, to provide a mechanism, but a mechanism that could speak to Paley – Design! As I read Young at this point, his case is that Darwin succeeds at this only by violating the canons of good science. Paley brought in God to explain design, and Darwin never really got rid of God!

Cambridge Professor of Geology Adam Sedgwick wanted to insist on the role of final causes in nature and asserted that natural laws were manifestations of the will of God. Like so many of those who seized on the anthropomorphic use of 'natural selection,' Sedgwick wanted to assimilate it to an active role for the Deity in sustaining and guiding the history of nature. Sedgwick was himself "unable to adopt Darwin's theory, but many others were able to do so because they interpreted Darwin in the very sense which Sedgwick was advocating."[12] Sedgwick was right on this point and Darwin was wrong. As we now start to move from the second part of Young's argument to the third and final part – the reception of Darwin's ideas, the inadequacy of Darwin's position becomes more and more overt.[13]

> It is clear from this and from many of the foregoing remarks by Darwin that the path by which he had come to his theory was causing grave difficulties and that, although he understood many of the objections, he was very unwilling to alter his mode of expression about natural selection. Although none of his correspondents was arguing for divine intervention in the crude form of catastrophist miracles, they were convinced that the course of evolution was guided by God's sustaining power and purposes. Darwin could grant this only if the Deity was identified with the principle of the uniformity of nature itself.

The problem is that bringing in God means bringing in teleology or final causes. And that is simply not acceptable in post-Scientific Revolutionary science. You can refer only to proximate causes. You can ask about the physiological processes that led to the eye. You cannot ask about the purpose of the eye. Its "final cause." Darwin's friend the American botanist Asa Gray spotted this. He, as it happens, was a Christian, so he was more than happy to bring in final causes. He congratulated Darwin on keeping them in. Unfortunately, instead of protesting indignantly that there are no final causes in post-*Origin* evolutionary theory, Darwin – the poor sap – went along![14]

> When, in 1874, Gray wrote that Darwin had done a 'great service to Natural Science in bringing back to it Teleology: so that instead of Morphology versus Teleology, we shall have Morphology wedded to Teleology', Darwin commented, 'What you say about Teleology pleases me especially, and I do not think any one else has ever noticed the point. I have always said you were the man to hit the nail on the head'

The point is that, to have up-to-date science, there should be no nails hitting any heads. It should now be "Morphology versus Teleology" and Morphology triumphing. So what was Darwin to do with his inadequate theory? Basically, he had to downplay natural selection – something easy to do given all the criticism it was getting (because of such things as an inadequate theory of heredity) – and rely more and more on the principle of the uniformity of nature!

> Darwin's mechanism in its nineteenth-century form and in its nineteenth-century context turned out to be a very frail reed, but in bending with the winds it allowed his real commitment to the uniformity of nature to contribute to the general movement of nineteenth-century naturalism.[15]

We end up with "a rather confused mixture of metaphysical, methodological, and scientific arguments which depended heavily on analogical and metaphorical expressions, they brought the earth, life, and man into the domain of natural laws."

In fact, we now see that the supposed mechanism of natural selection was no mechanism at all! And by the time things were over, Darwin and everyone else recognized this. Evolution triumphed, but this was because of the belief in the uniformity of nature – something that earlier evolutionists had already endorsed![16]

> In proposing the theory of evolution by means of the mechanism of natural selection he was not really supplying a mechanism at all. Rather, he was providing an abstract account at a general level of how favourable variations might be preserved. He had to keep his account at a certain

level of abstraction since, as he confessed, he could neither specify the laws of variation nor the precise means by which variations were preserved. The acceptability of his account depended on its plausibility and its ability to explain in very general terms the sort of process which was involved. He could neither show evolution at work nor provide a complete example of the stages by which it had worked.

So much for Robert Young's take on the Darwinian Revolution. I was hugely excited by it and, nearly 50 years later, rereading his seminal article on natural selection, I can understand fully my excitement. It really is an impressive piece of work, and its pretensions at least are major. Once we understand the social context of Darwin's thought – the British social context of Darwin's thought – all else falls into place. We see why it was that people after the *Origin* became evolutionists and yet, almost to a person – including Darwin himself! – rejected natural selection. There was gold in them, Thar hills, and Robert Young was the man who found it and mined it. That the gold then turned out to be dross, if anything, adds to the credit of Robert Young.

So, 50 years later, what do we say? What has all those days of labouring in the archives, reading the pertinent material, arguing with fellow scholars, taught us. How well does Bob Young's thesis stand up? I see three different responses.

Response one: agreeing with Young

The first tells us to go along with Young's arguments and conclusions. I won't say I was parroting Bob Young, but at the end of the decade, in 1979, I published an overview of the Darwinian Revolution – the book, I joked, I would have liked to have had when I started into the field. One place where I did go beyond Bob was in philosophy. He stayed away from it. Not that this was a great loss.

> Furthermore, the deliberations of some of the most eminent scientists, philosophers, editors, and men of affairs in the period at the meetings of the Metaphysical Society (1869–80), led to the common conclusion that 'The uniformity of Nature is the veil behind which, in these latter days, God is hidden from us.'

I am a philosopher, so I wasn't having any of that! Aided, I should say, very greatly by Sydney Smith, I delved into the pertinent philosophy of the day, especially the writings of John F. W. Herschel and William Whewell. Much to my satisfaction, I came up with very strong evidence of the influence on the structure of the *Origin* by the ideas of these two men.[17]

I was, and still am, very proud of this. Although obviously, in itself, I was just confirming Bob's thesis about the influence on Darwin of his British background. They were both Cambridge men, even though Herschel had a Germanic name thanks to his German father, William Herschel. I should say that my ideas have given a lifetime's pleasure to my good friend, Jonathan Hodge.[18] Hodge has excoriated my thinking – cursed by bell, book, and candle – through conference after conference, article after article, book after book.[19] A Cambridge man himself, I am amazed that he can so downplay the importance of two fellow Cantabrigians.

Philosophy apart – or rather philosophy confirming – I toed the Young line through the book. Darwin came from a British background and the clues to everything are to be found there. Natural selection was a bit iffy. (I should say that, for 50 years, I have been wrestling with the problem of teleology; later, I will show you how I think I have solved it.) And the theory of the *Origin* was no great success. It was battled and belittled until it was in a very sorry state. Natural selection was a bust and it was the fact of evolution that triumphed – and Darwin was but one of many, before and after the *Origin*. The person who has taken Bob's thinking to new heights is his former student – he was an undergraduate in Kings College – Peter Bowler. Focusing on the time after the *Origin*, recently, I wrote: "What about the time after 1859? The historian Peter Bowler has made somewhat of a cottage industry out of this one."[20] Actually, he seems a bit torn. Sometimes the suggestion is that Darwin did have some effect, but it was almost universally bad. Bowler's latest book is called *Darwin Deleted*!" If the young naturalist Charles Darwin had fallen over the side of the Beagle in the early 1830s, what would have happened? Much that is familiar. "Darwin certainly rocked the boat, but he did not steer it onto a completely new and dangerous course." Things would probably have been smoother. "There would be less tension between science and religion, since one of the major battles in what we see as the war between them would never have been fought."[21] At other times, the suggestion is that Darwin didn't really have much effect at all, and as for natural selection, what a misfit! At best, an idea before its time. It calls for a Trump Tweet. Bowler writes of "the myth of the Darwinian Revolution," concluding his discussion saying it "seems unreasonable for historians to claim that the turning point in the emergence of modern culture should be called a 'Darwinian Revolution.'"[22]

So much for Chuck Darwin and his theory of evolution by natural selection!

Second response: ignoring Young

A second response is to refuse to accept Young's premises. This is the approach taken by the Chicago historian of science, Robert J. Richards. He will have none of this British-background nonsense. Darwin was cosmopolitan and his greatest debt was to those in his youth furthest along in the evolution debate, German romantic figures. Focusing particularly on the explorer Alexander von Humboldt – about whose influence Darwin spoke effusively in his *Autobiography* – Richards sees Romantic thought throughout Darwin's life and work. In a recent discussion – debating me and my benighted views about the British influences – Richards writes[23]:

> There are four general features of Humboldt's conception that attracted the young Darwin: the sense of adventure and possibility in the study of nature; the notion that nature had to be understood as expressing systematically related laws; the awareness that aesthetic considerations offered a complementary approach to nature; and finally, that nature exhibited properties that had, in orthodox theology, been assigned to the deity.

The Youngian bogey of purpose is confirmation of Bob Richards's view of things.[24]

> The nature that Darwin experienced through Humboldtian eyes did not clank along in the manner of a mechanical contrivance, nothing like a Big Ben of the Pampas. Rather Humboldt's nature and Darwin's as well bespoke intelligence, aesthetic depths, and even moral character. That nature was a cosmos, where land, climate, rivers, and mountains pulsated with the organic patterns of life. And through the exotic beauty of that cosmos, Darwin detected at the center the hegemonikon, the purposive principle of mind.

Richards continues[25]:

> Ideas flowing from both the German Romantic tradition and from more orthodox natural philosophy gave essential form to Darwin's theory. Even good historians have been blinded by the light of modern evolutionary theory when attempting to give an account of the historical Darwin. In that brilliant glow coming from our contemporary science, those historians have constructed his doppelganger, a creature who has become ubiquitous in historical introductions to biology textbooks and in the more casual approaches to the *Origin of Species*.

With a build-up like this, little wonder that Richards has little trouble demolishing the "Darwin as failure" hypothesis. What others take as non-Darwinian, Richards takes as the apotheosis of good Darwinian thinking. Above all, there is the German evolutionist Ernst Haeckel. Central to Haeckel's thinking was the so-called "biogenetic law," ontogeny recapitulates phylogeny. This is the epitome of Romantic biology: *Naturphilosophie*. Harking back to Plato, all is one. Hence the emphasis on homology – archetypes – over function – adaptations. The biogenetic law is the story of the history of life condensed into the individual, and the individual reflecting the history of life. All is connected. That is the organic way.

And Darwin was right into this. Thus, the *Origin*[26]:

> Agassiz insists that ancient animals resemble to a certain extent the embryos of recent animals of the same classes; or that the geological succession of extinct forms is in some degree parallel to the embryological development of recent forms. I must follow Pictet and Huxley in thinking that the truth of this doctrine is very far from proved. Yet I fully expect to see it hereafter confirmed, at least in regard to subordinate groups, which have branched off from each other within comparatively recent times. For this doctrine of Agassiz accords well with the theory of natural selection.

Need one say more?

Third response: criticism

And so to the third response, that of the penitent sinner Michael Ruse. I continue to affirm the truth of Young's claim that Darwin came out of his British culture. That seems to me to be ever-more well established. I continue to agree that natural selection came from artificial selection, even though there have been those who (based on a careful reading of the private notebooks) doubt this. Darwin even read and noted an earlier breeder who made the connection.[27]

> A severe winter, or a scarcity of food, by destroying the weak or unhealthy, has all the good effects of the most skilful selection. In cold and barren countries no animal can live to the age of maturity, but those who have strong constitutions; the weak and the unhealthy do not live to propagate their infirmities, as is too often the case with our domestic animals. To this I attribute the peculiar hardiness of the horses, cattle, and sheep, bred in mountainous countries, more than their having been inured to the severity of climate ...

Darwin took careful note of this passage, and even though he could not quite see the full import grasped that, if something like this went on long enough, we would get full-blooded species.

> Sir J. Sebright – pamphlet most important showing effects of peculiarities being long in blood. ++ thinks difficulty in crossing race – bad effects of incestuous intercourse. – excellent observations of sickly offspring being cut off so that not propagated by nature. – Whole art of making varieties may be inferred from facts stated.
>
> —(Barrett et al. 1987, C, 133)

The artificial/natural selection analogy ran deep. (I do not accuse Darwin of plagiarism. Sebright was not thinking in terms of evolution.)

Parenthetically, Bob Young came to his position on the influence of British culture on Darwin thanks to his Marxism. I am not a Marxist. I am a John Stuart Mill, Fabian socialist. I have never got on with *Das Kapital*. My feeling about British culture is part of my childhood and especially the influence of six years away from home at a boarding school. History and literature classes paid a lot of attention to the nineteenth century, when the Empire was at its peak and Britain ruled the waves. Even in scripture, we did Plato's *Republic* so we could prepare for the philosopher-king role of ruling in far-away places. (This was ten years after the fall of the Raj!) As a result, I still read Charles Dickens and Anthony Trollope for pleasure and my favourite building in London is St Pancras Railway Station (now the terminal of the Eurostar). For me, the combination of Darwin and Britain was a natural.

I agree that final-cause thinking went across the Darwinian Revolution, before and after the *Origin*, that this was due to natural selection, and the reason is that selection was speaking to the design theory of Paley. I used to think this a big problem and in my first book, *The Philosophy of Biology* – written before I knew Bob Young – I really tied myself into knots on this issue. I no longer think it a problem. Although Darwin thinks in terms of final cause – explaining things by the future – I don't think he is into the problematic Aristotelian notion of final cause – where there is some kind of *élan vital* directing things forward – nor a Platonic super-mind designing things. It is, as Immanuel Kant pointed out, a metaphor. I regard adaptations as if they were designed. The future to which they refer – as in "the eye is for seeing" – is an anticipated future, not a real future, and it is anticipated because we expect the future to be like the past. A law of uniformity, but more than Young presumed. Kant was right. The teleology of biology is heuristic.[28]

> The concept of a thing as in itself a natural end is therefore not a constitutive concept of the understanding or of reason, but it can still be a regulative concept for the reflecting power of judgment, for guiding research into objects of this kind and thinking over their highest ground in accordance with a remote analogy with our own causality in accordance with ends; not, of course, for the sake of knowledge of nature or of its original ground, but rather for the sake of the very same practical faculty of reason in us in analogy with which we consider the cause of that purposiveness.

And Darwin was right. Natural selection brings about – through proximate causes – design-like effects and so the metaphor of design is appropriate. Final causes, but not problematic.

So, what then of the time after the *Origin*? Because there was no need of the metaphor of design in the world of professional biology, much of the work did not use natural selection. If one is doing morphology, adaptation is in respects a nuisance. It conceals true connections as yielded by archetypes. But there is more to the story than that. In the world of professional biology, those working on fast-breeding organisms were fully into natural selection. The classic case is that of Henry Walter Bates, Alfred Russel Wallace's naturalist traveling companion in the Amazon. He came up with the theory of camouflage, where non-poisonous butterflies mimic poisonous butterflies to escape predators (birds). This was entirely selection-driven, as were like pieces of work, for instance that of the German biologist Fritz Müller.[29]

What leads our attention away from this very active area of research, in the post-*Origin* era, using natural selection, is that, although the work may have been professional, the people doing it often were not. They were amateurs who collected butterflies and the like, and then tried to make sense of what they had found. One such amateur was the civil servant Albert Brydges, who wrote to Darwin on the topic of industrial melanism.[30]

> My dear Sir,
> The belief that I am about to relate something which may be of interest to you, must be my excuse for troubling you with a letter.
> Perhaps among the whole of the British Lepidoptera, no species varies more, according to the locality in which it is found, than does that Geometer, Gnophos obscurata. They are almost black on the New Forest peat; grey on limestone; almost white on the chalk near Lewes; and brown on clay, and on the red soil of Herefordshire.
> Do these variations point to the "survival of the fittest"? I think so. It was, therefore, with some surprise that I took specimens as dark as any of those in the New Forest on a chalk slope; and I have pondered for a solution. Can this be it? It is a curious fact, in connexion with these dark specimens, that for the last quarter of a century the chalk slope, on which they occur, has been swept by volumes of black smoke from some lime-kilns situated at the bottom: the herbage, although growing luxuriantly, is blackened by it.
> I am told, too, that the very light specimens are now much less common at Lewes than formerly, and that, for some few years, lime-kilns have been in use there.
> These are the facts I desire to bring to your notice.
> I am, Dear Sir, Yours very faithfully,
> A. B. Farn
> Letter from Albert Brydges Farn on November 18, 1878.

For all that Bob Young was rather contemptuous of those that grub about in archives, something like this suggests that he might not have been entirely wise in his dismissal.

What is fascinating is that Darwin seems not to have replied to this letter. Had I been Darwin, I would have brought out a new edition of the *Origin*, with this letter on the title page. His non-response, coupled with the fact that, although he much appreciated Bates's work – he even got the man a job as secretary to the Royal Geographical Society – he didn't introduce it until right at the end of the *Origin*, rather supports a supposition that I have long had. Darwin as a scientist was not much of a Darwinian! Think about his major scientific work done after he had discovered his theory and written out a 250-page version, very similar to that of the *Origin*. He then spent eight years on barnacles. One can certainly see evolution if one looks but, by and large, as for other morphologists, adaptation was a nuisance concealing homologies, and so natural selection was not needed. After the *Origin*, there was no empirical work with selection. Had I been he, in the late forties, I would have set up a breeding establishment in Downe – he could afford to do this – and see if he (or his assistants) could do such things as breed inter-sterile varieties. I think Young was right that Lyell did have a big influence and that one part of this was the belief that change is slow and not to be observed in our lifetimes. So, breeding experiments were essentially useless.

Here, in the world of the lepidopterists, natural selection is flourishing. Another place is in the public domain. I had not realized this until I wrote a book on Darwin and literature – a happy accident, thanks to spending four months in Stellenbosch in South Africa.[31] I found – surprise! surprise! – that the university library was mainly in Afrikaans. So, abandoning my intended plans, I switched to a project I could do from my computer. Within seconds, I would have a novel by Thomas Hardy or a poem by Emily Dickinson. And, looking now at this material as a Darwinian and not just as a reader seeking entertainment, this was a total revelation. I had not realized the extent to which, not just evolution but natural selection got into the public consciousness in both Britain and the US. In the year after the *Origin* was published, Charles Dickens's weekly magazine *All the Year Round* – circulation 100,000 – carried several articles explaining natural selection, in a very friendly manner. I quote from what I wrote[32]:

How, asks Mr. Darwin, ... have all these exquisite adaptations of one part of the organisation to another part, and to the conditions of life, and of one distinct organic being to another, been perfected? He answers, they are so perfected by what he terms Natural Selection — the better chance which a better organised creature has of surviving its fellows — so termed in order to mark its relation to Man's power of selection. Man, by selection in the breeds of his domestic animals and the seedlings of his horticultural productions, can certainly effect great results, and can adapt organic beings to his own uses, through the accumulation of slight but useful variations given to him by the hand of Nature. But Natural Selection is a power incessantly ready for action, and is as immeasurably superior to man's feeble efforts, as the works of Nature are to those of Art. Natural Selection, therefore, according to Mr. Darwin — not independent creations — is the method through which the Author of Nature has elaborated the providential fitness of His. How, asks Mr. Darwin, ... have all these exquisite adaptations of one part of the organisation to another part, and to the conditions of life, and of one distinct organic being to another, been perfected? He answers, they are so perfected by what he terms Natural Selection — the better chance which a better organised creature has of surviving its fellows — so termed in order to mark its relation to Man's power of selection. Man, by selection in the breeds of his domestic animals and the seedlings of his horticultural productions, can certainly effect great results, and can adapt organic beings to his own uses, through the accumulation of slight but useful variations given to him by the hand of Nature. But Natural Selection is a power incessantly ready for action, and is as immeasurably superior to man's feeble efforts, as the works of Nature are to those of Art. Natural Selection, therefore, according to Mr. Darwin — not independent creations — is the method through which the Author of Nature has elaborated the providential fitness of His works to themselves and to all surrounding circumstances.

The author, David Thomas Ansted (1814–1880) was a professional geologist and long-time acquaintance of Darwin. It is stressed that there is nothing to cause worry for the religious, and the status of Darwin as a scientist and his worth as a human being are likewise strongly underlined. Although the pieces are ostensibly agnostic about Darwin's work, opponents are referred to as "timid" and overall the sentiment is very positive.

> We are no longer to look at an organic being as a savage looks at a ship— as at something wholly beyond his comprehension; we are to regard every production of nature as one which has had a history; we are to contemplate every complex structure and instinct as the summing up of many contrivances, each useful to the possessor, nearly in the same way as when we look at any great mechanical invention as the summing up of the labour, the experience, the reason, and even the blunders, of numerous workmen.[33]

I see two major inroads into popular culture, both brought about by natural selection. First religion. Darwin was not a New Atheist. He did not disprove

God nor did he intend to. Higher criticism was doing a good enough job on that front. What Darwin did do was make God indifferent towards us. In a world ruled by the struggle for existence, a good, all-powerful God just didn't make any sense. By 1866, Thomas Hardy, raised a good Anglican, was picking up on this.[34]

> If but some vengeful god would call to me
> From up the sky, and laugh: "Thou suffering thing,
> Know that thy sorrow is my ecstasy,
> That thy love's loss is my hate's profiting!"
>
> Then would I bear it, clench myself, and die,
> Steeled by the sense of ire unmerited;
> Half-eased in that a Powerfuller than I
> Had willed and meted me the tears I shed.
>
> But not so. How arrives it joy lies slain,
> And why unblooms the best hope ever sown?
> —Crass Casualty obstructs the sun and rain,
> And dicing Time for gladness casts a moan. . . .
> These purblind Doomsters had as readily strown
> Blisses about my pilgrimage as pain.

The post-*Origin* God was like the God of Job cubed. He just doesn't care about us (Hardy 1994).

Second, there is no doubt that everyone picked up on natural selection, and sexual selection, even more. This is a poem by Constance Naden, written in the 1880s.

> I HAD found out a gift for my fair,
> I had found where the cave men were laid:
> Skulls, femur and pelvis were there,
> And spears that of silex they made.
>
> But he ne'er could be true, she averred,
> Who would dig up an ancestor's grave—
> And I loved her the more when I heard
> Such foolish regard for the cave.
>
> My shelves they are furnished with stones,
> All sorted and labelled with care;
> And a splendid collection of bones,
> Each one of them ancient and rare;

One would think she might like to retire
To my study— she calls it a "hole"!
Not a fossil I heard her admire
But I begged it, or borrowed, or stole.

But there comes an idealess lad,
With a strut and a stare and a smirk;
And I watch, scientific, though sad,
The Law of Selection at work.

Of Science he had not a trace,
He seeks not the How and the Why,
But he sings with an amateur's grace,
And he dances much better than I.

And we know the more dandified males
By dance and by song win their wives—
'Tis a law that with avis prevails,
And ever in Homo survives.

Shall I rage as they whirl in the valse?
Shall I sneer as they carol and coo?
Ah no! for since Chloe is false
I'm certain that Darwin is true.

We are a very long way from Shakespeare's sonnets.

Shall I compare thee to a summer's day?
Thou art more lovely and more temperate.
Rough winds do shake the darling buds of May,
And summer's lease hath all too short a date.
Sometime too hot the eye of heaven shines,
And often is his gold complexion dimmed;
And every fair from fair sometime declines,
By chance, or nature's changing course, untrimmed;
But thy eternal summer shall not fade,
Nor lose possession of that fair thou ow'st,
Nor shall death brag thou wand'rest in his shade,
When in eternal lines to Time thou grow'st.
So long as men can breathe, or eyes can see,
So long lives this, and this gives life to thee.

From the "darling buds of May" to fossils and dancing. This is a new world. Darwin's world. Bob Young – and the infant Michael Ruse – were dead wrong on this.

Incidentally, showing how new ideas and movements can have lives of their own, with effects quite beyond those intended by the innovators, can I draw attention to the fact that Constance Naden was female? In 50 years of writing on the Darwinian Revolution, once in a very rare while have I mentioned females. Rosemary Grant working with her husband Peter Grant on the finches of the Galapagos. Or the wives of great men, such as Emma Wedgwood who married her first cousin Charles Darwin. Working on literature and Darwinism, at least a third (if not more) of the writers were female – Mrs. Gaskell, George Eliot, Emily Dickinson, Edith Wharton, right down to the present. Sexual selection was much discussed and fictionalized, as in Naden's poem above.[35] Darwin in the *Descent* is conventionally sexist when it comes to discussing sexual selection. Not so the creative writers. In Naden's poem, it is the (male) narrator who seems a bit of a twit. A new world indeed. Although I was hardly alone in all this insensitivity, I am sure that that aforementioned boarding school had a hand here. For boys only – as was the custom in those days – we may have lusted after girls, but not one of us had any doubt that there is an ordering of the species and females are not at the top. Before I start knocking Darwin – also the product of an English, all-boys boarding school – perhaps I should make sure that my own greenhouse windows are in good order.

I have written far more than I intended. But you can see why the thinking of Bob Young has been so important to me – and to others – and why I mourn his passing but celebrate his life.

Notes

1 Acknowledgements to *The Cambridge Encyclopedia of Darwin and Evolutionary Thought*, 2012.
2 Gertrude Himmelfarb, *Darwin and the Darwinian Revolution*. New York: Anchor Books, 1962.
3 Gavin De Beer, *Charles Darwin: Evolution by Natural Selection*. London: Nelson, 1963.
4 Karl Marx and Friedrich Engels, *Selected Correspondence*. Moscow: Progress, 1965.
5 Robert C. Olby and Charles Darwin's Manuscript of Pangenesis. *The British Journal for the History of Science* (1963) 1, no. 3: 251–263; Peter J. Vorzimmer, *Charles Darwin: The Years of Controversy*. Philadelphia, PA: Temple University Press, 1970; Sandra Herbert, Darwin, Malthus, and selection. *Journal of the History of Biology* (1971) 4: 209–217; Sandra Herbert, The place of man in the development of Darwin's theory of transmutation: Part 1. July 1837. *Journal of the History of Biology* (1974) 7: 217–258; Sandra Herbert, The place of man in the development of Darwin's theory of transmutation: Part 2. *Journal of the History of Biology* (1977) 10: 155–227.
6 Robert M. Young, Darwin's Metaphor: Does nature select? *Monist* (1971) 55: 442–503.
7 Robert M. Young, *Darwin's Metaphor: Nature's Place in Victorian Culture*. Cambridge: Cambridge University Press, 1985, p. 44.
8 Young, Darwin's Metaphor.

9   Thomas Kuhn, *The Structure of Scientific Revolutions*. Chicago: University of Chicago Press, 1962.
10 Young, *Darwin's metaphor*.
11 Ibid. p. 449.
12 Ibid. p. 473.
13 Ibid. p. 477.
14 Ibid. p. 485.
15 Ibid. p. 500.
16 Ibid. p. 469.
17 Michael Ruse, Darwin's debt to philosophy: an examination of the influence of the philosophical ideas of John F.W. Herschel and William Whewell, On the development of Charles Darwin's theory of evolution. *Studies in History and Philosophy of Science* (1975) 6: 159–181.
18 Hodge, incidentally, deservedly, has just been awarded the ISHPSSB David Hull Prize, honouring him for his "extraordinary contribution to scholarship and service that promotes interdisciplinary connections between history, philosophy, social studies, and biology."
19 Jonathan S. Hodge, The Structure and Strategy of Darwin's 'Long Argument'. *British Journal for the History of Science* (1977) 10: 237–246; and his *Charles Darwin and Natural Selection*. Cambridge: Cambridge University Press, 1997.
20 Peter. J. Bowler, *The Eclipse of Darwinism: Anti-Darwinism Evolution Theories in the Decades around 1900*. Baltimore, MD: Johns Hopkins University Press, 1983; Peter. J. Bowler, *The Non-Darwinian Revolution: Reinterpreting a Historical Myth*. Baltimore, MD: Johns Hopkins University Press, 1988; Peter. J. Bowler, Revisiting the eclipse of Darwinism. *Journal of the History of Biology* (2005) 38; and Peter. J. Bowler, *Darwin Deleted: Imagining a World without Darwin*. Chicago: University of Chicago Press, 2013.
21 Bowler, p. 279.
22 Michael Ruse, *The Darwinian Revolution (Cambridge Elements)*. Cambridge: Cambridge University Press, 2019, p. 39.
23 Robert J. Richards and Michael Ruse. *Debating Darwin*. Chicago: University of Chicago Press, 2016.
24 Richards and Ruse, *Debating Darwin*, p. 102.
25 Ibid. p. 115.
26 Darwin, *Origins of the Species*, p. 228.
27 John S. Sebright, *The Art of Improving the Breeds of Domestic Animals in a Letter Addressed to the Right Hon. Sir Joseph Banks, K.B.* London: 1809. Privately published, pp. 15–16.
28 Immanuel Kant, *Critique of the Power of Judgment*. (Ed.) P. Guyer. Cambridge: Cambridge University Press [1790] 2000, p. 247.
29 William Kimler and Michael Ruse, Mimicry and camouflage. *The Cambridge Encyclopedia of Darwin and Evolutionary Thought*. (Ed.) Michael Ruse, Cambridge: Cambridge University Press, 2013.
30 Darwinian Correspondence Project 11747.
31 Michael Ruse, *Darwinism as Religion: What Literature Tells Us About Evolution*. Oxford: Oxford University Press, 2017.
32 Anon, Natural Selection. *All the Year Round* (1860) 3, 63: 293–299.
33 Anon, Species. *All the Year Round*, p. 299.
34 Thomas Hardy, *Collected Poems*. Ware, Hertfordshire: Wordsworth Poetry Library, 1994.
35 Constance Naden, *Poetical Works of Constance Naden*. Kernville, CA: High Sierra Books, 1999.

Part 2

Politics of History and Technology

Chapter 5

Paradigm at bay

Robert M. Young and the dialectical development of science and technology studies

Kurt Jacobsen

If you have any scholarly passion at all, a liberating glee arises when you first approach the intrinsically polyglot field that became known as Science and Technology Studies (STS). In this intellectually effervescent realm Bob Young became "one of the central founders of critical science and technology studies," attests Donna Haraway. "His pursuit of the issues where they led, rather than his pursuit of an orthodox academic career, has, in my view, been his greatest strength." Alas, as is the way with these things, it was also, speaking Machiavellianly, his greatest weakness insofar as wielding durable scholarly influence. The STS field, soon morphing into an umbrella term including sociology of scientific knowledge (SSK) and the social construction of technology (SCOT), has been a many-splendored, multiply interpreted and fascinatingly contested thing, but no longer is one where Young's radical take on science comfortably fits, except in disguise.[1]

The whole point of STS is that science – an endeavour that innocents and ideologues alike portray as angelic in motive and practice – is embedded in social processes, in accompanying ideologies, in unconscious motives, and in constricting rules imposed in professional (e.g. positivism) and national (e, g, Lysenkoism) settings.[2] Science gatekeepers seemed to prize variance, and its measurement, in all things except science itself. For them, at the time, a unitary science, not man, was the measure of all things, including man. Feyerabend, with J. S. Mill as his guide, made good sport of that institutionalizing conceit throughout his own maverick life.[3] "For neither the whole truth nor the whole of good is revealed to any single observer," as William James earlier deduced.[4] "Even prisons and sickrooms have their special revelations." What James said here for a single observer is true of paradigms too, which is a lesson Young took acutely to heart.

Young made his formal entrance into science studies in the early 1960s with a fellowship at Cambridge, though his Yale influences, such as a young Richard Rorty, had much to do with preparing him for the transformative studies he undertook in nineteenth-century brain research and on Darwin – amply addressed in earlier essays in this volume. History of science then was a tiny discipline usually housed in the few History departments where

DOI: 10.4324/9781003204244-8

arcane ventures were humoured. The 'internalist' versus 'externalist' debate was the key divide one encountered at the start of Young's academic life, as rendered at the time in sociology of science by Robert K. Merton or Barry Barnes and quite differently by Hilary and Steven Rose who operated in a more radical vein (which they believe conflicted with Young's work).[5] The notion of external influences on the practice of hermetically sealed science, especially in pre-Kuhnian days, was an extremely touchy, if not taboo, one. It was, among other things, code for Marxism.

Science supposedly was disinterested, cumulative, logical and rigorously tested, as near to an infallible institution as we are likely to get on a post-papal authority planet. How science, which prized questioning above everything, itself became a locus of unquestionable authority is an ironic story that Young could not help but notice and address. The succession of religion by science too was worrisomely clear enough to Noble, Feyerabend, and others. It's not that science was whatever scientists made up, it was that science in the twentieth century had poured into it all the hushed ecclesiastical fervour formerly reserved for medieval cathedral rites.[6]

Secular leaders obligingly imbue science with a quasi-divine aura so long as their own interests and legitimation purposes are served, and how could it be otherwise for the paymasters? (A theme of Harry Collins' and Trevor Pinch's *The Golem* books much later is that overvaluing science in this way courts the danger of a widespread public disenchantment when science falters, though they treat what they deem true science as a Platonic ideal more than as a socially embedded phenomenon.)[7] The burden of proof began to shift. A new norm arose in the late twentieth century that science is seen as embedded in and dependent on its supporting social context, but insulated in its practices from the influence of that context.[8] Bob quickly came to repudiate depictions of science & technology research as separable or insulated from social context, and not just in the slippery sense that social constructivists try to embrace. His explorations soon brought him to Marxian writings. The defining feature of such approaches to the history of science is that the "history of scientific ideas, of research priorities, of concepts of nature and of the parameters of discoveries are all rooted in historical forces which are, in the last instance, socio-economic."[9] Still, his concerns went even deeper than then standard Marxist concerns. He adopted Marxist analysis insofar as it served the ruthless critique of everything existing (for humane purposes). Bob also was drawn to what the young Marx called species-being (in Bob's terms, human nature), focusing on values as essential in critical analysis, and indeed in any truly dialectical analysis.

Bob ultimately argued that (1) social context mattered, as in Malthus informing Darwin, (2) that science was not separable from political economy, as Bernal also contended, (3) that we usually are prisoners of our intellectual indoctrinations, and thus (4) we often cling to our indoctrinations for purposes that serve psychic needs – making departures from beaten paths all the more difficult. To counter these cumulative inertial forces upon us, and to 'move on,' Bob argued, as did the critical theorists and Feyerabend, that we need to embark on the construction of a counter-reality and an alternative cosmology.[10] The reason we need a fictitious counterworld is because we are otherwise trapped in a myopically rational world shaped by others for their antagonistic purposes. In this regard, Horkheimer similarly wrote,[11]

> To realize an explicit interest in a future rational society the prerequisite is that the individual abandon the mere recording of facts, that is, mere calculations; that he learn to look behind the facts; that he distinguish the essential from the superficial without minimizing the importance of either; that he formulate conceptions that are not simple classifications of the given, and that he continually orient all his experiences to definite goals without falsifying them: in short, that he learn to think dialectically.

By the 1970s, when Bob launched the *Radical Science Journal*, critical theorist Jurgen Habermas' early work became a parallel source of kindred criticism of the siren song of socially skewed rationality.[12]

"We are struggling," Bob duly reckoned, "to integrate science and values at the same time that we are prevented from doing so by our most basic assumptions." An earlier educative seduction had taken place of which most of us were unaware and which was hard to shake. The twin spectres that Kuhn in 1962 highlighted, and, as a methodological conservative, strenuously fended off, were the prospect of the incommensurability of paradigms, and, no less upsetting, the ever fainter line between science and ideology, which were disturbingly similar in that science too was a sociological and cultural enterprise whose adherents and sponsors could misconstrue or deliberately distort what they do. Since then the internalist/externalist debate largely resolved itself in the favour of a recognition, at least, of the need to address external influences – with an attendant explosion of scholarly inquiries and enterprises in the intersecting areas of history of science, sociology of science and philosophy of science. In the remainder of this essay, I look at Bob's necessarily ambivalent attraction to dialectical thinking, underline the tacit role of his psychoanalytic studies (for he was not yet a clinician) in his STS concerns, compare his work with better known and marketed rivals and end with a few reflections.

The making of a 'Marxist outlaw'

No one I know of who calls themselves a Marxist would call Bob one, though quite a few erstwhile colleagues, who may have leafed through the Communist Manifesto once upon a time, behaved as though Bob might be the come-lately sixth member of the Cambridge Five spy ring. Yet, if Bob was a

Marxist, it was of the emphatically unorthodox kind that Alvin Gouldner termed Marxist outlaws.[13] Bob initially drew inspiration from, above all, Whitehead, E A. Burtt and in-house ruminators, such as Heisenberg and Planck, on the meaning of quantum theory, which sowed corrosive doubts about textbook renditions of science as automatically cumulative, progressive and human-proof.[14] Recall that this simple celebratory view of science went hand in hand, for example, with widespread Western acceptance of eugenics until the Second World War.[15] Bob always was insistent that critiques of science within capitalism in no way precluded critiques of science within an authoritarian socialist society such as the Soviet Union, however much it formally aspired to a democratic socialist regime.[16] Marcuse offered a similar critical stance in his *Soviet Marxism*.[17]

The internalist/externalist debate, once it was deemed legitimate, was succeeded briefly by a related but far more controversial one: that nature, at least in part, might be subject to our own conceptions of it, that it was not just out there. One hardly got more radically ontological than that. Engels, and his *Dialectics of Nature* and *Anti-Duhring*, was the chief whipping boy for irate opponents on both the Right and the Left. Bob take on this question was accordingly careful, responding,

> It is probably the case that all 'facts' are theory-laden, but it is certainly true that some facts are more theory-laden than others. The reader who comes to these popularisations for guaranteed social and political wisdom supported by the authority of science is making a very grave mistake. Let us have the debate on the social meaning of biology, but we must strip it of the specious aura of scientific objectivity.[18]

For Young, positivism was a profoundly dubious shortcut that actually impedes science as a knowledge-seeking enterprise.

Young appreciated that Britain somehow provided a haven for alternative thought that he never would have chanced upon, let alone been able to explore, in the US when he resided there.[19] In Britain, there was a tradition to hark to in the work of J.D. Bernal, Joseph Needham, J.B.S. Haldane, Hyman Levy, P.M.S. Blackett, Laurence Hogben, and others.[20] Bernal was influenced by the 1931 meeting with Bukharin, Boris Hessen, Ernest Kolman, and others of a roving bent in dialectical materialism, unshackled as yet by Stalinist diktats and most of whom, for their free thinking ways, came to sticky ends.[21] Curiously, in an event Young likely noticed, surviving former delegate and scientist Kolman defected in 1976 to Sweden where he castigated the Soviet regime but affirmed the utility of dialectics for his research.[22] (Bernal, incidentally, later is said to have rejected the notion that Young was his successor, which was okay with Bob, given certain tendencies of this ever more rigidified Stalinist Peace Prize winner.) The task was to peel away the cumulative detritus of dogma, and justifiable derision of it, to find the dynamic dialectical core of the Marxist approach, which attracted intellects of that calibre in the first place, before ossification set in.

The Social Function of Science, the Roses attest, made Bernal the founding figure in the now huge enterprise of science, technology, and society studies.[23] But, and here is a key point, Bernal's rendition of scientific socialism spoke to, and evoked, elitist instincts, and so Bob rejected it, as he did the notion of science as unmarred by ideology and interest.[24] Science, for Bernal, was fettered by capital, and needed to be set free. For Bernal, as for Thorstein Veblen, planning by experts was the only reasonable way forward, and neither gent seemed to bother overly much about assuring democratic approval or oversight.[25] Trusting elites is just what Bob was not prepared to do. No one who knew those flawed elites up close, however charming and couth at dinner parties, was likely to trust them either – at least, not on their own and at their word.[26]

Only in 1976 was the discussion, for example, of science and ideology thoroughly reopened, the Roses claim in a piece in which they do cite Young's Science is Social Relations.[27] The estimate is a bit unkind since Bob had launched *Radical Science Journal* several years before. 1976 was also the year Bob departed Cambridge for full-time publishing and activism in London. Bob targeted a fundamental contradiction in the dominant scientific, positivistic worldview,

> between science as an objective sphere, separate from the vicissitudes of subjectivity and clashes of values and interests — the servant of policies which are supposed to be determined elsewhere and science, at the same time, as the basis, the model, and the guide for society — eliminating uncertainties, achieving the 'correct' solutions, and reconciling conflicts and priorities by neutral means. In trying to have it both ways, the proponents and practitioners of these approaches... thereby collude with the propagation of values constituted by the production and reproduction of social relations in the capitalist mode of production, while believing themselves to be humble seekers after truth and progress — models of disinterestedness, fully deserving their mandarin role, status and perquisites.

Here is where Young's work departs markedly from rivals SCOT, SSK, and others. What was his dialectical approach, and why did he adopt it? And how does dialectics square with a pluralist sensibility?

The politics of dialectics

Young figured that dialectical materialism is not, and never has been, a programmatic method for the solution of particular *physical* problems, which, while Marxist eminences like Lukacs and Marcuse, agreed, is not entirely accurate. The prize whipping boy for what many deem dialectical delusions is Friedrich Engels who outlined general laws of dialectical development of society and nature, consisting of the trusty litany of the transformation of quantity into quality (and vice versa); the interpenetration and unity of opposites, and the negation of the negation – all scorned by various critics as general to the point of evanescence. Engels carefully noted, though, how he omits from each general principle the peculiarities of each individual process, indicating a great remaining latitude for scientific research.

For Engels, dialectical principles were rough but unignorable guidelines, not dogmas, and it was practice, not theory alone, that makes perfect, even if perfect is going to be provisional.

> Knowledge is essentially relative inasmuch as it is limited to the perceptions of relationships, and consequences, of certain social and state forms which exist only at a particular epoch and among particular people, and are of the very nature transitory so that anyone who hunts out absolute truths will bring home but little, apart from platitudes of the sorriest kind...[28]

Bernal's praise of Engels was not utterly misplaced. Loren Graham and others even testify that Soviet era scientists, apart from the notorious Lysenko episode, made innovative contributions based on a dialectical approach and more openly and squarely faced the implications of their philosophic assumptions than have scientists elsewhere.[29]

Lysenkoism was both a key lesson and impediment, deeply misunderstood in the West.[30] "If we could fight off the complacent liberals — East and West — who use Lysenkoism as a self-congratulatory object lesson," Young argued,

> to reinforce their own elitism and false consciousness about the autonomy of the content of science, *and* if we could fight off the scientism of both vulgar and 'rigorous', theoreticist, structuralist Marxists, we could use Lysenkoism to learn more and more about the single domain of enquiry.[31]

Lysenkoism, Graham noted, presented not a primarily a struggle between philosophers and scientists but one crossing these academic lines on both sides, between genuine scholars on the one hand and ideological zealots on the other.[32] No necessary link exited between Lysenko's Michurinist biology and dialectical materialism, and the latter was not incompatible with chromosomal theory. While the case for dialectics does not rise or fall with applications to natural or physical sciences, it is worth noting that it does not necessarily fall even there.[33]

Graham laid out dialectical guidelines in that sphere:

(1) The world is material, and is made up of what current science would describe as matter-energy; (2) The material world forms an interconnected whole; (3) The World is constantly changing, and, indeed, there are no truly static entities in the world; (4) The changes in matter occur in accordance with certain overall regularities or laws; (5) The laws of development of matter exist on different levels corresponding to the different matters of the sciences; (6) and therefore, one should nor expect in every case to be able to explain some complex entities as biological organisms in terms of the most elementary physico-chemical laws; (7) Matter is infinite in its properties, and therefore man's knowledge will never be complete; (8) The motion present in the world is explained by internal factors, and therefore no external mover is needed; (9) Man's knowledge grows with time, as is illustrated by his increasing success in applying it to practice, but this growth occurs through the accumulations of relative – not absolute -truths.[34]

Similar themes abounded outside the old Soviet Union: the whole is greater than the sum of its parts; the knower participates in his/her knowledge; evolutionary development produces differences in kind as well as in form; knowledge is absolute only insofar as it is compressed into rigid categories. Overlappings were many even if the entire program was not shared. Soviet biologists, in turn, readily acknowledged kinship to Ludwig Von Bertalanffy's organismic interpretation and to Whitehead's process philosophy. Here, it's best to quote Young himself who renders many or all of Graham's listed principles in his own style[35]:

Dialectical analysis provides us with an overview and a set of warning signs against particular forms of dogmatism and narrowness of thought, Young contended. It tells us: remember, that history may leave an important trace; Remember that being and becoming are dual aspects of nature Remember that conditions change and that the conditions necessary to the initiation of some processes may be destroyed by the process itself; Remember to pay attention to real objects in space and time and not lose them utterly in idealised abstractions; Remember that qualitative effects of context and interaction may be lost when phenomena are isolated, and above all else,

"Remember that all the other *caveats* are only reminders and warning signs whose application to different circumstances of the real world is contingent," all points which Bob even then calls too modest.

They are too modest, especially if one elides the political dimension, because dialectical materialism is a philosophy of nature, persons, and society with labour at the heart of its ontology, while the conception of dialectical processes (interpenetrations and mutual constitutiveness rather than simple causalities and mechanical interactions) is an alternative world view to that of the positivism of the integrated conceptions of capitalism and its science and technology.

While still at Cambridge, Young – who trained in psychiatry for two years at Rochester – remained interested in psychoanalysis, as attested by essays at the time on R. D. Laing and Herbert Marcuse. In biographical notes, he lists psychoanalysis among the doctoral topics he helped to supervise. Anyone this psychoanalytically astute was alert to the conceits, self-delusions, and other unacknowledged forces driving the search for knowledge, especially through institutional structures with all their seductive incentives.[36] Norman O' Brown's *Life Against Death* appeared around this time, with its acid ruminations on the motives of scientific work. Young never really viewed Kuhn as ground-breaking, though Kuhn problematized the paradigms that determined how professional researchers viewed and treated the world. It's not that, as for Stephen Toulmin and others, Kuhn went too far but that for Young, he did not go far enough. The dialectical core of Kuhn was utterly clear to anyone who bothered to grasp it, and his classic book boosted STS studies, consciously or not.[37] Where else was there to go from there but Marx? Bob and a small cohort set to work on the task of a sophisticated rendering of history of science via especially the *Radical Science Journal* (later, *Science as Culture*).

Conventional STS generally sidesteps, if not shuns, any link to what are, almost by definition, and no matter how supple and sophisticated, vulgar Marxist formulations. That way does not lie tenure. David Noble in his career was quite an exception to the general rule in explicitly examining development of engineering and manufacturing technologies.[38] Langdon Winner, no Marxist, certainly absorbed the best lessons in Marx (and many another thinker) in his *Autonomous Technology* and after. Young was especially drawn into the labour process literature launched by Harry Braverman.[39] The waywardness one detects in the development of STS since the 1970s is that it led away from dialectical materialist inspirations and toward less tainted but also less potent renderings. Where is the ineradicable politics of technology?

Why, for instance, aren't headlines featuring the threat by automation to owners, instead of work forces, a regular feature in newspapers? It's not a crazy question. The technology is available to enable the rest of the work force to dispense with office autocrats and the investor class, as adumbrated in fine works such as Zuboff's *In the Age of the Smart Machine*, which zeroed in on resistance against automated processes by endangered middle management, using surrogate Marxist tools without ever actually mentioning radical sources or pursuing all the pertinent questions.[40] I've no idea whether Zuboff ever read Young in particular, but in other cases, Bob's work was inspirational but went uncited. One cannot overemphasize the widespread academic impulse to use citations not only as self-promotional ploys and for group bootstrapping but as punitive or protective exclusion opportunities.

Looking for the overlooked is what dialectics assigns one to do, which is the dead opposite of the sacralized principle of parsimony, which has lot to answer for (though the eminently parsimonious proposition, Follow the money, is an excellent cynical substitute for dialectical wisdom that too few investigators heed). So too is E. M. Forster's exhortation only connect, but connecting had to include the fact that the development of science always has a social content: as such, it is always relative to the state of the productive forces, always linked to class struggles (often by remote links), always expressive of the interests and consciousness of a class. Was that so hard to do?

SCOT, Latour, and dialectical flirtations

The well-worn path to officially approved – or tolerable – sociological investigation of scientific activity is to incorporate every element of Marxist/neo-Marxist studies – attentiveness to material base, accommodation of "superstructural" and ideational influences, successions of frameworks – but denude them of all telltale verbiage and of any hint of teleology, except the always welcome teleology of progress. The goal was performing dialectics without using the word. Bob had the temerity to notice this and point it out. Cambridge evidently pressured Young to dump his distressing adventures with dialectics, or else leave. The Sixties sensibility burned brightly well into the Seventies and so he left, with transformative hopes, if not income, intact.

The key interveners were Trevor Pinch, Wiebe Bijker, Harry Collins, David Bloor, Simon Schaffer, and related others such as Steve Shapin, Thomas Hughes, and Donald MacKenzie who entered the fray with accounts of technological development collectively labelled the Social Construction of Technological Systems SCOT) or the "strong programme," though not all the forenamed subscribe to every letter of it. They divided over emphases on either historical reconstruction or on detailed micro lab-oriented science studies. The three Golem books were successive clarion calls for the technology-oriented branch.[41] A good deal of interesting and even excellent work has emerged from scholars variously affiliated with SCOT. Since all human activity takes place within society, all science and technology has society at its centre – and then they drop it and its implications. They opt for expertise, with some fringe lay expertise available as mild corrective agents. Bloor states 4 key elements of the "strong programme"[42]:

1   *Causality*: it examines the conditions (psychological, social, and cultural) that bring about claims to a certain kind of knowledge.

2   *Impartiality*: it examines successful as well as unsuccessful knowledge claims.
3   *Symmetry*: the same types of explanations are used for successful and unsuccessful knowledge claims alike.
4   *Reflexivity*: it must be applicable to sociology itself.

One can be mystified as to how this quartet improves upon the guidelines set out by Young and Graham. Causality (No. 1) reasonably allows that social influences matter in scientific and technological development while Reflexivity (No. 4) is a welcome recognition if rarely practiced. Both are watered-down versions of givens in dialectical studies, even if they are advances on the previous mainstream history and sociology of science. Impartiality (No. 2) promises but does not deliver comparative historical investigations of competing technologies; Symmetry (No. 3) is agreeable almost by rote. To be fair, even these positions were regarded as *risque* but not quite *outre* in the wider academic sphere.[43] The social constructivists smartly navigated themselves into a position between the subversive predilections of Young and his associates, and the rest of a staid and wary scholarly community.

Still, the acutely observant Landon Winner pinpointed troubling absences in the agenda, noting that, among other things, it exhibited almost a total disregard for social consequences of technical choice, no concern for moral choice, no room for evaluating alternative technologies versus those chosen, no attention to groups outside the immediate developmental process, and no allowance for deeper social forces working on those immediate groups on a particular technological device or arrangement – all of which are uppermost in Young's dialectical vision.[44] Edgerton, reviewing MacKenzie's otherwise excellent book on missile precision guidance systems, likewise skewered the SCOT devotees for ignoring historical alternatives, and the reality of technical choice.[45] He notes regarding accuracy, that "it was a human construct, a particular line of development is enforced by social interests, which predict a line of development and make it come about."[46] The key impediment stems from not wanting to distinguish the technical from the social, from exiling politics. One did not need SCOT or SSK to understand the politics of alternatives. Young was relentlessly radical while these ascendant rivals were insipid.

Elsewhere, and with a degree of not unprovoked antagonism toward Bloor and Barnes in SSK, Latour made his own way into dialectical territory, portraying daily life and work as an anthropological matrix in which we exist in which nothing can be split tidily between nature and culture where most things are hybrids.[47] Scientific facts are "networked," established on the basis of professional communities as Kuhn argued but in no way are, for example, the laws of physics for either Latour or Kuhn merely social conventions. In hybridized, socially determined but somehow materially grounded forms, Latour, who, like Young, detests postmodernism, refers to "imbroglios" of science, politics. economy. law, religion, and technology.[48] Latour was famously at odds with SCOT analysts on philosophical grounds and prized intricate case study method even more so than they, but an activist political ingredient is usually only latent in his intriguing work.[49] His long list of interests at play in "making a difference" in, for example, Pasteurisation, while akin to Young's (and Feyerabend's) work, was perhaps a tad too heterogeneous.[50] "However, I have learned over the years that all methodological questions are based on metaphysics," Latour writes, echoing Young, "and that every metaphysics is at heart a moral and political issue."[51]

So, by no means does one wish to imply Young and his associates were alone in their quest. Dialectical ideas, for a while, were in the air and taken up, however gingerly or obliquely, in the UK at the Sussex Science Policy Unit overseen by the redoubtable Christopher Freeman and also in the US by the adherents of the social structure of accumulation school.[52] However, scarcely anyone in the US paid attention to the Sussex people then or now, and the social structure of accumulation school in the US remained firmly on the fringes.

Positivism, abstract empiricism, and any spin-off of purely formal theorizing were anathema to Young. He approached Marxist thought with an open inquisitive spirit. "Just as the concept of a hard, discrete fact has had to be given up in the philosophy of science and the pure sensation in psychology," the notion of objectivity needs scrutiny such that I would "equally argue that the case for the role of such factors depends on presenting evidence which convinces a morally concerned and critically thinking man, Young asserted."[53] "The point is that there is no escaping the political debate, a debate which extends to the definition of ideology but also to that of science and its most basic assumptions." A glum Young appreciated that it ironically is a touch Ivory Tower-ish these days to insist on addressing the real world of power. In that respect, SCOT practitioners are nothing if not strong proponents of case studies of real events. Let's see what is to be made of a recent one.

The strange case of the origins of Covid-19

No one at the time of writing knows for certain the source of the Covid-19 pandemic. So, a dialectical student of science and technology must wonder why a maximum security Chinese lab complex, whose explicit mission is modifying viral materials for gain of function purposes (the gains being increasing lethality and infectiousness), and located very near Wuhan, was disregarded peremptorily as a possible culprit? Following several early pandemic appraisals, one a World Health Organization (WHO) document and another a collective statement in The Lancet, the mass media pried no further and blamed a bat disease for pouncing all by itself on humanity like a movie Dracula on a starlet's neck. This accords with journalist I. F. Stone's old saw regarding governments that one shouldn't believe anything they say or do until it is officially denied. Any hint of a laboratory leak of a modified microorganism drew withering official contempt (and even was initially banned by the Facebook police) and all the more so because former President Trump notoriously backed the leak allegation. According to his eminent foes, nothing Trump said or did could be trusted, which was true enough, but did confer on them a license to believe what they wanted instead.

The reigning narrative was that wild bats transmitted the disease 'zoonotically' to intervening animals – pangolins were a candidate – and then in a lethally altered and vastly more transmissible state to people via a so-called wet market in Wuhan. A zoonosis is an infectious disease that has jumped from a non-human animal to humans, according to the WHO. Zoonotic pathogens may be bacterial, viral, or parasitic or may involve unconventional agents and can spread to humans through direct contact or through food, water or the environment. Nothing else to see here, folks. Move along.

Yet, even someone so solopsistic as Trump randomly can hit it right. Critics, first forced to the sidelines, in the molecular genetics profession eventually managed to point out that the initial WHO report relied on Chinese-approved evidence and that the authors of several precipitously dismissive documents regarding lab origins included implicated scientific agents who had steered U.S. National Institute of Health funds into Wuhan biological research.[54] How's that for a conflict of interest that many authorities might like to keep quiet?[55] Given such added US funding, Covid-19 afterward hardly could be labelled a pure Chinese virus, even if it is proven to have emerged from the Wuhan labs. Chinese authorities obviously oppose the revisiting of the origins of Covid, belatedly urged in the Spring of 2021 by President Biden, the G7 and the WHO itself. The fleeting timeline of this imposed consensus was quite similar to that of the WMD charge justifying the invasion of Iraq – about a year and a half of shutdown of debate. In both instances, many people who knew better kept quiet, or were kept quiet, or were ridiculed as cranks. Only a vulgar Marxist evidently would suspect that high-value military-oriented research labs would have either the temerity to perform reckless research, or to deny accidents if containment of their products went awry, or so it seemed.

It is not as if biological laboratory accidents are rarities. In the US during 2008–2012, more than a thousand unintended releases of bacteria, viruses, and toxins were reported to regulatory agencies, some resulting in localized outbreaks. The University of North Carolina, which collaborated with Wuhan, reported six US accidents involving lab-created coronaviruses between 2015 and 2020. In military labs at Fort Detrick in Maryland, researchers have been harmed or even died from lab infections. Some scientists long had worried that dangerous viral enhancement activities at high security labs, such as the Wuhan Institute of Virology, would spill someday into a worldwide catastrophe. China had a single special high security lab while the US itself hosts at least 11 such experimental sites. Upon recent reassessment, there were no bats in the Wuhan wet market and the nearest live critters nested hundreds of miles away. Tracing origins is even more even vexing given that Dr. Robert Baric, a coronavirus expert involved in Wuhan, observed that the sophistication of bioengineering today is such that enhanced viruses would carry no sign of human crafting, much as Edward Snowden revealed about NSA tampering capabilities with internet traffic.

Biological weaponry is long banned but research is not.[56] One instructive active project revolved around recreating the 1918 Spanish Flu. Why exactly? Well, because they can, as even social constructivists might concede. Authorities have insisted on creating these hyper-lethal diseases on the grounds that they need to anticipate new diseases, meaning that bioweapons labs are weirdly tasked to protect us from devilish microorganisms that they themselves are inventing or intensifying. So, are we in good hands with experts? That scientific personnel benefit from the money devoted to these bizarre purposes means that the scientific community isn't the most reliable ethical guardian, as Young warned.

One among several likely alternative explanations is that hapless Chinese miners contracted a bat-borne disease which then was captured and genetically engineered in Wuhan into immensely infectious form and somehow escaped.[57] In 2014, these blandly termed gain of function experiments were halted by the US government until strict guidelines could be devised, but in December 2017, under Trump's watch, the ban was lifted, which hardly makes Trump look good in retrospect. The government ban halted funds for any research that was reasonably anticipated to have enhanced pathogenicity and/or transmissibility in mammals via the respiratory route, which was a gapingly huge loophole any savvy high administrator could saunter through. Critics futilely point out that this ambiguity about what one could reasonably anticipate allowed for related research that resulted in gain of function, while not directly aiming at it. Authorities usually can be counted on to exploit such ambiguities for their own ends.

An aspect very worthy of inquiry is whether during the 3 year pause, US agencies diverted money to Wuhan so that this highly risky research could continue without impediment. Weaponizing bio-research likely just proved too tempting.[58] The sainted Dr. Anthony Fauci happened to be director of the National Institute of Allergy and Infectious Diseases, a subdivision of the National Institute of Health, at the time exemptions were made for Wuhan research, though he denied the funds were for gain-of-function goals. The overall story looks less like one of good versus bad guys, or careful versus reckless ones, or Chinese versus Americans, than of the combined thrust of avid actors in state posts and in science to devise prized weaponry, and not let anything or anyone else get in the way. It's not difficult to reckon how Young, and anyone with dialectical attunement and some knowledge of history, would react to the original soothing claims. If there was a peep out of the social constructivist ranks as to their initial credibility, we are not aware of it. It's not their job to fret about anything beyond the execution of the technological task, once experts make their selection.

By Spring 2021 public opinion turned in favor of Biden 's then ordered investigation of Covid's origins, which in August that year came up with an aggravatingly inconclusive report.[59] The stakes are extremely high given the question of responsibility for millions of deaths worldwide, which potent institutions would much prefer to blame on feckless wildlife. Keep in mind that, even if it were somehow proven that the pandemic had a non-laboratory origin, all the preceding research projects exist and continue, for the most part, unchecked, which already was a huge issue. In particular, we must begin to see the central place of the institutional and ideological role of science in maintaining the most basic features of our anti-democratic society, Young argued all along.

> Once we have begun to see, every one of us must decide what, if anything, he or she is going to do about maintaining, reforming, or transforming the present order of society, beginning with the institutions in which he or she is most directly involved — labs, departments, colleges, communities.

Conclusion

Bob Young disdained what he termed "the usual piecemeal approach to the study of science and society" because rivals to dialectics failed to stir awareness of metaphysical assumptions underlying science, sidestepped the influence of potent players and economic systems, and lacked meaning and concern for those that never purely technical decisions affected. Like Winner, Young detected that "the methodological bracketing of questions about interests and interpretations amounts to a political stance that regards the status quo and its ills and injustices with precision equanimity."[60] In a dialectical approach "the sharp distinction between science and technology vanishes so that all is mediation – mediation of social and economic forces involved in the production and reproduction of real life." Science is inside society, inside history.

Given our Mills epigraph, it seems there should be a contradiction lurking in the twin propositions that dialectics is the best investigative way forward while also allowing that a Feyerabendian plurality of paradigms (including psychoanalytic ones) is needed.[61] Yet, these propositions are reconcilable on, funnily enough, dialectical grounds. A dialectics that isn't reflexive regarding its own blind spots simply is not dialectical. In recognizing the remit for, and value of, Marxist outlaws, Gouldner aptly pointed out that "Marxism's ideology critique powerfully illuminated the limits of one form of ideology, that based on idealistic objectivism, but Marxism itself generated a materialistic objectivism and remains bound by the specific linguistic, nonreflexivity of a materialist ideology."[62] There clearly were limits on knowledge other than class interest for which resort to additional frameworks, such as psychoanalysis, is needed.

A dialectical approach cannot be the entire or satisfactory answer to our questions about the development of science and technology, but attempted answers lacking a dialectical attunement are bound to be misleading and sorely incomplete. It is a matter of primacy, not exclusivity. In discussing Foucault, for instance, Young surmised that the question of how to conceptualize the relationship between knowledge and society is an open one that remains to be investigated: "For a Marxist, in the elusive last instance the question is not an open one. The arrow of causality must point, *however circuitous its path*, from the production and reproduction of real life to knowledge, whether theoretical or applied" (emphasis mine).[63] So long as that matter is addressed, nothing obstructs concern about any explanatory element that in Latourian terms "makes a difference." Young could not have been more adept especially in later years juggling (Kleinian) psychoanalytic interests with his longer-standing one in the philosophy, history, and sociology of science. They informed, refined, and enriched each other.

Notes

1 I exclude from this analysis Bob Young's students and close colleagues, several of whom are contributors to this volume, because my concern is his influence outside their thin ranks. Other exceptions become obvious as I proceed.
2 On different national "styles" of science administration, see Sheila Jasanoff, *Designs on Nature: Science and Democracy on Europe and the United States.* Princeton: Princeton University Press, 2005.
3 See Paul Feyerabend's, *Against Method.* New York: Verso, 1973 and *Science in a Free Society.* New York: Verso: 1978. Also see Kurt Jacobsen and Roger Gilman, "The Dialectical Philosophy of Paul Feyerabend." In Kurt Jacobsen, *Dead Reckonings: Ideas, Interests and Ideas in the Information Age.* New York: Prometheus Press, 1997, pp 3–22.
4 Cited in Russell Jacoby, *On Diversity.* New York: Seven Stories Press, 2020, p. 170.
5 Barry Barnes, *Interest and the Growth of Knowledge.* London: Routledge, 1977, Hilary and Steven Rose, *Science and Society.* London: Penguin, 1970; Robert K. Merton, *The Sociology of Science.* Chicago: University of Chicago Press, 1973.
6 See David Noble, *The Religion of Technology.* New York: Random House, 1997, Feyerabend, *Science in a Free Society,* and Ian Barbour, *Issues in Science and Religion.* New York: Basic Books, 1973. More recently see Adrienne Mayer, *Gods and Robots: Myths, Machines and Ancient Dreams of Technology.* Princeton: Princeton University Press, 2018 and Erik Davis on 'technomystical impulses' and the unacknowledged mix of nature and culture in technology in his *TechGnosis: Myth, Magic and Mysticism in the Age of Information.* New York: North Atlantic Books, 2013.

7 Harry Collins and Trevor Pinch. *The Golem at Large: What You Should Know about Technology.* Cambridge: Cambridge University Press, 1998, p. 151; also see their *The Golem: What You Should Know about Science.* Cambridge: Cambridge University Press, 1993. They seem much more worried about preserving the legitimacy of science as an institution, no matter what it does, than they are about getting at the (however provisional) truth of matters.

8 "The Social Dimensions of Scientific Knowledge," *Stanford Encyclopedia of Philosophy.* https://plato.stanford.edu/entries/scientific-knowledge-social/.

9 Robert M. Young, "Marxism and the History of Science." In R. C. Olby, et al., eds., *Routledge Companion in the History of Sciences.* London: Routledge, 1990, p. 77.

10 Robert M. Young, "Science is social relations." *Radical Science Journal* 5, (1977) pp. 65–129. Also Feyerabend, *Against Method*, p. 31.

11 Max Horkheimer, *Critical Theory: Selected Essays.* New York: Seabury Press, 1972, p. 181.

12 See Jurgen Habermas, *Towards a Rational Society.* Boston: Beacon Press, 1970, *Knowledge and Human Interests.* Boston: Beacon Press, 1971 and *Legitimation Crisis.* London: Heinemann, 1976.

13 Alvin Gouldner, *The Dialectic of Ideology and Technology.* New York: Seabury Press, 1976, p. 21.

14 Max Horkheimer, *Critical Theory: Selected Essays.* New York: Seabury Press, 1972, p. 181. See Roger Smith's essay in this volume on the influence, especially of Whitehead and Burtt.

15 Kurt Jacobsen, *Technical Fouls: Democratic Dilemmas and Technological Change.* New York: Routledge, 2000, Chapter 3.

16 On this point, see Kendall Bailes, *Science and Technology Under Lenin and Stalin.* Princeton: Princeton University Press, 1979.

17 In Soviet Marxism "the function of dialectics itself … has been transformed from a mode of critical thought to a universal world outlook and universal method with rigidly fixed rules and regulations, and this transformation destroys the dialectic more thoroughly than any transformation. Herbert Marcuse, *Soviet Marxism.* New York: Vintage, 1961, pp. 121, 122.

18 Robert M. Young, "Review of Eros and Civilization." *New Statesman*, no. 78, (1969) pp. 666–67.

19 See the interview with Young in the appendix.

20 Robert M. Young, "The Relevance of Bernal's Five Questions." *Radical Science Review* and, for overviews, Gary Werskey, *The Visible College.* London: Allan Lane, 1978.

21 Nikolai Bukharin, ed. *Science at the Crossroads.* London: Cass, 1971, orig. 1931.

22 *London Times* (6 October 1976).

23 Steven Rose and Hilary Rose, "Red Scientist: Two Strands from a Life in Three Colours." In Francis Aprahamian and Brenda Swann, eds., *J. D. Bernal: A Life in Science and Politics.* London: Verso, 1999, p. 49. But where Bernal saw Communism as an inevitable consequence of the scientific and technological revolution, today's radical intellectuals see pollution, chemical and biological warfare, and genetic reductionism. Where Bernal lauded an abstract rationality, today's radical intellectuals see the instrumental rationality of capitalism with science as its uncritical servitor and seek to rebuild both science and rationality as socially and environmentally responsible. Lastly, where Bernal saw scientists as potential organic intellectuals, today's radical intellectuals see them as a divided group of elite managers on the one hand, and casualized research workers on the other.

24 "A mandarinate without moral rudders is reminiscent of the people who did as they were told in dictatorial regimes and other who just did not make waves and endanger their positions in questionable companies and other institutions. My experience is that the places where I have worked in television, publishing, academia and the helping professions are full of such rudderless careerists." Robert M. Young, "Meritocracy: A critique." *Science as Culture*. http://www. psychoanalysis-and-therapy.com/human_nature/papers/pap133h.htm.

25 Thorstein Veblen, *The Engineers and the Price System*. New York: B. W. Huebsch, 1921.

26 Robert M. Young "On Quantification." In John Irvine, Ian Miles and Jeff Evans, eds., *Demystifying Social Statistics*. London: Pluto Press, 1979, pp. 63–74.

27 Rose and Rose, "Red Scientist".

28 Friedrich Engels, *Anti-Duhring*. Moscow: Foreign Publishing House, 1947, p. 131.

29 Loren R. Graham, *Science and Philosophy in the Soviet Union*. New York: Vintage, 1974, pp. 3–4. Also see George Fisher, *Science and Ideology in Soviet Society*. New York: Herder and Herder, 1972, p. 49.

30 See Graham, *Science and Philosophy in the Soviet Union*; David Joravsky, *Soviet Marxism and Natural Science*. London: Routledge and Kegan Paul, 1961; Dominique Lecourt, *Proletarian Science? The Case of Lysenko*. London: New Left Books, 1977; Zhores Medvedev, *The Rise and Fall of T. D. Lysenko*. New York: Columbia University Press, 1969; G. Jones, "British Scientists, Lysenko and the Cold War." *Economy and Society* 8, (1979) pp. 26–58; and Richard Lewontin and Richard Levins, "The Problem of Lysenkoism." In Hilary and Steven Rose, eds., *The Radicalisation of Science*. London: Macmillan, 1976, pp. 32–64.

31 Robert M. Young, "Getting Started on Lysenkoism." *Radical Science Journal* 6–7, (1978) p. 82.

32 Graham, *Science and Philosophy in the Soviet Union*, p. 22.

33 On the reciprocal and dialectical relationship of organism to environment, see Richard Levins and Richard Lewontin, *The Dialectical Biologist*. Cambridge: Harvard University Press, 1985.

34 Ibid. pp. 63–64.

35 Young, "Marxism and the History of Science," pp. 59–60.

36 See Kurt Jacobsen, "The Return of Determinism: Science, Power and Sirens in Distress." In Michael Thompson and Greg Zucker, eds., *Anti-Science and the Assault on Democracy*. New York: Prometheus Press, 2018, pp 180–197

37 Thomas Kuhn, *The Structure of Scientific Revolutions*. Chicago: University of Chicago, 1962. "A paradigm governs, in the first instance, not a subject matter but a community of practitioners."

38 David Noble, *America By Design*. New York: Oxford University Press, 1979 and *Forces of Production: A Social History of Industrial Automation*. New York: Oxford University Press, 1986.

39 Harry Braverman, *Labor and Monopoly Capital*. New York: Monthly Review Press, 1974.

40 Shoshanna Zuboff, *In The Age of The Smart Machine*. New York: Basic Books, 1989, and see my review of it in *The New Statesman*, 24 October 1989.

41 Also see Wiebe E. Bijker, et al., *The Social Construction of Technological Systems: New Directions in the Sociology and History of Technology*. Cambridge: MIT Press, 2012. Then there is Steven Shapin, *A Social History of Truth*. Chicago: University of Chicago Press 1994.

42 David Bloor, "The strengths of the strong programme." In James Robert Brown, ed. *Scientific Rationality: The Sociological Turn*. Netherlands: Springer, 1984, pp. 75–94.

43 See Alan Sokal's occasionally misplaced jeremiads.
44 Langdon Winner, "On Opening the Black Box and Finding it Empty: Social Constructivism and the Philosophy of Technology," *Science, Technology and Human Values* 18, no. 3, (Summer 1993) p. 368.
45 David Edgerton, "Tilting at Paper Tigers." *British Journal of History of Science* 26, (1993) p. 68.
46 Ibid., p. 68.
47 Bruno Latour, *We Have Never Been Modern.* Cambridge: Harvard University Press, 1993, p. 2. Also especially see Bruno Latour's and Steve Woolgar's *Laboratory Life.* Princeton: Princeton University Press, 1979 and Bruno Latour, "For Bloor and Beyond – A Reply to David Bloor's Anti-Latour." *Studies in History & Philosophy of Science* 30, no. 1 (March 1998) wherein he concludes that, in order to keep absolutist fancies at bay, "we need a complete reworking of the notion of 'nature'" (p. 127).
48 Latour, *We Have Never Been Modern.*
49 See Ava Kofan, "Bruno Latour: The post-truth philosopher, mounts a defense of science." *New York Times,* 25 October 2018.
50 Bruno Latour, *The Pasteurization of France.* Cambridge: Harvard University Press, 1993.
51 Latour, "A Reply to Bloor." p. 126.
52 For assessments of both, see Kurt Jacobsen, "Microchips and Macropolicy: The political economy of high technology." *British Journal of Political Science,* 22, (July 1992) pp. 497–519.
53 Robert M. Young, "Evolutionary biology and ideology: Then and now." *Science Studies* 1, (1971) pp. 177–206.
54 Bret Weinstein, "Why we should welcome the lab leak hypothesis." *Unherd* (5 June 2021). https://unherd.com/2021/06/why-we-should-welcome-the-lab-leak-theory/.
55 "An Interview with Richard Ebright." *Independent Science News* (24 March 2021). https://www.independentsciencenews.org/commentaries/an-interview-with-richard-ebright-anthony-fauci-francis-collins-systematically-thwarted/.
56 See Robert Harris and Jeremy Paxman, *A Higher Form of Killing.* London: Arrow, 2002 and Edward Spiers *Agents of War.* London: Reaktion Books, 2021.
57 Jorge Casesmerio "By Investigating itself the US can answer many of the key covid-19 origins questions." *Independent Science News* (8 June 2021). https://www.independentsciencenews.org/commentaries/by-investigating-itself-the-us-can-answer-ma.
58 Sam Husseini, Peter Daszag's "EcoHealth Alliance has hidden almost 40 million in Pentagon funding and militarized pandemic science." *Independent Science News* (16 December 2020). https://www.independentsciencenews.org/news/peter-daszaks-ecohealth-alliance-has-hid.
59 Saliditya Ray," Biden Reportedly receives an Inconclusive Report on Covid Origins from Intelligence Agencies" Forbes 25 August 2021. https://thehill.com/hilltv/what-americas-thinking/566577-poll-a-plurality-of-voters-say-us-hasnt-done-enough-to.
60 Winner, "On Looking inside the Black Box and Finding it Empty," p. 372.
61 This is not to say that Young welcomed *every* competing paradigm. Far from it.
62 Gouldner, *The Dialectic of Ideology and Technology,* p. 43.
63 Young, "Marxism and the History of Science."

Chapter 6

"Science *is* social relations"

Reflections on the essay and the intervention

Maureen McNeil

Introduction.

Returning to Bob Young's opus is a strange experience for those of us who knew him and worked with him: evoking memories, ghosts, and assorted emotions. Focusing on Bob's article – *Science is social relations*, which evolved from a talk given at the BSSRS (British Society for Social Responsibility in Science) conference – *Is there a socialist science?* – held in February 1975, to the essay which was published in *Radical Science Journal* No. 5 in 1977, proved to be particularly evocative in countless ways. Gary Werskey's description of this essay as 'possibly his [Bob's] most outrageous piece of writing' gave returning to this essay a further edge.[1]

Bob Young's 'most outrageous piece of writing'

Countervailing Werskey's assessment is Bob's own decidedly more positive retrospective appraisal of the essay, registered in his introduction to it in his impressive website:[2]

> Of all the essays I have written, this is the one of the two or three which I most enjoyed writing. I know it is dated, but I stand by its main argument, one which I believe was influential in the development of the social constructivist way of seeing science and all forms of expertise. Most social constructivists omit the radical science perspective which is integral to the argument, in fact, it came first. Whenever I ask myself where my basic approach can be found the answer is here.

In the obituary published in the *Independent* Roger Smith described the 'Science *is* social relations' article as 'perhaps his [Bob's] key political paper'.[3] Inevitably these rather different evaluations have informed my own revisiting of this essay. While this is evident in the discussion that follows, I have pursued my own trajectory: teasing out features of the article, deciphering its relationship to Bob's life and times, and offering my own appraisal of the text.

DOI: 10.4324/9781003204244-9

Taking a cue from Werskey's appraisal, Bob's distinctive mode of writing in that piece merits attention. Bob himself commented about this – telling readers that the article was experimental and there are a number of interjections that form a meta-commentary on his uncertainty about his mode of communication. He pronounced that the article was in style 'sometimes weird'.[4] It certainly was very different in mode and presentation from his preceding publications in the history of science (his book *Mind, Brain, and Adaptation* and his earlier articles).[5] This publication was distinctive not just in the avoidance of what had become his characteristically 'long, discursive' footnotes' – a feature which he foregrounds.[6] Reading this essay, it is striking to find how adept Bob was at coining distinctive slogans and aphorisms. Indeed, perhaps he missed his opportunity to produce a distinctive range of commodities – particularly t-shirts (of a kind which he himself might have modelled). There are many of these aphorisms and slogans, but each is distinctive and merits consideration. They begin with the title: *'Science is social relations'*.

There follows a long list of others: 'Science is not value neutral', *'Science is* ideological' (p. 70); 'demystification of science entails the demystification of its reifications' (p. 71); 'DARE TO STRUGGLE, DARE TO WIN, DARE TO SNUGGLE, DARE TO GRIN' (p. 78); 'Science as Domination'; 'Science and the Division of Labour' (p. 82); *'my* science, *my* findings, are mediations of social relations' (p. 83); 'The weight of tradition *can* be lifted...analysis can help us take its measure' (p. 88); 'Which Marxism?' (p. 90); 'theorise our own experience and experience our own theories' (p. 93); 'Prefigurative struggle' (p. 98); Make 'political work relations more personal AND personal relations more political' (p. 99); 'Only socialist processes can produce socialist results' (p. 99); 'Discipline and work should come from commitment... rather than authority or hectoring' (p. 100); 'No mental labour without manual labour' (p. 100); 'Criticism and self-criticism are central to struggle' (p. 100); 'Texture AND structure' (p. 101); 'Power is not to be seized but dissipated; knowledge is to be socialised' (p. 100); 'Prefigure the ends in the means' (p. 100); 'We must combine relentlessness with forgiving struggle' (p. 102); 'Decide which contradictions to confront and which to live with for now' (p. 102); 'We are constrained, squeezed, and fucked up in all sorts of ways by our contexts and ourselves' (p. 102); 'Productive Change or Reproductive Stasis' (p. 102); Be wary of: 'the path of value neutrality and isolated theoretical work' (p. 103); 'One can't get on one's horse and ride off in all directions at once' (p. 103); 'If we don't prefigure, we'll reproduce the existing society' (p. 103); 'Theory without action is arrogant and empty; Action without theory is truculent and blind' (p. 105); 'The critique of the factory applies equally to the laboratory' (p. 105); 'existing science, technology, lifestyles and consciousness are...imminently alterable sets of conventions' (p. 110); 'demarcate the scientific from its illegitimate overgeneralisation – the scientistic' (p. 111); 'All experience, including perception, is metaphysical and metaphysics is ideological' (p. 110); 'Marxism

needs freaks' (p. 110); 'Fear of relativism is a liberal's expansion of the moment between demystifying one cosmology and commitment to another'
(p. 112); 'demystify marxist scientism' (p. 112); 'We treat our social relations
as if they were laws of nature....treating the laws of nature as though they
were laws of nature' (p. 113); '[There's] no place to go but forward' (p. 113);
'dismantling the whole structure of the existing world' (p. 113); 'take sides
against the actual' (p. 113); 'We must learn to theorise our own practice and
to practice our own theories' (p. 113–14); 'Struggle. Compassion. Solidarity.
Organisation' (p. 114); 'Ask not if your comrade has arrived but if s/he is
struggling' (p. 114); 'To be "impersonal" is to be alienated from oneself and
one's comrades' (p. 115); 'prefiguring the ends in the means' (p. 116); 'We're
going to have to get a move on' (p. 118).

Turning from fantasies of t-shirts and trendy commodities, surveying this
remarkable assemblage and considering both the more substantive features
of this essay and situating it in relation to Bob's work as a whole suggest
further observations about Bob's distinctive skills and his influence. These
reveal continuity between his earlier research and publications and this ostensibly 'outrageous piece of writing'.[7] First, it seems clear that it was Bob's
impressive capacity for synthesis which was evident here and which links all
of his publications – at least those in the history and social studies of science.

The very definition of aphorism as: 'a pithy observation which contains
a general truth', is directly relevant here. In fact, many of the would-be
slogans and invocations quoted above constitute precisely what that definition encapsulates – 'pithy observations' – which, in most cases, are insightful, stirring, and sometimes unnerving. This is what Bob was so good
at and it was this, sometimes eerie, capacity that made interactions with
him – intellectually and politically – so stimulating, challenging, and often
disturbing – in both good, and, sometimes not-so-good, ways.

The substance of the essay: a time-capsule and transitional retooling

With reference to Bob's work as a whole and to the contemporary setting the
'*Science is social relations*' article could be characterised as a rich time cap-
sule which represents many components and features of the British radical
science movement of the mid-to-late 70s. Retrospective perspectives may
be fine, but Bob himself presented the essay as an 'exploratory argument
for seeing science *as* social relations' (p. 66) and as an 'exploratory working programme' (p. 95). His exploration was a transitional exercise which
documented the thinking, informing his move from being 'the bright spark'
in history of science and the lauded – if rather controversial – Darwinian
scholar, to radical science activist, strategist, and theoretician.

Bob had resigned from his fellowship at King's College and the assistant directorship of the Wellcome Unit for the History of Medicine at the

University of Cambridge on 31 December 1974.[8] This article marked his move from contextual studies of the history of ideas and scientific theories to Marxist critiques of science (and as he insisted throughout the piece, of technology and medicine as well). He explained that he set out to 'describe science as much as possible in terms drawn from marxist political economy and from the critique of industry and the division of labour' (p. 67). As he himself might have observed at the time: he was retooling – intellectually, politically, and personally.

Moreover, the rhetorical 'we' of the piece indicates that he was speaking to and, to some extent, on behalf of a political constituency. This was a document of and for the nascent radical science movement. In a 2015 interview, reprinted in this volume, he explained the background to this move and implicitly to this 1975/77 essay. Referring directly to the British Society for Social Responsibility in Science, he commented: 'I eventually left Cambridge in the 1970s so I could work with this movement. It changed what I thought, what I wrote. I wrote manifestos.' His reference to writing manifestos is significant and directly relevant to his 1977 RSJ article which was, as Smith observed, 'perhaps his key political paper'. Bob articulated this in a characteristic formulation that was both provocative and ambitious [a familiar Bob Young combination], in terms which circulated in the left at that time, explaining that: 'the project is to elaborate a strategy of revolutionary practice for people whose mediating role is based on expertise' (p. 68).

In substance, this article constituted a restless (conveyed by the frequent injunctions about 'needing to move on' that Les Levidow (this volume) highlights) and relentless set of encounters with theories, concepts, movements, and examples as Bob considered what they might offer the project and the movement. Sifting, critically evaluating, resourcing – these are the moves which animate the piece. The resourcing was to be both theoretical and practical. However, it is also useful to distinguish and specify the kinds of resourcing and encounters which make up the article. These are discussed below with reference to: the template, theories, movements, and popular cultural illustrations that shape the essay.

The template

This was a Marxist project and Bob emphasised that Marxism was his and the radical science movement's primary resource and reference point. He observed that Marx, Engels, and Lukacs had 'made transparent' (p. 72) the social relations of bourgeois economic theory and had shaken assumptions about the established capitalist social order. He reflected that:[9]

> Sets of human conventions are presented in bourgeois economic theory as unalterable, natural determinations, and marxism demystifies these. Now we must apply that same analysis to the laws of nature themselves

and demystify the existing conceptions of unalterable natural determinations and the attendant scientism, fatalism and deference to powerfully authoritarian experts.

The ambition of the project was clear: the vision was the extension of Marxism in a parallel project which would demystify capitalist science and the laws of nature as Marx and Engels had demystified economic theory, the laws of the economy and capitalism. In this sense, Marxism was not merely a resource, it provided not only intellectual and political insights and inspiration; it was *the template* for the whole project.

Theories

Nevertheless, Bob also investigated and mobilised in a more detailed way elements of the Marxist theoretical and conceptual repertoire. He pursued the concepts and strands of Marxist theory which he found most promising in analysing science, technology, and medicine and in addressing their entanglements with capitalism. These included conceptions of: class, the capitalist mode of production, private property, reification, fetishism, commodification, mystification, alienation, misplaced concreteness, domination, ideology, the labour process, the division of labour, hegemony, and mediation. He disabused 'vulgar Marxism' and Althusserian and other attempts to conjure scientific Marxism and identified his own take on Marxism as broadly 'libertarian'. He borrowed thoughtfully from Marxist commentators including: Braverman, Colletti, Gorz, Gramsci, Mandel, Marcuse, Marglin, Ollman, Sohn-Rethel, Edward Thompson, and Raymond Williams. The version of Marxism on offer in this essay was informed by the reading and discussion groups that had mushroomed within the *Radical Science Journal* collective and the Conference of Socialist Economists (which formed in the 1970s with some members of the *RSJ* collective, including Bob as members).[10]

Marxism may have been his deepest reservoir, but it was not the only theoretical and conceptual well from which Bob drew. In this essay, he registered and reviewed other intellectual sources which might offer insights relevant to the project of demystifying science. These included sociological and anthropological theories and research – notably deviance theory, sociology of knowledge and education, and comparative anthropology of knowledge systems. He referenced the theories of one of his long-time favourites – the philosopher Edwin A. Burtt (who Roger Smith [this volume] has noted was so crucial to Bob's thinking) – before chastising himself lest he be diverted into 'bourgeois philosophy of science' (p. 94). There were even nods towards the sociology of science as Bob noted recent work by David Bloor and Paul Forman (p. 83). While he demonstrated that there were insights which merited attention in these fields, he did not hesitate to label some of this theory 'bourgeois', he warned against the deference to the natural sciences which could taint them, and he expressed no reservations in insisting that Marxism was his ultimate touchstone.

Movements

Bob's trajectory was not exclusively conceptual, and the essay incorporated a remarkably wide-ranging review of social and political movements, as he adjudicated their features, strengths and weaknesses. This included: the Old and New Left (1st and 2nd generations), industrial struggles and trades unions, alternative technology and anti-science movements, visionary socialism from the C19 and C20 (Blake, Ruskin, Morris), life-style politics, anti-psychiatry, situationist, and new cosmological movements. Although this survey was broad, it is notable that his main reference point throughout the piece was industrial struggle and the trade union movement. He underscored the importance of the unionisation of scientific, technical, and university workers/experts and of links between theoretical analysis and scientific/technical experts and industrial struggle. Nonetheless, he maintained that the development of more specific forms of politics for 'mediators' – experts, scientists, and other knowledge workers – was crucial. There were also passing and somewhat anecdotal references to feminism and the women's movement, to anarchism, and to civil rights and anti-imperialist movements.

Considering the array of social and political movements that figured in Bob's review, some of his assessments are striking and some are amusing. He is generous in his treatment of life-style politics and alternative technology movements but snide about some of the old New Left. This related to his earlier exposition of the neglect of science and forms of scientism in the writings of some members of the British old New Left (including those of Perry Anderson and E.P. Thompson) which he had traced in his earlier essay "*The historiographic and ideological contexts of the nineteenth-century debate on man's place in nature*".[11] But perhaps it was his concern with prefigurative politics which was paramount here. While he undertook an explicit exposition of preceding and some contemporary political movements, he also drew attention to emerging political activities which emanated from and sustained the British radical science movement, especially the Radical Publications Group and the Publications Distribution Co-op. (He and some other members of the *RSJ* collective were participants in these.) Along the way, he noted flash points for the radical science movement: the Flixborough (1974) and Seveso (1976) disasters and, more positively, the promise of the Lucas Industrial Plan.[12]

Werskey has emphasised that Bob's sorting resulted in the disabusing of certain distinctions ad positions, notably: use/abuse, internalist/externalist, science/ideology – to which could be added: fact/value, positivism, scientism, technological determinism, vulgar Marxism, as well as notions of value-free or value-neutral science. Werskey foregrounds the negative orientation of the sifting exercise. Nevertheless, Bob also positively identified crucial synthesis: theoretical and agitational, laboratory and industrial struggles, research and applications, trade union activities and life-style politics, and various forms of prefiguring lifestyle.

Popular culture illustrations

Finally, Bob mobilised his own more personal resources drawn from popular culture in assembling his working programme. He quoted lyrics by some of his favourite singers (Paul Simon, Arlo Guthrie, Bob Dylan), proffered a list of recent films (around deviance), and inserted some repurposed and original cartoons. He even offered a few jokes, several of which were rather agitprop in orientation.

Science is social relations: invocation and legacy

This final set of reflections pertain to the assertion and title of the article: *Science is social relations.* There is a real sense in this essay of Bob saying: 'Up yours!' to the established world of the history, philosophy, and sociology of science that he had left behind. This article is significant as a vehicle for his personal and political transition from the academic world of the history of science and in it he does express outrage about the world he is leaving. The reasons for this emerge from the collection Bob edited with Mikuláš Teich, *Changing Perspectives in the History of Science*[13] and the 'state of the field' reviews in both the co-editor's introduction there and in Bob's *Man's place in nature* article.[14] In the latter – his own contribution to the collection – Bob summarised his survey of key texts, contending that 'these works [of the late 50s and early 60s] …made up a formidable orthodoxy in favour of treating the history and philosophy of science in relative isolation from their social, economic, and political contexts'.[15]

In a much later overview, another key figure in the history and sociology of science, Steven Shapin was scathing about the state of the field, noting that science studies researchers of the 1930s to 1950s had been engaged in 'defending and justifying some current arrangements of science in society'. He extended his assessment, contending that: 'the generation which began coming into the history and sociology of science from the mid-1970s…have tended to be more interested in performing rites of disciplinary purification than in changing the world'.[16]

Gary Werskey joined this critical chorus when he observed: 'The history of science, first at Cambridge and then more widely, was established on an explicitly anti-Marxist and "internalist" historiography….as an intellectual movement driven by the achievements of isolated, aristocratic geniuses'.[17]

(James Secord, in this volume and elsewhere, offered his own overview of the state of the history of science in the 1960s and 1970s.[18]) Without making sweeping assessments of a complex and diverse field here, there are good grounds for seeing continuities between these commentaries and Bob's project in this essay. Hence, Bob's title and invocation: *Science is social relations* – can be read as a passionate and determined assertion – as he insists – to the history, philosophy, and sociology of science community and others – that science *IS* socially embedded and constituted.

But perhaps the insistence conveyed by this invocation also betrayed Bob's own more personal frustrations not just with the state of the field but also with his own efforts within it. Bob himself seemed to be scouring and scurrying in dealing with this injunction in his efforts to discern ways of working with it. In his *Fragmentation of a common context* essay (first published in 1973), he was already reflecting that perhaps he was at the end of his own path in and through the history of ideas. He writes there of coming[19]:

> up against the limits of the legitimate explanatory power of the history of ideas...The questions I have raised cry out for consideration from the point of view of social, political, and economic historical research. These are perspectives which historians of science have yet to adopt in a serious and sustained way on most topics...In order to carry my own research further I now realize that I must embark upon a process of self-education for which there has been no preparation in eleven years as a student (and five as teacher) of philosophy, science, medicine, and history and philosophy of science – all of which were taught without reference to the historical forces at work in the socioeconomic order.

From the perspective of the history and sociology of science, Marxism both enriched and complicated Bob's position. Quite obviously as the *Science is social relations* essay demonstrated: there were rich pickings within the Marxist coffers for probing the social making of science – and this is certainly a big part of what this *RSJ* article was about. On the other hand, and again the *RSJ* essay makes this clear, the immersion in Marxism upped the stakes considerably. His project was no longer one of pushing or pulling an academic field along – it was about changing the world!

Werskey's take on this is that Bob and the radical science movement ran with 'the Labour Process Perspective' because it enabled the analysts of this movement to 'talk more systematically about the structuring of social relations, in and out of scientific practice'.[20] To some extent, this was the case, Bob having enthusiastically reviewed Braverman's *Labour and Monopoly Capital* (1974) in the preceding issue of *RSJ*.[21] But as Werskey indicated, further detailed research on the history of science as social relations was still required from the end of the 1970s and Braverman's insights did not sustain the field on the right [or left] track as Shapin's subsequent appraisal suggests.

This brings us to the question of the legacy of the *Science is social relations* invocation and here I can offer a few rather inconclusive suggestions. Bob's own C21 assessment might be a good place to begin. As the comment quoted above from the introduction to this text on his website registers, he assessed that the argument of the article had been 'influential in the development of the social constructionist way of seeing science and all forms of expertise.' But he also reflected that: 'most social constructionists omit the radical science perspective'. The personal, political and historical background to Bob's appraisal is complex and beyond the scope of my undertaking here. Nevertheless, I would dare to offer my own reflection that basically Bob was right on both counts. The '*Science is social relations*' argument does provide a crucial underpinning for social constructionist analyses of science, technology and medicine. However, as he himself recognised, Bob's contribution to such perspectives has not been adequately acknowledged.

Bob declaring the significance of his contributions to sociological and historical studies of science and lamenting the field's failures to acknowledge them is a pattern that was experienced and repeated in many contexts. Indeed, as others have noted, Bob continually felt undervalued by the academic community of history and social studies of science and technology.[22] It is beyond my remit and capacity to unravel the complex reasons for this. Bob bristled easily and tended to decide quickly that you were either for or against him. He was scathing and often dismissive in his judgments of the academic world he left behind - particularly of the history of science and Darwinian studies. But, as many evaluations and testimonials make clear, his challenges spurred on and reshaped the field.[23] Indeed, some of the most interesting reviews of his work and testimonials to his accomplishments have highlighted and probed aspects of this pattern.

While I retrospectively endorse Bob's broad-based conclusions and leave it to others to undertake more detailed investigations of his academic legacy, I shall finish with a few general observations about the significance of this particular essay.

1   '*Science is social relations*' – was a powerful rallying call. Nevertheless, if Bob would forgive this rather capitalist and now somewhat dated metaphor, it was and, perhaps remains, something of a blank cheque. It *could* and probably continues to haunt, inform, and encourage those setting out to critically analyse science, technology, and medicine. However – crucially, it does not chart how to proceed in doing this.

2   Perhaps it is the emphasis and tone of Bob's injunction which matters most. The article makes it clear that there is a lot at stake in understanding, working in, and living with science, technology, and medicine. The tone of Bob's injunction and the substance of the piece cautions against versions of, encounters with, and interpretations of science which deny or lose sight of the social and the political – becoming positivistic,

scientistic, technocratic, etc. To adapt Shapin's terminology – it cautions against forms of 'purification' both within science and within science studies.[24] We might be mindful here of Steven Shapin and Simon Schaffer's concluding comments in *Leviathan and the Air Pump: Hobbes, Boyle and the Experimental Life*: 'The language that transports politics outside of science is precisely what we need to understand and explain'.[25] In this sense, *Science is social relations is* a cry of outrage, but it is one that is too important to be dismissed as *merely* 'outrageous'.

Notes

1 Gary Werskey, 'The Marxist critique of capitalist science: a history in three movements?', *Science as Culture* (2007) 16, no. 4 (December): 438.
2 R. M. Young, http://psychoanalysis-and-therapy.com/human_nature/paper/index.hmtl.
3 Roger Smith, 'Robert M. Young: Science historian and Darwin scholar who wielded great influence on the cultural left', *Independent* (19 August 2019). See his essay in this volume.
4 R. M. Young, 'Science *is* social relations', *Radical Science Journal* (1977) 5: 66.
5 R. M. Young, *Mind, Brain, and Adaptation in the Nineteenth Century: Cerebral Localization and Its Biological Context from Gall to Ferrier.* Oxford: Clarendon Press, 1970.
6 Young, 'Science *is* social relations', p. 67.
7 Werskey, 'The Marxist critique of capitalist science', p. 438.
8 James A. Secord, 'Revolutions in the head: Darwin, Malthus and Robert M. Young', *The British Journal for the History of Science* (2021), no. 54: p. 51.
9 Young, 'Science is social relations', p. 72.
10 The Radical Science Journal Collective, 'Science, technology, medicine and the socialist movement', *Radical Science Journal* (1981) 11: 3–70.
11 R.M. Young, 'The historiographic and ideological contexts of the nineteenth-century debate on man's place in nature', in M.Teich and R.M.Young (eds) *Changing Perspectives in the History of Science: Essays in Honour of Joseph Needham*. London: Heinemann, 1973, pp. 344–438.
12 The Lucas Industrial Plan was a proposal produced in 1976 by Lucas Aerospace workers lead by the shop steward, Mike Cooley. Addressing the threat of layoffs, the proposal entailed detailed plans to convert the activities of the company from arms production to socially useful products and to thereby save jobs. Although never adopted by Lucas Aerospace, the plan was widely discussed and influential within the radical science movement and in diverse political settings (including the Greater London Council) in the late 1970s.
13 Teich and Young, *Changing Perspectives in the History of Science. Essays in Honour of Joseph Needham*. London: Heinemann, 1973 (1973b). Introduction in *Changing Perspectives in the History of Science: Essays in Honour of Joseph Needham*, pp. ix–xxi.
14 Teich and Young, *Changing Perspectives in the History of Science*, pp. 418–419.
15 Young, 'The historiographic and ideological contexts', p. 355.
16 S. Shapin, 'Discipline and bounding: the history and sociology of science as seen through the externalism—internalism debate', *History of Science* (1992) XXX: p. 357.
17 Werskey, 'The Marxist critique of capitalist science', p. 418–19.
18 Secord, 'Revolutions in the head'.

19 R. M. Young, 'Natural theology, Victorian periodicals, and the fragmentation of a common context' (1985, lst published, 1973), in Robert M. Young, *Darwin's Metaphor: Nature's Place in Victorian Culture*. Cambridge: Cambridge University Press, 1985, pp. 128–129.

20 The Radical Science Journal Collective, 'Science, technology, medicine and the socialist movement', p. 38; quoted in Werskey, p. 437.

21 Bob Young, 'Labour and Monopoly Capital', Harry Braverman [review], *Radical Science Journal* (1976) 4: 81–93.

22 M. Ruse, 'Robert M. Young and Darwin studies', *Free Associations* (2020), 80, pp. 43–45, Secord, 'Revolutions in the head'.

23 Ruse, 'Robert M. Young', Secord, 'Revolutions in the head'. Smith, An obituary.

24 Shapin, 'Discipline and bounding'.

25 S. Shapin and S. Schaffer, *Leviathan and the Air Pump: Hobbes, Boyle and the Experimental Life*. Princeton: Princeton University Press, 1985, p.342.

Chapter 7

"Let's move on"

Bob Young's contribution to radical science concepts and practices

Les Levidow

"Let's move on" is a memorable phrase from Bob's comments in group discussions and articles. The phrase combined a friendly invitation with a sometimes scary challenge to contest and abandon conventional concepts. They were perpetuating systems of capitalist domination, variously disguised as neutral objectivity, as the natural order, as technoscientific progress, etc. His invitation meant a joint task to substitute different concepts and practices prefiguring a post-capitalist society. This meant collectively creating pathways and methods for such a future, while addressing anxieties about uncertainties.

'Move on' arose especially in discussions within the Radical Science Collective. The same phrase began his 1977 essay, 'Science *is* social relations', where he enjoined readers[1]:

> It is time to move on both in theory and in practice. ... It is time that our theories and our lives expressed struggle towards socialism and prefigured that social order in the process.

Social order? Even for its advocates, a move towards a future socialist order was experienced as potential disorder – at once exhilarating and frightening. To inspire a transitional process, Bob formulated several aphorisms, e.g. 'Make political work relations more personal *and* personal relations more political', and 'Prefigure the ends in the means'.[2] As pithy observations, these aphorisms were at once insightful, stirring and unnerving, as noted by Maureen McNeil (this volume).

Bob's phrase 'move on' expressed a close engagement with his colleagues, readers, societal change and practices seeking to prefigure post-capitalist futures. In Gary Werskey's history of radical science generations as 'three movements', he compared Bob Young's role with J.D. Bernal's prominent role in the 1930s movement. Gary reflected on this role as follows[3]:

> As a thinker and writer on often highly abstruse subjects, Young had the gift of being clear and entertaining enough to keep you hard at

DOI: 10.4324/9781003204244-10

work trying to follow him. He could, by turns, also be disarming or – to some – intrusive in his personal revelations of weakness or confusion, or confronting when enjoining his readers to 'move on' with him. However, the deeper hallmark of his style was that of a perpetual dialogue between, himself, his material, and his audience about how we might make more sense of the world/ourselves, in order to change the world/ourselves for the better. Young's texts are nearly always presented as unfinished, open-ended, and – while not inconclusive – never at rest. For those looking for definitive answers and certain foundations, his approach was bound to frustrate. But he could not be more encouraging of the need for others to criticize and join him in thinking important subjects through to better conclusions, however interim.

For the aim of moving on, Bob initiated or facilitated in several collective projects:

- The *Radical Science Journal (RSJ)* Collective, later extended to the journal *Science as Culture* with its Editorial Board.
- RSJ seminars as interventions within the wider radical science movement, especially the British Society for Social Responsibility in Science (BSSRS) and its various thematic working groups.
- The Publications Distribution Cooperative (PDC), established jointly by radical periodicals for ensuring their distribution in bookshops, playing this crucial role for a couple decades.
- *Crucible*: Channel 4 documentary series on technoscientific issues with an accompanying Pan Books series in the early 1980s (e.g. *The Gene Business*).
- Free Association Books (FAB), whose name linked Freud's key methodological concept with Marx's reference to communism as 'the free association of the producers'. FAB published books especially on psychoanalytic and radical science themes.
- *Free Associations* journal, linking various critical psychoanalytic perspectives and eventually the stimulating annual conferences on Psychoanalysis and the Public Sphere.
- All these initiatives were opportunities for developing or promoting critical analyses of capitalist science, anti-capitalist alternatives and practices.

Radical science as engagement with Marxist traditions

Bob's writings analysed how professional knowledge embodied societal values and power structures while disguising them through various appeals to scientific objectivity, technological progress and human nature. He analysed their philosophical basis in a Cartesian dualism which conceptually separated the rational mind from physical nature. Hence, he highlighted the paradox that a non-spatial mind somehow knows a spatial world (Smith, this volume). As Bob understood, 'Values vanish into this ideological universe, becoming invisible as they are absorbed into nature, including the nature of things', as noted by Karl Figlio (this volume).

So he sought means to contest stereotypical binaries – such as mind/body and fact/value – as both practices and ideas.[4] Looking beyond representational mystifications, he argued that ideological roles are institutionally embedded and reproduced. Indeed, ideology derives from everyday practices. As he argued, effective opposition had to go beyond even the most critical philosophy.

De-naturalising value systems meant disrupting everyday institutional practices. This awareness stimulated Bob's political-intellectual engagement with Marxist concepts in order to deploy them strategically. To facilitate moving on with colleagues, he extended and linked three Marxist traditions: Critical Theory, labour process perspectives, and psychoanalytic Marxism. Let us consider each in turn.

Critical Theory: reification and fetishism

The term 'libertarian Marxism' has been used to encompass a wide range of Left-wing movements and ideas over several decades. It encompasses 1920s anti-Stalinist Communists (especially the ideas of Karl Korsch and Antonio Gramsci), the Frankfurt School's Critical Theory (including theories of Herbert Marcuse, as well as Horkheimer & Adorno),[5] Italian workerists & autonomists, the latter sometimes called autonomous Marxism. In each historical period, those movements and theorists opposed authoritarian agendas imitating the physical-biological sciences, invoking their putative objectivity and justifying capitalist work discipline – all in the name of Marxism.[6]

To counter authoritarian agendas, those movements revived Marx's dual concepts of reification and fetishism. As Bob noted, 'demystification of science entails the demystification of its reifications'.[7] Marx had theorised reification and then fetishism as follows:

> A definite social relation between people assumes the fantastic form of a relation between things.... This fetishism of commodities has its origin in the peculiar social character of the labour that produced them.[8]

Indeed, for Marx, these phenomena were not illusory misrepresentations of reality. Rather, they were reproduced in everyday practices, especially in commodity exchange, which structured waged-labour exploitation by extracting surplus value. This insight informed Bob's inquiry into capitalist metaphors in scientific concepts. Applying Marx's concepts to technoscientific production, he analysed facts as fetishised forms of human labour. Rather than inquire whether facts are true, as in empiricist philosophy, he changed the question. For example: What social values become embodied (and thus fetishised) as properties of things? How does scientific knowledge reify relations between people as relations between things? As a political task, then, how can collective action de-fetishise and de-reify scientific knowledge?

Together we posed such questions as tasks for the radical science movement and beyond. These questions stimulated our interest in the labour process as the form and role of technoscientific production.

Labour process perspectives: capitalist relations within forces of production

Drawing on various traditions since Marx's *Capital*, Harry Braverman elaborated a labour process perspective to analyse contemporary capitalist agendas for restructuring production, work and everyday life.[9] This approach was taken up systematically by the Conference of Socialist Economists (CSE) as the basis for a research agenda which included a study group, booklets, journal articles and books.[10]

From the RSJ Collective's engagement with the CSE, together we analysed changes in physical production systems within a global restructuring agenda. Then we extended this perspective to technoscientific activity and concepts. These more subtly embedded capitalist aims and designs through capitalist social relations, e.g. hierarchal division of labour, intellectual property, customer-contract principle, etc.[11]

Our perspective inverted key concepts, especially 'forces and relations of production', as they were commonly understood. According to the dominant Left formulations within Stalinism and Social Democracy alike, capitalist social relations of production were external constraints on inherently progressive forces of production, reductively equated with technology. By contrast, we investigated how capitalist social relations were designed within and manifested as forces of production, which Marx understood broadly as 'the general intelligence'. Such forces included: new knowledge-systems for both expelling and disciplining labour, the new international division of labour, Taylorised professional labour, digital-financial metaphors of nature, etc. This critical perspective opened up questions about how non-capitalist social relations could redesign the forces of production through different metaphors of nature.

Psychoanalytic Marxism

Conventional Marxism generally presumed a rational model of humanity. It attributed capitalist ideology to 'false consciousness' or irrationality as misperceptions of reality. For example, individual competition obscured collective interests, and racial or ethnic divisions obscured class interests. This rationalist diagnosis warranted more effective ways to 'expose' capitalist ideology as misperceptions.

Looking more deeply, psychoanalytic Marxism has sought to understand how capitalist social relations become internalised and naturalised within everyday emotional life, in ways which generally remain elusive or hidden. As this perspective suggests, capitalist value systems become naturalised through subconscious processes, which can be understood through various psychoanalytic concepts. Bob cited Habermas: 'Psychoanalysis is relevant to us as the only tangible example of a science incorporating methodical self-reflection'.[12]

As one entry point, an early contribution came from Joel Kovel.[13] He combined political theory and Freudian psychoanalytic concepts to illuminate his patients' insights. He analysed how capitalist oppression was internalised in everyday emotional lives along class, race, and gender lines.

Bob found more helpful the Kleinian theory of object relations, emphasising projective identification and splitting.[14] Regardless of which theory was elaborated, psychoanalytic writers sometimes succumbed to the same scientism underpinning other knowledges; they slipped into a reductionist, trans-historical reification of human nature. Bob readily applied his critical insights to such loss of critical perspective (Figlio, this volume). Highlighting historical change, he identified political-economic drivers which were being implicitly served, disguised and naturalised.

Building on the legacies in the 1980s

Bob invited us to 'move on' by developing and linking the three Marxist traditions outlined above. By doing so, the RSJ Collective abandoned various conceptual obstacles and diversions. We criticised banal binaries, e.g. between use/abuse (of science), externalist/internalist approaches, science/ ideology, fact/value, etc.[15] Likewise, we moved on beyond epistemological battles about the truth of scientific knowledge. Instead our revived Marxist concepts provided a stronger basis for engaging with new capitalist strategies and anti-capitalist revolt.

That re-orientation led us to these trans-historical observations about historical change:

- Historical change (especially class struggle) is the motor of technology, whose design and artefacts embody historically specific value choices.
- Nature likewise is always an historical category yet is portrayed as eternal.
- Natural science (like nature itself) entails historically specific categories and social relation, which become reified as the 'objectivity' of scientists.
- Scientific concepts are products of labour processes and are thereby shaped by its social relations.

Accordingly, 'moving on' meant identifying recent political-economic changes within those historical processes.[16] In particular, we recognised the following trends:

- The current historical phase features greater capitalist reconstitution of science and technology, being jointly redesigned to restructure global economies and thus strengthen capitalist domination.
- Key areas of capitalist restructuring (ICTs, biotechnology, reproductive technology, reparative medicine, etc.) are being promoted and portrayed as technological process, conflated with societal progress.
- Capitalist domination has new forms setting narrower limits on the scope for relative academic freedom.
- Class struggle increasingly centres on capitalist restructuring: people resist while potentially creating alternative technological designs and concepts of Nature.

From those trends, we tried to engage more effectively with professional experts, critics of technoscientific developments and resistance movements.

Today's legacies of the radical science movement

Four decades later, 'the radical science movement' is remembered as such by few people. Nevertheless, its insights (especially Bob's contributions) remain more relevant than ever before. They resonate with new critics targeting an ever-wider range of technoscientific innovations as deceptive or oppressive. As critics emphasise, such innovations are variously designed to exploit waged labour and fragment people into individual consumers. Such innovations today include: mass surveillance being justified as 'security', the gig economy justified as 'self-employment', the 'internet of things' justified as individual freedom, etc.

In the past decade, a critical network has been *Breaking the Frame*. Its name echoes the original Luddites who sabotaged weaving frames which were degrading craft skills and then faced heavy penalties from the 1812 Frame Breaking Act. Likewise, the name contests the dominant frame of technoscientific progress in today's capitalist strategies. The group has held numerous events engaging with various social movements and opposition campaigns.[17] In particular, it has recovered the historical memory of the 1970s effort by Lucas Aerospace workers to shift the company's priorities towards socially useful production and employment; such events have stimulated debate on analogous efforts today.[18]

In many such campaigns and critiques, there are echoes of ideas from the radical science movement, even if it's unclear by what trajectory they forged such links. Alongside such continuity, however, earlier critical concepts have become fragmented by campaigns separately targeting each technoscientific development. Thereby lost is Bob's agenda to integrate critical concepts: libertarian, labour process and psychoanalytic.

Many historical resonances are apparent likewise in the academic field of Science & Technology Studies (STS), especially given the radical politics that originally motivated some STS academics. Werskey noted wider intellectual contributions from the radical science movement but also its practical limitations since the 1980s neoliberal assault[19]:

> While some of the movement's ideas and projects – stripped of their theoretical moorings and political critique – have since moved into the mainstream of STS and science policymakers, they were rarely seen on scholarly and political agendas twenty-five years ago. It is also important to acknowledge that the RSJ programme was only a prolegomena to a more adequately theorized and rigorously applied framework for theoretical and agitational work, which never materialized.

As an important sequel, STS scholars have been analysing how neoliberal technoscience extends capitalist social relations to more areas of everyday life and living matter.[20] Scholars have been designing critical research with opposition movements and discussing strategies for such collaborations.[21] Sometimes called the 'New STS', academic-activist joint efforts have been reported in the journal *Engaging Science Technology and Society* (ESTS).[22]

In 2019, North American activists relaunched the organisation and magazine *Science for the People* from three decades earlier. As its first new issue emphasised, critiques and resistance have always contested science, sometimes shaping its trajectory. This caveat echoed earlier lessons[23]:

> .... a radical analysis must not theorize strategy in isolation from radical critiques of science's applications, epistemic features, and material basis. What is to be done can be realistically decided only by accepting an important lesson of critique: that the way to understand the different parts of science, and therefore to *change* them, is to understand the whole of science, particularly its integration in global systems of power and capital.

Hence, 'a radical analysis must offer lessons for how to transform science in a revolutionary direction'.

As these recent developments indicate, there will be more opportunities to recover and extend radical science legacies, including efforts to learn lessons from past advances and setbacks. From such analysis, we can better 'move on', as Bob had urged.

Notes

1 R. M. Young, Science is social relations, *Radical Science Journal* (1977) 5: 65, http://www.psychoanalysis-and-therapy.com/human_nature/papers/sisr.html.

2 Young, Science is social relations, pp. 99, 101.
3 G. Werskey, The Marxist critique of capitalist science: a history in three movements, *Science as Culture* (2007) 16(4): 435.
4 R. M. Young, Darwinism is social, in D. Kohn, ed., *The Darwinian Heritage.* Princeton and Nova Pacifica, 1985, pp. 609–638, http://www.psychoanalysis-and-therapy.com/human_nature/papers/paper60.html.
5 M. Horkheimer & T. Adorno, *The Dialectic of Enlightenment.* Redwood City, CA: Stanford University Press, 1972.
6 L. Levidow and L. Pellizoni, Technoscience: divergent Marxist perspectives, in *The Sage Handbook of Marxism*, edited by Beverley Skeggs, Sara R. Farris, Alberto Toscano. London: Routledge, 2021. Chapter 51 (pp. 940–58), https://www.researchgate.net/publication/343501514_Technoscience_divergent_Marxist_perspectives
7 Young, Science is social relations, p. 71.
8 K. Marx, *Capital: A Critique of Political Economy.* Vol. 1. Translated by Ben Fowkes. New York: Penguin, 1985, p. 165.
9 H. Braverman, *Labour and Monopoly Capital.* New York: Monthly Review Press, 1976.
10 CSE. 1976. *The Labour Process and Class Strategies.* London: Conference of Socialist Economists, 1976.
11 RSJ Collective. 1981. Science, technology, medicine and the socialist movement, *Radical Science Journal* 11: 3–70, http://www.psychoanalysis-and-therapy.com/human_nature/papers/pap100.html.
12 R. M. Young, Whatever happened to human nature? Chapter 1 of *Whatever Happened To Human Nature?*, (1997), http://www.psychoanalysis-and-therapy.com/human_nature/human/chap1.html.
13 Young, Whatever happened to human nature?
14 J. Kovel, The Marxist view of man and psychoanalysis, *Social Research* (1976) 43(2): 220–245; J. Kovel, *The Radical Spirit: Essays on Psychoanalysis and Society.* London: Free Association Books, 1988; J. Kovel & I. Craib, Marxism and psychoanalysis – an exchange, *Radical Philosophy* 55 (Summer 1990). https://www.radicalphilosophy.com/article/marxism-and-psychoanalysis-an-exchange.
15 D. King & L. Levidow, Introduction: contesting science and technology, from the 1970s to the present, *Science as Culture* (2016) 25(3): 367–372.
16 RSJ Collective.
17 Radical Science and Alternative Technology: From the 70s to the Present, Breaking the Frame conference, 2015. http://breakingtheframe.org.uk/radical-science-and-alternativetechnology-april-11th-2015.
18 Celebrating the Fortieth Anniversary of the Lucas Plan, Breaking the Frame national conference, 2016. http://breakingtheframe.org.uk/lucas-plan/.
19 Werskey, The Marxist critique of capitalist science, p. 440.
20 D. L. Kleinman and K. Moore, *Routledge Handbook of Science, Technology, and Society*, 2014; L. Pellizzoni and M. Ylönen, *Neoliberalism and Technoscience: Critical Assessments.* Farnham/Burlington, VT: Ashgate, 2012.
21 K. Moore, Capitalisms, generative projects, and the New STS, *Science as Culture* 30(1): 58–73, special Forum, 'From Radical Science to STS'
22 A. Kinchy, STS currents against the "anti-science" tide, *Engaging Science Technology and Society* (2020) 6: 76–80, https://estsjournal.org/index.php/ests/article/view/305/211; L. Levidow, *Science as Culture, EASST Review*, February 2018: 25–30, https://www.easst.net/article/science-as-culture/
23 H. Zhao, What is a radical analysis of science? *Science for the People* (2019) 22(1), The Return of Radical Science, https://magazine.scienceforthepeople.org/vol22-1/what-is-a-radical-analysis-of-science/.

Part 3

Psychoanalysis

Chapter 8

Bob Young and the Free Associations project

A personal recollection

Barry Richards

I offer some observations on Bob Young's work as editor, publisher and author in leading a project which sought to expand the influence of psycho-analysis beyond its base in small clinically-focussed networks. The project involved contributing to a new space that was opening in intellectual culture in the 1970s and 1980s, in which earlier efforts to bring psychoanalytically-based knowledge to bear on the study of society, culture and politics were starting points for wide-ranging enquiries. This was done in a spirit of strong engagement, professionally, culturally and politically, and also involved a reflexive consideration of psychoanalysis and its clinical practices in their social contexts. These observations are drawn mainly from my involvement in that project from the late 1970s to the early 2000s. There will be other, different evaluations of that project, and of Bob himself. The account here is based only on my direct personal experience, though I hope it adds a little texture to this particular piece of intellectual and social history.

In one of the autobiographical illustrations which Bob sometimes used in his writing, he recalled a young man whose piety might surprise some of those who knew him later[1]:

> You can imagine what a shock it was for me to go East to university (1749 miles from home) and be told in a course on religion that the Gospels contained innumerable inconsistencies. I took the trouble to go up after the first lecture when this was said and patiently explained to the pro-fessor that he was mistaken, since every word in the Bible was true. He was unshaken and gentle, and I spent a difficult period reconstituting my world-view to make allowance for uncertainty and mixed opinions.

This poignant picture of him as an earnest young Christian reminds us of how far the social and cultural journey of his life took him, from Presbyte-rian Dallas to psychoanalytic Islington, and suggests that in parts at least the journey was a painful one. Sixty years later, he still insisted on exactly how far away from home he had been then and how unprepared for the world.

DOI: 10.4324/9781003204244-12

When I first encountered him, he seemed formidably prepared, standing with a clear sense of purpose on the platform of intellectual authority which he had built at Cambridge. This was around 1976, when I joined the *Radical Science Journal* (*RSJ*) Collective. It had been publishing its journal since 1974, but like many 'collectives', it was not the internally levelled group which the name implies. Bob was clearly its nucleus and leader, even though some of the members were senior academics with strong reputations.

Some people experienced the Texan largeness of his presence as indicating self-importance. And on occasion, he was more than capable of pointing out his achievements. At the very large conference of the new Socialist Society in London in 1981, when Bob was working on the *Crucible* series of TV science programmes, he stood up and, following the convention of floor speakers introducing themselves, said 'I'm Bob Young, I'm a TV mogul'. The humour of the delivery was lost on most people there, who would have heard the self-congratulation and missed any element of self-parody. In general, however, in the contexts in which I knew him, it seemed to me that Bob was more interested in being right than in being admired by others. Being right, that is, not so much in the sense of scholarly accuracy, though that was part of it, but in the moral sense. Being right in that way probably brought from his superego much of the admiration he needed.

The breadth and depth of his erudition as a scholar, writer and teacher has been much remarked on, and this was manifest not only in scholarly publications and presentations, but how, for example in his many spontaneous asides in seminars or informal discussions, he might capture something essential and telling about a particular theory or writer. His powerful intellectual searchlight could be quickly trained on a concept, illuminating it from different historical and philosophical angles. If he was doing this partly to perform, as erudition may sometimes be used, the performance passed me by, as I was noting how helpful it was for those of his listeners who were trying to get a better understanding of things, and how Bob's contributions – which did not feel like condescension, nor attempts to control the discussion – routinely brought succinctness, clarity and depth to group discussions and to my own thinking, whether I agreed with them or not.

His need to be on the side of moral rightness, and the starkness with which he might at times define where the right side lay, was one of the factors which led him into conflict with others, or at least created distance between him and them. It certainly did not win him much goodwill, and it gave grief to some of those whom he saw as somehow falling short of his standards. In this, he was perhaps an example of the radical dissenter whose authoritarian part of the superego arrived at the barricades ready for service in the struggle against authoritarianism.

The *RSJ* Collective, as a cultural and intellectual space created and curated by Bob, had an open-ended and open-minded feel, but this was very much within the parameters of 1970s dissident subcultures. The then widespread capture of idealism and curiosity by Marxist or para-Marxist outlooks meant that the pursuit of moral or intellectual depth was typically fused with Marxist militancy, and so was snared within the factionalism of radical politics. The *RSJ* was part of the then-burgeoning radical science movement, of which the major part was the British Society for Social Responsibility in Science and its journal *Science for People*. The *RSJ* was the very radical part of this radical wing of the British intelligentsia; it was based around the idea that science was much more radically shaped by its social context than most of its social critics believed. The BSSRS critique tended to focus on how the applications of science and its research priorities were determined by particular political and business interests, and so were complicit in exploitative and oppressive practices. *RSJ*, however, saw the imprint of capitalism at a deeper, epistemological level, in the formation of its very concepts; the journal's position was summed up in a claim reflecting Bob's previous work at Cambridge on the history of science: 'science *is* social relations'.

In the political context of the time, such differences of understanding took on a factional quality, and the *RSJ* Collective probably had, in its experience of itself, a sense of privileged insight and integrity. However, it was a creative and diverse group, and rather than ossify itself inside its initial terms of reference, whereby it would surely have disappeared within a few years, it underwent a mitosis in 1983–84, with the emergence of the journal *Free Associations* and the transition of the *RSJ* into the more richly titled *Science as Culture*. In edition number 6/7 of the *RSJ*, in 1983, four members of the group had written an essay review of Juliet Mitchell's landmark book *Psychoanalysis and Feminism*.[2] Thus, psychoanalysis made an appearance on the radical science stage; it was not likely to prosper there, and the following year saw the launch of *Free Associations,* both as a special issue of *RSJ* and as the pilot issue of itself.

This creation of the *Free Associations* journal came about through a combination of three factors. First, the idea of using psychoanalysis to understand society, politics and culture was beginning to flourish, especially in the USA (in the works of Christopher Lasch, Norman O. Brown, Russell Jacoby, Joel Kovel, Victor Wolfenstein, Jean Bethke Elshtain, Bruce Brown, Eli Zaretsky and others), though with Mitchell's work and that of Michael Schneider in Germany amongst other very important contributions. This employment of psychoanalysis outside the clinic was not a new idea, of course, but a radical return to Freud, to a particular Freud, the one of his *Group Psychology* essay, and of *Civilisation and its Discontents*. And it was a return to Freud equipped with a sympathetic feminism and with political sensibilities shaped by the Vietnam War, the Cold War and the deepening of consumer culture. Second, within the RSJ Collective, a subgroup had formed of people for whom psychoanalysis was a central or major concern (Karl Figlio, Les Levidow, Barry Richards, Tony Solomonides, Margot

Waddell and Bob Young). Third, one of those people, Bob himself, had the vision, energy and resource required to imagine a new journal, defining a new field, and to set about creating it. Once this was underway, the *FAs* editorial group (those above with the addition of Paul Hoggett and of Joel Kovel as transatlantic member) separated out from the RSJ Collective (though some retained membership of both as *RSJ* morphed into *SaC*).

Bob was at the helm of both journals, which corresponded to the two major territories in which he spent his intellectual life. Although he continued to think and write about the topics in the history and philosophy of science around which his academic reputation had been made, my guess was that his intellectual centre of gravity, while always located on human nature and how we know it, had by this point shifted to back to his early interest in psychoanalysis, seeded in his time at Rochester Medical School by psychoanalytic psychiatrists there. He was about to move into clinical work by becoming a psychoanalytic psychotherapist, and the *Free Associations* journal was to be central to the intellectual, cultural and political project of which he was the major initiator and leader from the early 1980s onwards.

He continued to practice psychotherapy for the rest of his working life. After around 20 years of the journal, he listed the articles, by various authors, which he was 'most proud to have published' in *FAs*.[3] Nearly all were on clinical topics, broadly speaking, were written by practitioners, and could have appeared in clinical journals. The clinical domain was clearly of great importance to him, as a space for the relief of individual suffering. Inevitably perhaps, given his level of engagement in it, the clinical world was also where his impulse towards confrontation with the 'establishment' sometimes found most active expression, and where his interest in the psychodynamics of organisations and groups was sometimes deployed in combative mode. Nonetheless, Bob's commitment to clinical work was as far as I could see an expression of his fundamental humanism, of belief in a common humanity and in the power of selfhood.

There was no obvious continuity or necessary link between the *RSJ* agenda on the one hand, and the *FAs* mission of developing a socially engaged psychoanalysis on the other. But there was a common element between the two journals, which was Marxism, though rather loosely speaking since as far as I knew we were mostly not intellectual card-carriers (I for one was undertaking a slow process of disengagement from the Marxist canon). Bob's use of the (arguably oxymoronic) term 'libertarian Marxism' was one way at the time of connoting the broad tent within which we gathered. And since our aim was to bring psychoanalysis into dialogue with analyses of contemporary society and its politics, we were bound to pay very close attention to the body of Freudo-Marxist scholarship, since that had been by far the most extensive previous attempt to bring together the insights of psychoanalysis with those of social, political and cultural critique. Our return to Freud was therefore often through the Frankfurt School, though crucially, some key authors such as Christopher Lasch were outside the Marxist tradition.

At the time, Marxism was a strong and direct influence in the higher education sector in Britain, at least in those departments where psychoanalysis might gain a foothold, namely those of the SSH (social sciences and humanities) disciplines. Yet often the Marxists were the most dismissive of 'bourgeois' psychoanalysis. So to be a Left Freudian was a double alienation, in which one was at odds both with the world and with most of those who for similar reasons to oneself were also at odds with the world. On top of that (and not to mention the splits amongst Marxists), there were amongst Left Freudians deep divisions between humanists and post-structuralists, between people of Lacanian, Kleinian and/or object relations, and Jungian persuasions, and (to a lesser degree) between those with clinical and welfare-oriented interests on the one hand, and on the other those interested in film, literature and other cultural matters (which was not quite the same as the clinician/academic divide). So the scope for factional splitting in this intellectually 'intersectional' world was considerable.

However, it was my experience that these divisions did not, in the early years at least, take up much time or energy in the work of the Free Associations project, by which I mean not only *FAs* the journal, but also Free Association Books, and the many activities and events which went on around the journal and the book publishing, especially the annual 'Psychoanalysis and the Public Sphere' conferences at the University of East London from 1985 to 1997. (Near the end of his life Bob, with Kurt Jacobsen, was working on a plan to renew these, and in September 2019 they resumed annually in collaboration with Ivan Ward at the Freud Museum.) In the *FAs* editorial group, which was both an editorial group and for some years a reading group, there was no sense of an 'us' as the true defenders of the faith.

We were certainly not without commitment to the societal importance of the ideas we discussed, wrote about and published, nor were we especially virtuous. So the absence of a bunker or sanctum mentality may have been due partly to the fact that the conditions for corrosive intellectual competition were not met. We were in a field that was just opening up, and there was plenty of territory to be claimed, and bandwidth available, to accommodate all of the relatively small number of activists in the field. We were also not numerous enough to populate camps of sharply defined competitor groups.

Moreover, there was a widely shared reason, amongst ourselves and others in the field, for becoming involved with psychoanalysis, which may have sustained sufficient sense of common purpose to limit fragmentation. As Bob wrote, many had 'come to psychoanalysis as the last refuge of the disappointed radical or revolutionary', after the failure of the 1960s protest movements to change the world politically by leading to a dismantling of capitalism. Undoubtedly, many more personal issues were involved in the turn to psychoanalysis, but those were coated with a broadly unifying political rationale. Perhaps also any practical and political implications of some of the doctrinal differences within psychoanalysis had not clearly emerged, especially in what was a period of deep flux and re-alignment in British politics, as de-industrialisation and neo-liberalism were re-shaping British society.

Another factor acting against any tendency to a factionalist outlook on the part of the *FAs* group more specifically was in a key difference from the *RSJ* Collective. Not only was there no specific shared political ideology, there was also no core position on or in psychoanalysis which the journal embodied. Bob Young was foundational to the whole thing, as he had been for *RSJ*, with his intellectual vitality and depth, his networks, and not least the resources of Free Association Books, the London publishing house that he had established in the physical space which was previously the office base for his time as a 'TV mogul'. But there was no psychoanalytic equivalent of his radical take on the philosophy of science as a defining principle on which the journal was built. Bob recommended that we all should 'hold our concepts loosely and wear them lightly.'[4]

So *FAs* was able to respond to and accommodate creative and insightful work on the many fronts where it was beginning to emerge, and individuals within the editorial group were able to develop their own work, as contributions to the Free Associations project, in different directions. In my case that meant exploring how psychoanalytic insights might be integrated with sociological and political analyses other than Marxist ones; I think Bob was more amongst those who remained in pursuit of psychoanalysis as a last-hope remedy for the shortcomings of revolutionary theory.[5]

At least one important thing was however shared within the *FAs* group: a sense of being part of a path-breaking enterprise. It was an exciting experience, to be active in this small but colourful space in which we felt we were making a substantial contribution to the promotion of contemporary psychoanalysis not just in academia but in intellectual culture more broadly. That project necessarily involved seeking to stimulate change in the psychoanalytic community, by encouraging clinicians to apply their understandings of people to phenomena outside the consulting room, and also to consider and critique the social contexts and functioning of psychoanalysis itself, whether as therapeutic practice or as a form of knowledge. *FAs* was at least as well networked in the London-centred psychoanalytic community as it was in the more dispersed community of academic promoters of psychoanalysis.

While indebted to Freudo-Marxism and other forerunners, this promotion of contemporary psychoanalysis was something new. At a broad sociological level, it was part of the increasingly 'therapeutic' culture that was by the 1980s becoming well established at least in societies of the West. Central to this important cultural shift, which continues globally today, is the wide prevalence of a psychological orientation to everyday life, particularly in concerns with emotional experience, personal relationships, personal histories, and the prospects for emotional growth and repair. It is evident across tracts of popular culture, many professional and organisational practices, and the SSH disciplines in academia. It is visible in the huge growth in 'talking treatments' of all sorts since the 1960s. For those of us with belief in the validity and importance of psychoanalytic understandings of human nature (which, as Bob would insist, is our historically contingent 'second nature'), the influence of those understandings in the shaping of therapeutic culture ought to be as great as possible. In mental health interventions, psychoanalytic sensibilities and skills can help to reduce the suffering of individuals and families, while the key ideas of psychoanalytic theory can deepen both elite and popular discourses about who we are and what kinds of society we might hope for.

So there was and is a lot at stake, albeit indirectly. The Free Associations project was one of the first strands in what is now a vast and variegated global fabric of activities exploring and supporting applications of psychoanalytic thought. It contributed through its publications to the development of psychoanalytically-based practices in clinical and organisational settings. It has also fed into changes within the psychoanalytic world, in which there is now much more sociological reflexivity and political consciousness than there was 40 years ago.

Alongside its contribution to these broad socio-cultural and professional spaces, the Free Associations project also played a part in the making of a new academic space. It contributed to the consolidation of psychosocial studies as a recognised area of interdisciplinary inquiry, one focussed on the integration of psychological knowledge with understandings based on the social sciences. Now formally embodied in the Association for Psychosocial Studies, this area had also first emerged circa 1983, in an undergraduate programme in the Sociology Department of the then North East London Polytechnic (later the University of East London), and there was considerable overlap of activity with *FAs*, particularly in the conferences mentioned above.

The Tavistock Clinic in London was a third organisational source of psychoanalytically-based psychosocial work, and had connections with both *FAs* and UEL. The development in 1992 of an MA in Psychoanalytic Studies between UEL and the Tavistock would probably not have happened without contextual momentum to which the Free Associations project made a big contribution.[6] And at the University of Essex, the establishment of a similar MA began a process of growth which, under the leadership of Karl Figlio, who was also key to the development of *FAs*, saw the creation of the Centre for Psychoanalytic Studies and eventually the Department of Psychosocial and Psychoanalytic Studies, with a number of undergraduate and postgraduate programmes. Not all psychosocial studies work is psychoanalytic; another theoretical approach in psychology may be used, as the complement to a social science input. But psychoanalysis in one form or another is a dominant influence.

So the Free Associations project had beneficial resonance with psychosocial developments in academia. And in Bob's conversation and writing, there was a strikingly ready binocularity, a fluent linking of attention to inner and outer worlds. He might often remark on an experience of his, or make a passing observation, in which the links between psyche and society seemed vivid. While this sometimes risked that his arguments would seem anecdotally based, his suggestion that biography should be a core method for the human sciences was strongly argued.[7] This suggestion has yet to be taken up more fully in the psychosocial field, though it is obviously in the individual life that the links between psyche and society (and soma) must ultimately be most clear and fundamental. If there were to be a biography of Bob, it would likely be a rich contribution to historiography, given the span of change around and within his life, and the intensity with which he embodied some of the forces which shaped his era, and the tensions between them.

While much of the work in psychosocial studies attempts to draw psychoanalysis into dialogue with sociological, political or cultural analysis, Bob's approach to psychoanalysis was shaped more by his work in the philosophy and history of science, and was driven by the wish to repair what he identified as a crucial deficit in scientific epistemology. In his book *Mental Space*, his main contribution to psychoanalytic thought, he explains how the physicalistic definition of 'space' provided by the Scientific Revolution restricted scientific investigation of the human subject to the body. While Cartesian dualism could acknowledge the realm of mind as different from matter, it 'leaves us with no language for speaking about mind.'[8] He saw object-relations psychoanalysis as able to provide such a language, and goes on in the book to argue that it can not only describe and illuminate the 'spaces' which mind occupies in its development and its relationships to others and to the world, but can also point to how the containing and facilitating functions of mental space may be strengthened.

Again, though here he rarely raises the flag of humanism as such, Bob the humanist speaks clearly in the book. He opens it with his critique of how positivistic science left no space for the lived experience of humanity, and ends it with the emphases on creative reparation and selfhood of a Winnicottian humanism. In his recurrent focus on the deleterious impact of scientism within psychoanalysis, Bob was a passionate endorser of Bettelheim's call to see the humanist in Freud's soul,[9] and wanted psychoanalysis to develop into a 'full-blooded humanism'. While deeply influenced by object-relations theory, he objected along with others to the terminology of 'objects'. His defence of the subject and its coherence, against postmodern claims that the subject was dead or illusory, was not worn lightly and was central to his thinking. The cultural and intellectual spaces which he created and supported as parts of the Free Associations project are the most obvious of his legacies, as they live on in their outputs and in the ongoing broader trends to which they have richly contributed. But in addition, a vital element in the content produced in those spaces, and something of broad and hopefully lasting significance, was his affirmation of a sophisticated and impassioned humanism.

Notes

1 R. M. Young, Fundamentalism and terrorism. *Free Associations* (2017) 71, 65–85.
2 M. Waddell, et al., Psychoanalysis, Marxism and feminism. *Radical Science Journal* (1983) 6/7, 107–117.
3 R. M. Young, (n.d.) Free Associations: some reminiscences. Unpublished ms.
4 R. M. Young, Biography: the basic discipline for human science. *Free Associations* (1988) 11, 108–130.
5 R. M. Young, Postmodernism and the subject: pessimism of the will. *Free Associations* (1989) 16, 61–96.
6 The developments at UEL of both psychosocial studies and the collaboration with the Tavistock Clinic are described in the chapters by Richards & Brown and Rustin in M. Rustin & G. Poynter, eds. *Building a Radical University. A History of the University of East London.* Chadwell Heath: Lawrence and Wishart, 2020.
7 Young, Biography: the basic discipline for human science.
8 R. M. Young, *Mental Space.* London: Process Press, 1994.
9 R. M. Young, Freud: Scientist and/or humanist. *Free Associations* (1986) 6, 7–35.

Chapter 9

Bob Young at Free Association Books

Ann Scott

Cambridge, 1971: my first sighting of Bob Young. I am a first-year un-dergraduate and, having had introductions to the left-wing community in Cambridge, I link up with a radical network. I attend a political meeting at a well-known commune. I enter a packed room; many people are sit-ting on the floor. The Rolling Stones' Sticky Fingers has just been released and 'Brown Sugar' is playing, the music loud, exciting, enveloping. The en-ergy in the room is intense. The meeting starts. In one corner, as though on thrones – although they were probably bean bags – are Bob and Sheila Young. Bob is holding court and holding forth. My memory is of a large, generous, charismatic presence. Bob commands the space.

Bob continued to command the spaces he was in, at times brilliantly and constructively, at other times less so. He was a colossus who could, as is well known, also be a persecutory figure. In my mind – and occasionally in conversation – I have compared Bob to Orson Welles, a man of stun-ning early achievement whose career seemingly faltered and who later found himself somewhat isolated, at times a perhaps peripheral figure. I had most contact with him when I worked for him as an editor at Free Association Books in the 1980s and again as managing editor of FAB in the early 1990s.[1] The 1980s were the glory days of the company, a time when Bob was at the peak of his powers as a publisher. He had left Cambridge in 1976 and had come to London, involving himself in a variety of 'familial, theoretical, cler-ical and manual aspects of Left solidarity' including *Radical Science Jour-nal* and the Radical Publications Group.[2]. His key paper, 'Science *is* Social Relations', interpreting science as part of the labour process[3] and taking up questions of cultural transformation, appeared in *Radical Science Journal* in 1977.[4] Free Association Books, formed in the early 1980s, emerged from the different strands in Bob's work, bringing together his activism, his work in the history of the human sciences and his knowledge of psychoanalysis both academically and in his personal life. He oversaw work in psychoanal-ysis by new young authors and commissioned edited collections of the work of senior figures in the field.[5] With colleagues, he started the journal *Free*

DOI: 10.4324/9781003204244-13

Associations, 'which complements the clinical literature with critical, theoretical and reflexive work on psychoanalysis in its historical, social and cultural relations, including group process in various contexts',[6] and developed *Radical Science Journal* into *Science as Culture*, 'a new quarterly journal on science, technology and medicine, broadly defined, as they relate to the rest of life'[7].

I knew Bob from the Radical Publications Group, of which I had been a member in the late 1970s, and some years later, he invited me to join FAB as a full-time editor. I did not know Bob in his early years as a historian and philosopher of science, but I knew that the reputation of his *Mind, Brain, and Adaptation in the Nineteenth Century* was outstanding and enduring.[8] Working in the company, one had frequent glimpses of his essentially scholarly turn of mind; I can still see his copy of Peter Gay's *Freud: A Life for our Time*, for example, entirely covered in pencilled comments and annotations.[9] His memory for cultural trends, theoretical positions, key debates in a field was prodigious. Conversations with potential authors ranged widely and Bob would invite authors to be part of an intellectual project, an intervention in the culture. Meetings with authors took place in his office, a large, chaotic, booklined space in which he would engage in a wider discussion about trends in the culture or the profession before funnelling down to the project in question. He wrote exceptional blurbs for new books, seemingly effortlessly capturing both what was original and what was affecting in the work. His knowledge of the history of psychoanalysis enabled him to identify out-of-print or lesser-known classics that deserved reissue, and he would use his wealth of contacts to secure new forewords by prominent contemporary clinicians. His political radicalism led him to publish the work of radical analysts, or analysts working in politically oppressed settings. At the same time, he cultivated links with senior analysts in the established analytic societies, a source of pride that sat uneasily with his distaste for the mainstream.

I don't recall his exact words but Bob would often say that he was pursuing an intellectual project that took the form of a capitalist enterprise, a publishing company. Bob had embraced Marxist political economy[10] and he would have been aware of the contradictions at the heart of the project. Nevertheless, we can see something pre-figurative in his aims for the company.[11] He was proud, for example, of the cooked lunches that we took it in turns to make, which he saw as a sign that we were a community in a way that was quite different from a conventional publishing company. It has to be said that we were in his house and that he dominated conversation at these lunches. And this leads on to one of Bob's weaknesses. While he was daring as a publisher and was committed to innovation – he was proud of his knowledge of typography and production processes and always sought a high aesthetic in the look and feel of FAB's books – he could bring a profligate approach to the business aspects of publishing. David Musson, who worked as Sales and Publicity Manager at FAB in the 1980s before moving to Oxford University Press, describes this well:[12]

> Bob was a brilliant publisher – in the sense of editorial and commissioning insight, and intellectual commitment. But unfortunately his skills did not extend to those required to run a stable well-grounded business. His grandiosity may have provided fuel and chutzpah for the vision, but it also led to serious over-reaching in running the business, and in turn the continuous search for money and investors.

Bob's dominant personality allowed for little discussion of his business approach. At the simplest level, it is why a number of authors ceased to publish with him. Royalties were significantly delayed, with Bob apologising and affirming his commitment to paying them, and in the end, some authors lost patience with the company. But it was not only this. Bob's capacity for personal attack cost him certain authors. Bob always gave himself permission to speak openly to people about themselves, and authors were sometimes no exception. He could be painfully accurate about one's shortcomings (I still wince at the memory of his comments about mine). Looking through some files one day for a certain letter, I came upon the terse reply from one author, a rising star, to Bob's lengthy critique: 'There is nothing to be gained by responding to your letter', was its gist, 'and I will not do so'. As I recall, the author published nothing further with FAB.

It is immensely sad to be remembering this. Some authors stayed loyal to him, recognizing him as a significant figure in the field. Others moved to mainstream publishers, to Bob's chagrin and contempt. There was so much loss: the loss of individuals whose publishing careers he really did start, who turned away from him. This cycle supported his bitter resentments and his tendency to speak in terms of the spitefulness of others. I do not think he ever understood how hurtful he could be, how casual with relationships of trust and of others' trust in him. It is hard, too, to square the mean-spirited man with the knowledgeable, witty, forceful man who could be found in conference discussions making by far the most interesting and radical contribution from the floor, gesturing expansively and smiling warmly. Or the man running the company who could, at times, show that he really did have your back.

An author whose manuscript I have completely rewritten composes his Acknowledgements, referencing me in relation to 'minor adjustments' of the text. I go to Bob, incensed and, of course, upset. Bob is magnificent. He informs the author that this is not acceptable and insists that my work is properly acknowledged. I am very grateful, and relieved. The published Acknowledgements are generous. The book quickly becomes a classic.

Many of the books Bob commissioned have indeed become classics – even if subsequent editions of them went on to be published by more mainstream publishers. In that sense, it is true, as is often remarked, that FAB revived psychoanalytic publishing as a whole, like 'a shooting star'.[13]

Bob was rightly proud of his publishing instincts. And he was able to use the company to support a work that was to make a significant intervention in the wider culture. The account Martin Bernal gives of Bob's audacity in publishing *Black Athena: The Afroasiatic Roots of Classical Civilization* illustrates Bob's bravery and fearlessness as a publisher, combined with a certain autocratic charm.[14] Bernal[15] describes a dinner party in London in 1983 where one of the guests was 'my old colleague at King's, Robert Young, whom I had not seen since we had parted on bad terms over ten years earlier'. Asked by Bob what he was doing, Bernal explained his researches into the Afroasiatic roots of Classical civilization and his difficulty in finding a publisher as many university presses had refused his manuscript. Bob told Martin that he was 'now running a small press, and he would like to have a look at it', saying "If I like it, I will publish it", and 'he did!'[16] The plan was to publish across three volumes. Bob readily accepted a suggestion that the title of the initial book should be *Black Athena*, not just the title of one chapter within it. Then, later, when Bernal was concerned on scholarly grounds that *African Athena* might be a more appropriate title than *Black Athena*, Bob refused to change it, wanting a title that was 'both dramatic and radical'[17] Bob told Bernal that[18]

> his ambition was to make *Black Athena* the equivalent to E.P. Thompson's *The Making of the English Working Class,* which would never go out of print. Therefore, he wanted to make the publication of *Black Athena* a first-class production...He ordered excellent thick paper and beautifully set out type. He created a physically attractive book that people wanted to pick up and hold.

Bob arranged a launch at the Institute of Contemporary Arts in London, chaired by Jonathan Miller. He negotiated with Rutgers for the US edition of Black Athena, and I remember him being taken with the news that its director, Ken Arnold, had the right to publish 'two books a year bypassing the usual academic filters'. Rutgers' publishing structure appealed to Bob; it validated his belief in the power of the individual voice. 'In both Britain and the United States', Bernal writes, '*Black Athena* was published without having to conform to scholarly orthodoxy'.

The comparison with Edward Thompson's *The Making of the English Working Class* shows Bob's keen sense of the historical and of the wider impact that a book might have. Bob discusses historical scholarship in 'Science *is* Social Relations'.[19]

We are interested in history for the agitation we can get out of it, for
the knots it can untangle about the origins and structure of our present
forms of deference and mystification......We look to history for lessons
and warnings and morale-boosting precedents – all thoroughly disrepu-
table motives for all but a few old left scholars. And the warmth of those
few shines through their work so that they can speak directly to younger
people; I am thinking particularly of E.P. Thompson, Raymond Williams and Stuart Hall.

In a different register, his impact was unmistakeable in our discussion about
a possible new book by the writer and painter Mary Barnes:

*Joe Berke introduces Mary Barnes to FAB. Mary wants to do another
book, following up on her original work with Joe,* Mary Barnes: Two
Accounts of a Journey Through Madness, *which FAB has reissued or
is in process of reissuing. Mary visits the office, bringing with her bags
of papers containing writings and notes. She appears hesitant and a little
unkempt. My sense is that Bob and I meet with her, and Bob and I discuss
the possibility afterwards. Bob is not enthusiastic, while I see the potential,
not least because of the significance of the earlier work and the intrinsic
value in both looking back to it and looking at what Mary is working on
now. Bob says: 'You can do it, if you want, but I think you're idealizing
madness'.*

The definiteness with which he spoke struck me forcibly and has always given
me pause for thought. Just as I can still visualize his copy of Gay's *Freud*,
I can still hear him saying 'I think you're idealizing madness', confidently,
straightforwardly. Bob was in no sense a relativist and had no qualms about
stating his views. Here again it was in 'Science *is* Social Relations' that the
context for Bob's views of madness was set out:[20]

What is it about the writings of Carlos Castaneda, about the Situation-
ists International, about *R.D. Laing's celebrations of mad perceptiveness*
which has been so attractive to the alienated but politically committed
bourgeoisie? .... When we found attractive the phrase 'the politics of experience', we did so because it finally expressed the rock-bottom realisation that experience itself *in its apparently raw and unmediated forms* is
part of a totality which is in the deepest sense political. (Emphasis added)

Bob had had a vacation job on the back wards of a psychiatric hospital as a
student. It was an unforgettable experience for him, always to be included
within the 'totality' of experience, and it informed his later thinking about
mental illness and its idealization. So his observation about me was thought-
provoking. *Was* I idealizing madness? I have often asked myself this. I don't

think I was – I think he and I may have had a genuine difference of opinion about Mary's life and work after Kingsley Hall – but I was impressed by his conviction about it. It allowed me to go on examining my inner responses and is an observation that has returned to my mind over the years, in relation to other parts of my work. Importantly, too, Bob's perspective did not preclude his backing as publisher for the project, which came out as *Something Sacred: Conversations, Writings, Paintings.*[21]

After I left the company in 1994, the contact between us lessened. We would come across each other at professional gatherings and at book launches. I do recall a long letter from Bob shortly after I left the company, occasioned by a change in the management structure of Free Association Books. It went into our history in detail, with comments on my character and doubtless on my behaviour over the years. I seem to remember that I tried to compose a response wanting to acknowledge all that he had made possible for me without being overly defensive about his criticisms of me. But I did not manage to complete one and time simply passed. I remember saying to someone who, like me, had known him well, that I must now have joined the list of outcasts, of those who had abandoned him, having failed to acknowledge their mistakes. As the years passed, however, the contact between us softened when we came across each other. But this was not always sustained.

At Bob Hinshelwood's retirement conference in 2009, at the University of Essex, Bob approaches me in a coffee break. I am taken to task for my disloyalty to him in relation to another writer (I cannot recall the details, now). As usual, Bob's uncanny ability to light on whatever ill-judged or muddled thing one may have said or done, months earlier, means that it will not be allowed to pass without comment and complaint. As usual, there is no easing in the atmosphere, only an awkward sense of the unresolved.

By this time, however, I was editor of the *British Journal of Psychotherapy* and in due course was to be in contact with Bob over his contribution to the conference, the papers from which were due to be published in the Journal.

In my role as Editor in Chief of the BJP, I am working on the papers from Bob Hinshelwood's retirement conference. Bob's contribution presents a problem, full, as it is, of personal details about named individuals, and comments about other people that in my view are potentially defamatory. I ask the journal publisher's legal team for comment, having identified the passages that concern me. The legal team share my view and advise me to seek modifications to the text. I ask Bob to make changes, which he refuses to do. Then he publishes an online critique of me, alongside his conference paper, 'Varieties of Hinshelwood Experience', on his website. More than one patient mentions having seen the critique, and understandably wonders what I am really like. It is possible to work with it clinically, and to allow my patients free rein for their fears about the me they have read about, and the issue subsides. But it is a disturbance in the work.

Bob's critique of me is still available on the internet at the time of writing.[22] What is striking about it, to my mind, is that it allows for no other reading of the situation than his. There *is* only one view. It is so *personally* aggrieved, so hostile to me as an individual, so little linked with the debates and norms, in the wider culture, about speech in the public domain. Referring to the conference programme, he writes:[23]

> I was surprised that none of the other speakers made much reference to their working relations with [Bob Hinshelwood]. I was even more surprised that Ann Scott, the editor of the *British Journal of Psychotherapy*, to whom the papers were entrusted for publication, made it a condition of including this paper in the special issue of the journal containing the conference papers, that I should bowdlerize my paper in various ways. I thought her requirements were variously humourless, craven or picayune. Moreover, I doubt very much that any of the people who gave talks at the conference thought for one moment that accepting her offer to publish them in the *British Journal of Psychotherapy* meant that she would treat them in any way as submissions, subject to her editing. Bob Hinshelwood ...tried to bring about a compromise, whereupon she required even more alterations, some of which I found truly bizarre.

I do not report this sequence to try and resolve anything – years after the fact, and after Bob's death – but because it illustrates so well the exquisite difficulty of a closer engagement with him. Bob's belligerence about publishing processes led to a situation where his contribution was indeed absent from the issue of the Journal celebrating his close colleague and friend. The sadness is that through a process of righteous self-exclusion he did become, in this issue of the journal, the peripheral figure I referred to at the start of this piece.[24] Authors whose papers need to go through a legal read are usually aware that this is designed to protect everyone – authors, editors, journals and publishers – but for Bob it could only be an affront. And I was no longer a junior editor working for him, but someone with power over the publication of a talk he had given. I suspect it was this that he found intolerable at some level, however primitively. It is often said that Bob had difficulty acknowledging the careers and standing of his former students – and in this case, a former member of his staff. However we might debate the boundaries of speech in the public domain, I continue to believe that this dimension was, very sadly, in play.

Our clash over his paper at Bob Hinshelwood's retirement conference made it very hard to reconnect. In the last ten years of his life, my contact with Bob was very occasional. We met, for example, at the funeral of his ex-wife Sheila Ernst.[25] I knew that he had become increasingly unwell and was rather removed from professional life. Our last meeting was a few months before his death.

I am relieved that my last encounter with Bob is benign, at a book launch at the Freud Museum. He is seated by one of the beautiful lacquer cabinets, bathed in light, receiving those who come to speak to him. We can't have seen each other for several years at this point, and I think the previous time has been difficult. I am chatting with one of his (and my) oldest colleagues, and this strengthens me in my resolve to approach him; I feel my colleague's solidarity and understanding. This time Bob is cordial and – strikingly – contained. He is able to ask me how I am and what I am doing, and seems pleased to see me. He smiles warmly. I am touched by his friendliness, and ask if I might call on him, which he says I can. I don't manage to, with the flow of time and all our usual demands, but am glad about the encounter.

I look back on this moment and am curious about my oddly archaic way of speaking to him: 'Might I call on you?' It came to me unbidden. I see it now as showing deference and respect to someone whom I had known for nearly 40 years. There was a quietly reparative quality to our exchange, after the barbs of the previous years, his smile the smile that I remembered from the 1980s.

I was deeply shaken by Bob's death, the loss of someone so complicated and so significant in my life and in the lives of so many others. I was flooded with memories. My dreams were immediately disturbed. In an email of condolence to someone who had been very close to him but who had also had a conflicted relationship with him, I described him as an extraordinary person. I was moved and consoled, at his funeral, by the reading, by one of his children, of two verses from Alexander Pope's *Essay on Man*. The verses spoke to Bob's devoted commitment to the purity of scholarship and to the debate on man's place in nature: 'Know then thyself, presume not God to scan;/The proper study of Mankind is man'.[26] This was a reminder of all that was splendid about him, as I wrote when introducing Bob Hinshelwood's Appreciation of Bob in the *BJP* and of all that linked him with the history of the human sciences.[27] This lifelong commitment to intellectual enquiry is also found in the simple, brief statement Bob made in one of FAB's catalogues in the early 1990s.[28]

We remain proud of our contribution to the understanding of nature, human nature and society…We feel that Free Association Books and the activities associated with it in the broader culture are unique and well worth the commitment of all concerned.

Reading this nearly 30 years later, I see only the potency in Bob's thinking, and the vision that sustained his innovations in publishing, a vision that linked the present moment – at every level – with its historical and cultural precursors across a range of disciplines. The difficulties that he created seem to slip away, and I see only his dedication, his seriousness and his brilliant, warm smile.

Acknowledgements

I am very grateful to Bob Hinshelwood, Prophecy Coles, David Musson and Joanna Ryan for comments on an earlier version of this paper and to David Musson for drawing my attention to some of the obituaries and appreciations published after Bob's death.

Notes

1 My records of my work with Free Association Books are in storage and because of the Covid-19 pandemic it has not been practicable to consult them. This piece is written from memory and from early FAB catalogues, journals and books, and Bob's website. Although I have not been able to fact-check or research the piece fully, my memories of Bob and of the company are vivid. I have tried to stay true to them in the piece, in the context of what I recall (and know) of the wider culture of the company.

2 R. M. Young, (1977b) 'Contributor's Note'. *Radical Science Journal* 5, p. 135.

3 Roger Smith, (2021) 'In Memoriam. Robert Maxwell Young (Bob Young) 26 September 1935 – 5 July 2019'. *History of the Human Sciences*, July 6 2020. Accessed online 1/10/21. histhum.com/robert-maxwell-young-bob-young-26-september-1935-5-july-2019/. Also see his contribution in this volume.

4 R. M. Young, (1977a) 'Science *is* Social Relations'. *Radical Science Journal* 5, pp. 65–129.

5 Take, for example, Isabel Menzies Lyth's Preface, the first volume in her two-volume *Selected Essays* published by FAB, Isabel Menzies Menzies Lyth (1988) *Containing Anxiety in Institutions, Selected Essays Volume 1.* London: Free Association Books – and including her celebrated paper on nursing and social structures as forms of defence:

> It would not, I think, have occurred to me that my papers were worth collecting, although the initial reception and continued demand for a few of them might have suggested there was something worthwhile in them. I am grateful, therefore, to Robert Young of Free Association Books for suggesting that a selection of my writings over the years should be published. (p. vii)

6 *Free Association Books Catalogue.* Autumn 1987/Spring 1988, p. 30.

7 *Free Association Books Catalogue,* p. 32. It is his work as a publisher that is my focus in this piece. The 'Psychoanalysis and the Public Sphere' conferences (1987–1998) under the auspices of North East London Polytechnic and *Free Associations* were an equally important part of Bob's project but I do not consider them here.

8 R. M. Young, (1970) *Mind, Brain, and Adaptation in the Nineteenth Century: Cerebral Localization and Its Biological Context from Gail to Ferrier.* Oxford: Clarendon Press. A comprehensive overview of Bob's scholarly contributions,

alongside Mind, *Brain, and Adaptation in the Nineteenth Century*, is provided in Secord, Smith, Sim and Ruse in this volume.

9 Peter Gay, (1988) *Freud: A Life for Our Time*. London: Macmillan, 1989.

10 R. M. Young, (1977) 'Science *is* Social Relations'. *Radical Science Journal* 5, p. 67.

11 'Along the way we must learn to theorise our own practice and to practice our theories – to combine the vision of an alternative world with pre-figurative struggle in our own daily lives.' Young, "Science *is* Social Relations", pp. 113–114.

12 David Musson, personal communication, 2021.

13 David Musson, personal communication, 2021.

14 Martin Bernal (1987) *Black Athena: The Afroasiatic Roots of Classical Civilization. Volume I: The Fabrication of Ancient Greece 1785–1985*. London: Free Association Books.

15 I am grateful to David Musson for alerting me to Martin Bernal's self-published autobiography, *Geography of a Life*.

16 Martin Bernal, (2012) *Geography of a Life*. Bloomington, IN: Xlibris Corporation, p. 423.

17 Bernal, *Geography of a Life*, p. 424.

18 Bernal, *Geography of a Life*, p. 424.

19 Young, 'Science *is* Social Relations', p. 85.

20 Young, 'Science *is* Social Relations', pp. 110–111.

21 Mary Barnes with Scott, A. (1989) *Something Sacred: Conversations, Writings, Paintings*. London: Free Association Books.

22 October 2021.

23 R. M. Young, (n.d.) 'Robert M. Young Online Writings. Varieties of Hinshelwood Experience'. Accessed online 1/10/21. psychoanalysis-and-therapy.com/human_nature/papers/pap152.html

24 Bob's conference presentation is available online. The online version strikes a more boundaried tone than I recall in the original. I suspect that Bob did, ultimately, edit the paper.

25 Formerly Sheila Young.

26 Alexander Pope, (1733–1734) *An Essay on Man*, edited and with an introduction by Tom Jones. *Epistle II*. Princeton and Oxford: Princeton University Press, 2016, p. 28.

27 R. D. Hinshelwood, (2020) 'Appreciation: Bob Young'. *British Journal of Psychotherapy* 36(1): 147–149; A. Scott, (2020) 'Editor's Comments', *British Journal of Psychotherapy* 36(1): 1–3.

28 FAB, 1993 inside cover.

Chapter 10

Money as the currency of value[1]

Karl Figlio

Introduction: the reduction of value to debt

In a book dedicated to the thinking of Robert M. Young, it is important to remember that his abiding concern was to find out how the human was lost into human nature and human nature was lost into nature, to be understood and investigated as nature. Torn from its human roots, nature lay outside human values, including the urge to do good.[2]

The loss of a human core, as if usurped by nature, is an estrangement of an integrating self, divided into components that no longer inhere in each other. Marx and Freud described this estrangement from different angles, external and internal.[3] Marx saw an estrangement from one's 'species being,' driven by the replacement of an inherent integration of one's capacities, embodied in labour, by abstract 'labour power.' Labour power could be bought and sold on the market. Use value – something inherent in labour and its products – was replaced by exchange value – its price in the market. The internal dynamics of estrangement were described by Freud. The self emerges into object relations that can deplete it as well as confirm it, an instability exposed in narcissism. Later, psychoanalytic theory and practice has described in detail the forms of narcissistic intrusion into the ego, for example, by projective identification.[4]

The external and internal dimensions come together in a market economy. Externally, money is empty, acquired from estranged labour or from money itself, rather than from productive labour. Internally, wealth can be amassed outside of relationships of generosity and indebtedness, reproducing a kind of estranged or empty labour. Having no inherent value, money reduces qualitative values to quantity. Quantity can be divided into quantities. Difference dissolves into equivalences, distinct only by more or less. It is what the anthropologist David Graeber called the replacement of a 'human economy' by a 'commercial economy.'[5]

I take the human economy to mean feeling loved at our origin and in our core – embraced by loving others from the outset. We begin our lives, at least in fortunate circumstances, as new, loved, and loving beings. We share

DOI: 10.4324/9781003204244-14

our labours in families and communities that are sustained by this mutual valuing. Many bring a new generation into being, as we had been brought into being, creating, as Jonas argues, a lineage with an ethic of responsibility across the generations.[6] I would add that, born into such an embrace, we are also born into a lineage of indebtedness, gratitude, and reparation, with an internal as well as external dimension. Of the internal dimension, Freud said 'To the ego, living means the same as being loved – being loved by the superego...'[7] What is handed down unconsciously as tradition is a lineage of the superego.[8]

I link the cluster of love, indebtedness, gratitude, and reparation to fertility, as the faith in life and its regeneration, and see it as kin to the creativity of un-estranged labour. The capacity for indebtedness, gratitude, and reparation depends on a sense of sufficient internal goodness and, mutually, on the goodness of the other – the good object in psychoanalysis – towards which they are directed: mother and the environment that supports her goodness. It is a benign circle of faith in the goodness of the self and the good object, which is anchored in the libidinal narcissistic core of the ego.[9]

But the narcissistic core of the ego is susceptible to depletion by the object world, as if in competition for a limited supply of libido. This 'pathological narcissism' – akin to the power of the market to replace productive labour with estranged labour power – builds a defensive shell around an emotional estrangement, one form of which is an anxiety of depleted fertility. In a theme common to the world of production and the world of emotion, the commercial economy estranges the indebtedness of human relationships, whether in the creativity of living labour or of generation and nurturance of life. It reduces love, indebtedness, gratitude, and reparation to debt, where debt and credit seem akin to a law of nature: one is born in debt to – mother? father? sibling? the owner of capital? nature? As Freud put it, '[E]veryone owes nature a debt and must expect to pay it.'[10] Debt brings the illusion of repayment, ultimately by financial compensation. But it also brings the idea of transcending debt, maybe by forcing onto others; so, too, in pathological narcissism, in which narcissistic grandiosity triumphs over the indebtedness of libidinal narcissism.

Pathological narcissism is the internal dimension of the infiltration of abstract market relationships into every corner of human life, so extreme in neo-liberalism. While paying off debt is rational in such a society, especially one based on capital accumulation and making money from money, it feeds a narcissistic grandiosity as a defence against dependence. The quality of indebtedness is transformed into a quantity of debt. Paying it off then supports an illusion of redemption, in a rational irrationality. We work to pay off debts and believe we can transcend its insufficiency – get ahead of the game, ultimately by making money from itself.

The transformation of indebtedness into debt is one of the situations in which the public disquiet that arises in society converges with the private world of anxiety in the consulting room, and the analysis proffered by the social scientist converges with that of the psychoanalyst. For the social dimension, I rely heavily on David Graeber's analysis.[11] In the analytic setting, I see a narcissistic current that runs alongside conscious thinking, which can disappear and elude analysis. Resentment at fees, for example, can be legitimately explained by limited resources, and availability for sessions can be explained by the realities of family and work. Shame of dependency and indebtedness hide inside this rational core; and while an interpretation along these lines might make good sense to the patient, a current of grievance can still persist. It is this current that points to a narcissistic dimension, in which the patient feels depleted by the analysis, whether or not by finances or obligations.

I will structure my argument around three themes, grounded in clinical examples: (1) money in servicing debt, as an annulment of indebtedness; (2) money as narcissistic fulfilment; (3) the encapsulation of an anxiety of depleted fertility in the servicing of debt.[12]

Money in servicing debt

The place of money at the core of market societies is typically attributed to the need of a common framework for exchange of products and services that are unrelated to each other. Money is so essential to the market, that it is hard to reflect on it. No doubt, extensive forms and chains of exchange could not have evolved without it. There could be no complex division of labour, no equivalences across classes of goods and services – any activities – without it. In that sense, a marketization of traditional relationships based on money must have been the precondition for growth of societies in size and complexity.

But there is another side to money. Graeber has provided extensive evidence in support of a different origin, one which has a resonance with psychoanalysis. Graeber argues that money, in a variety of currencies, did not emerge as the medium of exchange, and exchange did not emerge in an autonomous market. The idea of an autonomous market, operating outside a sphere of human relationships, and of its bringing money into existence to support it, is a creation of an economic orthodoxy.[13] This orthodoxy did not discover the autonomous market as an abstract medium of exchange but invented it as its object of study.

Currencies have existed at least as far back as there are records, but, until recently, they were part of what Graeber calls a 'human economy.'[14] In such an economy, there have been customs for distributing products without currency within groups of familiars, and symbolic mediums for transactions between non-familiars. Currency exchanges have been forms of managing debt and credit, both moral and material. To be in debt was to be obligated to another, but with this difference: 'that a debt can be precisely quantified.

This requires money. Not only is it money that makes debt possible: money and debt appear on the scene at exactly the same time...[A unit of currency] is effectively an IOU...[It] is not the measure of the value of an object, but the measure of one's trust in other human beings.'[15] To be able to measure an obligation in monetary terms was to be able to settle a debt that otherwise was unmeasurable and could be infinite.

Outside the market, currency is a human currency, a measure of credit and debt in a human relationship. The most elemental debt is a life for a life: if a member of one clan has murdered a member of another, then the only equivalent of the victim's life is the loss of a perpetrator's life. The earliest currencies were to offer a pawn, perhaps a wife or daughter or an indebted stranger, or even oneself, into servitude at the disposal of the aggrieved. Various inanimate currencies have also been substituted: perhaps hides, brass or wooden rods or cloth, but typically objects of no intrinsic value; though in such unmarketized societies, they tended to be used for adornment, as if to represent a desired form of a creditor. More generally, whoever/whatever disturbs the equanimity among people, the injustice must be assuaged by an equivalent disturbance imposed on the agent of the disturbance.

Paying a debt by pawn offers an interim compensation that could extend a final – albeit impossible – settlement into the indefinite future, so that, in effect, it dissolves. But no payment, whether by forcing an equivalent injury on the perpetrator, or by offering a pawn or other proxy, can redeem a loss. The idea of equivalence between injury and payment by pawn rests on tearing her out of her human context, leaving 'a generic value capable of being added or subtracted and used as a means of exchange.'[16] Such an abstraction is on the path to money as currency.

As an equivalent to an injury, as well as an abstract medium of equivalence in general, money forces a commercial economy into human economy. Debt can be compensated and ultimately forgiven, but in its commercial form, compensation gapes with deficiency. Abstracted from the human economy, money becomes the medium of marketized debt. Money exposes the raw contradiction in debt: inflaming injury while assuaging it.

Even replacing lost money cannot restore the injury of its theft, which is a violation. One could argue that no restoration can annul a loss: that it would be more appropriate to think of forgiveness rather than restoration. For Hannah Arendt, 'The possible redemption from the predicament of irreversibility – being unable to undo what one has done though one did not, and could not, have known what he was doing – is the faculty of forgiving.'[17] Moreover, she argues that 'Forgiving and the relationship it establishes is always an eminently personal...affair in which *what* was done is forgiven for the sake of *who* did it.'[18] Forgiveness has a 'revelatory character' akin to respect, in which the forgiven is valued as him/herself (I have explored the relationship between forgiving and reparation in a forthcoming work).[19]

Nonetheless, the aim of monetary restoration stands apart from any other, in that money is so wholly abstract, so wholly lacking in a human bond between agent and victim, that payment for loss as easily repudiates the injury committed, as recognize it. The character of the offender/debtor is thereby blemished by the compensation, as would be any nominal forgiveness based upon it alone. It tarnishes a human economy, which remains a set of dependent relationships from conception on. We begin and remain indebted and attract the indebtedness of others. But indebtedness can shade into debt, while reparation towards the life-sustaining, good object, along with redemption of the self, can shade into retiring a debt. And while debt can urge a process of redemption with the stirrings of reparation, it can also urge a triumphal repudiation of one's own indebtedness and the forcing of debt onto others. So, too, with reparation. Reparation is driven by guilt[20] and the urge to make better, but guilt can be intolerable, experienced as a dishonour that must be forced onto an other. In that case, it is manically triumphal, not reparative.[21]

This marketization of relationships lies at the heart of a distinction between compensation and reparation. Compensation is based on an illusion of equivalence between loss or injury and payment. Reparation is an urge to make better. Both compensation and reparation are deficient, but in different ways. Compensation leaves a grievance unsatisfied, undermining faith in goodness. The reparative urge, driven by guilt, aims to make better, sustaining love for a damaged, but good object. Money in a marketized economy, more so in an economy based on accumulation, erodes faith in reparation. It promotes instead an avoidance of indebtedness in relationships, replacing it with debt and the illusion that it can be measured. This conversion of quality – of values – into quantity, adds the illusion that indebtedness as debt can be paid off.

Money as narcissistic fulfilment

Libidinal narcissism remains objected-related, bolstering the value of objects and self-esteem. Pathological narcissism facilitates the *amassing* of wealth in itself as an abstract form of self-value. In both forms, money as an abstraction with no property of its own, and the costing of objects in money, undermines value as the product of creative labour. On the libidinal side, however, a producer, trader, or customer can use money without losing a sense of being a needing, valuing person whose longing is partially satisfied by the production or purchase of an object. But in pathological narcissism, the value of oneself as a person, satisfied through producing or acquiring a needed object, is replaced by the dissatisfaction of feeling robbed in not acquiring an experience of self-value. More wealth repeats the cycle and drives it forward.

Money can support the ego when income is held in relation to goods and services that enhance the experience of belonging to caring groups. In that case, we can speak of healthy, libidinal narcissism. Money can also be stored up or acquired from monetary transactions, as in the amassing of wealth. In this case, we can speak of pathological narcissism. The balance of these two attitudes in any one individual can be expressed by speaking of normal narcissism when it leans towards the former, and pathological narcissism when it leans towards the latter.

The socio-economic environment of the commercial society promotes an illusion of an autonomous market, governed by its own abstract laws and driven to accumulate capital. It supports a narcissistic illusion of esteem in economic growth, forming an alliance that hides inside an appearance of the reality of a money economy as a closed system. The apparent economic rationality puts money and amassing wealth beyond critique. It becomes rational that an economy cannot remain stagnant. It must grow or diminish for no reason beyond the attraction of investment by an economy in growth, and the disinvestment from an economy that threatens contraction. But this very economic feature enacts the narcissistic imperative to invest or disinvest as the narcissistic self-as-capitalist seeks to amass self-capital in the form of wealth.

A recent Office of National Statistics study reported that net financial wealth in the form of stocks and shares, savings in banks or money in hand – not physical possessions, not comparison with others, not increasing property or pension values – correlated most strongly with well-being. It seems that having the universal measure of wealth and of the amassing of wealth, in itself, grounds a sense of well-being, which links with security and esteem more than any object with inherent properties.[22]

Money is a narcissistic broker. Anything can act as narcissistic capital, and anything can act as money. First, money stands in for any recompense; second, in doing so, it offers no recompense because it is not anything, surely not even a pretence of, or an approximation to, what has been lost. These two features lead to a curious paradox: money is a magical substance that offers everything and nothing. It is illusion, shadowed by disappointment. Abolishing debt with money replaces reality with a world of illusion, and in the process, it re-enforces a fundamental grudge that one has not been recompensed despite having been offered a fair price.

There is a precedent to this paradox in Freud's formulation of money as a sublimation of anal-erotism.[23] The character traits of anal-erotism – orderliness, parsimony, and obstinacy – are reaction-formations to the infantile pleasure in playing with faeces. The pleasure of retaining, expelling, and manipulating faeces is apparently revoked by orderliness, cleanliness, and conscientiousness, but in fact the two currents co-exist in the unconscious. In this paradox of opposites, the shininess of gold is equated with the muddy filth of faeces. Along with rationality in individual and social life, the amassing of wealth through the acquisition of ever more money retains the equation of gold = shit. As Ferenczi puts it, 'the capitalistic interest, increasing in correlation with development, stands not only at the disposal of practical aims – of the reality-principle, therefore – but ... the delight in gold and in the possession of money... also satisfies the pleasure principle.'[24]

Ferenczi presents a stunning clinical vignette of the persistence of these two strands of anal-erotism.[25]

> A patient could not recall any kind of coprophilic manipulations, but... related...that he took a special pleasure in brightly shining copper coins, and had invented an original procedure for making them shine; he swallowed the piece of money, and then searched his faeces until he found [it], which during its passage through the alimentary canal had become beautifully shining. Here the pleasure in the clean object became a cover for satisfaction of the most primitive anal-erotism [, about which he] was able to deceive himself.

But although the anal stage provides the anatomical, physiological, and functional substrate for becoming a self through controlling the retention or release of bodily content – idealizing and denigrating faeces – the earliest paradox lies before anal-erotism. In the narcissistic dimension, the loss is not of an object, but of the ego – an ego stolen, added to the mother's wealth. Freud implied as much, in speaking of the loss of the breast at the moment the mother appears, not as breast, but as mother.[26] At an even more primal level, perhaps 'everyone owes nature a debt and must expect to pay it.'[27] One's birth creates a debt and one is born in grievance or in triumph. Based on striking clinical material, Eric Rhode argues that birth, in phantasy, is accomplished through a double annihilation – of mother and a twin – and that the placenta and cord, as lifeline to the pre-birth mother, incarnate the annihilated pair for the baby.[28]

Although the subsequently offered breast might compensate for loss, it does not restore what was lost. Object-relating is the prototype of dependence on provision and therefore of generosity and gratitude; but narcissistically, as amassing wealth, it is the prototype of irredeemable grievance born in the wellspring of love and life. Otto Fenichel drew attention to the insubstantial dimension of the desire to amass wealth. 'Now among all human needs whose satisfaction can be bought with money, particularly conspicuous are those which we call "narcissistic"...In the deeper layers of the mind, the idea of possessions refers to the contents of one's own body, which could be taken away.'[29]

> In so far as the drive to amass wealth appears to be a means of the ego for increasing self-regard, or for preventing a lowering of its level, this desire can be looked upon first as a derivative of that primitive form of regulation of self-regard in which the individual requires a 'narcissistic supply' from the environment in the same way as the infant requires an

external supply of food. Money is such a supply. [I]n the present-day economic system, especially with...illusions...of getting rich, the idea of being wealthy becomes an ego-ideal. The attainment of wealth is fantasied and striven for as something bound up with an enormous increase of self-regard.

(pp. 95–96)

Objects that enhance self-regard are possessed as if part of one's body and bodily ego, possessions 'through which one's own ego is set off from the rest of the world. *Possessions are an expanded portion of the ego.*'[30] 'The drive to amass wealth seems to be a special form of the instinct of possession... The possessive instinct is a special form of bodily narcissism and expression of the fear of bodily injury, [expressed through the] social function of possessions.'[31]

Fenichel takes the pleasure in anal retention to be the clinically demonstrated origin of the desire for possession and of possession as a defence against the injury of having a portion one's body-ego torn out of oneself. Money, however, is not just an object of erotogenic pleasure in possession, but a social tradition that also fulfils the instinctual function of amassing a possession. The capitalist, argues Fenichel, is driven by the rational need to increase his capital in competition with other capitalists, and money serves this function so well because

the attitude toward introjections of every kind can be projected on to money...In the unconscious mental life money can represent not only possessions but everything that one can take or give; therefore it can represent relations to objects in general and everything through which the bodily ego feeling, and with it...self-regard can be increased or diminished.

(pp. 99, 100)

The first object that can be taken or must be given over is the breast; the second is faeces. The quality of money fits it to stand for all processes of taking-in, losing and giving-out, and it could not serve this function were it to become an object in its own right. The drive to amass wealth becomes an unlimited substitute for the reality of an actual object and of the body-ego as a self-possession. Money and capital lock into place an unstable illusion that amassing is the same as possessing and securing one's ego and object, and a defence against ever-threatened loss. But in narcissism, self-possession is lost from the outset, even before the loss of the breast, eroded by the very presence of an other. Amassing wealth must therefore continue relentlessly.

The narcissistic core of indebtedness starts with the dependence on the breast as a part-object; challenged by loss to mother perceived as a whole object; brought to a head at weaning; backed with agency in anal conflict over retaining or giving over faeces; and reinforced phallically and locked in through a money economy.[32] From this angle, money fills a narcissistic deficit. The fit between the money as a narcissistic illusion and the narcissism of an irrational desire for amassing wealth is tight. Since illusion can only be maintained through amassing wealth, money also fits tightly with the need of capital to grow. The narcissism of amassing and the narcissism of capital growth define money as the bearer of this illusion, in which risking capital also unsettles the insubstantiality of narcissism.

The financial crisis of 2008 strikingly illustrates the catastrophic crashing of illusion. In April 2006, the IMF's Global Stability Report stated that 'the dispersion of credit risk by banks…has helped make the banking and overall financial system more resilient.'[33] On July 21, 2007, the huge Merrill Lynch organization felt quite secure. Two weeks later, they realized there was no reality to their position.[34] The price of credit then evaporated, when France's largest bank, BNP Paribus, suddenly halted withdrawals from money market funds worth $2 billion because the assets were largely backed by US mortgage loans.[35]

These events were illusions, collapsed into a moment when the banks lost trust in each other and in the assets they had to back further lending. It would be better to say that trust was catastrophically broken, because it was supported by illusion. The whole economy, based as it was on continuing investment, lending, profiting from lending – on milking illusory profits from illusory wealth – ceased functioning. It was not that the link between producers, buyers and goods was broken: it was the collapse of trust between the bearers of illusion, a loss of a defence against dependence.[36]

Esteem, indebtedness, debt, and the anxiety of fertility: clinical evidence

Etymology offers an insight into the connection between relationship, indebtedness, and fertility, on the one hand, and the instability of narcissism, on the other. The German *Geld* (money) brings out a cluster of meanings. One leads to the English, to *geld* meaning to castrate, and through that act, to eliminate fruitfulness. The other leads to the English, to 'yield' as the fruitfulness of a crop as the yield of the land and/or of animals. But the same word refers to submission to a greater power, in what must be surrendered or handed over – yielded. The ambivalence of 'yield' comes out: indebtedness for the benevolent gift of fertility and the payment of a debt imposed on the indebted – something that must be given over. Geld as money is the bearer of value with roots in fertility, but which, in its phallic omnipotence, is fragile to the core through castration. Human relationship, in conception, nurturance, and growth, is based on fertility; amassing wealth is based on omnipotence.[37]

The sphere of indebtedness, debt, and fertility is a situation in which social disquiet converges with the private world of the consulting room, and the analysis proffered by the social scientist converges with that of the psychoanalyst. With indebtedness, a narcissistic current runs alongside conscious thinking. Clinical vignettes offer a glimpse into the bonding of a narcissistic current to everyday life, in the form of money.

Haydée Faimberg reports a moment in an analysis in Argentina during a serious economic crisis, when purchasing dollars was favoured to protect against devaluation of the peso. Her analysand, Mario, however, seemed unconcerned up to the following moment, when he became anxious that he could not continue his analysis.[38]

> [S]omeone who was trying to persuade him to buy dollars had asked him if he knew how much a dollar was worth. Mario had answered that a dollar was worth two pesos. [Meanwhile] he made a hardly perceptible gesture with his hand, as if to make sure that something in his pocket was still there, a loving gesture accompanied by a tender and secret smile. At the same time, with an absent, indifferent attitude, he said his friend told him that a dollar was worth five thousand pesos. He did not seem concerned that he did not know the value of the dollar...[and he] indicated he was aware of his desire to continue with his analysis as well as of his anxiety at...what he believed to be its inevitable loss.

Mario continued to do nothing. Instead, he 'tenderly caressed his pocket when talking about those "two pesos" dollars, [appearing] "[to keep] in his pocket" the secretly cherished and treasured dollars [valued at] "two pesos"' (p. 100).

I present this example as a vivid scene, which suggests a line of enquiry evoked in my reading of the case, not Faimberg's. What stands out for my argument is Mario's devaluation of his internal world, represented by currency devaluation, and his attempt to repair it by identifying his good object with his two testicles. But his ignoring the devaluation of the peso created an ersatz fertility in the form of illusory money, which allowed him to substitute a shaky, insubstantial narcissistic omnipotence for his and his analyst's valuing him and his analysis, and for recognizing his indebtedness to his analyst as a valuable good object. Following this key period, Mario moved into a more reparative mode, which included sorting out the significance of his transference figures (I have set out this interpretation in detail elsewhere).[39]

In another analysis, here of an indulged son of a wealthy merchant, the value of the German Mark suddenly collapsed, but the analyst, Franz Alexander, did not raise his fee.[40] The patient loosed a torrent of abuse against him and asked for a referral. The new analyst demanded ten times Alexander's fee. Meeting Alexander on the street a year later, the patient 'gleefully [said] he had been relieved of most of his complaints.' It is a reasonable guess that he had gained an illusory stability through an amassed wealth, the existence of which had nothing to do with money in the bank, but rather with his finding in his new analyst the needy son whom he supported.[41] In current language, Alexander's ex-patient had found a repository for projectively identifying his depleted narcissistic self in his new analyst.

Such cases as the above reveal the paradox in which money is the medium of financially rational irrationality. Even Alexander's ex-patient, on the surface, seemed to assert the rationality of recouping income lost through devaluation by expecting his analyst to raise his fee. He seemed to suspect Alexander's rationality and perhaps his competence when he did not raise the fee. But his flight from Alexander and his pleasure in telling Alexander of the success of the new analysis, with a greatly raised fee, suggest the unconscious motivation referred to above. A narcissistic triumph over Alexander shines through, which cancelled any indebtedness to Alexander by an illusory amassing of wealth equivalent to the higher fee he now paid to his needy analyst.

I will supplement the cases above with some evidence from my own work. I have often listened to rational accounts of restricting the frequency of sessions and of resentment at the analytic fee or of paying for missed sessions. Typically, they are incontrovertible in their own terms and difficult to separate from an underlying complaint. I have come to think that one dimension of the bond between the rational economic stance and the underlying complaint is a negative narcissistic[42] kernel of a self that feels the expenditure of money is equated to the loss of self. Expenditure, reversible by retaining or amassing wealth, which includes finding a repository for depletion, ties the economic and narcissistic currents together.

Mr R was a committed, hard-working farmer. At our first meeting, he said that his wife had suggested he contact me on account of his emotional distance. From his side, he felt swamped by female figures that scrutinized his interior world, but was also concerned that he might burden his wife with a distancing, deadening aspect of himself. I said I thought he might hope we could protect his marriage by lifting this burden off his marriage and bringing it here. At the end of the initial consultation, I explained the few, usual boundary conditions, were we to continue. It was several months before I heard back from him.

Mr R spoke at length about farming. He ran an ancient farm – a true heritage site – owned over generations by his natal family, and he aimed to hand it on in a better state than he received it. He felt ground down by his father, whom he admired and criticized, and by whom he felt criticized. He worked tirelessly, continually planning and implementing new ideas – letting fishing rights, establishing a farm shop, meeting Soil Association criteria, setting up an organic vegetable business, installing a new drainage system, harvesting straw for thatching and making briquettes – but he felt they came to nothing: in father's words, they were 'hare-brained schemes.'

Only later did I learn of another current: one that would remain unresolved. After our initial consultation, he had pondered indecisively over whether to proceed. He delayed because he had been angered by the conditions of the setting, such as paying for missed sessions. Did I intend to annoy him as a strategy to provoke him or was his tendency towards annoyance the very problem he brought; was I trustworthy?

He suspected that I watched him critically, but he focused his complaint on his father. Although father had retired from the farm, he routinely reviewed the accounts, questioning expenditure that, to Mr R, were improvements, but to father, were risky schemes. More broadly, his relationship with his superego was projected into the farm. It was the external representation of his internal world: the site of his diligence but also, from superego-father's angle, the site of his 'hare-brained' schemes. Sessions were filled with the problems of a grudging farm, which he struggled to make better and secure as a good object.

A strand of this representation was so obvious that it remained invisible. For a farmer, planting seeds and nourishing growth was routine. He rarely spoke about his anxiety that *his* fertility was damaged, along with need for improvements of the farm. I refer to fertility because it is life itself, fundamental to any idea of value, whether in the capacity of life to continue or in the vitality of any creativity. Over the years of our work, his anxiety over his fertility – not wholly assuaged by the evidence of three healthy children – surfaced (I explore seminal anxieties elsewhere).[43]

The leading theme was the tough job of sustainable farming. The farm was marginally solvent in the current account but always in debt to the bank. There was, however, another theme, kept quite separate: apart from the farm, the family was established and seemingly wealthy. I knew that he supported children in private schools and that his wife was also in treatment and paid a higher fee than mine. He occasionally and vaguely referred to pursuing a compensation claim in the millions of pounds. I would occasionally point out that he suggested the family seemed to be wealthy, yet he was on the verge of impoverishment that threatened his analysis. He rarely replied.

After several years, I suggested we add a session, and some time later, that we consider a rise in my fee. These changes brought us on course to termination. He based his decision on financial grounds, but another reality pointed elsewhere. I never doubted his account of bank debt, but by now, his wife had ended her sessions and only one child remained in private education. Nonetheless, the strain in time and money was, he avowed, too much to continue.

In his business dealings, he could tolerate a debt owed him, but being in debt was intolerable. His wife once criticized him for delivering a ton of potatoes to a client in debt to him, but he countered that farmers were honest, and it was important maintain the community of trust. He could invite trust and dependence but could not himself trust and be dependent. He ran the farm but complained that the family dipped into its resources for their satisfaction, as if replenished by him without limit. He saw me as extracting ever more from him. On a balance sheet, he so to speak tried to hand on the debt, into which I and the bank had landed him.

In a session just after a short break, he wasn't sure whether to tell me something and began instead by saying he had felt bubbly that morning, but that his wife looked 'down.' What followed was no surprise, because he often saw his own gloom in his wife and would hope to see her cheerful after even a short absence. He said he had over a long time declared an interest in renting 100 acres of organic land from a neighbouring farmer. Today, he had phoned the farmer, only to learn that the farmer had let the land to someone else. Mr R was desolate and felt betrayed. He thought he had been too nice, and he wished he could walk away, saying 'stuff it.'

The session carried on until I felt ready to bring his desolation, betrayal and wish not to be nice, into the transference as my betrayal. In response, he first compared sessions unfavourably with all the healthy activities of which his sessions deprived him, then continued with farming, then returned to his despair. Recently, about to leave the farm for the day, he had left his farm manager instructions not to cut down a particular ash tree. He returned to find it cut down. He said that miscommunication must have been the cause. I said that, when things went wrong, he felt they could not be made better. He turned to his wife's gloominess. He might buy her a gym membership at his gym, but he learned there would be no special deal for adding her membership to his. He could not afford it for her (and in my view, funding me). I think Mr R could not walk away from the loss of hope, which he had 'perceived' in his wife's gloom; from the loss of organic land to revitalize his store of healthy, fertile soil; from the loss of the ash tree, which was desolation itself. But in this state, he also felt he no longer had resources to invest, whether in improving his wife's gloom or his gloomy sessions with me – or his organic farming. He had lost confidence in his reparative capacity as he was run down by debtors.

Later, in the closing phase of our work, certain earlier episodes took shape, which revealed a deep, primal insecurity. Coming for a session well before the events above, he had seen, through the glass panels of my front door, that the waiting room was dark. Although he had mentioned the dark room at the time, not until much later did he add that he had panicked – immediately and physically – with no awareness or thinking: just the re-action. I recalled other panics for him: although he had come to value the additional session, at the time I suggested it, he had shot back, 'It is inconceivable!' Similarly, when I had proposed to raise my fee, he again rejected it with ballistic force, and when we compromised on a fee, he wanted to reduce the frequency of his sessions.

As the Christmas break approached, I gave my re-starting date, as if we would continue after the break. He felt panicked by neediness and feeling suffocated. 'Oh, no: I can't decide, I can't think about it, I just want to get away!' The present moment of dependency then reached back and tapped the panic of the dark room. But by the following session, the panic had vanished, and he reverted to money in deciding to end his analysis. His panic at involvement – the issue that had initially, after a delay, brought him into analysis – was now alive between us, but mastered by financial 'reality.'

I acknowledged his financial hardship but reminded him of his panic and his need to get away, with which money was confused. Yes, he thought that was so. He said it was similar to how he felt about coming four times/week, and it was the same panic that he felt when he saw the dark waiting room. I reminded him of its being 'inconceivable' as an immediate feeling, not open to thinking.

We began to review his panic at dependence, abandonment, and betrayal, now as a living reality. He stuck to his plan to end our work, and he did so in a perfectly reasonable and wholly irrational way. He went over the tough situation on the farm, which had occupied his sessions for some time, and was a wholly reasonable fear that his farm had been thrown into serious hardship. Continual rain had turned the growing season into a disaster of crop failure with its economic impact. The economic reality of the frequency of sessions, of the (increased) fee and of continuing with our work, comprised a debt he could no longer afford.

In my view, he also could not afford the disaster of betrayal that he had experienced at the dark waiting room – a raw, physical panic. The idea of continuing was close to his hope in restoration in the face of gloom, which I have linked with fertility as revitalization, as in the 100 organic acres. But his desolation was a loss of a hope: hope that could be betrayed. Now, unlike the night of the dark room and unlike the moment he learned that the 100 acres of organic land had gone to someone else, he could walk away.

The panic evoked by the dark room was – by definition – overwhelming and incomprehensible. One might say that it was not a measured experience and could have no measure; nothing could divide its totality into pieces, or move it to the side of his ego, against which the ego could restore itself as an agent in an object-related world.[44] My proposing an increase in session frequency and, separately, in fee, also provoked a panic. They were, as Mr R said, 'inconceivable.' These three incidents swamped his ego. At an objected-related level, he reacted to my actions, but in the immediacy of the moment, they depleted his ego. Bringing the two levels together, one could say that I depleted his ego.

Conclusion

I see this depletion of Mr R's ego by me as a moment of negative narcissism, and it is in this moment that money binds the external and internal dimensions together. The rational man judged that he could not afford to continue with an expenditure that depleted his bank account, especially when weather had destroyed the wealth in his crops. The man gripped by negative narcissism panicked at the loss of ego, especially when his internal wealth had been depleted by incidents that, though separate in consciousness, merged in his unconscious to swamp him. Money mediated these two levels of awareness. Although he could spare his bank account by finishing his session, in my view, he also amassed internal wealth. Unlike his compliant response to the lost 100 acres, he could walk away. He could, by projective identification, leave me impoverished as his betrayed ego (the first and second themes in my list).

To be clear: Mr R faced a tough reality with which he struggled, and through which he sought independence of mind and control over his environment. My point is that his environment was internal and interpersonal, as well as external and physical, and he nourished an illusory control over his situation. Money mediated the relationship between the two roots. He hated being in debt. He converted debt quickly from feeling obligated, appreciative, or dependent, into a financial arrangement. Money now tamed inconceivable indebtedness as a measurable quantity of which he remained the illusory master. He could also pass the debt on, projectively depositing it in repositories, including me, and he could amass wealth by refusing to indulge my hare-brained scheme of continuing our work.

I admired Mr R's dedicated work to make the farm better for his children, as he continued the lineage from generation to generation. My point is that his dedication to its improvement also portrayed an internal world in which he unconsciously felt that his fertility as procreative and reparative was compromised (the third theme in my list). As libidinal narcissism, the farm was an ego-ideal with which he joined his ego in a loving bond that overflowed: into farming organically, into the produce of the farm, into the family, and into object relations in general. As negative narcissism, the farm depleted him with its demands, its condemnations of his capacity to farm successfully and in his feeling depleted by object relations in general. Money became the arbiter between himself and his object world. It measured his self-esteem as profit and loss in abstract currency, devoid of any value in itself, in a different dimension from valuing in human relationships.

Mr R's internal economy – his self-value and self-esteem – was locked into the economy of the farm, which was locked into the economy of farming; that, in turn, was locked into the commercial economy of a modern, neoliberal society. At all levels, money as abstract currency facilitates exchange and the settlement of debt. As the settlement of debt, however, it transforms indebtedness, gratitude, and reparative urges into compensation for an unnameable loss. The conversion is, in fact, a violation, a breach of anticipated human caring, based on trust and love. In an alienated form, debt could be paid off, as in his debt to the bank, to the farm, to family, to me, and it could also be passed on, so that creditors become debtors. Amassing narcissistic superiority over debtors is always vulnerable to a crash, whether in the individual or in the market. Grievance persists inside apparent resolution and calls for more compensation, more amassed narcissistic wealth, more money.

Notes

1 This paper is a substantially revised an expanded version of a presentation to the New Imago Forum, Oxford, September 12–13, 2015.
2 R. Young's writings are voluminous. I will cite three: his first publication, in the history of science, R. M. Young, *Mind, Brain, and Adaptation in the Nineteenth Century: Cerebral Localization and Its Biological Context from Gall to Ferrier*, 2nd ed. Oxford: Oxford University Press, 1990 (originally pub.1970) and two recent papers on nature and human nature with particular reference to psychoanalysis: R. M. Young, Psychoanalysis, Values and Politics. *Free Associations: Psychoanalysis and Culture, Media, Groups, Politics* (2018) 74, pp. 23–31; R. M. Young, Whatever Happened to Human Nature? *Free Associations: Psychoanalysis and Culture, Media, Groups, Politics* (2019) 76, pp. 1–16 (Originally published in *Ethical Record* 100(1), 1995).
3 R. D. Hinshelwood, Projective Identification and Marx's Concept of Man. *International Review of Psycho-Analysis* (1983) 10: 221–226.
4 In Mourning and Melancholia, Freud describes an ego overwhelmed and devalued in a narcissistic identification with a disappointing object, with the merged pair judged by a critical agency. S. Freud, Mourning and Melancholia. *The Standard Edition of the Complete Psychological Works of Sigmund Freud* (1917) 14: 237–258. See R. Britton, *Sex, Death and the Superego: Updating Psychoanalytic Experience and Developments in Neuroscience*, 2nd ed., Abingdon, New York: Routledge, 2021, pp. 111–134 on narcissistic vulnerability; for overviews of the large field of projective identification, see K. Figlio, Projective Identification – An Overview. *Encyclopedia of Critical Psychology*. New York: Springer Verlag, 2013; R. D. Hinshelwood, *A Dictionary of Kleinian Thought*, 2nd ed. London: Free Association Books, 1991.
5 The distinction that Graeber draws between societies in which markets do not appropriate the 'human economy' of social relations, and those in which markets transform social relations into a 'commercial economy', has earlier roots, for example in Michael Polanyi's (1944) formulation, in which 'instead of the economy being embedded in social relations, social relations are embedded in the economy' D. Graeber, *Debt, the First 5,000 Years: Towards an Anthropology of Value*, 3rd ed. Brooklyn/London: Melville House Publishing, 2014 and Kindle edition . Also see K. Polanyi, *The Great Transformation*. Boston: Beacon Press, 1944, p. 57.
6 H. Jonas, *The Imperative of Responsibility: In Search of an Ethics for the Technological Age*. Chicago/London: University of Chicago Press, 1984.
7 S. Freud, The Ego and the Id. *The Standard Edition of the Complete Psychological Works of Sigmund Freud* (1923) 19: 58.
8 S. Freud, *New Introductory Lectures on Psycho-Analysis. The Standard Edition of the Complete Psychological Works of Sigmund Freud* (1933) 22: 66.
9 Narcissism embraces everyday and technical meanings. There are two broad currents of the theory of narcissism, roughly categorized as 'normal', 'healthy' or 'libidinal' narcissism and 'destructive' or 'pathological' narcissism. Healthy narcissism is an ego feeling of affirmation, esteem, and satisfaction with one's personality, which is carried forward from the earliest experience as a reservoir

of libido. It is mainly associated with ego psychology, espoused by Paul Federn. Federn also discriminated a pathological, excessive narcissism, which became an omnipotent defence against disillusionment at the hands of reality, compensating for the lack of esteem and strength of deficient libidinalization.

> Healthy narcissism is employed as countercathexis to the object strivings and for their support (for example, hope, ambition), but not as their substitute. The more narcissism functions as a substitute, the more pathological it becomes. See P. Federn, On the Distinction Between Healthy and Pathological Narcissism. *In Ego Psychology and the Psychoses*, edited by Edoardo Weiss. London: Imago, 1953; Karnac, 1977, p. 361.

In a more object-relational mode, Abraham observed an enhanced libido, some time after a loss. Compensation here takes the form of triumphing over the lost object. See K. Abraham, Letter from Karl Abraham to Sigmund Freud, *The Complete Correspondence of Sigmund Freud and Karl Abraham 1907–1925*, London: Routledge, 2002 (March 13, 1922): 452–454; and (May 2, 1922): 457–458.

Similarly, for Melanie Klein, a manic defence is the first step in 'normal' mourning. See M. Klein, Mourning and its Relation to Manic-Depressive States. (1940). In *The Writings of Melanie Klein*, vol. 1. London: Hogarth and the Institute of Psychoanalysis, 1975, pp. 344–369. Rosenfeld highlighted a perverse attraction to a protective and exciting cover offered by an internal gang of shady customers, whose promise includes trashing the object. In this way, he linked the 'normal' but defensive, manic – melancholic – phase of mourning with the perverse excitement of an ego overriding any dependence on the (lost, any) object. See H. Rosenfeld, A Clinical Approach to the Psychoanalytical Theory of the Life and Death Instincts. *International Journal of Psychoanalysis* (1971) 52: 169–178; reprinted in *Rosenfeld in Retrospect: Essays on His Clinical Influence*, edited by John Steiner. London: Routledge, 2008, pp. 116–130. Also see H. Rosenfeld, On the Psychopathology of Narcissism: A Clinical Approach. In *Psychotic States*. London: Hogarth, 1965.

In the Kleinian school, Rosenfeld and Britton have held to the existence of both libidinal and destructive narcissism. See R. Britton, What Part Does Narcissism Play in Narcissistic Disorders. In *Rosenfeld in Retrospect: Essays on His Clinical Influence*, edited by John Steiner. London/New York: Routledge, 2008 and Britton, *Sex, Death and the Superego*, pp. 112–115; 118–120.

So, in both traditions, there is a theory of a normal ego, energized, supported and experienced either as the source of itself as an independent agency, or embraced in a loving relationship with good objects; and a theory of an ego that cannot tolerate dependence and overrides it in an illusion of autonomy as superiority. That surmounting of dependence of an object by narcissism can be more or less triumphal, denigrating, annihilating to the object, and more or less drawn into a perverse relationship with exciting internal objects that substitute excitement for the experience of degrading dependence.

10 S. Freud, Thoughts on War and Death. *The Standard Edition of the Complete Psychological Works of Sigmund Freud* (1915) 14: 288.

11 Graeber, *Debt*.

12 Arendt says of love in relation to fertility, that the 'world-creating faculty of love is not the same as fertility, upon which creation myths are based' H. Arendt, *The Human Condition*. Chicago/London: The University of Chicago Press, 1958, p. 242 n. 82. From a psychoanalytic angle, I think this disjunction underplays the creative intercourse of the parental couple.

13 For Graeber, Markets aren't real.

> They are mathematical models, created by imagining a self-contained world where everyone has exactly the same motivation and the same knowledge and is engaged in the same self-interested calculating exchange ... The problem comes when it enables some ... to declare that ... since we live in a market system, everything (except government interference) is based on principles of justice: that our economic system is one vast network of reciprocal relations in which, in the end, the accounts balance and all debts are paid. Graeber, *Debt*, Kindle ed., loc. 2346–2354.

14 Graeber, *Debt*, Kindle loc., 2681–2688.
15 Graeber, *Debt*, Kindle, loc. 500–501, 974, 996.
16 Graeber, *Debt*, loc. 3285.
17 Arendt, *Human Condition*, p. 237.
18 Arendt, *Human Condition*, p. 241 (Arendt's emphasis).
19 K. Figlio, Forgiveness in the Recognition of Actuality. In A. Novakovic and R. Britton, (eds.) *Forgiveness*. London: Routledge, forthcoming.
20 The depressive guilt of conscience, not the persecution of a destructive super-ego. See Klein, Mourning and its Relation to Manic-Depressive States.
21 Graeber shows that debt is often a form of dishonour forced upon a victim by violence, exacerbated by the creation of an abstract, autonomous area of exchange – a market of debt – in the midst of a human economy (see especially Graeber, *Debt*, loc. 3372–4348). If sufficiently powerful, perpetrator societies retain their honour by forcing others into the dishonour of debt. While previously, victors in war could take slaves, victors in the market, perhaps following victory in war or the threat of war, can force monetary debt on weaker economies. I am restricting my attention to the individual's experience of indebtedness and trying to alleviate it by compensation for a debt and by handing the debt on. Alleviating indebtedness is reparative, urged on by guilt; compensating debt is manic, urged on by triumph. See H. Segal, Manic Reparation. In *The Work of Hannah Segal: A Kleinian Approach to Clinical Practice*. New York: Jason Aronson/London: Free Association Books, 1986, pp. 147–158.
22 Office of National statistics. (2015) Relationship between Wealth, Income and Personal Well-being, July 2011 to June 2012. http://www.ons.gov.uk/ons/dcp171776_415633.pdf accessed 5 September 2015, reported in the Financial Times Weekend, Saturday 5 September–Sunday 6 September 2015, p. 1.
23 S. Freud, Character and Anal Erotism. *The Standard Edition of the Complete Psychological Works of Sigmund Freud* (1908) 9: 167–175.
24 S. Ferenczi, The Ontogenesis of the Interest in Money. In *First Contributions to Psycho-Analysis*. London: Hogarth, 1952, p. 331.
25 Frenczi, The Ontogenesis of the Interest in Money, pp. 329–330.
26 S. Freud, *Three Essays on the Theory of Sexuality. The Standard Edition of the Complete Psychological Works of Sigmund Freud* (1905) 7: 222.
27 Freud, Thoughts on War and Death, p. 288.
28 E. Rhode, *Psychotic Metaphysics*. London: Karnac, 1994, pp. 89, 112. For additional clinical evidence see A. Piontelli, *From Foetus to Child: An Observational and Psychoanalytic Study*. London/NY: Tavistock/Routledge, 1992, pp. 17–18.
29 O. Fenichel, The Drive to Amass Wealth. *Psychoanalytic Quarterly* 7: 69–95, reprinted in *The Collected Papers of Otto Fenichel*, 2nd series. New York: W. W. Norton & Company, 1954, p. 91.
30 Fenichel, The Drive to Amass Wealth, p. 97. (Fenichel's emphasis).
31 Fenichel, The Drive to Amass Wealth, p. 97.

32 K. Figlio, The Financial Crisis: A Psychoanalytic View of Illusion, Greed and Reparation in Masculine Phantasy. *New Formations* (2010) 72: 33–46; also in D. Bennet (ed.) *Loaded Subjects: Psychoanalysis, Money and the Global Financial Crisis*. London: Lawrence and Wishart, 2012, pp. 34–51.

33 A. Turner, *The Turner Review: A Regulatory Response to the Global Banking Crisis*. London: Financial Services Authority, 2009, p. 42.

34 A. R. Sorkin, *Too Big to Fail: Inside the Battle to Save Wall Street*. London: Penguin Books, 2009, p. 146.

35 Sorkin, Too Big to Fail, p. 88.

36 The illusory character of the market was known in economic circles long before the crash of 2008, but also not known (disavowal). In 1992, Hyman Minsky articulated his financial instability hypothesis, in which he showed that markets were inherently unstable. The financial world 'knew' that deflation was inevitable. There was particular concern for so called 'collateral debt obligations' and financial 'derivatives', which were forms of selling packages of debt on to other banks or insuring them. But as the packaging of debt moved further away from the original institution and client, so did capacity to assess the assets on which the debt could be repaid. There was no empirical basis for the value of these new financial products, but the 'market men' nonetheless generated 'rational' models to set prices, assess risks and insure against them. The models were illusions. The breach of trust in the world of illusion brought the economic system down, not the personal debt of people investing in the substantial reality of housing. Here is where the function of money as the embodiment of narcissistic illusion is flushed into the open. See H. P. Minsky, *The Financial Instability Hypothesis*. Working Paper no. 74, Jerome Levy Economics Institute of Bard College. Annondale-on-Hudson, New York: Jerome Levy Economics Institute; *Handbook of Radical Political Economy*, edited by P. Arestis and M. Sawyer. Aldershot: Edward Elgar, 1993.

37 This fragility hovers around the distinction between phallus as the instrument of an omnipotence, so easily stolen by castration, and penis as the instrument of testicular potency. Nature engenders a burgeoning wealth in reproduction and growth, yielding crops and the multiplication of animal and human life. The idea that human beings can enhance wealth on the basis of phallic omnipotence is counterfeit wealth and is vanity. I think the reason Freud stuck to castration as cutting off the penis, not cutting off the testicles, was to emphasize the phallic narcissistic dominance attributed to the male genital (On phallic versus testicular potency, see K. Figlio, Phallic and Seminal Masculinity: A Theoretical and Clinical Confusion. *International Journal of Psychoanalysis* (2010) 91(1): 119–139.

38 H. Faimberg, The Telescoping of Generations:—Genealogy of Certain Identifications. *Contemporary Psychoanalysis* (1988) 24: 99–117. In H. Faimberg, *The Telescoping of Generations*. London: Routledge, 2005, p. 100.

39 K. Figlio, Devaluing and Repairing the Internal World. *Psychoanalysis, Culture & Society* (2012) 17: 87–91.

40 F. Alexander, Some Quantitative Aspects of Psychoanalytic Technique. *Journal of the American Psychoanalytic Association* (1954) 2: 685–701.

41 Alexander, Some Quantitative Aspects, pp. 692–693.

42 I speak of 'negative narcissism', not pathological narcissism. I have used 'pathological narcissism' to refer to that pole or moment of narcissism at which the ego feels depleted by the object and seeks to triumph over it. I use 'negative narcissism' to refer to that pole as an unconscious current in everyone, not a pathological personality.

43 K. Figlio, Phallic and Seminal Masculinity. Also see K. Figlio, *Masculinity from Toxic to Seminal*. London: Routledge, forthcoming.
44 Federn distinguishes between fear and anxiety, on the basis that:

> In fear, the sensation of danger exists only at the ego boundary threatened by that danger. The seizure of the total ego [– in anxiety –] by the feeling of danger, or...by hallucinated terror, interferes with observation in the direc-tion of the object from which the danger threatens.
>
> (Federn, On the Distinction Between Healthy and Pathological Narcissism., p. 348)

Chapter 11

Schizophrenia *in* history

Outsiders, innovators and race

Peter Barham

Schizophrenia and the crisis of value

The alignment of schizophrenia with history may at first reading appear jarring, oxymoronic even, since in the conventional psychiatric wisdom the schizophrenic is assumed to belong to a class of natural kinds that reflects the network of causal laws and, in the words of the philosopher Ian Hacking, 'represents nature as it is'[1]. The ambition of some of the most influential theories in the human sciences has been to model the study of human beings on the natural sciences. However, drawing on critiques of the foundations of modern epistemology such as Richard Rorty's *Philosophy and the Mirror of Human Nature (1980),* Alasdair MacIntyre's *After Virtue* (1981), and Charles Taylor's *Sources of the Self (1989),* I have tried to demonstrate the limitations of an approach to mental disorder that is circumscribed by naturalistic assumptions about what it is to think scientifically[2]. The legacy of scientific naturalism has served as weapon and mask in the project of psychiatry by severing the links between the suffering of mental patients and the wider human community of which they are part in the name of a supposedly neutral and value-free line of enquiry. Though we have been taught to suppose that the intellectual revolution of the nineteenth century was in essence an epistemological one, on Charles Taylor's argument, it was in equal measure an ethical and moral one. To make any headway in clarifying the kind of problem that schizophrenia is, we must be willing to range across and engage, key questions and considerations on a number of fronts, not least in the definition of what it is to be human, so as to cut through the illusions and distortions imposed by a wholehearted dependence on a naturalist picture of human life and action.

In actuality, what has traditionally been called the 'course of schizophrenia' more closely resemble a life process that is open to a great variety of influences than an illness with a determined course[3]. Schizophrenia is not, after all, an all-encompassing illness which sets the patient apart from other human beings. Accordingly, we must recognize that what has been called schizophrenia exists *in* history and we must contemplate those human beings who have been designated chronic schizophrenics as historical agents. To

DOI: 10.4324/9781003204244-15

achieve this, we must grapple with the vicissitudes of the ideological project of schizophrenia and hence with the social and intellectual history in which the problem of schizophrenia emerged and was formulated. As Robert M. Young has amply demonstrated over the years in numerous writings[4], the history of a science such as psychiatry cannot be written in independence from a history of morals or from an interrogation of questions of value. It is against this background that I am all the time preoccupied with distinctions of worth or value in my discussions of mental patients and, in equal measure, with uncovering the suppression of such distinctions in the writings of others. One of the main findings (and, from a treatment angle, challenges) in my research concerns the lack of worth, or crisis of value, among people with a schizophrenia diagnosis that (at the time I was first writing in the early 1980s) was insufficiently addressed by the prevailing approaches, both theoretical (many of them an ironic reflection of just that negative outlook) and practical, both inside and outside the hospital.

In my own discussions of schizophrenic lives, I say a good deal about the schizophrenic person's sense of worth or value. In the 1970s, I worked with a very disturbed, but human and engaging, hospitalized, working-class schizophrenic whom I call Joseph K. Joseph K.'s deepest preoccupation was with his sense of his own value. 'If things get worse', he stated on one occasion, 'I won't be able to cope with my direction gear. I see myself heading for the life of a recluse, being valued at 7 and ½ pounds per calendar month'. As I construed it, Joseph's desire was to be permitted to participate in social life on terms that took account of his need both for shelter or retreat (for asylum in the proper sense) and equally for recognition as a valued person who was as much capable of bestowing care and consideration on others as he was in need of care himself. One morning, for instance, he surprised me by saying that in return for all that he believed I had done for him, he would now like to do something for me, and that if I had a sick animal, perhaps I would like to bring it to him to take care of. The notion of himself as a 'carer' possessed a very necessary function for him as a mean to give expression to his own deep-rooted, and authentic, concern for others and, equally, as a counterbalance to the idea of himself as a sick person; as though he could contrive a conception of himself as someone who was indeed severely ill (as he knew himself to be) and yet was not wholly defined, or taken over, by his condition.

Learning from the work of the Canadian philosopher Charles Taylor (1989), I realized that the question of value pervaded, and hence linked, domains that traditionally have been demarcated and treated quite separately, such as the ontological and the epistemological, or the clinical-cum-existential against the intellectual and doctrinal.[5] Schizophrenics, scientists and ordinary human agents are more connected with each other than illusions of scientific privilege and detachment have led us to suppose. 'To be a full human agent', Taylor declares, 'to be a person or self in the ordinary meaning, is to exist in a space defined by distinctions of worth'. Being a self is 'inseparable from existing in a space of moral issues, to do with identity and how one ought to be. It is being able to find one's standpoint in this space, being able to occupy, to *be* a perspective in it'.[6] A focus on distinctions of worth provides the key to a reading of the history of scientific and philosophical consciousness in Western societies since the seventeenth century. Scientific naturalism is ultimately a moral project grounded in a commitment to a particular set of background distinctions of worth that esteem, especially, a disengaged image of the self. As Taylor argues, it is not a question of trying to demonstrate that the attachment to a disengaged identity is simply wrong or misguided, but rather of freeing it of its 'illusory pretensions to define the totality of our lives as agents'.[7]

Emil Kraepelin and dementia praecox

In the 6th edition of his *Psychiatrie*, published in 1899, Emil Kraepelin established a paradigm for psychiatry that would dominate the following century, sorting most of the recognized forms of insanity into two major categories, dementia praecox (subsequently to be renamed schizophrenia by Eugen Bleuler) and manic depressive illness. In the 8th edition (1909–1913) of his handbook, the exposition of dementia praecox as a 'special disease unit' occupied some 300 pages, now taking centre stage in the mobilization of psychiatry as a cutting-edge medical science.[8] Though he later allowed some qualifications, Kraepelin thought of dementia praecox as an essentially deteriorating illness that was unresponsive to environmental intervention.

For most (though certainly not all) psychiatrists of the late nineteenth, and early twentieth centuries, and for many of their successors, the type of what became known as the chronic schizophrenic did not pose any problems of historical understanding, but served only to confirm the operations of a natural and inexorable disease process. At a meeting of the Royal Medico-Psychological Association held in 1909 to review Kraepelin's clinical portrait of dementia praecox, a Dr Devine captured the mood of the gathering in stating that Kraepelin's scheme enabled the psychiatrist to predict 'by observation of symptoms what will probably eventually happen to a patient'. Though one sometimes comes across what on a first encounter appear to be recoveries, 'this does not destroy the value of the conception', for 'it is necessary to carefully watch the future of the patient and to see if he is really as useful a social unit as he was before, and if this is merely a remission, a temporary arrest, as it were'. Kraepelin's descriptions of clinical decline have, he believed, 'given a meaning to the incoherent mutterings, the gait, attitude, conduct of even a terminal dement, all these features having acquired a significance which previously they had entirely lacked'. In consequence, 'one finds it hard to look on dementia praecox, to which one owes so much, as an "undesirable alien"'. Dr Hayes-Newington concurs, taking the term 'dementia praecox' to 'admirably denote the quiet collapse of jerry-built brains under the strain of their own weight or on the first contact with the responsibilities of adult life'.[9]

'Insanity', Brower and Bannister asserted in their textbook in 1902, 'is a more or less permanent disease of derangement of the brain producing disordered actions of the mind'. The 'general course of all adolescent insanity is towards more or less complete mental breakdown'.[10] Two decades later, in their textbook of psychological medicine, Craig and Beaton could find in the disorders of dementia praecox 'no other cause than the patient's failure to master life'. At a certain point, perhaps after some critical life event, the loss of a job or a girlfriend:

> the patient whose behaviour had hitherto been regarded as "neurotic" or "idiosyncratic", and treated accordingly, begins to show conduct which is definitely psychotic. He becomes irritable and liable to emotional outbursts on no apparent provocation: he is negligent, dreamy and self-absorbed. His habits become individualistic and asocial; he masturbates frequently, avoids other people, shuts himself away or wanders from home.[11]

If the 'shell-shocked' in this period were cast as the ineffectual 'fall-out' from the system of modern warfare, the dementia praecox patient, or subsequently the chronic schizophrenic, was cast in a similar role in the sphere of social and industrial progress. William Alanson White, superintendent of the Government Hospital for the Insane in Washington DC, confided in 1916 that dementia praecox 'is nothing more than a waste basket into which we throw all the cases we know nothing about'.[12] The theory of degeneration tended to dissociate radically the mentally ill from normal humanity. Mental disease and mental health were mutually exclusive, rather than points on a continuum. The picture of humanity drawn by these nineteenth-century physicians was almost of two different species, 'physically alike but mentally different'.[13] A blood relationship with a psychotic was often shameful and stigmatizing, stimulating doubts about 'one's place in the brutal dichotomy between well-being and disease'.[14]

The history of schizophrenia: what are we to make of it?

Writing some 50 years later of the attitudes towards schizophrenics in this epoch, the distinguished Swiss psychiatrist Manfred Bleuler, the son of Eugen Bleuler, who coined the term schizophrenia, and who, like his father, served as director of the famed Burghölzli Hospital in Zurich, described how the schizophrenic was conceived as suffering from a 'final and irrevocable loss of his mental existence':

> So it happened that the clinician became increasingly accustomed to seeing in his schizophrenic dementia cases an autistic attitude on the part of the patient. The patient and those who were healthy had ceased to understand one another. The patient gives up, in abject resignation or total

embitterment, any effort to make himself understood. He either no longer says anything or says nothing intelligible. In so doing the naïve observer declares, out of hand, that the patient has lost his reasoning powers.[15]

The late 1970s saw the publication in translation of Bleuler's magisterial *The Schizophrenic Disorders: Long-term Patient & Family Studies* (first published in 1972). Not only did Bleuler produce a far-reaching study of the long-term course of schizophrenic disorders, he also delivered an incisive and critical account of the history of schizophrenia, notably the dogma of 'incurability in principle' that held sway in the inter-war years, and the plethora of dogma and mistaken biases in which the lives of schizophrenic people have become entangled. And entwined with both of these strands is the narrative of Bleuler himself reflecting on his struggles to understand his patients, and on the intellectual and institutional currents with which he has had to contend.[16]

As the distinguished historian and psychiatrist German Berrios and colleagues have shown in a closely-argued conceptual history of schizophrenia (2003), the prevailing view within the psychiatric community of a linear progression down the years, through successive definitions culminating in the present, does not hold up and is a myth. According to the 'continuity hypothesis', schizophrenia has always existed, and nineteenth- and twentieth-century alienists have merely busied themselves in refining its blemishes and impurities, 'culminating in the DSM-IV definition which can be considered as a paragon of a real, recognizable, unitary and stable object of enquiry'. The role of this continuity story has been 'to flatter and justify the present'. Sadly, however, historical inquiry reveals that in actuality there is little conceptual continuity between the theories of Morel, Kraepelin, Bleuler and Schneider. The current view of schizophrenia is not, after all, 'the result of one definition and one object of inquiry successively plucked by various psychiatric teams' but instead is 'a patchwork made out of clinical features plucked from different definitions'.[17]

As the cultural historian of medicine Sander Gilman (2010) has argued, nothing coherent can be constructed from the often contradictory views about the nature of schizophrenia that have been proposed and held. Instead, there is a dialectic in operation in the construction of the disease concept of schizophrenia whereby theories react to other theories. No composite theory of schizophrenia can be extracted from this discursive melee and most likely none will ever be produced, The creation of a 'disease entity' called *schizophrenia* is an artefact of the ideologies implicit in late nineteenth-century medical nosologies. 'It is not the semiotics of an "objective" set of symptoms that is of interest to the historian of *schizophrenia* but rather the ideology associated with the entire structure of disease that is extrapolated (correctly or incorrectly) from this set of phenomena' (ibid.: 462). The best one can do, Gilman concludes, is to 'understand how the various concepts have evolved historically', and how, at one level or another, they are related to each other.[18]

Schizophrenia and modernity

The demonstrable failure of *schizophrenia* to cohere as a domain of science with 'a real, recognizable, unitary and stable object of enquiry' and, instead, to resemble a patchwork, as Berrios describes it, a creation composed of many variegated elements, likens it to a quintessentially modern methodology, or technique of art creation (originating, some would claim, with Picasso and Braque in 1912), such as collage, which introduces fragments of externally referenced meanings, such as newsprint, into juxtaposition, producing a collision, or mingling, of signifiers that bring the incongruous into connection with the ordinary and that, through an assemblage of different forms, meanings, and resonances, may generate a new whole.

This is to suggest that schizophrenia and modernity are rather more closely connected, and inter-woven, than the conventional epistemology of psychiatry might lead us to suppose. The important work of the clinical and philosophical psychologist Louis Sass has, after all, over a number of years sought to expose and explore just such connections.[19] To phrase it slightly differently, schizophrenia, in all its varieties, is an integral part of the performative fabric of modernity, of the complications and distortions that inhere in the effort to make out humanly within the fabric of modern life. The disorder that we call schizophrenia may be a distorted form of addressing, or of disavowing, the disorder of modernity itself. The disorder of schizophrenia is certainly not reducible to the disorder of modernity itself, but nor is it wholly separate from it. Within the disturbance that *is* modernity, schizophrenia has for more than a century played a wholly ambivalent role, variously as symptom, as messenger or, more typically, perhaps, as a disavowed fragment. Thus, the clinical and humanistic psychologist Sarah Kamens proposes that, rather than mistakenly focussing inquiry about schizophrenia on the disorder-as-object, and the search for an elusive empirical object, we must instead recognize that schizophrenia is located in social-discursive meanings and in the socio-historical evolution and structural reproductions of the debate as such.[20] Or, as the cultural critic Des O'Rawe argues, we must understand mental illness 'as a sociological phenomenon rather than a biomedical fact, a consequence of capitalism and its peculiar structures rather than the product of diagnosable neurochemical and emotional disorders'.[21]

The psyche and the group, the part and the whole

As the pioneering group analyst Malcolm Pines (1999) described in a Maxwell Jones memorial lecture in 1998, in the inter-war period the limitations, and falsehoods of a positivistic science that succeeds only in morcellating, or repressing, the myriad ways in which the psyche and the social world were inter-connected, were being increasingly recognized. The closed system of nineteenth-century science was being replaced by field theory and dynamic conceptions of the environment. Object Relations Theory was exploring connections and disconnections in the psychic life of infants, and the idea that society shaped, and was, in turn, shaped by, the psyche was starting to gain acceptance. In 1927 already, Trigant Burrow, an early innovator in group therapy and analysis, was adopting an outlook that connected the individual life to a larger whole: 'Under no circumstance is the reaction of anyone regarded as isolated or separate'.[22] A focus on the group as a whole, and on the 'here and now', were to become shibboleths in the approaches of W.R. Bion, S.H. Foulkes and their associates, and in the allied traditions of the Institute of Group Analysis and the approach to group relations, influenced by Melanie Klein and W.R. Bion, adopted by the Tavistock Clinic and the Tavistock Institute of Human Relations after the Second World War (in which I trained). All these connected traditions share a recognition that primitive, psychotic processes are at work in all of us all the time. In a stimulating 2000 essay, originally a lecture at the Tavistock Clinic, Robert M. Young engages with primitive, psychotic depths as they have been explored through the countertransference, and in his therapy with schizophrenic patients, in the writings of the pioneering American psychoanalyst Harold Searles.[23]

The effort at reconnecting the part, or the disavowed fragment, with the whole resides at the heart of the inspiration behind the therapeutic community movement in which, by contrast with the social arrangement of the traditional hospital, where patients are 'robbed of their status as responsible human beings', the capabilities and energies of all community members are brought into play.[24] In his account of the famous Northfield experiment, psychiatrist and group analyst Tom Main relates how the idea of the therapeutic community suddenly burst upon him: 'One evening I suddenly realized the *whole* community, all staff as well as all patients, needed to be viewed as a troubled larger system which needed treatment'.[25] This is precisely the kind of insight that might have reached out to, and connected, with the mad psychotics – 'mad saluters' and others – whom I wrote about in my study of the psychiatric aftermath of the First World War,[26] and also with Joseph K., languishing on the back ward of a mental hospital in the North East of England, with whom I worked in the early 1970s,[27] all of whom were palpably reflecting the unacknowledged troubles of a larger system but were, instead, mostly spurned, treated as isolates, and inhibited or obstructed from making, or exploring, potentially productive connections or from playing responsible roles.

In the early 1980s already, the political scientist and critical commentator on mental health, Peter Sedgwick, had questioned the legitimacy of a community-based psychiatric practice based largely around the 'individualistic administration of medicaments by the authoritative and qualified to the powerless and deferential'.[28] As has been remarked there is a deep and insidious form of colonialism in motion here in this use of medication.[29] In subsequent years, with the gathering pace of neoliberalism as, in the words of the political philosopher Wendy Brown (2015), 'the rationality through which capitalism finally swallows humanity', Kantian individuals, considered as ends in themselves, and intrinsically valuable (if ever such existed), have been supplanted, as Brown adumbrates in a skilful analysis, by a subject who becomes human capital for itself, 'at once in charge of itself, responsible for itself, yet an instrumentalizable and potentially dispensable element of the whole', at 'persistent risk of failure, redundancy and abandonment through no doing of its own', for whom 'there is nothing to being human apart from "mere life"'.[30] 'It is not the therapeutic spirit of Hippocrates, but the capital-accounting ethos denounced by Marx and hymned by Weber', avers Peter Sedgwick, 'which in different phases of capitalist development herds the multitude inside asylum walls and expels them again when the operation becomes too costly for a fiscally overextended social order'.[31]

The remarkable David Kessel: physician, poet, activist & chronic schizophrenic

To offer a vantage point on the experience of someone with a long history of schizophrenic illness in struggling to plot a course, and salvage resources for hope, amidst the debris and vacuity of late capitalist society, let me illustrate briefly the example of David Kessel, born in London in 1947 and died in March 2022, a former GP, a published poet, a socialist, and a mental health activist, whom I knew for some years and was privileged to count as a friend.[32] The son of a famous surgeon, Kessel recovered from a breakdown in his late teens before embarking on his medical training, subsequently working in the psychiatric unit at Hackney Hospital, and after that as a GP, for several years, until another breakdown put paid to his medical career.

David Kessel is defiantly unfashionable in identifying himself as a 'chronic schizophrenic', a label, or a self-definition, that some today may consider wrong-headed or, even, offensive. Yet, in his embrace of it, this is no abject surrender to a psychiatric inquisitor, as much as an instrument for interrogating the various dimensions –biological, existential, cultural and political – of what he holds to be the 'truth' of his situation. Kessel, it is, perhaps, worth emphasizing, has a double identity, or destiny, in relation to the universe of schizophrenia, both that of a direct participant and equally that of a trained and experienced clinician, accustomed to observing and diagnosing the suffering of others, who has learned the medical mind-set from within. Though his personal experience has certainly led him to be very critical of psychiatric orthodoxy, equally he has in part been shaped by the knowledge, and cast of mind, that his professional formation has given him.

Kessel wrote about schizophrenia on various occasions over the years, generally quite brief but dense remarks, not necessarily always easily understandable but invariably thought provoking, comprising a form of prose-poetry allied to David's own definition of a poem as a 'grammatical-emotive nexus', the 'clotted truth' of a personal or political circumstance or problem. 'I argue', Kessel writes, in an essay called *Schizophrenia: A Personal View*, 'that schizophrenia is not merely a mental illness, it is also a mystical

interpretation of life'.[33] Because 'vicariousness is the emotional half of civ-
ilised life', it is mostly an interpretation of life from within a condition of
suffering, for 'sometimes it seems that schizophrenia is one long inner and
often inaccessible essay in vicariousness, of vicarious suffering'. From Kessel, we can learn something about the nature of emotional suffering which is
very real, and personal, but is at the same time intimately, and inextricably,
entangled in the skeins of an ambiguous, and constantly evolving, social
and cultural world. It is always a suffering *in*, and may sometimes reflect the
suffering *of*, a social field. By no means is it a fixed reality, but rather a flux,
a 'becoming' or sometimes a 'waning', frequently a surplus, or excess, that
is ignored, or not accounted for, in official appraisals, quite at odds with
official outlooks and proffering an entirely divergent perspective.

The experience of 'being schizophrenic' in our type of society is, above all,
marked by 'futility' and 'invalidation', so Kessel believes. 'Any meaningful
care', he writes, 'has to fundamentally meet the chronic invalidation and sense
of futility which mark this condition'. In his moving and reflective foreword to
the posthumous complete poems of Howard Mingham [*Waters of the Night*,
Caparison, 2012], a friend of Kessel's, and, like Kessel himself, a socialist and
a schizophrenic, he identifies futility as 'the emotional mark of serious mental
illness and chronic poverty'. Acquiring insight into the nature, and origins,
of this predicament is inevitably painful, but at the same time 'the "painful
bits" are the useful living bits. Pain tells us that we are natural creatures, not
deluded Gods or fairies, but part and parcel of the natural world around us.
Existential pain is the personal starting point of healing, of which poetry –
naturalistic, metaphorical, or ironic – can be an essential part'.[34]

What, Kessel asks in another essay, would Christopher Caudwell, the
Marxist writer and poet who was killed in the Spanish Civil War, and whom
he admires, have 'thought of Britain and the world today where human solidarity is broken up at every turn and individuality has become, for many, a
digit on a computer screen?' As the creator of a *Schizophrenic Salvation Network*, Kessel is acutely aware both of the need for fellowship ('must associate
to counter loneliness and stigmatisation') and to the threats to solidarity
experienced by schizophrenics on the current scene ('very often invalidated
and demonised and often both together. Could become the modern Jews?').
With the closure of the asylums, many schizophrenics who were 'resettled'
in the community died within a year from dislocation, neglect and cold, he
observes. 'The inadequate, friendly, simple schizophrenics; the emotional,
devastated hebephrenics; the intense and wordy paranoids....we are not told
about them!' [These are older terms for identifying subtypes of schizophrenia, familiar to me from my training at much the same period as Kessel, but
not much in currency now]. To engage with the problems of 'chronic invalidation' and 'futility', the resources of the therapeutic community tradition
are essential. As for the writings of radicals such as R.D. Laing and David
Cooper, they are 'truly great philosophically' but in most cases they are

'downright dangerous therapeutically'. Kessel does not shirk from insisting that on occasions even ECT may be an essential ingredient of modern treatment, along with 'appropriate minimal medication'.

If much of this sounds rather downbeat, that is not at all how Kessel intends it for he believes passionately in what he calls the 'utopianism of the schizophrenic', and the idea that the schizophrenic has 'an existential duty towards the community in communicating by word, organisation or art his or her particular richness'. 'Poetry butters no parsnips. A fancy excrescence', he sardonically remarks. 'At best a mere condiment, a chutney'. He laments the almost unbridgeable chasm between labour and culture today. 'Poetry, which is the coming into consciousness of life, new life, the living thread which is inchoate, highly complex, both painful and wonderful, is regarded as a bourgeois enclave'. All the same, in the teeth of contemporary misery, writing poetry 'may be organically linked to the healing of schizophrenia, that abused and ill understood condition', and hence make the schizophrenic a contributor in the 'inalienable task of poetry to confront the despair and deadliness within existence, and transform it in a matter of fact way into everyday and millennial hope'. Over many years now, David Kessel endeavoured to fulfil his own existential duty by communicating with immense richness, variously as poet, thinker and activist, about his experience as a self-identified 'chronic schizophrenic', an experience of life in which 'schizophrenia' and 'hope' prove to be ironic bed-fellows. These lines from his poem '*In Memoriam Salvador Allende*' (2010) poignantly convey the mutual entanglement of 'person' and 'history' that is integral to Kessel's outlook:

'*We are all alone, but not separate*
from each other in street and parks.
We live in the spaces of other's lives'.[35]

Institutional psychotherapy at Saint-Alban

Through the combination of his writing and his activism, David Kessel evinces a potential for connection between the psychic and the social or, more accurately, the political that is, perhaps, more radical than anything accomplished by the British therapeutic community tradition, and more closely resembles the therapeutic experiments associated with the theorizers and practitioners, such as Jean Oury and Francois Tosquelles, of what became known as institutional psychotherapy, at the hospital in Saint-Alban in central France, and its associated clinic of La Borde, where Tosquelles worked from his arrival as a Catalan refugee from Franco's Spain in 1941, carrying Jacques Lacan's thesis on paranoid psychosis among his hastily gathered possessions, through to his death in 1994. Oury, Tosquelles and their collaborators were profoundly influenced by their experience of war, fascism and occupation from which they understood that occupation was not simply a physical condition but also a state of mind. Recognising that historically psychiatry had mostly functioned as a vector of power, they insisted that therapeutic care be viewed critically within an understanding of the asylum as a locus of symbolic power.[36] Institutional psychotherapy, declared Oury in 1970, 'is perhaps best defined as the attempt to fight, every day, against that which can turn the collective whole towards a concentrationist or segregationist structure'.[37] For Tosquelles, psychiatry and politics opened the possibility of accomplishing a form of true freedom through the 'disoccupation' of the mind in which Marx and Freud were complementary figures in the struggle towards what Tosquelles called 'une politique de la Folie', 'a politics of madness'.[38]

A paramount objective was the creation of an environment conducive to collective transference in which typical hierarchies and boundaries were constantly challenged so as to ensure that the object of transference was not simply the individual psychiatrist or therapist but the group as a whole. The point was to consider the psychic potential of the hospital environment in its totality as a vehicle for engaging with madness as a social problem. Among the innovations introduced here was the Club Paul Balvet, founded in 1947 as a patient-run cooperative structure, that took charge of organizing all activities within the hospital. Marius Bonnet, a nurse at the time, recalled how during meetings of the club 'when a patient, without warning, would begin to talk about his problems, the meeting agenda was dropped and everybody listened.....You see, at Saint-Alban, everything was a pretext for dialogue and not only in these meetings. Elsewhere, also, in daily life. The gardener, the cook, the secretary, the nurse, the electrician...everyone on the staff intervened in the system of psychotherapy'.[39] There was also a weekly journal, *Trait d'Union*, which ran from 1950 to 1981, featuring theoretical, literary and poetical texts, together with drawings, recipes, advertisements and letters. All these creations and activities were designed to facilitate the emergence of a 'horizontal' collectivity, a horizontal, as opposed to a vertical, vision of society that would bring about a new space of transference – a 'transferential constellation' – and an alternative form of treatment for the psychotic patient. As the historian Camille Robcis recounts, for Francois Tosquelles 'institutional psychotherapy was 'not a rigid and all-encompassing model but rather, an ethics, a way of thinking and living. Constantly evolving, adapting, and always revisable, institutional psychotherapy was a form of permanent revolution of politics, society, and psychic life, all at once'.[40]

Franco Basaglia and the radical psychiatry movement in Italy

The outlook that animated the tradition of institutional psychotherapy is in many respects reminiscent of the movement that got under way in Italy in the 1960s, inspired by the legendary psychiatric reformer, Franco Basaglia, involving a whole host of actors and groups from diverse walks of life, to transform the institutional landscape of Italian mental health care that was dominated by repressive and decaying lunatic asylums, or *manicomi*, and also, and more daringly, to transform the society that had brought such deficient institutions into being in the first place. Like Oury and Tosquelles, Basaglia and his associates belonged to a post-war, anti-fascist generation who cared deeply about human rights and were shocked by the violence and squalor that confronted them in these institutions, the utter disregard, not to say the wilful repudiation, of the humanity of its inmates.

The 'essence of psychiatry', remarked Giorgio Antonucci who worked with Basaglia at Gorizia, 'lies in an ideology of discrimination'.[41] Basaglia interpreted mental illness as a socio-political problem, and drew upon Husserl's concept of 'bracketing', the suspension of judgement in the first encounter with reality, in his approach to mental patients, maintaining that it was essential to establish a relationship with the individual patient independently of the label by which that individual had been defined. Along with phenomenology, Basaglia also turned to Gramsci and other Italian Marxists to understand the complex nexus of contradictions (institutional, ideological, ethical, medical, political, and social) in which madness was embedded. The movement of *Psichiatria Democratica* he inspired took the political engagement of mental health reform to a new limit, linking with, and becoming a rallying point for, wider social protests, so lending the movement an overtly revolutionary and, in the minds of its critics, an extremist, or 'ideological', character, eventually succeeding in 1978 in bringing about legislation, the notorious Law 180, that led (though the process took some twenty years to complete) to the closing down of all psychiatric hospitals in Italy.

Though the movement began around the asylum in Gorizia, in actuality its scope and reach went far beyond the story of Franco Basaglia and Franca Ongaro, Basaglia's wife and long-time collaborator. The story of the Italian reform movement has been subject to considerable misrepresentation and mythologizing, in Italy and especially in Britain, where it has frequently been subjected to vitriol and derision, and it is only recently that a critical study has appeared by John Foot, a distinguished historian of modern Italy, subjecting the history of the movement to scrutiny, detailing the contests over meanings, interpretations, and even over the definitions of facts themselves, involving numerous agents and agencies, from mental patients to psychiatrists to politicians to the media, that have contributed to the making of the popular legend around Franco Basaglia.[42]

Foot embarked on his research with a focus that was initially Basaglia-centric but soon discovered that the movement as a whole, in its rich and jostling diversity, and not least the processes implicated in the creation of the Law 180, were more complex and multi-valanced than this. In the last years of his life (he died prematurely of a brain tumour in 1980), Basaglia felt himself to be the prisoner of a myth, variously extolled or derided by the press as the man who either freed or abandoned the mad, burdened by hopes and expectations on which he could not possibly deliver. In deconstructing this legacy of myth and misrepresentation, and telling the story of a movement that was inspired, but only partly led, by Basaglia himself, Foot to an extent mimics the gesture of a small museum (now sadly closed) in the grounds of the asylum at Trieste which included a bust of Franco Basaglia that was intentionally covered with a sheet.

As Foot is at pains to convey, Basaglia never envisaged the closure of *manicomi* as a solution, only as a stage, though obviously a crucial one, in a series of moves towards a different conception, and treatment, of people with mental illness and society's responsibilities towards them. 'The destruction of the madhouse', Basaglia wrote, 'does not imply that patients will be abandoned, but it creates the conditions under which they can be looked after in a better way in terms of their real problems'.[43] One of the flagships of the movement, the hospital at Trieste was not just closed down, 'its whole raison d'etre was undermined, built as it was on separation, exclusion and silence'.[44] Historically, it is in any case, a mistake to conflate the closure of asylums with the abandonment of patients since lunatic asylums *themselves* had come to exemplify a culture of abandonment. The anti-institutional movement with which Basaglia was associated was not so much about creating a new kind of mental health system, as a new kind of society, a new way of being in life, that would not necessarily eliminate mental illness or severe mental distress, but would foster more productive, and hopeful, ways of dealing with it, and would to that extent possess a definite preventative function. Inevitably, there were some 'excesses' in the Italian experiment and, quite properly, Foot acknowledges that the legacy of the movement remains controversial, and even divisive, though it must be borne in mind that this is surely true of the history of psychiatry as a whole.

Schizophrenia and Black madness

A consideration of schizophrenia *in* history must, perforce, engage with the category of race for, to an extent that has still to be properly acknowledged, the history of psychiatry as a whole, as some recent studies amply attest is a racialized history.[45] There is an unspoken dimension here for it is *whiteness* that is steering the plot. Modern reason is above all *white* reason. In Britain, nearly 50% of in-patients are now detained on an order under the Mental Health Act. Black people are four times more likely to be detained than whites. Moreover, black patients are subjected to Community Treatment Orders at nearly *ten* times the rate of white patients.

Black radical thinkers like Saidiya Hartman have shown how 'black lives are still imperiled and devalued by a racial calculus and a political arithmetic that were entrenched centuries ago. This is the afterlife of slavery – skewed life chances, limited access to health care and education, premature death, incarceration and impoverishment'. Concludes Hartman: 'I, too, am the afterlife of slavery'.[46] Mad exclusion and black exclusion together are *constitutional* of capitalist modernity, and they are part of the fabric, wired into the hardware, that keeps the show going.

Revealingly, the subtitle of Jonathan Metzl's powerful study *The Protest Psychosis* is: '*How Schizophrenia Became a Black Disease*'.[47] As Metzl relates, when Kraepelin's terminology of dementia praecox reached the United States in the 1910s and 1920s, 'the emphasis on brain biology fit easily into existing beliefs that "Negroes" were biologically unfit for freedom'.[48] For example, in 1914, Arrah Evarts, a psychiatrist at the Government Hospital for the Insane in Washington DC, published an article entitled 'Dementia Praecox in the Coloured Race' in which she described dramatic increases in the condition in coloured patients which she linked to the pressures of freedom, for which, she claimed, Negroes were biologically unfit. In reality, she concluded, the bondage of slavery had been a 'wonderful aid to the colored man', since 'the necessity of mental initiative was never his'.[49] Of course, European colonizers had for two centuries and more been arguing that colonial servitude aided blacks by civilizing them, but Arrah Evarts and other physicians from the 1910s and 1920s dressed up this lineage in 'modern' Kraepelinian terminology.

Over the years from the 1920s through to the 1940s, the impression given in the popular press was that most people with a schizophrenia diagnosis were members of a category called white, not because there were no black schizophrenics, but because in an age of profound segregation the countless men and women diagnosed with schizophrenia who resided in segregated, southern 'Negro hospitals' were mostly invisible, suffering outside public awareness, the media rarely deigning to mention the dismal conditions in black mental hospitals.[50] In an expose in *Ebony* magazine in April 1949, the Negro wards at Milledgeville State Hospital in Georgia were described as the worst in the nation, unbelievable 'this side of Dante's inferno'.[51]

The 1960s and 1970s, argues Metzl, represented an era in which psychiatry's symbolic order shifted in immutable ways, bringing about an alignment between protest and psychosis in which schizophrenia became associated with aggression, hostility, rage and Black Power.[52] In 1968, psychiatrists Walter Bromberg and Frank Simon published an article on 'protest psychosis' in *Archives of General Psychiatry* in which they contended that black men developed 'delusional anti-whiteness' after listening to the words of militants such as Malcolm X, requiring psychiatric treatment as a result, since their symptoms threatened not only their own sanity but the social order of white America. Advertisements for the anti-psychotic drug Haldol from the 1970s depicted black men with clenched fists and bore the legend: 'Assaultive and belligerent? Cooperation often begins with Haldol (haloperidol), a first choice for starting therapy'. Even in an era dominated by neuroscience, Metzl maintains, diagnosis remains a projective act combining scientific understanding with a complex set of ideological and political assumptions. Though psychiatric definitions may provide clarity for some patients and families struggling to understand painful life events, overall for black mental patients especially, 'wholesale acceptance of psychiatric terms and frameworks involves entry into a potentially racially subjugating symbolic order in which biomedical definitions of illness supplant cultural ones'. In consequence, through a process of attrition, persons with a schizophrenia diagnosis 'become doubly stigmatized, both by a disease that carries a poor prognosis and by a medical system that forces acceptance of hegemonic descriptors of well-being at the expense of autobiographies of protest or survival. To enter the doctor's rhetorical system, rhetorically speaking, is to give up the fight'.[53] Drawing on a Blues tradition in which going crazy was a way of resisting white authority during slavery, among contemporary rappers schizophrenia possesses multiple meanings. Rappers turn the notion of a protest psychosis on its head, concurring that they are indeed black, male and violent, 'but this violence is not *our* pathology –it is a response to *yours*'. And in rap lyrics, 'schizophrenia' and 'schizophrenic' connote not so much a disease as an identity 'claimed in response to a system that misperceives survival strategies as insanity'.[54]

In conclusion

There can be no real conclusion to a discussion of this kind. Professor Robin Murray, the doyen of schizophrenia studies at London's Institute of Psychiatry, announced in 2017 that he expected to see the end of the concept of schizophrenia soon. 'Already the evidence that it is a discrete entity rather than just the severe end of psychosis has been fatally undermined'.[55] For Joseph K., David Kessel and their confederates, though, it is very much a case of *a luta continua*! And it is here, perhaps, that we are brought back to the category of 'the political' which informed the movement for institutional psychotherapy inspired by Francois Tosquelles and his followers, understood as 'the essence of all community, that which founds the being-together or the being-with [*l'-etre-ensemble ou l'etre-avec*], how it is constituted and how we can think it'.[56]

This understanding is, I believe, very much in tune with what the great Swiss psychiatrist Manfred Bleuler is getting at when he remarks that the treatment methods that have 'proved their worth with schizophrenics' are those that 'consist of emphasizing the distinction between "I" and "we", and between "you" and "all-of-you" in an active communal relationship'.[57] And alongside these utterances, we may place the proposal by the historian of disability Lennard Davis for an alternate standpoint in life to that of the colonial norm, based now on the partial and incomplete subject, whose realization is no longer autonomy and independence, but dependency and interdependence. 'Dependence is the reality and independence grandiose thinking', Davis writes.[58] Psychoanalysts like Jean Laplanche have argued that, far from being autonomous and bounded selves, we are instead constituted in relationality. When I try to tell the story of myself, I am made aware that another story is already at work in me.[59] I discovered only very recently that there is a remarkable affinity between Laplanche's ideas and the philosophy of 'Ubuntu', an African world view, much extolled by Nelson Mandela and Desmond Tutu, based on the idea that 'a person is a person through other persons'. Historically, as scholars like Celia Brickman have shown, psychoanalysis has been decidedly ambivalent about the 'primitive', or the African if you like, in the emotional life of all of us.[60] But in the writings of Laplanche and others, perhaps rather belatedly, we are at last being granted an intimation of a black or African Freud. In the teeth of the continuing marginalization and exclusion of people with psychosis, psychoanalysis has a compelling moral obligation, I believe, to renew and maintain such an ethic of interconnectivity. May we, perhaps, look to a re-discovery and re-invigoration of 'the political' in a practical solidarity of the partial and the incomplete? And it is not, I believe, farfetched to suggest that such an ethic is in the spirit of the kinds of discoveries that Robert M. Young was making on his long journey through the human sciences into psychoanalysis and therapeutic practice.

Peter Barham, April 2021

NOTES

1 I.Hacking, 'A tradition of natural kinds', *Philosophical Studies,* 61 (1/2): 109-126, 1991

2 P. Barham, *Schizophrenia and Human Value: Chronic Schizophrenia, Science and Society,* London: Free Association Books, 1993, 2nd edition with new preface, first published Oxford: Basil Blackwell, 1984; A. MacIntyre, *After Virtue*, London: Duckworth, 1981; R. Rorty, *Philosophy and the Mirror of Nature,* Oxford: Basil Blackwell, 1980; C. Taylor, *Sources of the Self,* Cambridge: Cambridge University Press, 1989

3 P. Barham & R. Hayward, 'Schizophrenia as a life-process', in: R.Bentall ed., *Reconstructing Schizophrenia*, London: Routledge, 1990

4 Notably in 'The naturalization of value systems in the human sciences' (1981), 'The moral and the molecular' (1996), and in a stimulating review, 'The divided science' (1966), of R.D.Laing's *The Divided Self*, all accessible on Robert Young's website: http://www.psychoanalysis-and-therapy.com/human_nature/papers/index.html

5 C. Taylor, *Sources of the Self,* Cambridge : Cambridge University Press, 1989

6 Ibid.: 112.

7 C.Taylor, *Philosophical Papers, Vol 1: Human Agency and Language*, Cambridge: Cambridge University Press, 1985: 7.

8 S.Gilman 'Constructing schizophrenia as a category of mental illness', in: E Wallace & J Gach eds., *History of Psychiatry & Medical Psychology*, Dordrecht: Springer, 2008: 461—483; S. Heckers & K.Kendler, 'The evolution of Kraepelin's nosological principles', *World Psychiatry*, 19 (3): 381–388, 2020; E.Kraepelin, Dementia Praecox and *Paraphrenia* (translated by R,M.Barclay) Edinburgh: Livingstone, 1919, originally published in 1913 as Psychiatrie (8th edn), Band III, Teil II, Kapitel IX.

9 T.Johnstone, 'The case for dementia praecox', *Journal of Mental Science*, 55: 64-91, 1909.

10 D.Brower & H.M.Bannister, *A Practical Manual of Insanity*, London: W.B. Saunders, 1902: 15, 303, 305.

11 M. Craig and T. Beaton, *Psychological Medicine* London: J & A Churchill, 1926: 117, 134, 128.

12 Cited in R. Noll, 'Psychosis', in G. Eghigian, ed., *The Routledge History of Madness and Mental Health* London: Routledge, 2017, pp 331—349, at p.340.

13 H.S.Decker, *Freud in Germany: Revolution and Reaction in Science, 1893—1907*, New York: International Universities Press, 1977.

14 J.Zubin, G.Oppenheimer, & R.Neugebauer, 'Degeneration theory and the stigma of schizophrenia', *Biological Psychiatry* 20: 1145—1148, 1985.

15 M.Bleuler, *The Schizophrenic Disorders: Long-Term Patient and Family Studies*, New Haven: Yale University Press, 1978: 417. First published as: *Die Schizophrenen Geistesstorungen im Lichte Langjahriger Kranken und Familiengeschichten*, Stuttgart; Georg Thieme, 1972.

16 For discussion see Barham 1993 op.cit.

17 G. Berrios, R. Luque, and J. Villagran, "Schizophrenia: A Conceptual History." *International Journal of Psychology and Psychological Therapy*, 3(2): 114—140, 2003: 134—135

18 S.Gilman, 'Constructing schizophrenia as a category of mental illness', op.cit: 462 & 478.

19 L.Sass, *Madness and Modernism: Insanity in the Light of Modern Art, Literature and Thought*, Oxford: Oxford University Press, 2017, revised edition, first published 1992.

20 S.Kamens, 'De-othering "schizophrenia"', *Theory & Psychology*, 29(2): 200—218, 2019: 209

21 D.O'Rawe, 'The politics of observation: documentary film & radical psychiatry', *Journal of Aesthetics & Culture*, 11 (1):1-18, 2019: 1.

22 Cited in M.Pines 'Forgotten pioneers: the unwritten history of the therapeutic community movement', *Therapeutic Communities*: 20 (1): 23—42, 1999. On Trigant Burrow (1875—1950), see Edi Gatti Pertegato & Giorgio Orghe Pertegato (eds), *From Psychoanalysis to Group Analysis: The Pioneering Work of Trigant Burrow*, forewords by Malcolm Pines, Alfreda Sill Galt and Lloyd Gilden, London: Karnac, 2013.

23 'Harold Searles', a talk given at the Tavistock Clinic, 28 March 2000. http://psychoanalysis-and-therapy.com/human_nature/papers/pap129h.html

24 See T.F.Main, 'The hospital as a therapeutic institution', *Bulletin of the Menninger Clinic* 10: 66—70, 1946, reprinted in Tom Main *The Ailment and Other Psychoanalytic Essays*, edited by J. Johns, London: Free Association Books, 1989; see also M Pines, 1999, op. cit.

25 T.Main, 'The concept of the therapeutic community: variations and vicissitudes', *Group Analysis*, 10 (2): S2-S16, 1977.

26 P.Barham *Forgotten Lunatics of the Great War*, London & New Haven: Yale University Press, 2004

27 P.Barham *Schizophrenia and Human Value*, op.cit.

28 P.Sedgwick, *Psychopolitics: Laing, Foucault, Goffman, Szasz and the Future of Mass Psychiatry*, London: Unkant Publishers, 2015: 237, first published by Pluto Press, 1982.

29 C.Mills, *Decolonizing Global Mental Health: The Psychiatrization of the Majority World*, London: Routledge, 2014: 69.

30 W.Brown, *Undoing the Demos*, New York: Zone Books, 2015: 44, 37, 38.

31 P.Sedgwick, 2015, op.cit.: 225. On these themes see also P.Barham *Closing the Asylum: The Mental Patient in Modern Society*, London: Process Press, 2020, 3rd edition, first published by Penguin Books 1992.

32 I shall draw here on my essay 'Poetry, Parsnips and Schizophrenia' in: *Ravaged Wonderful Earth –A Collection for David Kessel*', produced by Outsider Poets & Friends of East London Loonies (F.E.E.L.), 2012.

   For a fine obituary of David Kessel by Alan Morrison see: https://www.therecusant.org.uk/obituary-for-david-kessel. A moving eulogy by his son, Tom Kessel, can also be found at: https://www.therecusant.org.uk/a-eulogy-for-david-by-tom-kessel.

33 A version of this piece was written as early as 1988-89 and included in Kessel's collection, *'O the Windows of the Bookshop Must Be Broken: Collected Poems'*, London: Survivors' Press, 2006.
34 H.Mingham, *Waters of the Night*, London: Caparison Books, 2012.
35 Warm thanks to Tom Kessel for granting permission to cite these lines.
36 See, notably, C. Robcis 'Francois Tosquelles and the psychiatric revolution in postwar France', Constellations 23 (2): 212—222, 2016 & C. Robcis, *Disalienation: Politics, Philosophy and Radical Psychiatry in Postwar* France, Chicago: University of Chicago Press, 2021. See also D. O'Rawe, 'The politics of observation: documentary film and radical psychiatry' *Journal of Aesthetics and Culture*, 11 (1): 1-18, 2019.
37 cited in Robcis 2016: 212
38 Ibid.
39 Ibid.: 219
40 Ibid.: 220
41 cited in John Foot, *The Man Who Closed the Asylums: Franco Basaglia and the Revolution in Mental Health Care*, London: Verso, 2015: 105.
42 Ibid. See also a review of Foot, 2015, by Peter Barham in *Reviews in History*, 2016: http://www.history.ac.uk/reviews/review/1883
43 Ibid.: 386
44 Ibid.: 366
45 See, among others, M. Summers, *Madness in the City of Magnificent Intentions*. New York: Oxford University Press, 2019, & M. Segrest *Administrations of Lunacy*, New York: New Press, 2020.
46 S.Hartman, *Lose Your Mother: A Journey Along the Atlantic Slave Route*, New York: Farrar, Strauss & Giroux: 6. See also C.Sharpe *In the Wake: On Blackness and Being*, Durham & London: Duke University Press, 2016.
47 J. Metzl *The Protest Psychosis: How Schizophrenia Became a Black Disease*, Boston, MA: Beacon Press, 2009.
48 Ibid.: 30
49 A.Evarts, 'Dementia praecox in the colored race', *Psychoanalytic Review*, 4: 388–403, 1914: 394.
50 J.Metzl, *The Protest Psychosis*, op.cit.: 40
51 Ibid.: 41
52 Ibid.: 190
53 Ibid.: 197.
54 Ibid.
55 R.Murray cited in S. Guloksuz and J. van Os, 'The slow death of the concept of schizophrenia and the painful birth of the psychosis spectrum', *Psychological Medicine*, 48: 229–244, 2018: 236
56 Cited in C. Robcis 2016, op.cit.: 213.
57 M.Bleuler, 1978, op.cit.: 470; P.Barham, 1993, op. cit. : 174.
58 L.Davis *Bending Over Backwards: Disability, Dismodernism and Other Difficult Positions*, New York: New York Universities Press, 2002: 31.
59 J. Laplanche, *Essays in Otherness*, London: Routledge, 1998.
60 C.Brickman, *Aboriginal Populations in the Mind: Race and Primitivity in Psychoanalysis*, New York: Columbia University Press.

Chapter 12

Values

Inner and outer

R. D. Hinshelwood

Not only is everything we see and think theory-laden, but every theory is value laden.[1] We hold a theory because we think it is true. And true is judged good, high value. But there are other values, often very implicit, un-expressed and unrecognised. Indeed, there are some that are purposely hidden for shameful reasons.[2] The core idea – that the central motivations of human beings come down to value systems – is the underlying principle of psychoanalysis. And I think Bob Young became fascinated with psychoanalysis as a 'technology of values'.

Bob Young as mentor

I was once a part of a small reading group, in the 1980s, organised by Arturo Varchevker that sought to place psychoanalysis in the wider cultural and philosophical traditions. We were not very good at it, and so we looked for a group mentor. Bob Young had left Cambridge and was in London in process of setting up a new career in publishing and psychotherapy. And so he agreed, in 1984, to join the group as teacher, mentor, leader. I want to set out in this chapter, something of what I learned from him, and what I have made of it.

There are several driving ideas that he brought to the fore for me. The first was the importance of the implicit subjectivity of humans that emerged as knowledge, grounded knowledge and claimed as refutable; the second is the way that these implicit attitudes and convictions had a social life that impacts across all those in a specific culture, whether nation or class. A third influence was the encouragement to build on Marxist ideas of private property. And in addition, he shared with us a conviction that psychoanalysis could be a fine weapon in exposing the falsity of aspects of class, race and gender consciousness, albeit with the risk that psychoanalysis itself could be complicit in aiding the falsity of such elitist cover-ups and be itself laden with biased values. Indeed, he got into many quarrels over the values that grew up in the cultures of psychoanalytic and psychotherapy

DOI: 10.4324/9781003204244-16

organisations, often his views being reduced to a simple anti-elitism, which offended many.

By the time I knew Bob, he had grown suspicious of the standard ways of publishing his thoughts and arguments, and he set out to first of all establish a publishing house that he could oversee for its biasing of the output; and second, he attempted to pioneer, especially with his own writing the use of the internet where much of his psychoanalytically inspired work can be found (this is currently to be found at http://psychoanalysis-and-therapy.com/rmyoung/index.html, but is in process of preparation for conventional publication as a series of books by Process Press).

Social construction of research

Despite his original intention to graduate from Medical School to become a psychoanalyst, he was waylaid by his interest in philosophy to come to the UK and wrote his PhD thesis in the history of science at Cambridge. This led to his interest in Darwin and the Malthusian metaphor that the mid-nineteenth-century commitment to market competition inspired the idea of evolution by natural selection. And in turn it grounded market economics in our biological nature. He saw this construction of economics as engineered by such social attitudes.

He was a social constructivist in everything, including the questions that science asks and the answers that count as answers to those questions. As he once said, "All meanings are social"; and "the question of ideology is the question of how societies construct and come to take for granted, their conceptions of nature, life, humanity and society".[3] Hence the way a culture puts emphasis on these fundamentals, so it will frame its understanding of the way science enquires into them. In particular, it is perhaps illustrative to look back to the date when Margaret Thatcher came to power in Britain, in 1979, followed very shortly by Ronald Reagan in the US in 1980, resulting in Reaganomics based on Milton Freidman's shareholder theory which has blossomed spectacularly.

For example, in the 1960s, the huge technological project to travel to the moon was certainly a triumph of the theories of physics and chemistry and electronics behind the achievement. However, it was driven by the cold war imperative between the US and Russia. Their nationalist and even imperialist rivalry came down to the simplistic competition of values – capitalism versus communism, one nationalism versus another nationalism. After the cold war, a different urge took over the US. George Bush declared the 1990s the 'decade of the brain'. Large Charities were encouraged to put huge resources into researching the neurology that produces our human consciousness. This political value coming out of the need for the US to re-define its hegemony of the planet after the collapse of Soviet influence, has not succeeded quite so spectacularly as the race to the moon, but has promoted the value of people and consciousness as cognitive machines based on Boolean algorithms.[4] The technology of consciousness is perhaps itself the 'technology' of value judgements.

Constructing/deconstructing the self

One significant issue I have been left with from my encounter with Bob Young's ideas is the issue of subjectivity. It is the route by which social attitudes (themselves dependent in some way on the hidden or explicit attitudes of individuals) infiltrate the persons so often in covert ways. This subjectivity of the individual person is inevitably highlighted as a crucial element in any of the human sciences. This points to psychoanalysis and the roles that social attitudes and the personal 'self' of individuals have in relation to (or interaction with) each other.[5] There are many aspects of this 1980s neoliberal reconstruction of value by a social movement.[6]

But significantly there was a redirection as a social movement to attributing the origins of personal value to some internal state. It is not that inward reflection has not been absent in the history of mankind. One can think of those outlines on cave walls of human hands. Those early human cave-dwellers made their mark on the wall by blowing charcoal powder against their hand pressed to the wall. What was their purpose, their value, in the minds of those proto-artists? It seems something of their capacity to recognise some part of themselves, or some survival of a part of themselves may have been a very early occupation 30,000–40,000 years ago. This propensity for self-reflection and representation also became socially used in the post-Mediaeval and early industrial period.

This glossy recounting of history may need a lot of refinement, but I am suggesting that marking the personal being in oneself has been a long-standing attribute of the human mind and that it could be built into a social construction of self and self-value at a time when it was needed. In Europe, that time seemed to be in the early-to-mid nineteenth century. With the help of psychoanalysis, that prioritising of self-value in terms of inner states of being has become a powerful pre-occupation from the mid-twentieth century. The value of being who you are has thus become significant for people formed in the Western world by the pressures of social construction.

Taking this line of thinking, there is a separation of what is socially constructed as a value, from what is *felt* as a valuable person. A person's own conscious and unconscious sense of being a valuable person is important existentially. In our contemporary world that inner sense of an individual person vies with the social construction of what a valuable person is. The social value constructed from the value of money may contrast with the inner sense of value, or may substitute for it, or may invalidate it, especially for a person in poverty. This kind of marriage contract between an inner construction and a social construction is, I suggest, a particularly powerful motivator of a person in society.

Being and production

Back to a little bit of history. Around the time when Protestantism was in full swing, there was investigation of the sense of being a person or losing that sense. Feuerbach exposed what he regarded as the essence of the human being, his 'species-being', as a religious sensibility that involved projection into the external world of the idea of gods.[7] Such an anti-religious thesis was adopted, in part, by Marx and Engels, who turned Feuerbach on his head (Marx 1845) and saw the human essence in very much more practical terms. Marx's correction was not that humans have an inner self that gets expressed as gods, rather that human essence and sense of himself and value is the *capacity for material production*. Interestingly, this feature of the human self-evaluation is reflected in Freud and the notion of the ego that begins to accept reality[8]:

> [M]otor discharge, which, under the dominance of the pleasure principle, had served as a means of unburdening the mental apparatus of accretions of stimuli... was now employed in the appropriate alteration of reality.

Instead of a simple stimulus-response in the environment, Freud added: "Restraint upon motor discharge... was provided by means of the process of *thinking*... It is essentially an experimental kind of acting".[9] Unlike animals, in the case of humans, their sense has involved the production of food with the thoughtful invention and use of implements and tools, etc. This specific attribute is our species-being, the essence of being human. It is the craft of producing the physical means of living. The notion of the human comes close in Marx and Freud. Thus, the inner sense of self was not just confined to religious proselytising, but in the atheist tradition the inner self has its presence in material production.

But at this crucial time in the nineteenth century, there was a realisation, notably by Marx, that the individual person could lose their species-being, their productive craft, and could enter a state of being a kind of non-person or alienated from his essence. This construction of 'alienation' by Marx was, he perceptively noted, at a time when the means of production was radically changing.[10] So much production was moving over to the function of machinery, and the organisation of production from a domestic setting to a factory organisation.

In Marx's view, therefore, the nature of a person was becoming confused, in terms of social constructions, with the inanimate nature of a machine. He postulated therefore that the species-being of human's was then regarded as little different from the nature of machines. The person lost his personhood amongst the machines and became alien. He was alienated from his own nature as a person. But Marx also spotted another deeply important process that was involved in this.

The value of persons

Not only is the individual worker valued merely in relation to the machine which the worker uses but there is another very subtle way in which he is alienated from his own value as a human person. It is the origins of what has reached its zenith in our present monetarism of Reaganomics. This concerns 'labour process'.[11] Humans do not just find their necessities in nature, but they attempt to change nature to their needs[12]:

> He opposes himself to nature as one of her own forces, setting in motion arms and legs, head and hands, the natural forces of his body in order to appropriate nature's productions in a form adapted to his own wants.

However, the way this planned production from nature is achieved varies with the kind of society and culture in which it operates. And significantly different relations grow up according to the particular method of production. The means of production most prevalent in Western society developed early on and progressed in steps, one later step was introduced by Friedman.

Marx (1867) had spotted the earlier steps in that method of production, and he called it 'labour process'. The pattern of relations is that the worker who produces in a factory will find his product taken from him: "the object that labour produces, its product, stands opposed to it as something alien".[13] Let us consider as an example a factory in which a man makes nails. He is paid a certain amount – X pounds – for his labour for a day's work; and he makes N nails during a day. The factory has other expenses as well as his wages – the site, the machinery, the raw materials, transport, investors and managers and so on – say Y pounds. When the factory sells the N nails (called the 'exchange value' = E pounds), that amount has to cover X + Y. If the factory is successful, then E will be more than X plus Y. If it is more (say S pounds per days production) then $E = X + Y + S$. So the profit for a days' work from the worker's production is S or the surplus value. Because the worker is paid her day, then S goes to the factory (or more importantly its owner), not to the worker. Thus, the worker passes over to the factory a quantity of nails equivalent to S. In this way, it is possible to *quantify* the value that the factory takes from the worker after all expenses are settled. In that process, the *quality* of the person is diminished.

Surplus value may therefore be disputed and the worker may claim he should have some proportion of S. Such debates that go on in industrial relations concern money, although as can be seen from the mention of the inner world, it is not just money value that the worker passes over, but a proportion of his own sense of self embodied in the object produced and now belonging to the factory. These relations, worked out in terms of wages and surplus value, implicitly convert the inner world sense of self into monetary value.

Since his act of production is a part of his essence, his species-being, then the removal of his product into someone else's ownership is a loss of his sense of being human: "The worker places his life in the object; but now it no longer belongs to him, but to the object".[14] There is something of the worker's sense of being is put into the object as he makes it. And as it passes to someone else, he loses something of his feeling of being himself, so that: "The more the worker exerts himself, the more powerful the alien, objective world becomes which he brings into being over and against himself, the poorer he and his inner world become" (Marx 1844, p. 324; see also Hinshelwood 1983 and the comparison between the separation of aspects of the self in both Marx's alienation and in the schizoid mechanisms, described a century later as projective identification, by psychoanalysis).

We have come a long way, today, from this early nineteenth-century beginnings of the social relations of self. Marx was aware that there was an interchangeability between this sense of self (the inner world, as Hegel called it) and money. So, that 'monetarisation' of self and one's personal being has proceeded now to the shareholder theory of 50 years ago that inspired low tax economics. But it has also resulted in what we now call the gig economy. Interestingly, the gig economy where workers are paid according to tasks an employer seeks to achieve for a customer, rests on a system where the worker responds to an algorithm in a computer. This expresses of course the need for efficiency but in the process, it implicitly defines the worker as a non-personal element controlled by electronic machinery. It is an encroachment of the alienation that started with the implicit equivalence of the nineteenth-century worker's self (embodied in his product) with the surplus value which separated him from an element of his being.

Even today in Western societies, there survives a highly regarded tradition of craft manufacture in which the craftsman retains his name in connection with the pottery or jewellery he makes. The artist signs his work. A painting by Leonardo da Vinci might be known simply as a Leonardo. This indelible link between creator and product is a hall mark of certain individualised productions. An essay like this one is identified by the writer. Such a tradition of identification of producer with product remains very strong in certain areas of production, including intellectual production. This self-conscious survival of the more personalised craft production occurred in the nineteenth century and survives today perhaps precisely because of a hangover of the personal kind of exchange system.

Exchange and anthropological speculation

A further strand to the psychoanalytic contribution to social-personal interaction is the idea of an exchange system. Psychoanalytically, this concerns the processes of exchange of aspects of the self, via projective and introjective identifications. This has been demonstrated in the discussion of industrial relations and the detachment of product from producer. This leaves both the product and indeed the worker himself as less than personal.

They are alienated and can be referred to as commodities. That is to say without the personal link between product and producer both are reified and become more like things. It is a process of depersonalisation as it might be regarded by psychoanalysts and shown in classical studies using psycho-analytic concepts to investigate working organisations.[15] The capacity to re-duce a person to something more like a thing is, it seems, prevalent amongst humans, the extremes being such a place as Auschwitz.

Marcel Mauss contrasted gift economies in non-West societies with com-mercial commodity based economies.[16] Graeber argued that in spite of Adam Smith's early speculations, there is no evidence that a barter economy exists or ever existed as a transition stage from a gift economy to a money-based economy.[17]

Gregory, an anthropologist, drew a distinction between the traditional tribal exchange systems (typically the exchange of gifts in ceremonies such as the potlatch or the kula) and the introduction of Western commodity exchange during the colonial periods. He summarised, somewhat bitterly perhaps[18]:

> [There is a] logical opposition between gifts (relations between non-aliens by means of inalienable things) and commodities (relations be-tween aliens by means of alienable things).

The exchange of gifts and of goods which remain perfused by the person-alities of the producer and user – and indeed giver – tends now to be an activity restricted in Western society to family life and close communities of friends and in particular personalised ceremonies such as birthdays, wed-dings and Christmases. They reinforce the inalienable links between people. Such gifts are highly personalised and take account more often than not of others' need.

In public life, the exchange of alienable commodities, produced anony-mously, and consumed anonymously, has more or less taken over.[19] And, that exchange system has been perfused by money, large quantities some-times, with an inevitable commodification.

Even with de-industrialisation, the effect has unfortunately not been to restore the sense of personal production and a fuller personhood. In fact, there are now countless people in lower or middle level management jobs instead who perform jobs which in the heart of heats they feel to be 'bullshit jobs' as Graeber called them.[20] It does not restore a sense of value to themselves, in fact the reverse. They remain with a sense that their job may contribute nothing. The reaction is to seek a sense of value in them-selves and social attitudes provide the answer that it is the accumulation of money and property. This need to find something to give value to the self, in this way, then, in turn, helps to promote money as the value to be sought.

One of the important ideas I took from Bob was the idea of a process philosophy. Not specifically Whitehead but the general notion that subjectivity is the mind in movement. But more than this, so is the body. From a medical background, biochemical systems are not linear causations, as they appear in a laboratory. In the body, they are self-sustaining cycles, adjusting to influences of chemical concentrations, acidity, temperature and pressure and so on. The body is a system of adjustments of these self-sustaining systems in exchange with each other as they sustain themselves. If you lie a living body down next to a corpse. The actual substances are all in much the same proportions in the same place in each body. But one has a system of processes interacting that give rise to a self-sustaining system – the corpse rots away, disintegrates and cannot sustain itself. Such a set of self-sustaining systems in incomparable complexity is 'life'.

It is easy to see how that complexity could be seen as a spirit inhabiting and bring to enduring life the matter of the body. The inspiration and expiration of the breathe is evidence of such a communication with a world of the spirit, as spiritual substance is in-spired or ex-spired. That emphasis on process has lasted in my thinking (inspired me, even) and drawn me to the theory of complex self-sustaining systems. It had seemed to me a more subtle way of approaching the kind of radical politics which led Bob Young to become so often confrontational.

Ideologies

Shareholder theory for which Reagan got Friedman the Nobel Prize is a simplifying idea of the way commercial businesses run – or should run. Thatcher's contribution was to try to apply the idea to public service in Britain Friedman wrote a 3,000 word article in the New York Times in 1970.[21] The fundamental principle of a business is to increase profits – as Freidman says "the social responsibility of business is to increase its profits". In fact, this is such a key point he made it the sub-title to the article. Shareholders who invest their money in a business are the prime priority and their dividends are the sole consideration. Any expense that the company makes for the benefit of employees, suppliers and even customers is regarded by Freidman as a 'tax' on the dividends due to shareholders. It is a simple one-dimensional principle for managers to steer their companies by. And, with the backing of the US government, it has been extremely successful in steering national economies around the world. It is the heart of what is now called neoliberalism. It places the shareholders benefits as the highest value for the commercial world.

It is an example of how a value dictates the direction of cultural change. The implicit value of Freidman's shareholder theory is the value of money, and not merely that, it is the value of those who own and invest their money.

Inner construction

This doctrine sets out a 'social responsibility'. It is both based on the value of money and in turn is an expression of how that principle gained leverage over greater and greater areas of economic and social life. It originated in an ideological belief in the value of money and is a significant example of the emergence of a social construction of a major element of the culture within which we live today – i.e., the neoliberal relations and values of the social classes.

It would seem the time had come for the idea that the really valuable principle and the really valuable people are money and the moneyed. Although that may seem self-evident to so many people today, it has not always been so. Going back to Mediaeval times value was assessed in a very different way. The construction of a valuable person was something to do with their relations with God. The lack of money, poverty and godly devotion could be entirely compatible then, and indeed, a special value might have been given to people who chose poverty – hermits, for instance, the choice of a chilly and sparse life in a monastery or convent, celibacy in favour of communion with God and so on.

As the Enlightenment took over, the social methods of assessing valued action and valued persons gradually changed, despite a widespread movement to rescue something of the Mediaeval construction of God. The Protestant movement all across Europe attempted to purify the corruption of the Church (often mediated by money) by relocating the presence of God within the individual. A direct access between the person and the value-making entity, God, became a personal affair rather than one mediated by the clergy.

The social construction of money

Money is the example, *par excellence*, of a social construct. It is the construction of value itself and is a form of abstraction of value seemingly not linked to any particular use value in itself, apart from the smooth running of a bargaining system where use values and exchange values can be juggled for the advantage of two negotiators. The advantage for these negotiators is served by the intermediary of money that smooths the negotiation and transaction. Such transactions do not occur in gift economies where the exact use value of products is not strictly compared. As Gregory says, money and the comparability of values in the exchange seems to come in especially in correlation with the alien forms of commodities detached from their personal reference points.[22]

I wish to develop briefly two main points about the development of money as a social construct of value itself. First of all, it may not be true that money has no use value in the classical sense. If use value is an attribute that leads to the creation of a product that has surplus value, then money can be used to create more surplus value. Perhaps since the beginning of the use of money, maybe 6,000 years ago, there have been money-lenders who use money to make money. And certainly, from biblical times such people who used money in that way have been disapproved of. Although it might be that such disapproval has waned over recent centuries, and the value of money to make money has increasingly been seen as a social asset. The fact that banks may lend something like eight to ten times their reserves enables the circulation of money on the basis of a loan system. Banks may recoup not just the loans they make but also interest on those loans even though they do not have reserves to cover those loans. It is a system of trust that there will not be a sudden demand for the cash from those who have loaned on trust. It is a trust that has begun to run out on occasions, for instance, Black Monday 1987, and in October 2008. Such a system based on a supposed use value of money itself is known therefore to be unstable, based on trust rather than on a physical use of a physical product.

The development of a system of money as a super-ordinate value seems to have been an inevitability. The evolving and developing of the system for exploiting money in this way is both based on the sense of money as super-ordinate and enhances that implicit social construction within the culture. It appears to be a positive feedback system both based on and in turn enhancing the social construction of what money is and how it can function. Having a self-sustaining feedback system as outlined, it appears to have a life of its own supported on the implicit socially constructed value system where money has come to the top. There appears to be little that can be done to change it.

Ethical conflicts

Moving on from this risky system of values constructed by our social attitudes, there is a second and perhaps more alarming consequence of the super-ordinate status of money. If money is indeed an implicit super-ordinate value in public life (as opposed to the dominance of the gift economy in the private life of family and friends), then we might need to be concerned about those values which are implicitly not super-ordinate and which infuse private life. It is a given within ethical systems that values may conflict and a judgement has to be made about which value should be given precedence on any particular occasion. For instance, a marital infidelity might be best kept secret. Loyalty to the marriage versus honesty is in conflict and which virtue should be followed is something to judge on the specific unfortunate occasion.

However, where we have a situation as in public life that there is a super-ordinate value which can therefore override other values, there is not a judgement to be made on each occasion. The super-ordinate value quite simply wins. Thus, there is little choice to be made between for instance, making money and a decent respect for looking after the unfortunate poor. A rich person is entirely entitled to pursue his money-making activity, however much it might further impoverish the poor. Or, more alarmingly, money-making can override honesty, with an entirely justifiable *ethical* resort to corruption! Whatever a legal system might say, the implicit judgement of the socially constructed value system is that making money wins over honesty in one's public dealings. It is hard to insert oneself in imagination into such a position, but increasingly it would appear that such an ethical requirement is compelling, even though it offends against a code of decency in private life.

However, where we have a situation as in public life that there is a super-ordinate value which can therefore override other values, there is not a judgement to be made on each occasion. The super-ordinate value quite simply wins. Thus, there is little choice to be made between for instance, making money and a decent respect for looking after the unfortunate poor. A rich person is entirely entitled to pursue his money-making activity, however much it might further impoverish the poor. Or, more alarmingly, money-making can override honesty, with an entirely justifiable *ethical* resort to corruption! Whatever a legal system might say, the implicit judgement of the socially constructed value system is that making money wins over honesty in one's public dealings. It is hard to insert oneself in imagination into such a position, but increasingly it would appear that such an ethical requirement is compelling, even though it offends against a code of decency in private life.

Conclusions

Bob Young's trajectory from would-be psychoanalyst to Cambridge scholar in the history of nineteenth-century science and back to a practitioner of psychoanalytic psychotherapy was a rather irregular circle. Whether he really reconciled his social constructivist position as a historian with his convictions about the psychoanalytic inner world is not completely clear to me. As someone deeply influenced by Marx, he could say[23]:

> In fact, the whole Marxist tradition can be described as one long battle against the economists and others who have tried to claim that existing social relations are based on the laws of positivist science.

But in turn he used psychoanalytic concepts, especially Kleinian ones, in a somewhat positivist way. He became, I think, fascinated with metapsychology and clinical practice as a technology of values. And although he paid a lip-service to psychoanalysis being itself value-laden, he seemed to be more interested in using his experience of psychoanalysis as a means of exposing the social constructions of values in the human sciences. Whilst I may seem to criticise his views as not completely consistent, I suspect he reached as far as it was possible to go.

I cannot claim to have confronted the conundrum that psychoanalysis is a model for thinking about social construction of values of the human sciences (and in much of the natural sciences) whilst accepting that psychoanalysis is itself a child of the social constructions of our times. The values of psychoanalysis are undoubtedly a challenge to the pervading value system of monetarism in its present form, and therefore it is a model that serves an important critiquing function in that respect. But there is little that can be found here about the implicit social influences on the values of psychoanalysis itself and thus how skewed its job of critiquing social values might be. As Bob was fond of saying: 'There is no position above the battlefield'. So, we are all in it together. Nevertheless, as a psychoanalyst, it has prompted me to engage in some critique of values in Western cultures and hopefully some attempt to engage in that critique from within might be worthwhile.

In the essay here, I have been explicit about my own debt to him and have tried to follow on some of the investigations that I have felt were in my scope. It is for the reader to reflect on the success of the kind of model I have tried to generate, and which I believe might be in accord with, and respectful of, Bob Young's own psychoanalytically based critical model.

Notes

1 R. M. Young, Science is social relations. *Radical Science Journal* (1977) 5: 65–129.
2 See G. Lukacs, *History and Class Consciousness*. Cambridge, MA: MIT Press, 1971.
3 R. M. Young, Science is a labour process. *Science for People* (1979) 43/44: 31–37.
4 M. Cobb, *The Idea of the Brain: The Past and Future of Neuroscience*. London: Profile Books, 2020.
5 R. D. Hinshelwood, Psychoanalytic knowledge and its production: Responding to Dreher, Briggs and Scott. *British Journal of Psychotherapy* (2019) 35: 107–113.
6 D. Harvey, *A Brief History of Neoliberalism*. Oxford: Oxford University Press, 2007.
7 L. Feuerbach, *The Essence of Christianity*. London: John Chapman, 1841 [1854].
8 S. Freud, Formulations on the two principles of mental functioning. *The Standard Edition of the Complete Psychological Works of Sigmund Freud, Volume XIII*. London: Hogarth, 1911, pp. 213–226.
9 Freud, Formulations on the two principles of mental functioning, p. 221.
10 K. Marx, *Theses on Feuerbach in Early Writings*. London: Penguin, 1975 [1845].
11 H. Braverman, *Labour and Monopoly Capital: The Degradation of Work in the Twentieth Century*. New York: Monthly Review Press, 1974; R. M. Young, Braverman's, *Labour and Monopoly Capital. Radical Science Journal* (1976) 4: 81–93.
12 K. Marx, *Capital*. London: Penguin, 1975 [1867], p. 283.
13 K. Marx, *Economic and Philosophical Manuscripts*. In *Early Writings*: London: Penguin, 1975 [1844], p. 323.
14 Marx, *Economic and Philosophical Manuscripts*, p. 325.

15   I. Menzies Lyth, The functioning of social systems as a defence against anxiety: A report on a study of the nursing service of a general hospital. *Human Relations* (1959) 13: 95–121. Republished 1988 in Menzies, *Containing Anxiety in Institutions*. London: Free Association Books; and in Trist and Murray (eds) *The Social Engagement of Social Science*. London: Free Association Books, 1990. Also A. Obholzer and V. Roberts, (eds.) *The Unconscious at Work*. London: Routledge, 1994.

16   M. Mauss, *The Gift: Forms and Functions of Exchange in Archaic Societies*. London: Routledge, 2002 [1925].

17   D. Graeber, *Debt: The First 5,000 Years*. New York: Melville House, 2011.

18   C. A. Gregory, *Savage Money: The Anthropology and Politics of Commodity Exchange*. Amsterdam: Harwood Academic, 1997, pp. 52–53.

19   C. A. Gregory, *Gifts and Commodities*. London: Academic Press, 1982. L. Hyde, *The Gift: Imagination and the Erotic Life of Property*. London: Vintage, 1983; J. G. Carrier, *Gifts and Commodities: Exchange and Western Capitalism Since 1700*. London: Routledge, 2012.

20   D. Graeber, *Bullshit Jobs*. New York: Simon and Schuster, 2018.

21   Available to read free online at https://www.nytimes.com/1970/09/13/archives/-a-friedman-doctrine-the-social-responsibility-of-business-is-to.html, (accessed December 2021) 13th September 1970.

22   C. A. Gregory, *Savage Money: The Anthropology and Politics of Commodity Exchange*. Amsterdam: Harwood Academic, 1997.

23   R. M. Young, Anthropology of science. *New Humanist* (1972) 88: 102–105.

Chapter 13

Primitive space

Paul Hoggett

Introduction

Bob wrote most of his book *Mental Space* in the early 1990s.[1] The threat of mutually assured nuclear destruction (MAD as it was called in those days) had only just receded with the collapse of the Soviet Union and the end of the Cold War. But the flowering of hope that followed the end of the 'iron curtain' was almost immediately crushed as the threat of genocide returned to Europe with the break-up of former Yugoslavia and the rise of virulent Croatian and particularly Serbian nationalism. That Bob's book should have a chapter named 'Primitive Space' was therefore entirely appropriate to the times in which he was writing.

Bob drew heavily on Klein and Bion in his exploration of the psychotic anxieties he felt haunted the political imagination but he also drew on his direct experience of participating in, and later staffing, Group Relations conferences. His exploration of the dynamics of group life proceeded partly under the guidance of Gordon Lawrence and David Armstrong, two highly original thinkers and practitioners both steeped in the work of Bion.[2] They both enjoyed a somewhat ambivalent relationship to the orthodoxy of the Group Relations tradition as embodied in the figure of Eric Miller at the Tavistock Institute. Naturally, Bob was drawn to such maverick figures rather than to the establishment.

Group Relations 'conferences' provided, and still continue to provide, a space for learning about the psychodynamics of groups, institutions and society. These 'conferences' are challenging events for both participants and staff; in my experience, they are at times infuriating, at times wildly exciting and at times terrifying. My first experience of being a staff member on such events came via invitation from Bob and Gordon. It was 1992 (I think) and Bob had developed a collaborative link with a network of radical psychiatrists in Bulgaria and, under the directorship of Gordon, Bulgaria was to experience its first taste of a Group Relations conference. It was an extraordinary event, held in deep midwinter in the Peoples Palace of Culture in Sofia, working with 50 or so participants virtually none of

DOI: 10.4324/9781003204244-17

whom spoke English. At that time, Bulgaria had the feeling of a collapsed state. Everything was rationed, power cuts alternated around the capital city, nothing seemed to work (including the Ladas and Trabbis that ferried us back and forth to the Palace). Even more bizarrely, hardly anyone present had any experience of participating in an autonomous group or community as every aspect of civic life under the former communist regime had been controlled by the state under Todor Zhivkov. It all felt a bit mad at times.

Fundamental to Bion's thinking about groups was his awareness of the constant interplay between the realistic, the creative and the deranged dimensions of group life. He captured this through his concept of group 'basic assumptions,'[3] which he believed underlined various forms of group mindlessness including flight and panic, fight and hatred, the anticipation of revelation and salvation and abject faith and helplessness. Speaking of his own early experiences as a participant in Group Relations conferences where such trends in group life come vividly alive, Bob wrote,[4]

> I continue to find this profoundly sobering. I also continue to ruminate it and am far from having digested the experience.
>
> (p. 91)

A double pandemic

The metaphor of *The Plague*, the title of the famous novel by Albert Camus, has been used by colleagues within the climate change community for some time.[5] Clive Hamilton used it to refer to the reappearance of an era of social breakdown, the plague that once accompanied genocide this time accompanying ecocide.[6] 'The plague' symbolises what occurs in such eras, one's which require an attitude of what Camus calls 'active fatalism' if they are to be borne. For myself, coming from a Group Relations background, I have pictured the plague in Bionic terms. When society is threatened with breakdown and fear seeps into everyday life like a rising sea, it is then that the plague is unleashed. We see it in small ways when breakdown threatens the life of the group and Bion's basic assumption mentality takes hold – groups become both frightened and frightening. Fear brings out the worst in us, as Yeats says in his famous poem *The Second Coming*, "the worst are full of passionate intensity."

In Europe, we last saw this with the break-up of Yugoslavia. Right at the end of the Bosnian war, I participated in a visit to Tuzla organised by the Helsinki Citizens Assembly as a demonstration of solidarity with the besieged Bosnians. After three years of war, Tuzla remained a model of a pluralist and multi-ethnic community, giving the lie to the prevailing Western narrative that this was a civil war between Serbs and Muslims.[7] We travelled inland from Dubrovnik up the valley of the Neva seeing burnt village after burnt village and imagining the tide of hate, lust and violence which must have surged up from Mostar. This unfortunately is what comes with social collapse. Roy Scranton, following Haraclitus, simply calls it strife, "such viral phenomena as nationalism, scapegoating, panic, and war fever."[8] In *Mental Space*, Bob Young invited us to consider the nature of what he called 'primitive space,' the space haunted by psychotic anxieties contained by "that thin and all too easily breached veneer that constitutes civility and stands between what passes for the social order, on the one hand, and chaos (or the fear of it), on the other."[9]

I'm writing this at the end of the year 2020, the day after Donald Trump seems finally to have accepted that he will be leaving the White House. Writing just after the US election Timothy Snyder, one of the foremost commentators on the history of European totalitarianism, tweeted that the USA stood on the very brink of a *coup d'etat*. Liberal democracy, the foundation of civility in the modern age, has been, and continues to be, under threat. This has been an extraordinary year. In front of the backdrop provided by the progressively deepening climatic and ecological emergency has appeared a resurgence of global authoritarianism on top of which has come the Covid pandemic. This has been a double pandemic, a biophysical and an emotional contagion, a re-enactment of Camus' plague. Primitive space is all around us. To use Bob's words once more, what is primitive space if not 'a world of human subjects haunted by demons'?[10]

The great derangement

The great sociologist of science Bruno Latour insists that we can understand nothing about politics today without placing climate change and its denial at the centre of the stage.[11]

As we enter what Latour calls the 'new climatic regime' – or what the climate science community tends to refer to as the Anthropocene – Latour suggests that our inability to imagine a common solution is driving us crazy, a madness symbolised by the election of Donald Trump in 2016.

From its very beginning, the development of capitalism was built upon the extraction and use of fossil fuels, first coal and then oil. Fossil Fuel Capitalism is now at its end, it has dug its own grave, and yet it holds on tenaciously, threatening to drag its own child, modern civilisation, down with it. As Roy Scranton vividly put it,[12]

> How do we stop ourselves from fulfilling our fates as suicidally productive drones in a carbon-addicted hive, destroying ourselves in some kind of psychopathic colony-collapse disorder? How do we interrupt the perpetual circuits of fear, aggression, crisis and reaction that continually prod us to ever more intense levels of manic despair?

In 2012, after a series of workshops and conferences and the prompting of Adrian Tait and later Judith Anderson, activist colleagues of mine, we helped to establish the Climate Psychology Alliance. The initial impulse was to establish a forum for therapists and activists to deepen our understanding of the West's paralysis in the face of worsening climate change. In the intervening years, it has steadily grown into a global network. It has taken on a life of its own and grown in directions that Adrian and I could never have imagined.

Members of the CPA have the option of participating in an online discussion forum. In 2019, our internal discussions and external interventions were preoccupied with 'climate' or 'eco-anxiety,' particularly among young people.[13] The year 2020, perhaps unsurprisingly, had been dominated by Covid and the links to ecological destruction, for after all this was a phenomenon that appears to have 'jumped' from the nonhuman world to the world of the human animal. We have understood Covid as a sudden eruption of the Lacanian 'real' or, in terms of classical psychoanalytic theory, in terms of a disavowed 'fact of life' suddenly breaking in upon the routinised going-on-being of we Moderns.[14] Some, perhaps more misanthropically inclined, saw this as the veritable 'revenge of Gaia.'

As the year went on and the US election approached, our CPA discussions increasingly focussed upon understanding what seemed like this 'Weimar moment' in US history. Then, in the last couple of months of 2020, something new began to surface on our online forum – concern about the spread of conspiracy theories – particularly within the alternative health/ new age/ deep green milieux which was part of the movement around the climate and ecological emergency in which we swam. More and more CPA members began posting about how clients, good friends or acquaintances had suddenly become susceptible to the most outlandish beliefs, some being actively spread by networks such as QAnon. The beliefs involved conspiracies about the nature and spread of Covid (including the idea that it was a hoax and didn't actually exist, that it did exist and was deliberately introduced by the Chinese/Bill Gates/the deep state/5G), about anti-Covid vaccines, about the wearing of masks, the 'real' reason for lockdowns, and so on. These conspiracies were increasingly entangled with another set of conspiracies about the Democrats having stolen the US election, which themselves led the believer to further conspiracies about the Democrats sponsoring child sex trafficking rings, and so on. This susceptibility of the alt-health/deep green/well-being movement to conspiracy theories during the pandemic has been given a name – conspirituality.[15] It is but one of many symptoms of the great derangement marking our entry into the Anthropocene.

An epistemological crisis

This is an extraordinary moment, one when Hannah Arendt's warning that in the pre-Totalitarian period "everything is possible and nothing is true" has come viscerally to life in front of us.[16]

We are living through a crisis of knowing. Bion imagined the existence of an anti-life force, -K, within the individual psyche, something inside all of us which rather than seeking the nourishment that truth provides, sought to destroy the truth. In this way, he attempted to give flesh to Klein's reflections on envy, 'the green-eyed monster that doth mock the flesh it feeds upon.'[17] Bion drew attention to that part of us which is contemptuous of the truth and seeks triumphantly to show that its own distortions, corruptions and perversions of reality have more potency and more vitality than the psychological growth that encounter with the truth can bring.

But what if we think psychosocially about this phenomenon, in a way which looks at the inner and outer reality? What social conditions support or militate against the love of truth? What happens when malignant social and cultural forces create the conditions in which that truth seeking part of us no longer feels supported, indeed may even feel threatened. Recently, I reported on the impact of Trump's election in November 2016 upon a patient of mine who spent much of his time online engaging, partly with fascination and partly in horror, with alt-right forums. In one session,[18]

> he began to think of 'flat earthers' and holocaust deniers, with only a very small element of irony he said that they just might have a point, so it was best not to dismiss them. A moment later he said that even though he accepted that they were "utterly and completely wrong" he nevertheless could imagine a world where the Trumps were right.

At first, I thought that this was a vivid illustration of disavowal, where one part of the mind sees and knows but another part says that it cannot be true. But on reflection, I wonder was this disavowal? If it was then what was being disavowed was not just a particular thought but the capacity to think. It was like he was saying "no I don't have a mind, please don't mistake me for someone who has one" – my patient was starting to believe that it was just too dangerous to own a mind in times like these.

In a vivid way this patient expressed the possibility that some family or social systems may make 'thinking for oneself' so dangerous that we are tempted to become mindless in order to feel safe. My reading of Bion suggests that he perceived the mind to be structured like a primitive society,[19] and it is no surprise to find that many analysts influenced by his work see the malignant or 'ego-destructive' superego operating like a gang in the mind (Meltzer 1986). I often find myself talking to patients with punishing and terrifying superegos that it is as if there is an inner dictator at work, as if they are living under an authoritarian internal regime where might is right. I am reminded of an exchange between Humpty Dumpty and Alice in *Through the Looking Glass*:

> 'When I use a word,' Humpty Dumpty said, in rather a scornful tone, 'it means just what I choose it to mean — neither more nor less.'

'The question is,' said Alice, 'whether you can make words mean so many different things.'

'The question is,' said Humpty Dumpty, 'which is to be master — that's all'.

Down the rabbit hole

Over the last decade or so, the alt-right has developed its own slang. One often used term is the phrase 'to be red-pilled' which comes from the film *The Matrix*. To be red-pilled is to have suddenly seen the light. In *The Matrix*, virtually everyone has become enslaved to a malignant AI which imprisons them in a virtual world. Only a small group of resistors have managed to avoid the spell cast by the Matrix. As one of them, Morpheus, says to Neo in the film, "you take the red pill, you stay in Wonderland and I show you how deep the rabbit hole goes." Paradoxically, given their rage at 'woke culture,' to be red-pilled *is* to wake up and to see the world as it really is, that is, as it is from a far right – nationalistic, misogynistic, white supremacist – perspective. It is the same language of revelation that woke liberals use in relation to climate change, trans rights and other progressive issues.

As many have commented when friends or acquaintances have become drawn to conspiracy theories, it all happens so suddenly. One moment they're talking about a particular yoga exercise they have found enriching or expressing interest in a Zach Bush podcast and then next moment they're avidly following cult alt-health guru Kelly Brogan and her team who, as Matthew Remski vividly describes it,[20]

> want to purify the world of GMOs, vaccines, masks, "victim narratives," and fear itself. They fret about the microwaves that beam their content to their followers' devices, then shoo the toxins away with slogans like "Community is Immunity."

Before you know it, your friend has disappeared down the rabbit hole where crazier stuff lurks. Here's an example. A post on the *Prepare for Change* website by Edward Morgan is called "7 Things Regarded as 'Crazy Conspiracy Theories' are Becoming Facts Right Now." In a section headed 'Microchips,' Morgan states that one of the seven alleged conspiracies which are actually becoming facts concerns the microchipping of the US population. The evidence? Well, Morgan correctly mentions the key element in anti-Covid vaccines is the ability to reprogramme mRNA molecules. He adds that these molecules are called 'messenger ribonucleic acid' molecules.

So, you might ask, how does this amount to evidence? Well, first you need to know that the *Prepare For Change* website believes that 'a New Society is being born into the Light of Truth' and that after 'The Event' 'the rising of planetary frequencies' will be accompanied by 'the planned mass arrests of the worldwide criminal cabal, politicians, big bankers and others who have committed numerous crimes against humanity.' If you read Edward Morgan's post literally you miss the point for the point is that you are not meant to read it literally, it is sufficient to put together Microchips, 'messenger ribonucleic acid' (the key term here being 'messenger') and reprogramming for any red-pilled reader to 'know' what Morgan is talking about. Microchips + mRNA + reprogramming = mind control.

Zach Bush and even Charles Eisenstein can function as the entry level drugs drawing truth seekers on towards the full red-pill. Kelly Brogan provides a fascinating case study. Brogan is what today is called a 'social influencer.' Through her website, podcasts, subscription based chat rooms and so on she has acquired a small but significant influence, particularly among middle class women in the USA. Championing 'natural' health as opposed to 'medicalised' health care, Brogan originally drew support from women opposed to a medical establishment which was seen as corporate and patriarchal. Medical expertise and authority was not to be trusted.

Then along came Covid and it was but a short slip from a largely harmless and slightly New Age critique of medical authority to an increasingly pernicious criticism of the public health profession in the USA and its representatives such as Dr Anthony Fauci. A criticism which started with scepticism about the purported virulence and contagiousness of the virus, quickly spread to opposition to lockdown, mask wearing and other preventative measures and then on to championing full blown anti-vax conspiracies involving the Gates Foundation, the use of nanotechnologies in the human bloodstream, etc.

Everything connects

In a fascinating article, internet game designer Reed Berkowitz takes the reader through the perverse logics of QAnon and other conspiracy generators. She describes how when she was once trialling a maze game with volunteer investigators she was disconcerted to find that random stuff she had strewn across the virtual creepy basement floor became interpreted as vital clues by her volunteers.[21]

> It was a problem because three of the pieces made the shape of a *perfect arrow* pointing right at a blank wall. It was uncanny. It *had* to be a clue. The investigators stopped and stared at the wall and were determined to figure out what the clue meant and they were not going one step further until they did. The whole game was derailed. Then, it got worse. Since there obviously was no clue there, the group decided the clue they were looking for was IN the wall. The collection of ordinary tools they found conveniently laying around seemed to enforce their conclusion that this was the correct direction......

> I stared in horror because it all fit so well. It was better and more obvious than the clue I had hidden.

Berkowitz then introduces the reader to a new term, *apophenia*. As the tendency to perceive a connection or meaningful pattern between unrelated or random things, *apophenia* appears to be one of the key psychological processes underlying the attraction of conspiracy theories. At first sight, this seems to be the very opposite of what Bion referred to as 'attacks on linking' (Bion, 1967) and the splitting processes that underline Klein's paranoid-schizoid position. In his admittedly abstruse paper, Bion hypothesises an internal force which attacks the capacity to link thought with thought, and thought with feeling. As a consequence, the possibility of a creative connection between reality and experience is denied leading to 'a severe disorder of the impulse to be curious on which all learning depends.'[22] The links and connections that should be made are not made.

In contrast with apophenia, it is as if everything connects. This feels like a kind of semantic promiscuity. What seems to be missing in apophenia is what the post-Kleinians would call 'thirdness,' i.e. the capacity to obtain perspective and to think critically, something I believe the Quakers call 'discernment.'[23] There is virtually nothing in the psychoanalytic literature on apophenia but the term was popularised by the German psychiatrist Klaus Conrad who saw it as a crucial feature of the early stage of schizophrenia. To cite Conrad,[24]

> Borrowing from ancient Greek, the artificial term 'apophany' describes this process of repetitively and monotonously experiencing abnormal meanings in the entire surrounding experiential field, e.g., being observed, spoken about, the object of eavesdropping, followed by strangers.

Conrad notes the grip of these meanings on the patient's mind is so powerful that it undermines their inability to transcend their current experience or shift their frame of reference. Returning to conspirituality, whilst those gripped by conspiracies such as The Great Reset might speak in terms of having an epiphany, the reality is that they are in the grip of an apophany. It is apophenia which makes possible the equation Microchips + reprogramming + mRNA = thought control.

Everything connects, hence the seductiveness of this style of thinking to the alt-health and deep green milleux with its emphasis on holism and integration. Indeed, the Prepare for Change website is clearly oriented towards the spiritual and deep green community, as it says

> Optimism and joy are creating peace in everyone as they are filled with an instinctive knowing of truth and humanity's potential for loving change.

And after 'The Event,'

> Clean technologies which had been previously suppressed by big corporations will be released, the natural abundance of this planet will be distributed for everybody, our eco-systems cleaned and this planet, along with all its inhabitants, finally healed and liberated.

This doesn't seem to be the language of alt-right white supremacists does it? But this is just the first step down the rabbit hole, before you know it you're into the demonising of Anthony Fauci, Covid restrictions as an attack on fundamental liberties, 'The Great Reset,' the valiant efforts of Donald Trump to expose what's going on... etc. And you can descend much further than this towards familiar global Jewish cabals, intergalactic struggles between forces of darkness and light and so on.

Jules Evans reminds us how rife this convergence of New Ageism, occultism and fascism was during the Nazi era. Evans notes the absorption of astrology, parapsychology, alternative medicine, 'back to nature' ecocentrism and nature-mysticism and organic farming into the Nazi worldview alongside conspiracy theories regarding the grip of a global Jewish cabal on the world economy, media and government.[25]

Up until quite recently, 'the left' tended to see the problem of false consciousness primarily in terms of a failure to make the connections, for example, between one's own disadvantage and structural issues such as class and power. Now, we seem to be presented with the opposite problem, people making the wrong connection rather than no connection.

Varieties of anxiety

I've been immersed in Kleinian thinking for almost 40 years now, first intellectually, later through my own training as a psychoanalytic psychotherapist at a Kleinian inspired training organisation. And throughout this period, I have struggled, and still struggle, to 'translate' Klein's distinctive language into a phenomenology or 'common sense' that is free of jargon and understandable to non-specialists. What exactly does she mean by psychotic anxiety? How does it differ to depressive anxiety? Where does persecutory anxiety fit with this? And catastrophic anxiety? What feeling states and thinking states are specific to each? I notice that Bob, when he referred to psychotic anxiety, linked it to 'survival of the self,' whereas depressive anxiety is concerned with the survival of the object(s) upon which the self depends.[26] (I find this helpful.) Ultimately then depressive anxiety leads us towards acknowledgment of our dependency on the human and the nonhuman environment, of our attacks upon this and our capacity for concern about these attacks.

But let's return to the survival of the self. In my clinical work, I am struck by the frequency with which patients report experiences which have the feeling of being a matter of life or death for them. Slights or rejections, sometimes real and sometimes imagined, are experienced as a catastrophe, as if I am in the presence of a small child which seeks the comforting words "there, there, it's not the end of the world." And yet to that individual at that point in time it does feel like the end of the world. What seems to the therapist like a small incident may lead the patient to take to their beds for an entire weekend or to begin a process of ruminating and chuntering that may last for days and sometimes weeks.

Thinking of the experience of catastrophe, one of the physical symptoms of the more severe cases of the coronavirus has been a lack of oxygen. Some hospital patients have been interviewed and have given a graphic depiction of the effect of this on them. They say that you feel that you are gasping for air, that there is just not enough getting into your lungs, it makes you feel very panicky. By all accounts, it's a terrible feeling, presumably that's why torturers conjure up a similar effect through waterboarding.

These thoughts take me back to the now rather neglected psychoanalyst, Michael Balint. Balint insists, contra the Kleinians, that in the prenatal and immediately postnatal environment, there are no hard or sharp objects, but rather a 'harmonious interpenetrating mix-up.'[27] He then offers two metaphors of such interpenetration, the fish in the sea and the air that a person breathes. In each case, we have a medium that the fish/person takes totally for granted. But, as with the coronavirus patient, deprive them of this medium and their response is vehement – it feels like a catastrophe to which they respond violently.

I'd forgotten how influential Balint had been for me when I wrote *Partisans in an Uncertain World*, my first attempt to bring together my psychoanalytic and political passions, a book that wouldn't have appeared without Bob's support and encouragement. At the time of writing it, 30 years back, I worked primarily as a consultant to groups and organisations, working very much along the lines of the Tavistock Group Relations tradition where agenda-less small and large groups are given the maddening task of doing nothing but studying their own processes in the here-and-now. What I had repeatedly noticed was how some people took to such groups and thoroughly enjoyed them whilst others thrashed about and sometimes sank without trace.

Using Balint's ideas, I began to develop the notion that the fundamental emotional task of the developing infant (and, later, the participant in a Group Relations conference) was to learn to swim in a new medium, no longer the amniotic sea but a 'primary social medium.' The agenda-less Tavi group strips everything away, leaving just this social medium. As I put it in Partisans[28]:

> Participants speak of being 'set adrift', of having the experience of being 'all at sea'. When participants attempt to share an experience with the group they find their words quickly 'sink without trace'. Others speak

of the difficulty of 'floating an idea'...Indeed, some ideas do float for a while but, the more people cling to them the more quickly 'they go under'. As a consultant, I am often tempted to say, 'Only those afraid of sinking need fear water'.

The nonhuman

Thinking of my kids learning to swim, and my own attempts for that matter, I am reminded of the phrase 'the medium will support you if you let it.' This calls attention to a basic trust involved when we immerse ourselves in this primary social medium, something Bion refers to as establishing contact 'with the emotional life of the group.'[29] This is a trust some people, usually because of failures in the early social environment, have never acquired or one that can be shattered by terrible experiences later in life.

Thirty years on and freer than I was from the solipsistic identity of a 'Modern,' I can see now that my idea of a primary social medium excluded the nonhuman or, rather, anticipated it without mentioning it. Following Harold Searles, I now believe that our very earliest experiences as sentient beings occur in the context of the nonhuman environment and via the realm of the senses – the smell or touch of a body, the light of a room, the pulsing of the foetal environment, the air passing by us and through us, perhaps a glimmering sense of space and time.[30]

The birth of modern civilisation is normally attributed to the shift from hunter-gatherer to pastoral forms of subsistence, the latter making possible fixed settlements and therefore rudimentary forms of society. Most commentators agree that this occurred with the passing of the last Ice Age 11,000 years ago and the inauguration of the Holocene period. We speak of 'the cradle of civilization' and through such imagery conjure the idea of something held or contained by a uniquely benign biophysical environment.[31] In a similar way, it is possible to think of the newly born member of this civilisation contained by its nonhuman environment. As Searles put it,[32]

> It is my conviction that there is within the human individual a sense, whether at a conscious or un-conscious level, of *relatedness to his non-human environment,* that this relatedness is one of the transcendentally important facts of human living,

And

> in terms of the chemical structure of his body as well as in terms of his fate-the inevitable return to an inorganic state when his life span is ended-an integral part of the fabric of all created matter, including the great inanimate environment of which our known Universe is predominantly composed.

If the fundamental task facing the human infant is to learn to be held by and to swim in a new medium, the primary social medium, then this is the challenge posed by our temporary emergence from the nonhuman into the human environment. And I now wonder whether this journey isn't haunted by the fear of catastrophe, that at any moment we might drown, suffocate or fall though space and that as a result, some of us never accomplish this task fully and never feel fully able to trust this social medium. Without its presence their life is precarious, at any moment like a fish out of water or a person without air, they might feel that their world is ending. I wonder if this is what Bion had in mind when he coined the term 'catastrophic anxiety.'[33] Meltzer wonders whether this might be the prototype of all anxiety, including psychotic and depressive anxiety, in which case I am left to assume that psychotic anxiety is primarily persecutory and paranoid and concerns a self busy relating to objects. But then this would be something which follows on from and is anticipated by a 'baby human' embedded in its nonhuman environment.

There is something in all of us which can be self-isolating, haunted by feelings of imminent catastrophe, longing to feel free of longing. R.D. Laing called this 'ontological insecurity,' a fault line running through one's sense of being, and to this day, his chapter in *The Divided Self* remains one of the best explorations of it.[34] I'm coming to believe that this fault line expresses the predicament of our civilisation, one now threatened to its foundations by the ecological and climate emergency. If you look back through history to the founding myths of European civilisation – the Garden of Eden (Paradise), the tree of knowledge, 'the fall' – the themes of catastrophe and longing are ever present.[35]

Ecological destruction and the end of the world

Now, catastrophic anxiety is very familiar to those of us involved in climate psychology.[36] The problem we constantly encounter is that individuals/societies 'deal' with the difficult thoughts and feelings connected to our deepening ecological and climate crises through denial.[37] But as the crisis deepens and floods, fires, droughts, famines and the news about them break in upon our comfortable world, then at some point, 'reality bites' and our defences are overwhelmed. The danger now is that we switch from denial to despair, from complacency to catastrophe and that 'end of the world' feeling. I believe that it is this anxiety which now increasingly characterises our collective psychology. It is becoming a structure of feeling[38] for the end times provoking a variety of forms of survivalism.[39] It connects to something in all of us. The survivalist in us fearfully imagines a coming social collapse, perhaps even the end of civilisation, but the catastrophe that drives survivalism is ultimately a catastrophe that lurks within us.

Catastrophic anxiety provides the conditions for survivalist ideologies, groups and practices to flourish. Today, survivalism assumes so many forms. It can be religious or secular, high or low tech, and it can involve an imagined escape to the hills, to New Zealand, to Mars or heaven or to the inner self.[40] Organisations and individuals become preoccupied with their survival at any cost and with what Lawrence called 'the politics of salvation.'[41] Survivalism infects the culture of the modern organisation which takes on the hue of living in an extreme situation – narrow your horizons, focus on what is immediately before you, travel lightly without attachments, be vigilant and so on.[42] It's not that Survivalists fear a coming catastrophe, the point is that they are already living the catastrophe. The end times have already arrived and conspiracy theories which reveal its secrets proliferate like Arachne's web. Catastrophic anxiety has become a cultural phenomenon, a structure of feeling of our age.

Notes

1 R. M. Young, *Mental space*. London: Free Association Books, 1994.
2 D. Armstrong, Names, thoughts and lies: The relevance of Bion's later writing for understanding experiences in groups. *Free Associations*, (1992) 26, 261–282; G. Lawrence, (2000) *Tongues of fire*. London: Karnac; G. Lawrence & D. Armstrong, Destructiveness and creativity in organisational life: Experiencing the psychotic edge. In P. Bion Talamo, F. Borgogno, & S. Merciai, (eds.) *Bion's legacy to groups*. London: Karnac 1998, pp. 53–68.
3 W. Bion, *Experiences in groups*. London: Tavistock, 1961, p. 141.
4 Young, *Mental space*, p. 91.
5 A. Camus, *The Plague*. London: Penguin, 1947.
6 C. Hamilton, What history can teach us about climate change denial. In S. Weintrobe (ed.) *Engaging with climate change: Psychoanalytic and interdisciplinary perspectives*. London: Routledge, 2013.
7 Y. Ahmad & P. Hoggett, The death of Bosnia and the birth of the new world disorder. *Free Associations*, (1995) 35, 416–419.
8 R. Scranton, *Learning to die in the anthropocene*. San Francisco: City Lights Books, 2015, p. 87.
9 Young, *Mental space*, p. 74.
10 Young, *Mental space*, p. 75.
11 B. Latour, *Down to earth*. Cambridge: Polity, 2008.
12 Scranton, *Learning to die in the anthropocene*, pp. 85–86.
13 C. Hickman, I'm a psychotherapist – here's what I've learned from listening to children talk about climate change. *The conversation*, September 15, 2019. https://theconversation.com/search/result?sg=0fd6151f-6272-42f1-9c27-da82 b7e39604&sp=1&sr=3&url=%2Fim-a-psychotherapist-heres-what-ive-learned-from-listening-to-children-talk-about-climate-change-123183.
14 S. Western, Covid-19: An intrusion of the real. *Journal of Social Work Practice*, (2020) 34 (4), pp. 445–451.
15 'Conspirituality' – the overlap between the New Age and conspiracy beliefs. Medium, April 17. https://julesevans.medium.com/conspirituality-the-overlap-between-the-new-age-and-conspiracy-beliefs-c0305eb92185.
16 H. Arendt, *The Origins of totalitarianism*. London: Penguin Classics, 1951, 2017.
17 Bion. *Learning from experience*.
18 P. Hoggett, The grip of the ideal. *British Journal of Psychotherapy* (2020) 36(3), 415–429.

19 P. Hoggett, The internal establishment. In P. Bion Talamo, F. Borgogno, & S. Merciai, (eds.) *Bion's Legacy to Groups*. London: Karnac, 1998. p. 13.

20 M. Remski, Inside Kelly Brogan's Covid-denying, vax-resistant conspiracy machine. Medium, Sept. 15, 2020. https://gen.medium.com/inside-kelly-brogans-covid-denying-vax-resistant-conspiracy-machine-28342e6369b1.

21 A. Berkowitz, A game designer's analysis of QAnon. *Medium*, Sept. 30, 2020.

22 W. Bion, Attacks on linking. In *Second thoughts: Selected papers on psychoanalysis*. London: Heinemann, 1967, pp. 106–107.

23 R. Britton, *Sex, death and the superego*. London: Karnac, 2003.

24 A. Mishara, Klaus Conrad (1905-1961): Delusional mood, psychosis, and beginning schizophrenia. *Schizophrenia Bulletin*, 36 (1), 9–13.

25 J. Evans, Nazi hippies: When the New Age and the far right overlap. *Medium*, Sept 4. https://gen.medium.com/nazi-hippies-when-the-new-age-and-far-right-overlap-d1a6ddcd7be4.

26 Young, *Mental Space*, p. 78.

27 M. Balint, *The basic fault: Therapeutic aspects of regression*. London: Tavistock, 1979, p. 66.

28 P. Hoggett, *Partisans in an uncertain world*. London: Free Association Books, 1992, p. 55.

29 Bion, *Experiences in groups*, p. 141.

30 H. Searles, *The nonhuman environment in normal development and schizophrenia*. New York: International Universities Press, 1960.

31 As Susan Kassouf recently explained, this idea that ontology may reproduce phylogeny was actively discussed between Freud and Ferenczi. Ses Kassouf, Psychoanalysis and climate change.... *American Imago*, (2017) 74(2), 141–171.

32 Searles, *The nonhuman environment in normal development and schizophrenia*.

33 D. Meltzer, *The Kleinian development: Part III, the clinical significance of the work of Bion*. Perthshire: Roland Harris Educational Trust, 1978.

34 R. D. Laing, *The divided self*. London: Pelican Books, 1965.

35 P. Hoggett, The grip of the ideal. *British Journal of Psychotherapy*, (2020) 36(3), 412–429.

36 P. Hoggett, Climate change and the apocalyptic imagination, 2011.

37 Or, more properly, through the process of disavowal. In disavowal, we 'know' about climate change but our knowing is split off from our feeling so that our knowing leaves us untouched, undisturbed.

38 Drawing on the work of Raymond Williams, sociologists have used the term 'structure of feeling' to refer to feeling states shared by groups, communities, sometimes whole societies, that endure over time. P. Hoggett, *Politics, identity & emotion*. Boulder, CO: Paradigm, 2009, pp. 13–15.

39 C. Lasch's examination of survivalism remains unsurpassed. Writing at the time when nuclear war threatened global civilization Lasch comments both on survivalism's visible forms (such as one's own private nuclear fallout bunker) and on the less visible and more insidious ways that it affects everyday life, culture and the psyche. Lasch, *The minimal self: Psychic survival in troubled times*. New York: WW Norton & Co.1984.

40 C. Lasch, The minimal self; B. Garrett, *Bunker: Building for the end times*. Allen Lane: Penguin Random House, 2020.

41 Lawrence, The politics of salvation and revelation in the practice of consultancy.

42 S. Cohen & L. Taylor, *Escape attempts: The theory and practice of resistance to everyday life*. London: Routledge, 1992.

Chapter 14

Robert M. Young

A farewell

Valerie Sinason

How we miss Bob Young. He was a giant of a man both literally and symbolically. A giant of a brain and a heart and sadly, over time his body became larger than life could manage. However, even carrying that extra burden he lived to the grand age of 84. I met him over 40 years ago when he was founder of Free Association Books and Editor of the quarterly journal *Free Associations*. I loved the intellectual freedom espoused by the journal which managed to keep a psychoanalytic core whilst being free to discuss areas that were not of mainstream interest then. He also carried a rather glamorous whiff of gossip about him – as a tall American with a Yale background, a Cambridge PhD, Director of the Wellcome Unit for the History of Medicine and for his partners – rather remarkable women – Sheila Ernst, then Margot Waddell, Em Farell and finally Susan Tilley. His house was filled with books and magazines and papers which spilled over the space, rather like the time he generously devoted to all of this, albeit at the expense of his private and domestic life.

He was also one of the first to publish my work in what was only the second issue of *Free Associations* when I was a trainee child psychotherapist at the Tavistock, writing on adolescent subculture. I was looking at the meaning of tattoos in adolescent gang members, something that could go through the skin to offer the idea of fidelity and security when it did not feel as if they existed in the heart. But from 1979, when I joined what was then called the Subnormality Workshop started by Neville Symington, Bob was riveted by the subject. He saw instantly that people with an intellectual disability were wrongly excluded from psychotherapy and that the eugenics wish towards them would be internalised. He invited me to give talks and encouraged my writing in this area. He was amused by my oedipal dilemma over the workshop.

My grandmothers were both illiterate refugees and my maternal grandmother, who lived with us, had a mild disability through trauma. Additionally, my father, a child of refugees, became a Professor of Mental Handicap having been a luminous and pioneering teacher before that. His landmark book *No Child is Ineducable* triggered both the Plowden and Warnock

DOI: 10.4324/9781003204244-18

reports and he was the first head teacher of a school for children with an intellectual disability to ban the cane – the assault weapon teachers were allowed to use. When Neville Symington started his Tavistock workshop, I worried if it was oedipal to join when it was my father's field and then I realised it would also be oedipal to deliberately not join! So I joined and felt deeply at home. Neville had created the workshop around a patient with a mild intellectual disability who had somehow been referred to him. He attracted a group of psychoanalysts who would not continue with the work but took on one patient each, inspired by Neville. Neville was as interested in the thoughts of as trainee (myself) as in the thoughts of the most senior training analysts. It was a wonderful workshop to join.

When Neville moved to Australia, after a brief gap, Jon Stokes, a psychoanalytic psychotherapist in the Adult department (where he later became Chair) and I (a trainee child psychotherapist in the Children and Family Department) took over the Workshop, using the new name that had appeared "Mental Handicap". I liked this term as it referred to a medieval game in which you took out from a cap something that would either bring a reward or a forfeit. It seemed to sum up the genetic lottery involved in disability. Although, of course, despite a certain amount of disability being organic or genetic or unaccounted for, the majority of all people with an intellectual disability had a mild disability and came from social class 5. It is therefore a condition with a concerning social implication. Violence to the mother before birth, foetal alcohol syndrome, poverty, racism, stress, lack of adequate housing all played their part in creating mild disability.

Bob's understanding that we were all embedded in socio-political situations and identities meant this did not get discredited by him as "political" and therefore "not proper psychoanalytic thinking". He cared about the politics, and he shared my linguistic fascination with the way terms for problematic subjects became unusable after a while. "Subnormality" became seen as an insult. My father, the late Professor S. S. Segal had worked with this group when the term was "backward" so I understood the psycholinguistic change from my own background However, despite a large number of papers on disability which I had published in the 1980s, my writing for Free Association was usually on other topics- including literary criticism and psychoanalysis, partners or millstones? (1986) and it took until 1989 for me to write on the psycholinguistics of discrimination.

In 1990, with several papers published on this subject, I went to discuss ideas of publishing with him. I was backed in this by Juliet Hopkins who said I should write a solo book. I had raised the idea of a combined workshop book with the work of Jon Stokes and I. However, when I nervously went to visit Bob with some of the titles of my case studies he very quickly said co-edited books were more work for him than solo books. He said I should write my book first and that I had more than enough material. He then immediately said he would publish it. He did not want a workshop book first. It was a flowing conversation.

That was one of the most wonderful days of my life. There was no complex writing to and fro or hidden hurdles. He was totally upfront. We were united in doing something to improve the inclusion of people with intellectual disability into the orbit of psychoanalytic therapy. The book was published to great critical success and a revised edition was published in 2011. I am now planning a further one. Jon meanwhile became Chair of the Adult Department and is work on organisational consultancy increased.

After this, my relationship with Bob increased on a personal level. As someone who had four major partners in his life, he was sympathetic when my first marriage to psychoanalyst Michael Sinason ended, and he continued to let me know how much he admired Mike's concept of a psychotic co-habitee. We shared concerns about fearfulness and rigidity in analytic institutions, the problems I incurred whilst undertaking the adult psychoanalytic training as a consultant child psychotherapist working at the Tavistock. There was a fearfulness about extreme abuse and working with disability. Whilst there were always individual psychoanalysts offering help, it was the institution which was problematic.

When I ended my first independent group analysis on completing the child therapy training I sought a Kleinian analysis for the adult training but because of disagreements this ended and I then found the right analyst in Mervin Glasser, a contemporary Freudian. Bob was a sympathetic and understanding ear. He had chosen a Kleinian training for himself and, like me, wanted what Brett Kahr called "Kleinacottian" understanding! The outside and how it was politically embedded in us, and the patient were crucial to understand. He was having similar problems himself. Essex University finally became such a good home for him, and he had such pride in the size of the library and staff group that was built up. He was a voracious reader and would update me on every phone call with books I ought to read or gossip about institutional cowardice. He welcomed my second husband David and happily included him in these discussions. We also could discuss our respective dieting problem! He always expressed pride in his children and their mothers but arrangements for seeing them felt a mystery. The overflowing of papers and books left little room physically or mentally.

The world is a little bit smaller with his loss, a little bit colder. There was a warmth in his voice, his bearhugs, the hugeness of his intellect and the delightfulness of his gossip! Thanks to Kurt Jacobsen and David Morgan for continuing his seminal contribution. The conference that produced this festschrift sweetly and poignantly brought Bob back into the room with us and reminded us of the magnitude of his legacy.

Conclusion

Bob Young and Regenerating his Project

Kurt Jacobsen and R. D. Hinshelwood

Clichés sometimes have their place, as do rituals, which are especially help-ful in the experiences of mourning and loss we all undergo. There is a fa-miliar rustic Irish lament (from an unapologetic sexist era) regarding any remarkable departed figure that "we will never see his like again," which seems all too fitting for Bob Young, who died on 5 July 2019 in Whitting-ton Hospital in London. In this volume honouring Young, we assembled a band of essayists in the quest to state concisely and sometimes contra-dictorily what he was all about. Luckily, Bob also insisted on making his books and essays available online free of pay barriers, like his reinvigor-ated journal *Free Associations*, so as to disseminate all the profound and arresting things he had to say as far and wide as possible. In the website (http://www.psychoanalysis-and-therapy.com/rmyoung/index.html), you'll espy in the upper left corner a tiny Sisyphusean animation pushing a boul-der up a steep incline again and again. It was kidding on the square. Bob certainly felt that way about his work but took Camus' view of imagining Sisyphus was happy or, better still, just could not act otherwise.

Entering his cavernous groaning room of books, computer and memora-bilia in Freegrove Road was to trespass into an alluring magisterial reality. Here was an authentic intellectual's "Life of The Mind" theme park, in the very best sense of the expression. All the exciting and terrifying rides you could ever crave were tucked up there on the dusty bookshelves, already thumbed through and threatening at any second to inundate you. Bob was chided for a complicated relation with "stuff" by people beset with our middle class minimalist IKEA sensibility about decor, but it wasn't hard to understand that the surroundings grounded him. He wore the decor like a million medals, and it suited him perfectly. If something was always tipping over or on the verge of it, well, that, as Lacanians, for whom he didn't care much, like to say, 'signifies' how real thinkers think. Nothing was quite fixed for Bob, except of course a core belief in human dignity and in the curative power of truth.

Bob distrusted, if not detested, clubs, from Bullingdon boors to pro-fessional cabals, with their compulsory complacency, groupthink and

DOI: 10.4324/9781003204244-19

self-satisfaction – mental barricades to going where unencumbered thought and experience takes you. He picked up this aversion from hard goings in the South. In High School, he rose to the ROTC cadet top status of Colonel, but he had the temerity to turn down West Point. Bob had glimpsed an escape route through a scholarship to Yale instead. It was a turning point for someone who ever after insisted on following his own path whatever the cost. A difficult early marriage plus his own budding zeal to investigate the history of medicine drew him from Rochester University medical school into a fellowship at Kings College, Cambridge in 1960, resulting eventually in *Mind, Brain, and Adaptation*. Cambridge invited him to stay on as a don until his resignation in the mid-1970s. Bob told one of us that the famous American sociologist Edward Shils, who held a dual appointment at Chicago and Cambridge, approached him one fine Cambridge afternoon to inveigle him to inform on American students there to US intelligence agencies. Bob kicked him out of his office. Shils, whom even his pal Saul Bellow could not resist lampooning later, no doubt thought Bob terribly rude and arrogant.

Bob, averse to arbitrary authority in all guises, became increasingly radical in politics as well as methodological approaches over this tumultuous period and quit to form *Free Associations* and *Radical Science Journal* (now *Science as Culture*), as described by Maureen McNeil, Les Levidow and Barry Richards, and start Free Associations Press, as vividly described by Anne Scott, which turned out some 300 books before he was elbowed out. Leftists, a mutual friend observed, might know how to analyse the business world but rarely know how to handle themselves in it. *Darwin's Metaphor* in 1985 located the ideological thrust of Darwinism not only in bourgeois Victorian culture but also in its meanest and most cruel expression, Malthusianism, as parsed out by Roger Smith, Jim Secord, Timothy Sim and Michael Ruse. Science is, in Young's oft-repeated phrase, social relations, and a labour process, attest and elaborate. For over a decade in the darkest Thatcherite days, Bob and comrades annually staged the inspiring and rambunctious "Psychoanalysis and Public Sphere" conferences, terminating with what was the false dawn of a New Labour government besotted with the black magic of a rigged global marketplace that steadily stokes inequality.

Bruising encounters with the cutthroat manoeuvring typical in high media circles during production of the ITV *Crucible* series propelled him into analysis, where he ultimately found a new profession: Kleinian psychotherapist, about which phase Bob Hinshelwood, Peter Barham, Paul Hoggett and Valerie Sinason share illuminating disciplinary insights and some personal experiences. He despaired at desertion by many former associates he regarded as sell-outs and climbers, perhaps unfairly in some cases, but true enough in others where people he had helped up the ladder carefully distanced themselves from this now toxic left wing genius. Still, he remained a generous, compassionate and questing spirit. One of us watched him get teary-eyed as he described the retrieval, shall we call it, of schizophrenics in the documentary *Take These Broken Wings*. On the other hand, co-editor Jacobsen learned that the ROTC colonel incarnation of Bob could make an occasional peremptory reappearance, but they quickly got past those rare eruptions. A life with several divorces was hardly an advertisement for the wonders of domesticity, but he took unambivalent pleasure in all his children and grandchildren. "If it goes right," he testified on the topic of raising kids, "as experiences go, it's one of the best.'" I suppose that if we ever do see his like again – and we will, life is like that – it will be precisely because his phenomenal and much-needed *oeuvre* has seeped into and seeded the culture, whether the culture likes it or not.

One of Bob's voiced concerns for his intellectual legacy was for a revitalised *Free Associations* Journal to carry on in its founding radical political spirit. With the psychoanalytically accomplished and politically astute David Morgan agreeing to fill Bob's spot as co-editor that wish is being fulfilled. In 2019, a sort of son of "Psychoanalysis and The Public Sphere" conference entitled "Psychoanalysis, Values, and Webs of Power" took place in London in conjunction with the Freud Museum, and with Ivan Ward as chief enabler. This really quite ill-disguised way of feting Bob, who was intended to deliver the welcoming address but died two months earlier, marked the rebirth, again with the help of the Freud Museum and David Morgan, of the Public Sphere conferences as a significant annual event.

Bob exerted a formidable presence whilst engaging others with intense personal interest. He had the physique of a Texan biker, a stubborn taste for Country-and-Western music, an impressive breadth of reading and a voracious appetite for absorbing himself in the subjects he chose, which he could accomplish at an extraordinary speed. With such a rainbow of talents, he was an attractive draw for many people, not least his women. There is nothing awry about personal recollections, some slightly at odds with each other or with him, of Bob's humanity and humanism in a festschrift of essays devoted to and cued by his scholarly achievements. For him, humanism was at the core of all intellectual endeavour, both its inspiration and its obdurate stubbornness. We do nothing without being human about it. And that means all intellectual activity has a moral responsibility for its contribution to the human conditions we create for ourselves.

Bob had an accomplished academic record and a fierce commitment to a humanistic view of the nature of scientific thinking. The latter he conveyed in his very first known publication in the student journal at Yale. Humanity inescapably thinks with beliefs and values as much as with 'facts.' He always claimed his interest in psychoanalysis started early, and if that was only a partial interest, he did convey he was as concerned about the way we made discoveries as in the discoveries that were made. 'Social responsibility' of science was really the social determination of science.

Young did not become a professor at Cambridge as perhaps he should, and if he felt in some way he failed or had been cheated, it would have been balanced equally by his sense that it was the University which had failed, and by his enthusiastic embrace of an exploratory Sixties culture still going strong at the time. His commitment to a new view of science and the way it pursues its trajectory took a new turn for Bob when he began making and presenting documentaries on his iconoclastic views of scientific progress. He was disappointed when his series was broadcast just once during the inhospitable Thatcher era. By the mid-1980s when Hinshelwood first made his acquaintance, Young was forging yet another career. Having edited a journal to present his radical view of science, he branched out to launch the psychoanalytically oriented *Free Associations*. In addition, he founded a fully functioning publishing house for psychoanalytic texts, *Free Association Books*.

Young tackled a vexing lifelong wheels-within-wheels problem: The question moved from 'How are the functions of the brain localised?' to 'where did we get the questions we ask the brain?' (Young 1994, p. 2). What sets of values bring people to ask the questions they do in science and medicine? Can we, as it were localise our questions about how we localise in the brain? If we have an idea of the person, we can ask who localises and how do we do it? This can seem silly, and I think it is. It asks us to apply the same kind of thinking to experiential data as we do to materialist data. And Young wanted to make that distinction; if we are curious about what 'this' is, can we be curious about why we are curious?

It is a specially human reflectiveness, and he rightly turned to psychoanalysis for answers. So, his third project was to embark on becoming a psychoanalyst or psychotherapist. This is where Hinshelwood came on the scene. Too old to be accepted for training at the London Institute of Psychoanalysis, Young set about putting together his own informal training. He had been in analysis with Colin James before he left Cambridge in the early 1970s. He believed he knew the academic side of psychoanalysis well enough but what he did need was supervision of clinical work. When Hinshelwood first met him, in 1984, he was looking for someone to take him on for supervised clinical work. Hinshelwood was running a psychotherapy department in the NHS and took him on as a volunteer under supervision for a couple of cases. And he joined a supervision group. Because he and Hinshelwood first met when he became mentor of a discussion group the latter was a part of, they were then in symmetrical positions. Each was leading discussions in a group of which the other was a member. Bob changed his analyst to Sydney Klein, a Kleinian (no relation) in London, and an analyst who had been one of Hinshelwood's own training supervisors 10 years before. It was perhaps this balance that enabled us to achieve a longstanding connection and relationship.

Hinshelwood learned a lot about Marx, Lukacs, Braverman and many others and felt a solidity taking place in his own radicalism. Bob was launching himself into the world of psychoanalysis. Publishing was a substitute public presence. It perhaps expressed the limiting subjectivity of our culture. He presented an opportunity for many would-be psychoanalytic writers who at the time had little outlet for their work. Together with Karnac, Free Association Books revolutionised psychoanalytic publishing in Britain and indeed the Anglophone world. It was, however, a career that faded into debt and had eventually and sadly to be sold off.

By the late 1990s, Young had built his psychotherapy practice, joined the Lincoln Clinic and was an established therapist. He was of course not content merely to do the job, but entered the more political aspects of the profession. He was generally seen as standing against the elitism of the discipline and critical of the closed shop that the Institute of Psychoanalysis appeared to be (and in many respects was). The fact that at that time, in the 1990s, nearly half of the psychoanalysts had part-time appointments in the NHS, social services, child guidance clinics, the prisons or charities providing services, was not lost on Bob and I think he approved of this engagement with the 'real' world beyond the couch. However, he constantly complained of the cliques that ran the psychotherapy organisations themselves.

As far as Hinshelwood knew, Bob was never allowed into those inner circles. He could challenge, but the grounding of his challenge did not always get communicated. His interest in psychoanalytic debate was to lever human experience out of the world of physical facts and place it within the realm of culture. And yet, culture is merely a framework, a template, for handling nature, what we think of as natural. The circularity is not necessarily post-modern. And it does not dissolve into vapid fog. It would be more to reconvene the conventionalist views of the material world and to humanise the reified conceptualisations we use. The medium we all swim in, mentally, is our culture, and we had better know it. Culture makes sense; it makes meaning or social meanings; and it constricts us to those meanings. The nature of mental space was the focal interest in his one major book from the 1990s on. It places the mind in a context in which the experienced entity, a mind, is socially constructed. What is that experience we have of ourselves which makes us reach for the word 'mind'? At the same time, how is it framed and shaped by the culture that minds create together.

Perhaps he did not pursue that as far as he might. Bob did not promote his 1994 book *Mental Space* in the way he vigorously promoted all those of the other authors he published. Once again, it is as if Bob ventured forward in a radical direction looking ahead in ways that were not popular, but were in fact important. And then somehow the momentum declined as if he was defeated, and he built in another direction.

On three occasions, Bob went to annual or biennial meetings of the International Network of Psychoanalysis: once in Zurich, once in Milan and once in Paris. I accompanied him together with Karl Figlio. The Network was a multinational collection of people around Europe who were trying to keep the progressive 1960s on life-support, 20 years later. This was inevitably a short-lived venture. Bob instead, and characteristically, invented his own substitute, the Psychoanalysis and Public Sphere conferences. On one of the European trips, the inevitable discussion of group dynamics came up, in which he objected to what he identified as Hinshelwood's scientistic views, and which led to an awkward silence. Hinshelwood had mentioned the Tavistock approach to group relations about which he thought Bob had been largely ignorant. Nevertheless, within a year, he had been to the Leicester Conference returning with considerable enthusiasm, and another project to create an embryo interest in group relations in Bulgaria, enlisting the support of Toma Tomov, a professor at the New University of Bulgaria in Sofia! It was another of his promising enthusiasms which sadly petered out. It was more, so far as Hinshelwood could see, to do with his impatience in putting across the problematic that drove him on.

It is matter of regret that the impetus of his intentions seemed frequently to run dry in the midst of frustrations which he not only did not understand but which instead he found wholly caused by the limitations and indeed blockages of others. Indeed, it was a sad pattern, and yet perhaps we can renew interest in his long-held concerns which might yet regenerate. The plight of the space of the essentially human mind is the need to overcome the constraints of imprisonment within the conceptualisations invented by the human mind. What sort of a mind might encompass that better than Bob's?

Bob Young was never an angry radical and rarely discussed party politics. He was more inclined to attract others' ire. Ultimately with his diabetes, his prostate cancer and his weight problem, he went downhill physically though he retained, until his final illness, an impressive lucidity. He was all open debate that could question accepted opinion – although not too open. The boundaries of social expectation encircled what he wanted to consider, and which limited the progress of new thought – but Bob always wanted to be the one to define – or redefine and broaden – those limits.

This volume has done its best to give a picture of the man and his thought. We as editors have been midwives of that emerging picture of a powerful influence in both the academic and professional domains that Bob chose. It has not been possible to merely give his thinking, but a flavour of his personality comes through as it did in all his dealings in life. And moreover, he would be the first to claim that it is the personal that makes the world of humanity. He believed in the human achievement despite all its destructive elements and his criticisms of individuals and institutions. It has been important to us to dedicate this volume to Bob Young and to his legacy of his ideas and his colleagues. We contend that there is not a single dated or unfruitful idea among his major (and many minor) works. Apart from books, Bob has strewn his essays and reviews with a multitude of arresting arguments and insights that most scholars would be proud to claim one of. The basic questions he addressed never go away, though they can be ignored in some camps. Any scholar can be enlivened and inspired and stimulated by his stances, whether initially agreeing with them or not. What sort of memorial this book will be can only gauged by the future, but his forceful contention that humanity steers what humanity discovers and knows is powerful enough to survive as his memorial anyway. "The end is nothing," as Willa Cather summed up. "The road is all."

Appendix

An interview with Bob Young

Kurt Jacobsen

An interview conducted with Robert Maxwell Young in 2015 in his home in London.

Conducted in 2015

Let's start as routinely as we can with family background, and your trail from the Dallas suburbs to Cambridge and then London.

It's so clichéd I hardly dare say it to you. My grandfather's father owned slaves. My grandfather became one of the richest men in Dallas because he had a lumber yard in a town that was burgeoning. My grandfather was more or less lassoed by my grandmother who was an orphan who worked in China at the time of the Boxer Rebellion. She came back with tuberculosis and therefore my granddaddy, who had lots of money, not billions, but, you know, lots of money, decided as was the thought at that time that they should go and live in the mountains where the air is pure. Think of....

The Magic Mountain?

Magic Mountain, thank you. My mother wrote an account of her childhood which is a very moving document. It was typed up for my 70th birthday, a hundred something pages. They lived on this ranch. My grandfather was a monster. When his wife wouldn't sleep with him, he got out his six guns in front of the children. And my mother was held responsible for the death of her 16 year old brother because my grandfather became interested in the Farmers' political movement in America at that time and left my mother when she was 16 in charge of her little brother who got ill. My mother rang the doctor who said give him some castor oil and he died. And they blamed her. Oh, and then when she married my father and they came back from their honeymoon, her sister rang her and said, 'I'm having trouble with my boyfriend,' who was somebody who came back from the war shell shocked. My mother, who said she had a terrible time on the honeymoon because my mother didn't know anything about sex – said 'I can't do this now.' That night the boyfriend killed himself. She thought she was responsible [for that death too].

Yipes. What a burden.

So they settled in Dallas where my mother's family was prominent – where they could have been debutantes and so forth – in a little cottage surrounded by vast mansions, and, boy, do I mean vast. I showed my partner some pictures of Dallas houses for sale in this suburb and you would not believe it. My High School is one of the top ones in the country and there still has not been a black student there. It's 2015 and still not one Black student in that High School. I don't know how they do it. It must be illegal. Well, I played with a black child until I was 5 when I was told that I couldn't anymore. We had a black servant all through my childhood, through my life. A devoted, absolutely wonderful person who got very politicized in the civil rights movement. I didn't know anybody in the working class. I didn't even know anybody in the lower middle class. Because you couldn't live in this suburb if you didn't have a certain amount of money. We were in the cheaper houses but I was still going to this wonderful school. And we had a swimming pool three blocks away. There was a creek that meandered near the house where I caught crawdads, and swam sometime. It was something straight out of Tom Sawyer.

How do you wind up at Yale instead of SMU?

I was a very good swimmer and I got a scholarship to Yale which was the leading swimming school at the time. So I went to Yale. I had never heard of trade unions, except that there the Unitarian minister in the neighbourhood gave me *Talking Union Blues* to listen to. My father said 'What are you looking at that for?' He worked for a company that made cotton gins. Trade unions were beyond the pale. My father used to say, 'You know what that president's real name is, it's Rosenfeld.' That's the atmosphere I grew up in. The people locally bankrolled [Joe] McCarthy. So ultra-right was common sense. So when I actually heard Pete Seeger, who used to come to Yale, it had more influence on me politically than any other single event. And I also met these New York intellectuals like Andre Schiffrin, who became a famous publisher at Pantheon, and Joel Kovel. You know him? And I was the local hick. They used to talk about Botticelli, I never heard of Botticelli. They'd be rattling off names that I never heard of. I was so ill-informed, so unread, that I used to read Classics Illustrated comics in High School when they assigned novels.

So did I on occasion.

Good for you. My first teaching assistant was Richard Rorty, and he took me under his wing because he saw something there. I don't know how but he saw something because I got a zero in my first test and they gave me a carrel in the library and put me in the philosophy section. I used to wander up and down the aisle pulling books off the shelves and quoting them in my essays. Completely innocently I got engaged in self-education. I went from zero to being in the top 10% of my class, then the top ten people in my class, and I did nothing but work. I had no girlfriends till my third year. And I was just loving it. I was reading books way over my head, like Cassirer and Alfred North Whitehead and *The Great Chain of Being.* You know, really proper senior level ace texts. And for some reason, I was so excited I managed to read them.

So you go from Yale to Rochester Medical School. Any sign of Freud there?

My medical school was dominated by psychoanalysts so I was steeped in psychoanalysis from the day I set my foot in the door of Rochester. And then I went to Cambridge to work on ideas from Freud's *Project for a Scientific Psychology.* There is not a word of psychoanalysis in my thesis, and yet that is the whole reason I wrote it! Then I went back to it in the 1980s when I got depressed when I was in London. The plug was pulled on a project I was involved with, making documentaries. I went back into it strictly as a patient. My partner had a job at the Tavi, so I suddenly got inspired to get involved with psychoanalysis. My mentor in this said, come and work with me. I did and the rest is history. In five years, I was a Professor. I'm telling you about a series of opportunities – chance favours the prepared mind, of course – but I had opportunities which really were openings out for me. And I'm still at it.

Could you go back to your first experience at a mental institution during a Summer off at Yale and how it affected you?

Well, my mother was mentally ill. I was planning to become a psychiatrist, or so I thought, and there was a wonderful opportunity to have a taster. I went to Arizona State Hospital which was one of the old-fashioned bins like the movie *The Snake Pit.* And it was dreadful. Except for the admissions ward and the old folks ward, all the others were custodial places. If a patient didn't eat fast enough they were not allowed to serve themselves and would have the food shovelled down them. And if you, as I did, sat down beside them and say, 'I'll sit with you while you eat,' they ate perfectly civilly and happily. If they said 'I want to be alone to take my bath,' they were not allowed to do so, and you had three people struggle with them to have a bath. And I said to them, 'What is it about this struggle to have a bath?,' and they said, 'I want to be alone.' I left them alone and it was all right. The [institutions] were used to bullying people. The wards were locked. I administered shock therapy, which went out of fashion. It's now back in fashion, by the way.

People were very crazy in these places because there weren't any drugs to mitigate their personalities. And that Summer, two drugs came in, Thorazine and Reserpine, and transformed the place. They unlocked the doors. People became civil, etc. But they weren't the miracle drugs they were made out to be any more than Prozac was in a later generation. So this place became a more humane institution. But you do know that not very long after this period – roughly the mid-fifties – they closed down all the old hospitals, claiming they were making the world a better place but put nothing in their place. So the people now inhabit park benches and ordinary hospital wards. So it's objectively worse. Better to have the old bins, in my opinion, than to have the nothing we have now.

There were at the time some people, like Searles and Bion and others, who were interested, or becoming interested, as the case may be, in talking cures.

But it wasn't widespread. It was little islands around the place. I read a book when I was in Yale which had a title which was later adopted as a title for a movie, *Rebel Without a Cause*. And it was a hypno-analysis of a criminal psychopath. And I read another one called *My Six Convicts*. So in England, you had these people who behaved well with one or two or a dozen patients but they didn't affect the institutional culture. There was one exception to this, a man named David Clark whom I knew at Cambridge, He was the superintendent of the local mental hospital and he was ace in his humaneness. I published his autobiography, by the way, and it was not anything earthshaking. They were just civil to the patients. They dressed in their own clothes. And no one forced them, and they gave them good food. No one was allowed to hit them. In one of the wards I worked, there was a guy who was like Carr, the floorwalker in *Cool Hand Luke*, who took the knobs off the television, and in order to get a knob you had to give him a cigarette. It was just demeaning, straightforwardly demeaning. God, was that man well cast.

Let's continue the journey. Why was England so attractive?

I came to England for two reasons. One of them is that I was too poor to go on Junior year abroad like so many of my University contemporaries. And I really wanted to go abroad. The other is that my wife was mentally ill and I couldn't carry on with medical school. You can't be a medical student and look after a young child because your wife can't handle it. So I made a smart career move and got a fellowship, a colossal fellowship, to go to Cambridge. And when I got there I can't tell you how wonderful it was! Graduate work in Oxbridge you have no obligations whatsoever. I had no lectures to go to, no languages I had to learn, no grades. You have a supervisor. You don't have to go see and see him. I could do anything I wanted. Go to any library in Cambridge. My wife had disappeared by this time. I could take my son to the nursery. Pick him up and then work late into the night. I was a free creative scholar for four years and I'm still living off the capital I built up over that time. I'm talking about the social sciences and the arts. You're just given the opportunity to do your bloody work and my thesis was published without a change of a single word. There's still in the published version [of *Mind, Brain, and Adaptation in the Nineteenth Century*] a misspelling of my supervisor's name. One of my examiners, who was a professor at Oxford, took it to Oxford University Press and it became famous. Not any revisions whatsoever because it was so carefully done.

I don't think that would have happened in America. I don't know how many people felt as liberated as I did but, my God, I did. For me it was academic freedom in the first instance and I suppose after my wife and I parted it was sexual freedom, Because I had an American friend in London who had parties all the time and he would say at the end of the party, 'Anybody who doesn't want to go to bed with the person they're dancing with, leave now.' I'm not kidding.

Sounds like the Sixties were well under way.

But the next thing to say to you is that the antiwar movement was an earthshaking matter for me and my friends and everybody had their different take on it. I was in something called the British Society for Social Responsibility in Science, and we were talking about the use of university computers to plan bombing missions. It eventually covered all aspects of the human sciences, the social sciences and the hard sciences because all sorts of academia were coopted. We set out to fight it and then we realized it wasn't just the division of labour, it was consensual framework of the social sciences and eventually the hard sciences [which needed criticism], which is what I was doing and still am. And all of that was a consequence of the presumption of the Vietnam war years, that they thought they owned the ideological and conceptual framework of the universe that represented this planet. And there were people – [Defense Secretary Robert] McNamara comes to mind – who were terribly repentant about what they did. And other people who were shame-faced about it. And there are people in the middle like Al Gore who try to have it both ways.

How does Darwin, of all people, figure in this liberation?

I eventually left Cambridge in the 1970s so I could work with this movement. It changed what I thought, what I wrote. I wrote manifestos – first about my discipline which was Darwin at that moment in my life. I relooked at how Darwin should be thought about. Lo and behold, he thanked a political economist, Malthus, for the heart of his idea and I said this in Cambridge and the guardians of Darwin's corpse, or whatever, said who does this guy think he is? They don't want to know. The theory of population created the model for the concept of natural selection. It's amazing. So I went around saying these things. I was a good scholar so they couldn't naysay me. The Wellcome Trust were very shocked they got somebody who was drifting into Marxism. I'm not talking about communism, but about Marxist theory of knowledge and so forth. We had a conference on self-management and science, for example. Labs are hierarchical institutions. We said, Why is it that way in science? Why does the supervisor get his name on every paper you write? I don't know if it's true in social science but it's true in natural science.

And you know how they throw ropes on an elephant if it's misbehaving? I didn't have any ropes on me from my past anymore. I came from perhaps the most reactionary place in America outside of the Deep South, Dallas. To come from a framework like that and to go and change it to something more leftwing, you got these ropes on you. Your thinking isn't as rich as it could be. Pardon my immodesty but my thinking is as rich as I could ever make it because I'm here [in the UK], not there. When the war ended, the liberatory aspects of it in the academic world disappeared like a puff of smoke. You must know this from your own experience.

I do.

It's very hard to be a leftwing intellectual in America. Maybe it's impossible. I don't know. There aren't many intellectuals in America talking with a full-throated left of centre, never mind ultra-leftist, epistemology in research. Don't you think?

Very few slip through, unless they do safe post-modern gibberish. People like Chomsky are miraculous exceptions.

So what I got in coming to England was freedom. And then I got to exercise my freedom in exploring Lukacs, Gramsci, and so on – and I'm still not done thinking about these things. Absolutely thrilled. And you have an effect on me. You'll say, what about this guy? Then you say, why are you reading that rubbish? I sometimes sneak off and read them anyway. I sense that I don't know the geography of the academic world [anymore] because its conformism is so well-established. You don't know that these people are creatures of some interest. You know, by contrast, I had a close friend who fracks and we can't speak to each other now. And he has no iota of doubt about what he is doing. He was president of the class, the head cheerleader. They're all working for his company and they are all rich as Croesus because they went to the right university, got into the right fraternity, and went into business in Dallas. And I could have done that. Somebody said, if you work for me, I'll make you my heir, and when he died, he had 800 million dollars. I got no regrets, by the way. Maybe I answered a broader question than the one you asked but that's what it did for me. Still is, by the way.

I want to ask you about R. D. Laing because of the novelized account Zone of the Interior *of him written by someone we both know, Clancy Sigal. Were you aware of Laing's work when you came to England?*

He must have qualified in 1960. Would that be right? I qualified in 1960 but I wasn't here in London. I was in Cambridge. It wasn't one single set of institutions because Scotland was different from the South and psychiatry was different from psychotherapy and both are different from psychoanalysis. Laing was in a very conventional setting at first and then moved into an extraordinarily facilitating one with people like Winnicott and Masud Khan and so on, who were themselves characters. And they qualified him over other people – I'm talking about psychoanalysis now – over other people's protests. Just as Winnicott had qualified Masud Khan over other people's protests. And he turned out to be a bad egg, a very bad egg. So I'm trying to say there were two worlds. There was a world of psychiatry, which I'm not familiar with really though I know people who have been through it, and then the world of psychoanalysis where he was treated as the brilliant young man.

When did you become aware of Laing?

I read *The Divided Self* when it first came out, and, by the way, I wrote a review of it which you are welcome to. And I was very impressed. I probably read it in 64 or 65. I had studied philosophy at Yale and I liked the idea of combining existentialist thinking with psychiatry and liked the idea of freeing things up. I had worked in one of the most horrible psychiatric bins in the gap between my third and fourth years at University, so I knew the world he was talking about and it was breath of fresh air. The thing we have to say almost immediately is, it painted a picture of what you could do with the freedom that he offered that turned out not to be – I won't say not to be true – but not as facile, as excellent as he and Esterson and others thought. It's much more refractory. We're now fighting a drug industry that wants to stamp out talking therapies because you can't package them into pills. Psychiatrists nowadays sell pills and psychotherapists don't have the right to prescribe, so it's changed a lot, mostly for the worse. Most psychiatrists hand out pills and see four to five patients an hour and that's because they can make four to five times as much money as if they were a psychotherapist seeing somebody at one an hour.

Going back to Laing, he was very, very liberating and was very charismatic and people followed him – I don't know – not necessarily slavishly because there were people like Clancy Sigal who were critical, and Joseph Berke who turned out to have a longer shelf life, if I can put it that way. He is still treating mad people with talking therapy, which is practically unheard of these days. I know. I do it. Laing's charismatic personality had a good side and a bad side. And the bad side eventually took him over.

Did you visit Kingsley Hall?

Yes, but only recently, Kurt. I was never there during Laing's time. What is interesting – and my take is very biased – about Kingsley hall is that Joseph Berke was never in the centre of Laing's followers although he was deeply influenced by him. And he's the one who took a properly mad person and worked with her, the smearing of shit on him and so forth, 24/7 sometimes, and this woman Mary Barnes became a very well-known and admired painter. They wrote a book together. A best seller. *Two Accounts of s Journey Through Madness,* It's called. And he was just influenced by the ambiance of Laing and then without it being any partnership at all he just went off and worked with this woman. It's the best thing that came out of Kingsley Hall so far as I'm concerned.

Clancy Sigal eventually came to you with this tell-all yet kind of sympathetic satire on Kingsley Hall.

Well, as you know, it's not in print in this country and that's because it let cats out of bags, including a plan to put LSD in the water supply, which wouldn't have made a particle of difference because you can only put it into distilled water. But that was the kind of stuff that revolutionaries, in inverted commas, were thinking of getting up to. Clancy is very charismatic too and a very curious – as in curiosity – person. I read that book and liked it a lot, partly for mischievous reasons, and he got in touch with me at some point when I was a publisher at the time and asked me to re-publish it. And I re-read it. When I went to Joseph Berke, he said, 'You won't be allowed to do that. We'll sue you.' Here I am a tiny little publisher with no lawyer and no backup for anything. I just said I can't possibly do this. When I told Clancy, he was very offended. It was as if I failed to join the revolution. And I felt wounded that he couldn't appreciate my position. I admired his work. Don't get me wrong. I suppose I just thought he was egocentric and couldn't make the imaginative leap to see why I couldn't publish something nobody else had published for as long as that. There must be a reason. It's interesting because Joseph Berke didn't take part in any of the naughty things that Clancy's book refers to. I don't know what else to say about it. I gather Clancy has just written another book. I ordered it, on Hemingway. Anyway, I'm looking forward to it. It sounds like classic Clancy looking at a rebel sympathetically, and I expect to be enlightened by it. He hasn't written much fiction, has he of late?

Screenplays and memoirs mostly.

How old is he?

Eighty-seven, I think.

He has a right to slow down a little. I'm slowing down a lot. I will say this. I met a woman who had been one of Clancy's women who gave me the impression that she felt hard done by him. And I think Doris Lessing didn't feel treated wonderfully.

As she related in great detail in The Golden Notebooks.

He's in there, isn't he? So I wonder if he's a bit egotistical and can give women the space they deserve, if I can put it that way. Is he in a relationship now, do you know? Yes? Well, people change.

He's got a teenage son.

For a man in his eighties, that's not bad going. Well, I have a daughter who is 18, so I must have been 60 when she was born.

You're scaring me.

Well, there are few better experiences out there if it works. I have a son with 2 BAFTAS as well by the way.

So what's your biggest gripe against Laing and his gang and what's their biggest merit, if any?

There was a kind of – you'll think I'm an old fart for saying this – a lack of gravitas about it. I think the [Kingsley Hall people] lost the respect of a lot of people. And I have a feeling, Kurt, and I speak as someone who worked psychotherapeutically with schizophrenics, I have a feeling they led people to underestimate what a hell of a job that is. Really, it's heartbreaking. For example, I see several people five times a week which is if they are in full analysis. And the problems with the parents and the problems with the patients are terrific. I've had a patient jump out a two story window. These are really, really difficult things to do. The idea that there is a charismatic solution is mistaken in my opinion. And I have a feeling he thought there was a charismatic solution. I have a soft spot for him but I lost respect for him, I have to say, because he blotted his copybook. Is that fair?

The blots are all people seem to recall these days.

Well, look. The larger picture is mental patients were badly treated. Mental institutions were bins. I recently re-watched *The Snake Pit*. Over half the state mental hospitals of America were revamped as a direct result of that one book and movie. So there's a change in the institutional setting of the mental hospitals. But before this change got anywhere near completing the thing it ought to have done, the government said, 'I know what we'll do. We'll close these places and we'll replace it with care in the community.' And they did the first but not the second. So now these people are sitting on park benches and that's horrible. Corrupt politicians behave that way, don't they? There're no mental institutions in this country. There're just empty buildings and a lot of selling off of property. I wish I knew what was happening in America. I wouldn't be surprised if it was the same. Do you know?

Exactly the same thing and it probably started earlier. What is worth retrieving from Laing?

The respect for the patient. Believing what the patient says. There's a guy named Peter Barham who wrote a book which I republished. He wrote a book about the history of the closing of the asylums. He's a remarkable man. Very gentle man and he said, in the wake of Laing, Don't think that psychotic people rant. Listen to what they say. Interpret it as if you were interpreting them as a psychoanalyst, not just as someone who tolerates their idiosyncrasies, and you will find out what is going on in their unconscious. Do not fail to attend to what these people say.

Still looks like a revolutionary thought.

And Laing had a lot to do with laying it before us. And I don't think many people would follow Peter Barham's advice. He is not a guru. He's just a man who said good things. I'm giving a talk in a few days about the relation between psychotherapy, psychiatry, and the drug industry. The drug industry is absolutely trying to wipe talking therapies off the map because they want everything to be pills. Pills don't do so much for you, you know. It isn't as if there are twenty new drugs since Thorazine and Reserpine. They tinker with the molecules. There is one good drug for manic-depressive psychosis. Lithium. But the drug industry is a lot of bullshit. So that was one thing Laing did, he fought the drug industry which got worse rather than better. I wish I could sing his praises more because I did love the man in a certain way but I felt badly let down by him. I mean, people think I am mad to do psychotherapy with schizophrenics.

So there are things that could be done in the spirit of Laing and should be done. I'm asking myself why I haven't done it, but maybe too late for me.

Because there was a place called Chestnut Lodge in Maryland where Harold Searles, the very best writer on schizophrenia ever, and Frieda Fromm-Reichmann worked. And there is a DVD called *Take These Broken Wings* about the kind of therapy I do with schizophrenics, and they cure them. They cure them. One of them was the woman who wrote *I Never Promised You a Rose Garden* and the other woman was a helper in a mental hospital. She is now a full time worker and is well. They had her husband on camera. 'Do you really think she is really well?' He said, absolutely. Why isn't there more of that? The answer of course, is that it costs the earth.

At least.

So I suppose what could be rescued from Laing is to have the kinds of institutions that Kingsley Hall tried to be. But I must tell you Joseph Berke set up something called the Arbour Centre and some other people set up a place in Hampstead. Now the Arbour Centre is closed. And the training is gone. It's a change in the zeitgeist. It's all drugs. Drug companies were fined thirteen billion pounds a year or two ago. It's chicken feed given how much they sell. The top ten drug companies make more money than the other 490 of the top 500 companies in the world. More than all of those. Now there must be something going on there and it ain't cure. The guy who was editor of the DSM-4 has written a book called *Reclaiming Normal* about 'stop pathologising people' because more people are being pathologised because of the drug companies. They want more diagnoses because they sell more pills. You know that in psychiatric training, there is no more psychodynamic or psychoanalytic training since about ten years ago. None. Niente, and that's all going the wrong way, colossally the wrong way. So I could say, under the banner of Laing, we could try to reverse this. But I think the zeitgeist take on psychoanalysis is about the reification of human nature. It's about the people who argue that wealth is good. I'm thinking of that film *Wall Street*, 'greed is good.' And nobody is doing anything about it. That means immiseration further down and the trickle-down thing is not true. It's false. So why did the *New York Review* publish critiques of psychoanalysis? Why did this English professor at Berkeley get listened to?

Frederick Crews.

Crews, yes. So I think it's a very large ideological shift for the worse. Because it's against the concept of the human soul by which I mean the inner world. They have no place for the inner world. Psychiatrists won't talk to their patients except to say 'How's it going?' and adjusting the dosage from time to time. I wish I was younger and more brave. I tried with my publishing house to promote some of these ideas.

While the Fifties freed you, at least in the UK, the Sixties are still your touchstone, you've told me before.

Well, I think it's in my heart still. My response is to soldier on. The people who were most politically active then, they're all professors now and they're all enforcing the norms of the culture. I'm talking culture at the highest level of culture. The 'What is your Ontology?' kind of thing.

You're talking about socially acceptable cynicism. Realists is their preferred term. Is it really any different in psychoanalysis?

Most of my writings since I became depressed are about psychoanalytic theory, hopefully on the most enlightened parts of psychoanalytic theory. When I encounter corruption in my subculture of psychoanalysis I wrote about it, but nobody, but nobody, has ever mentioned those writings, even though I was telling the goddam truth. Psychoanalysis was a radicalizing force for a time, wasn't it, in the 1950s? Certainly in my medical school it was. Most psychoanalysts now are conformists. They are probably apolitical or at best liberals. But I don't think it's snuffed out in everybody's mind.

Index

Note: Page numbers followed by "n" denote endnotes.

For Product Safety Concerns and Information please contact our EU
representative GPSR@taylorandfrancis.com
Taylor & Francis Verlag GmbH, Kaufingerstraße 24, 80331 München, Germany